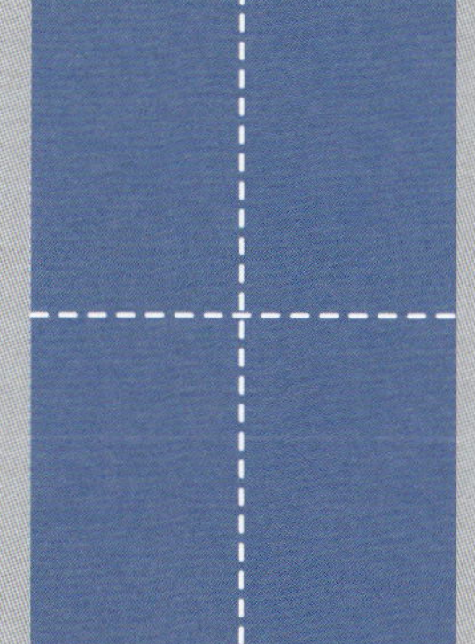

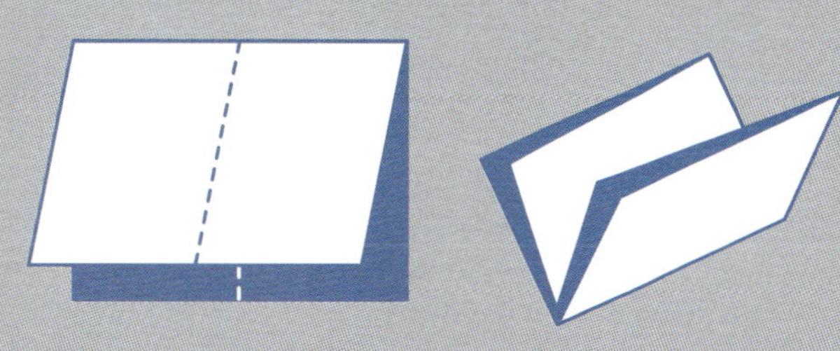

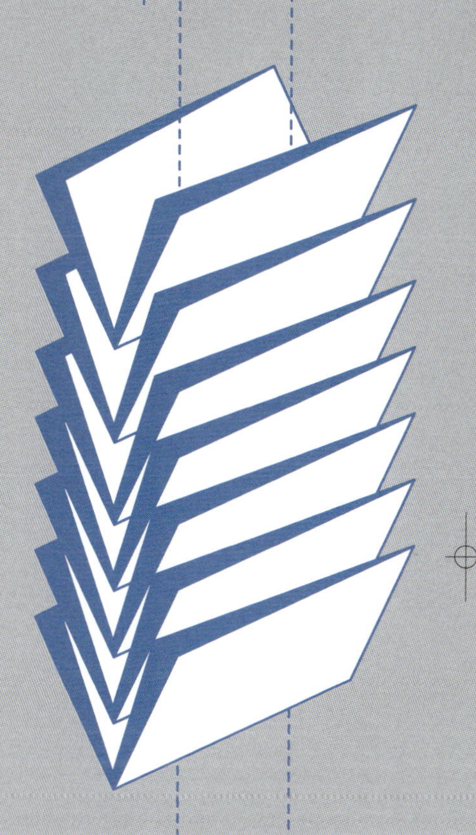

FOLDING

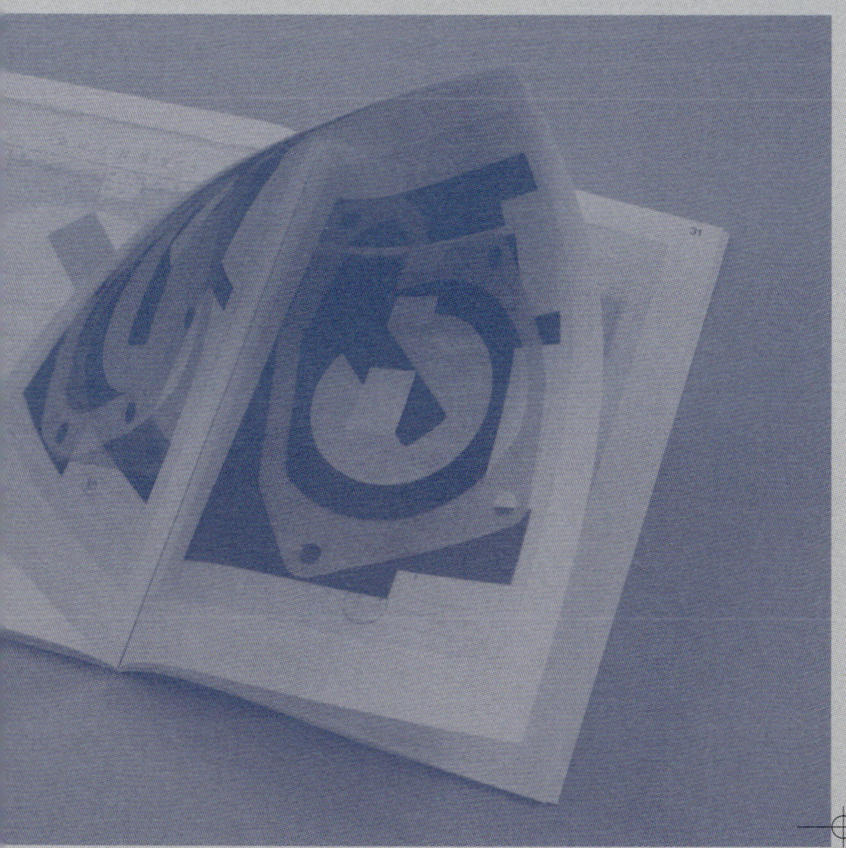

Folding is a common way to manipulate paper. It enables a 2-page paper to actually include more pages. Choosing an appropriate way of folding helps to better convey messages. After lots of experimentation with folding, there have emerged various established ways to fold a paper for publication. Examples include valley fold, gate fold, accordion fold and french fold, to name only a few. Creators can select a corresponding folding technique according to the contents and the application scenarios of the publication. It should be noted that one should fold along the direction of the fiber in paper, so as to avoid paper cracks. In the field of book design, creators can achieve the following effects through folding:

1. Reduce the size of publications, giving them greater portability.
2. Divide 2-page paper into several pages, each of which serves as a single page. In this way, creators can make full use of the space of each page, as well as better separate and classify the contents.
3. Control the reading order through different ways of folding, providing a smooth reading experience.
4. Enhance the interactive function of publications and improve the overall style of the design.

INSERT

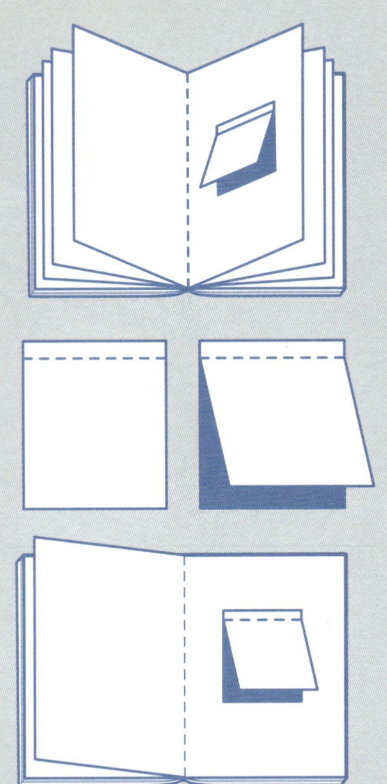

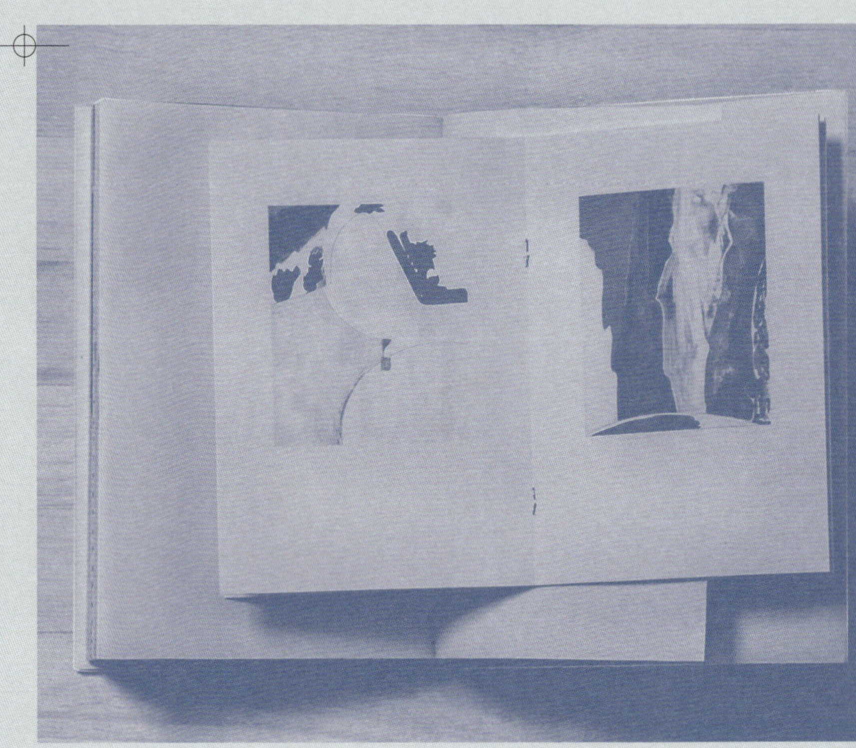

Insert usually refers to pages printed separately and inserted inside publications. These pages are printed with images or contents related to the theme of the publication. It also refers to pages printed on papers or with colors that are different from those used for the main part of the publication. There are two kinds of inserts: collective insert and scattered insert. Functions of insert are as follows:

1. Present contents that are different from the main text with a unique size and design, and classify information in a more intuitive way.

2. Add extra information in the insert without influencing the original layout.

3. The size of insert is different from that of the inside page, making the whole publication more interesting by creating a perceptual change for readers.

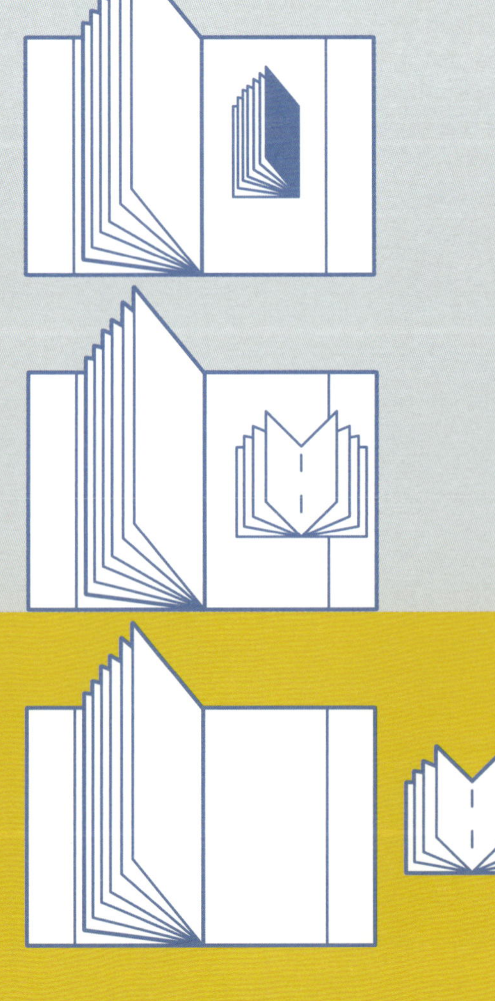

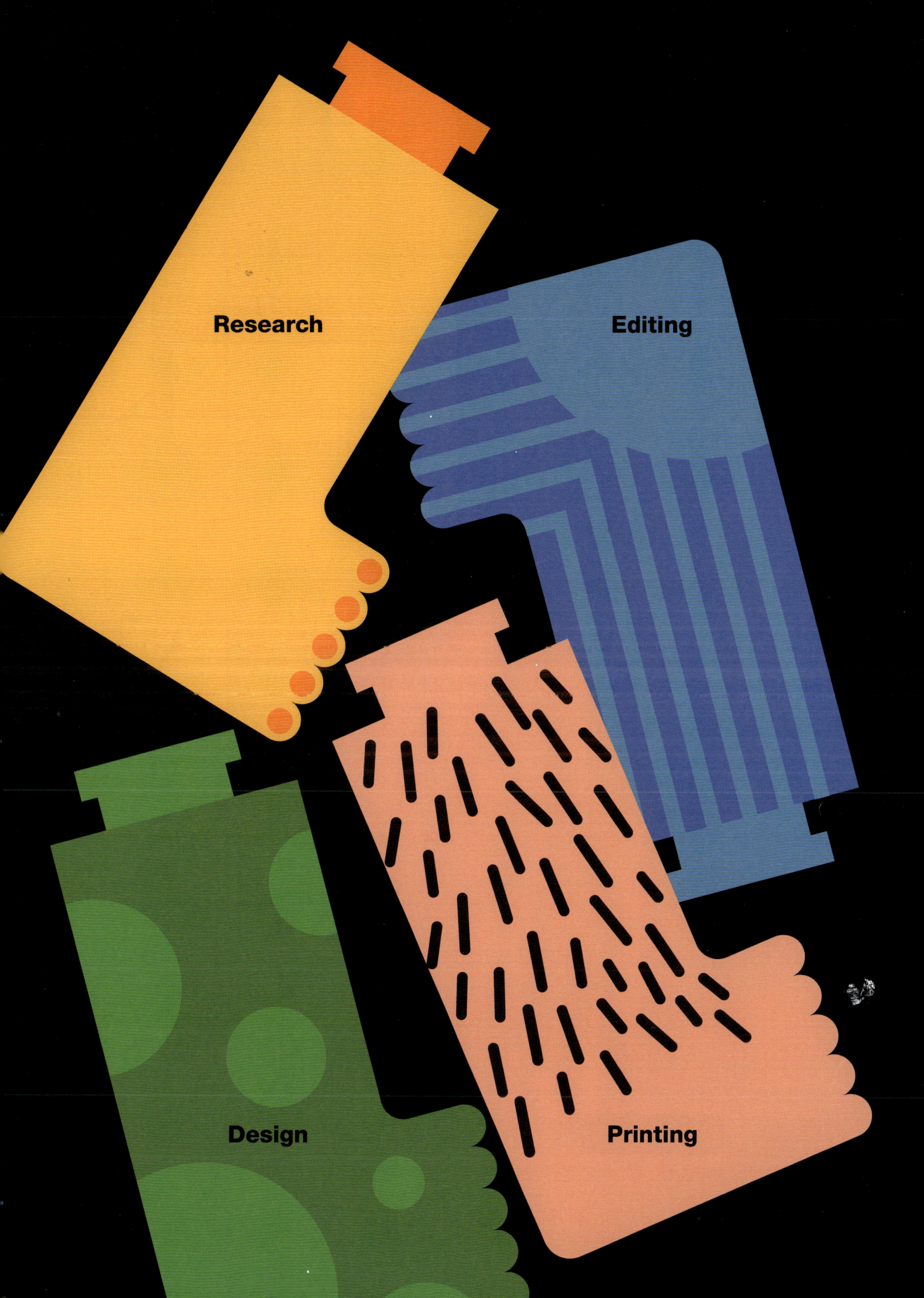
Research
Editing
Design
Printing

CREATE A SPATIAL PAPER ZONE

Editor
Gakky Luk

Can you imagine how a book is made just by holding it on your hands? Generally, the publishing process includes steps like topic selection, editing, design, proofreading, printing and binding. Through these steps, the initial vision and concept can be turned into a physical book. It also means that the book represents an integration of the various opinions of different parties and the revisions they made before the final publication takes shape. Nevertheless, creatives can, through self-publishing, centralize all of these roles and hold them all in their own hands, so that they can freely present their works in a more personalized form. In addition to conveying messages in the most direct textual way, they can also communicate on an emotional level through details that may be easily ignored, such as typeface, paper, material, craft and so forth, which have a wordless communication with readers and convey invisible messages to them.

The more we become familiar with something, the more we are likely to weaken our imagination and underestimate its possibility. We might be surprised to discover its infinite charms after we clear our preconceived notions about it. Taking paper as an example, various types of paper are the most fundamental and common publishing material. Different materials, textures, thicknesses and weights of paper can meet the various needs of the creative minds behind the publication. Apart from applying the fundamental features of paper, people can greatly improve the playfulness of the publication by breaking through the flat design and endowing paper with a spatial zone, thus stimulating people's design inspiration in a surprising way.

(All the examples in this article are from the projects featured in this issue.)

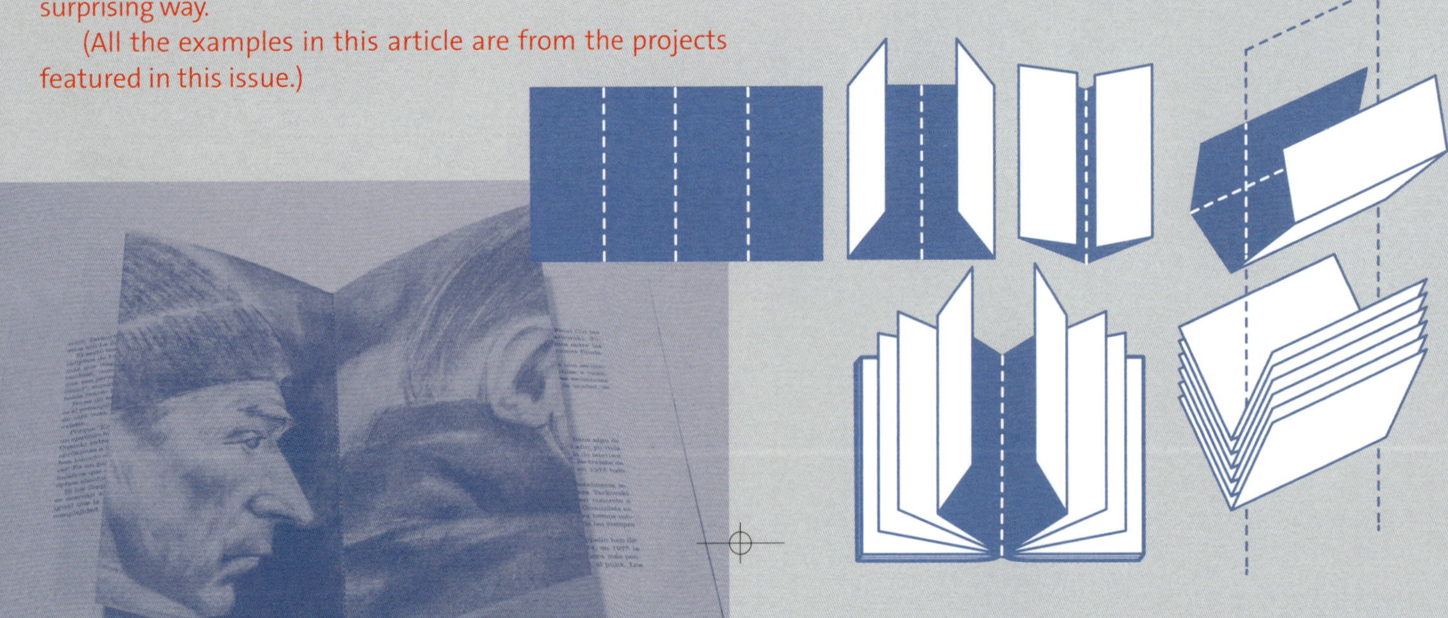

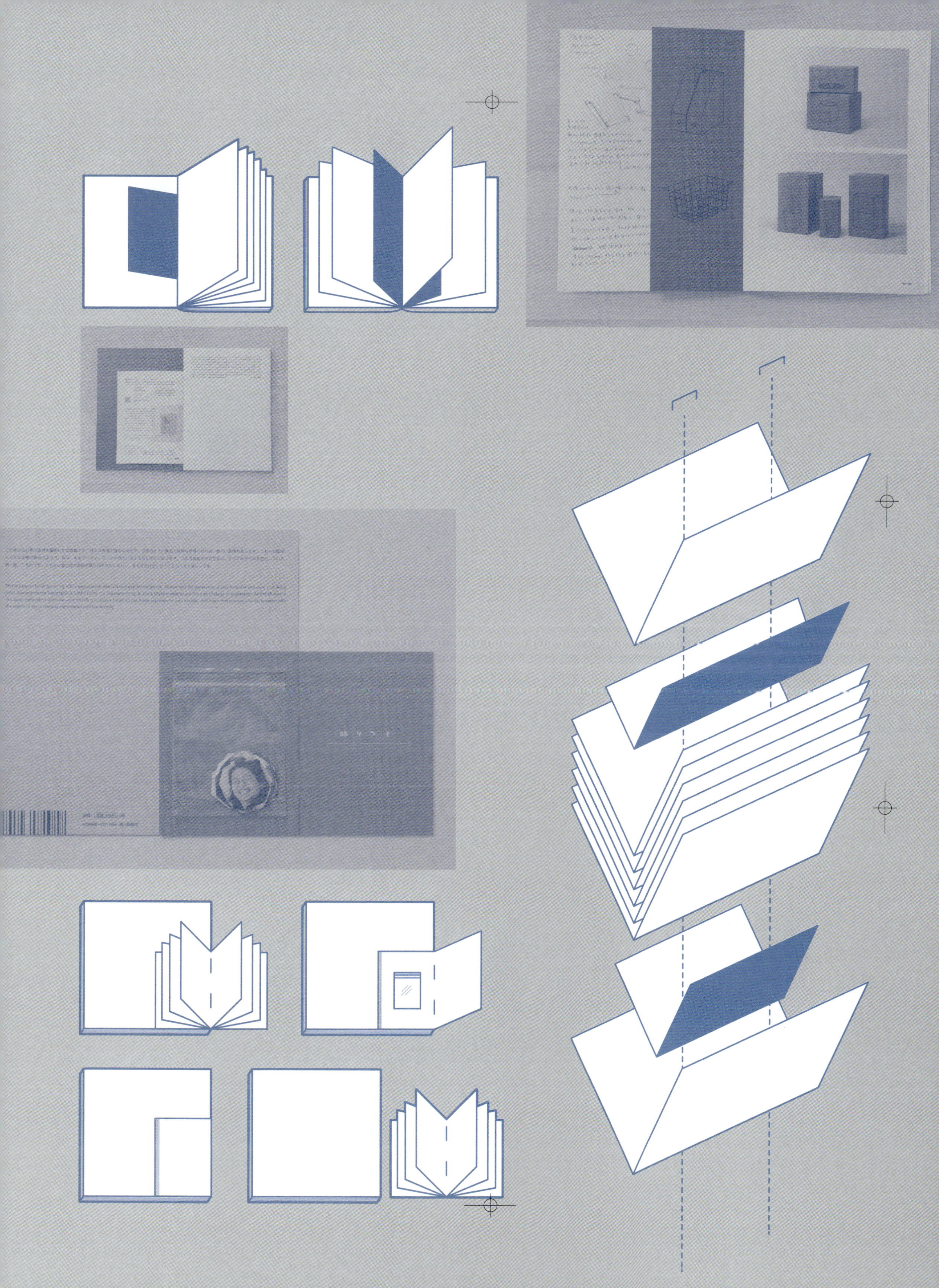

Folding and insert are two common methods to process the papers. The flexible combination of these two ways can facilitate the use of more creative structures, endowing the publications with an interactive function, and enlivening paper painting. Besides, selecting an appropriate binding can also have many benefits. Basic binding techniques include thread stitching, perfect binding and saddle stitching. In addition to these types of bindings that require extra binding tools, there is also another option: no binding at all. It can make a book with only one piece of paper or leaflet, which cannot only spare the cost of binding, but also present the project in a flexible way. Therefore, many creators prefer to choose this kind of binding for publications with relatively small print runs.

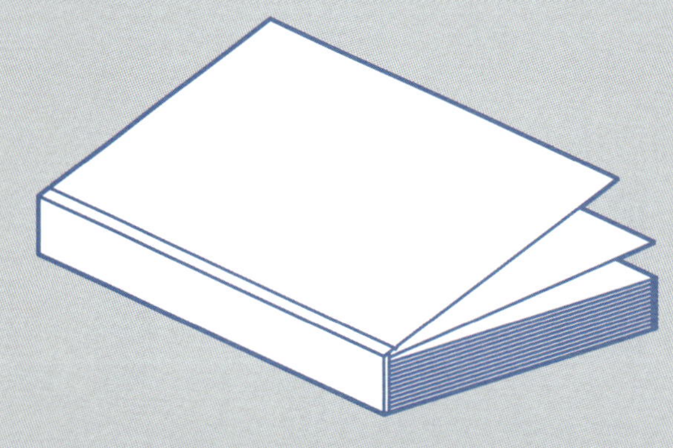

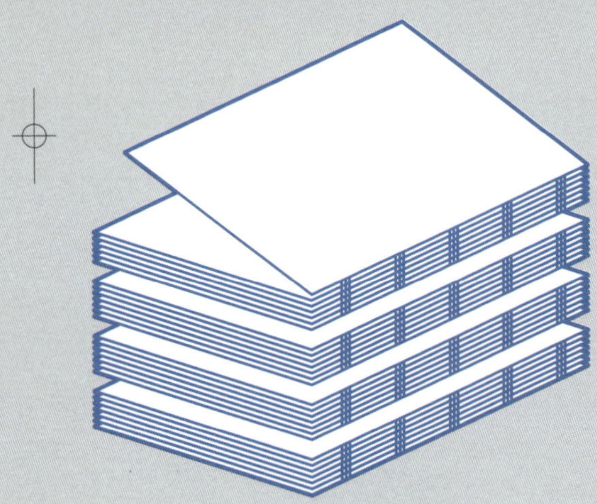

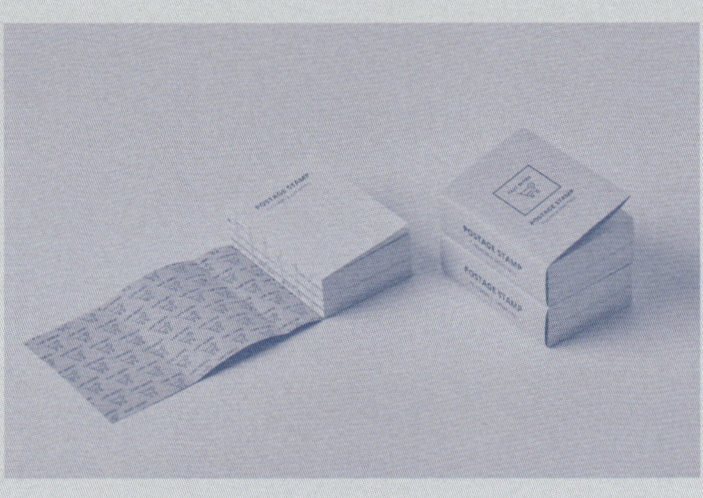

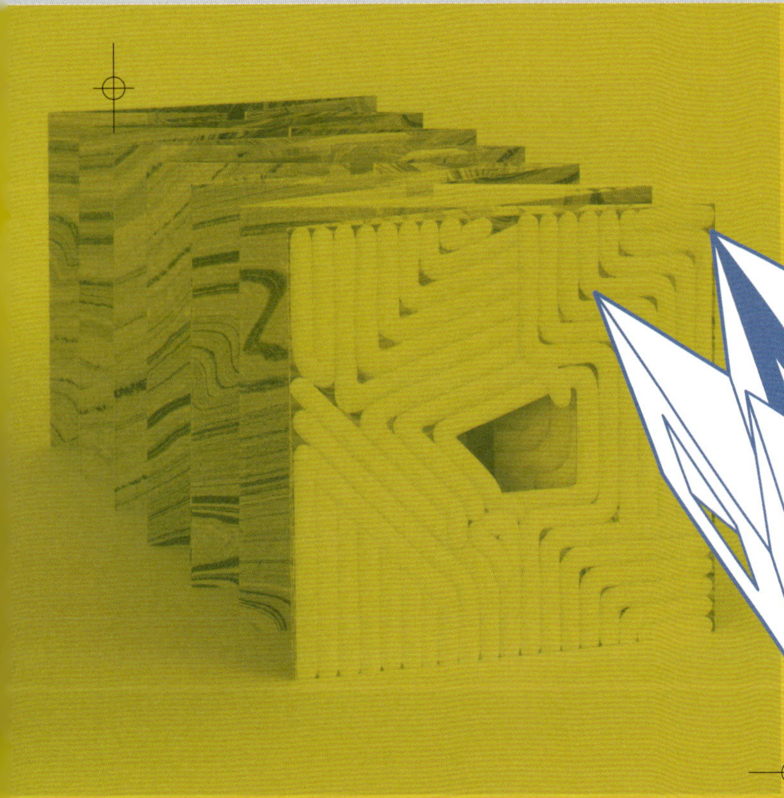

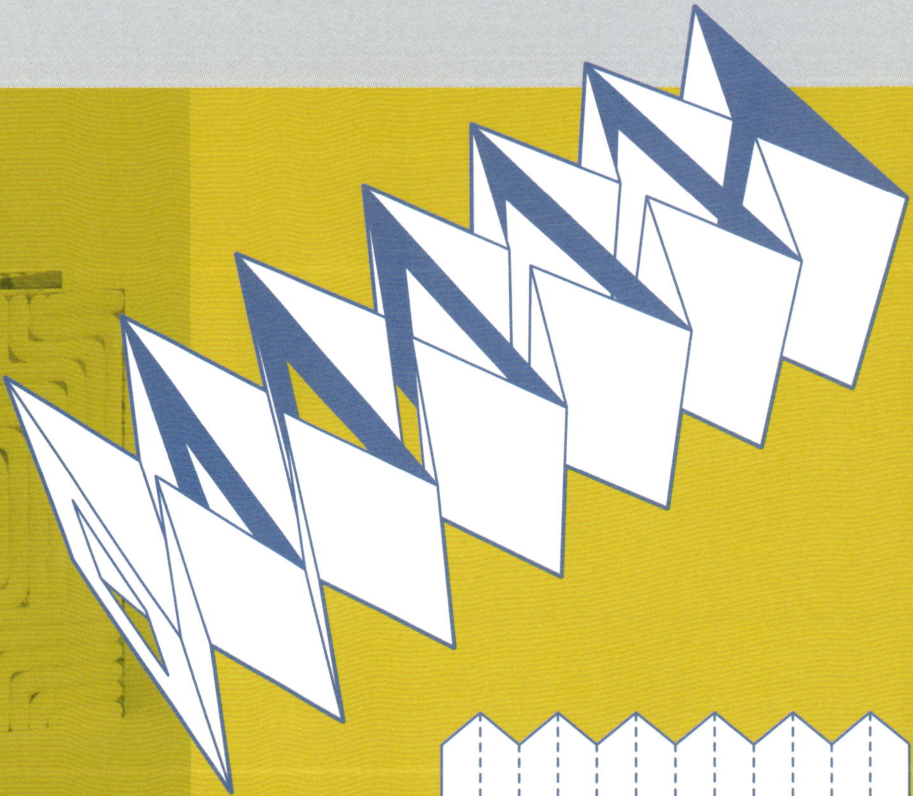

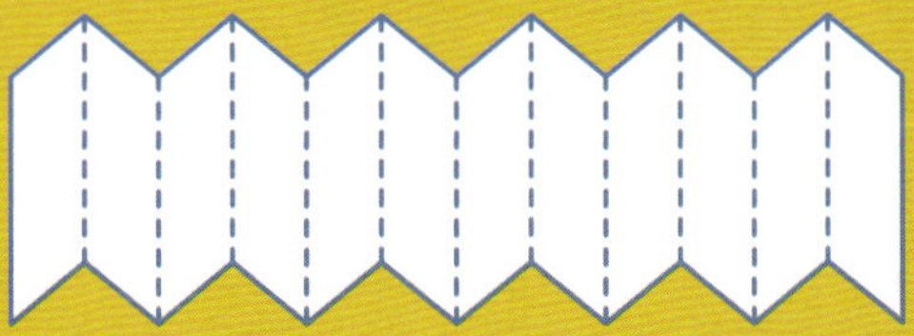

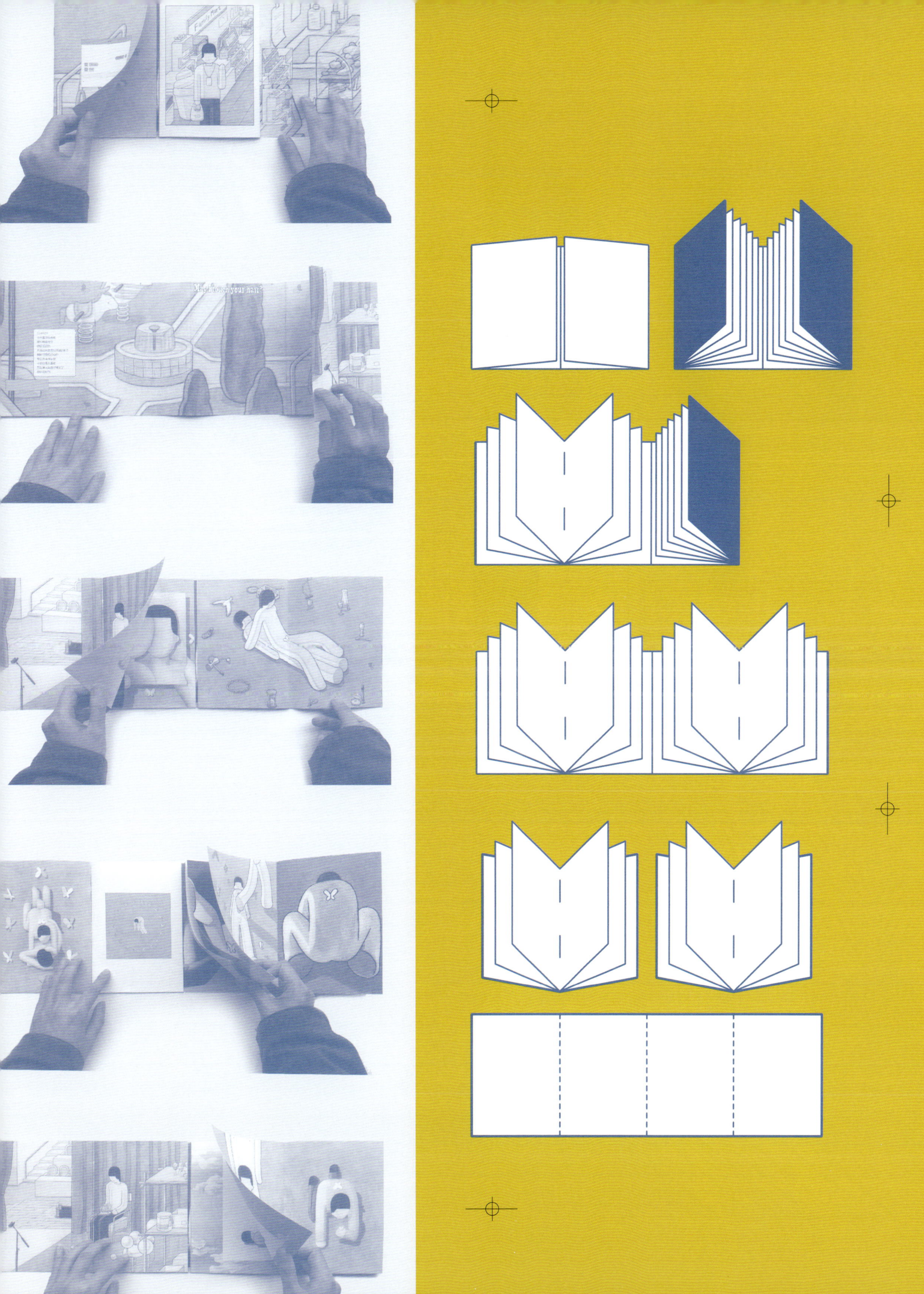
May I touch your hair?

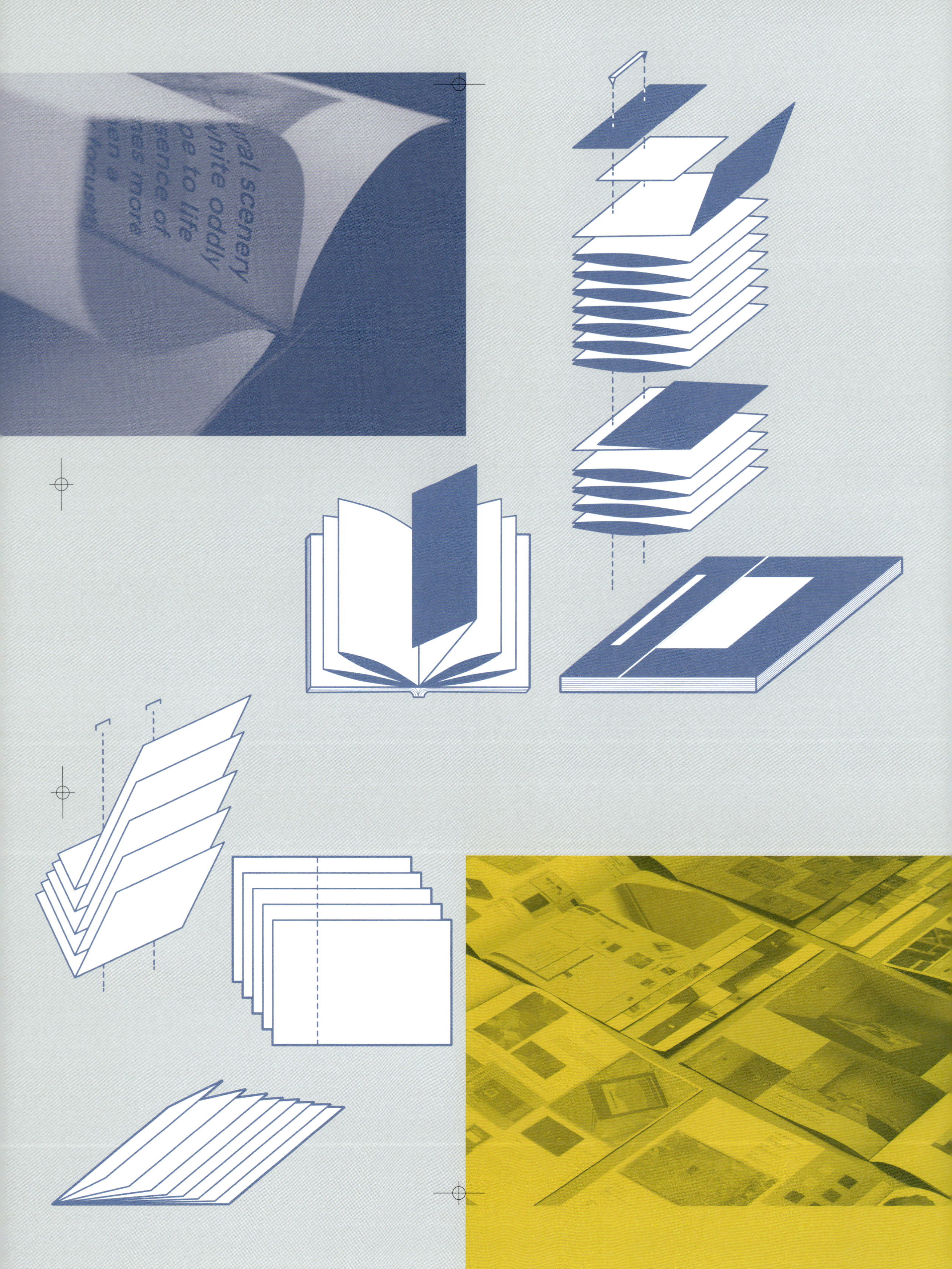
ural scenery
white oddly
pe to life
sence of
nes more
en a
focused

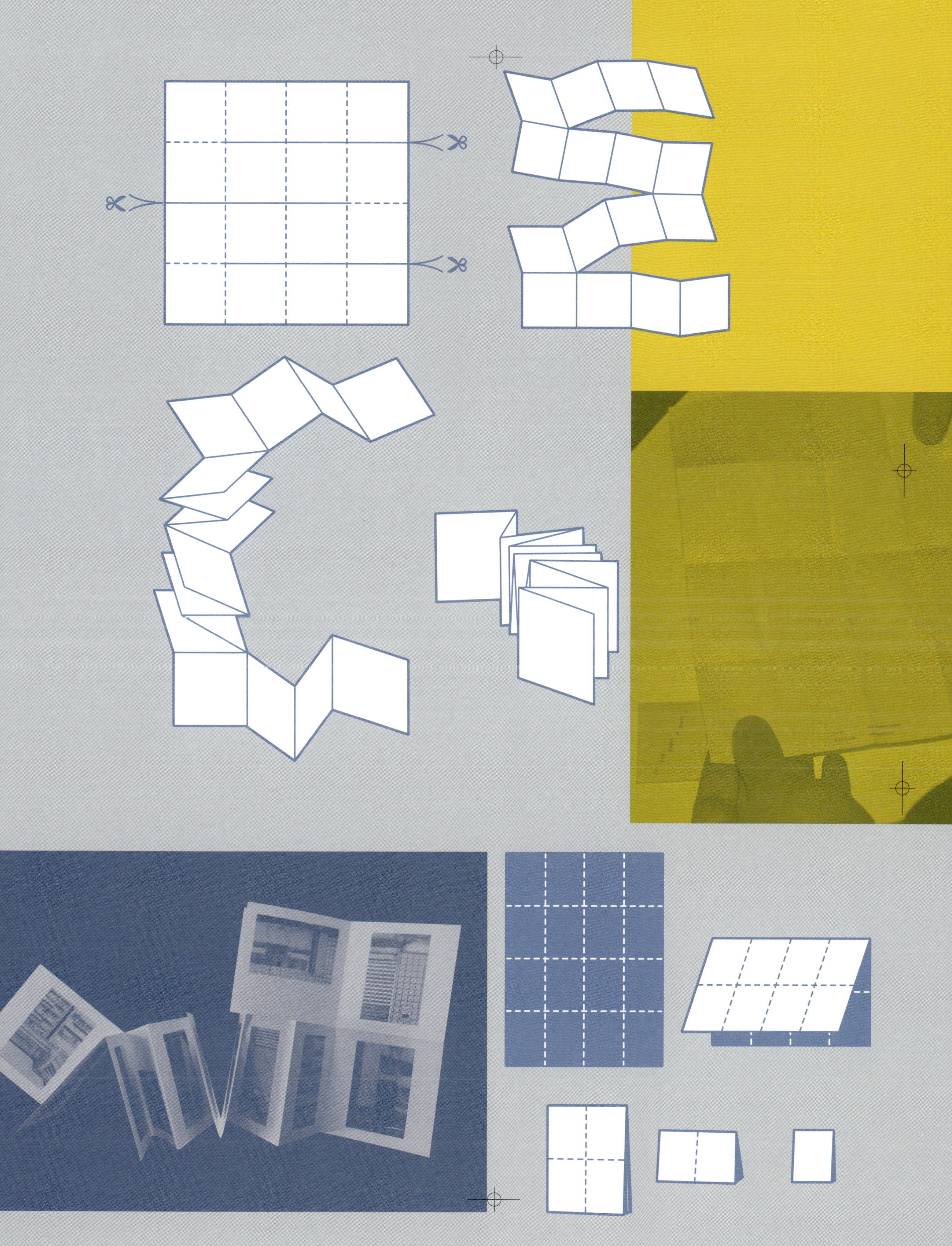

FOUR LEGS OF SELF-PUBLISH

Issue 57

AD
Art Director
CD
Creative Director
D
Designer
P
Photographer
VA
Visual Artist
DS
Design Studio

Editor-in-Chief
Nicole Lo

Nicole.Lo

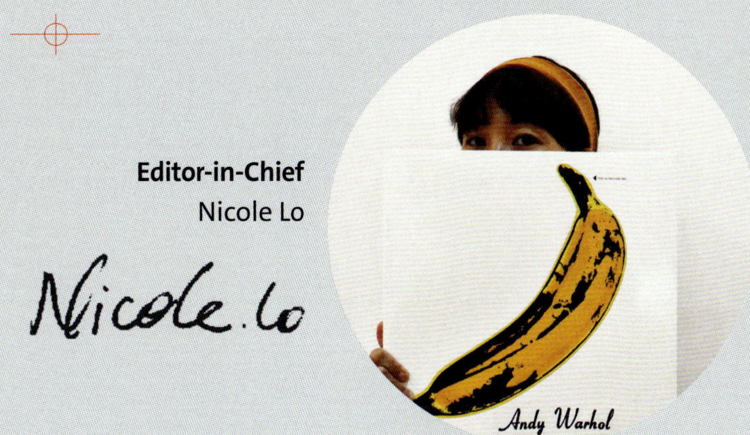

Hear the Voice of Self-Publishing

What is self-publishing? I think it could be defined as self-publishing if a publication is not completed with the assistance of established publishing houses.

Someone says: "Self-publishing is like a grassroots carnival." Do you agree with it? To me, if it is a grassroots phenomenon, it must be characterized by vitality. Art book fairs have become popular in recent years and have been held in various cities, which has blazed a new trail for the publishing industry. It has also attracted the attention of creatives in various fields, and has motivated them to participate. They have great enthusiasm for producing a book by themselves. Compared with traditional publishers, self-publishers still show their qualifications and professionalism in this field. Through bookstores, we also find that there has been more and more excellent self-publications emerging in recent years. At the same time, lots of uniquely positioned bookstores started to appear in cities. We are excited to see this new developmental model in the publishing industry.

I think it is too narrow a view to ignore this model and to think that the publishing is somehow a sunset industry. Although traditional publishing is still the mainstream today, readers are making clear their more individual demands. This all leads to a situation that the publishing houses, editors and book designers redefine the publishing content and the format of books. There has even been a change in the bookstore sector. I think self-publishing is like a catalyst: it is bringing vitality to the publishing industry and changing it for the better. Everyone knows that there is only one sun, even if it is a setting sun. But one can always embrace the same sun rising in a brand-new day if he or she can see things from another perspective. The optimization of self-publishing provides creatives with more creative space. More and more people will accept and respect the differentiation in the editorial logic. Indeed, it requires courage and a suitable environment for self-publishers to express their ideas. I believe that more and more publishing legends will appear in this field.

No wonder some people say that "Self-publishing is like a child prodigy—it can run about madly the moment it is born." Is it because it has four legs? Four legs of self-publishing are research, editing, design and printing, which make a self-publication from an untouchable thought to a physical book, just like four edges define a specific page. In this issue, we will explore and appreciate the unique charm that characterizes self-publishing!

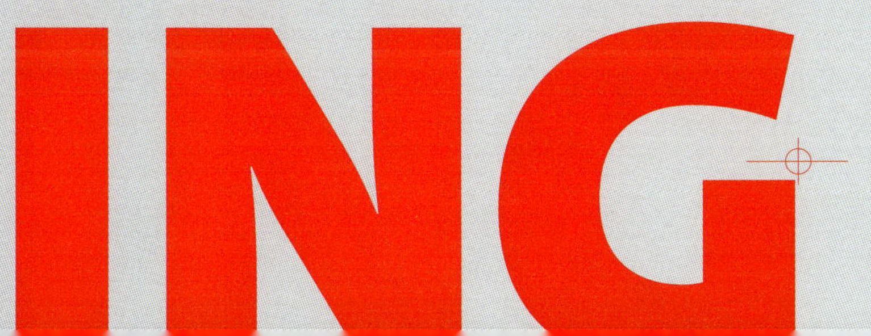

CON

TENTS

DESIGN × SELF-PUBLISHING PROJECTS

P090—197

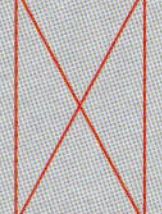

34×60mm—140×205mm

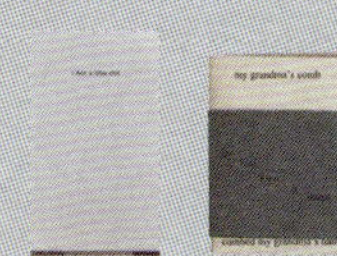
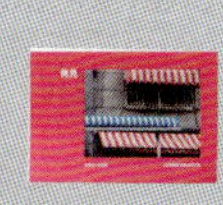
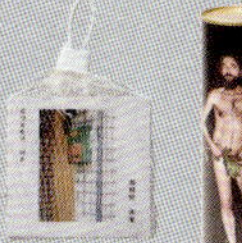
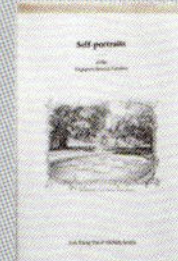
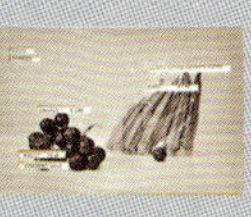
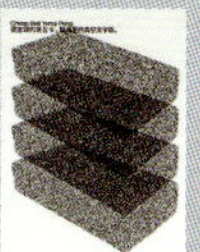
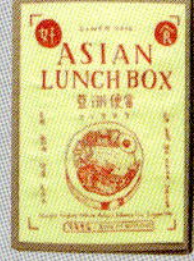

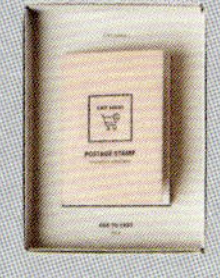
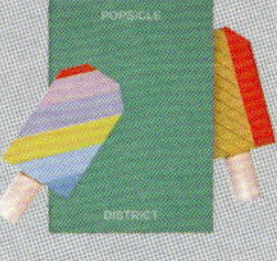
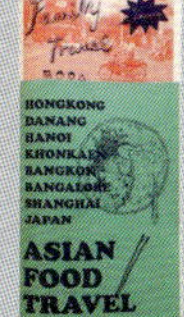

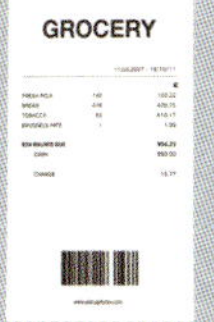
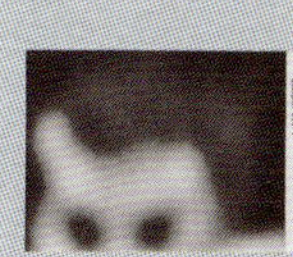
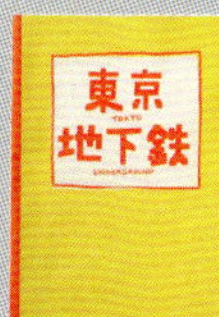

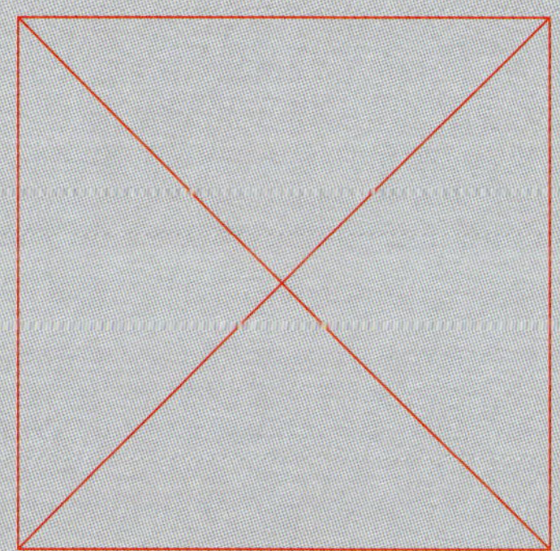

170×170mm—100×500mm

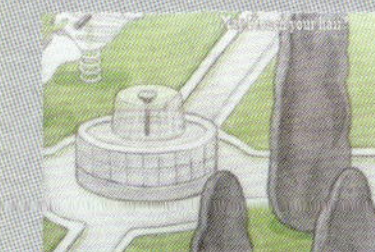
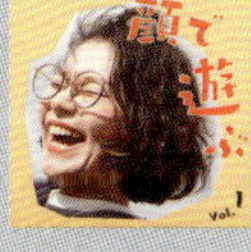
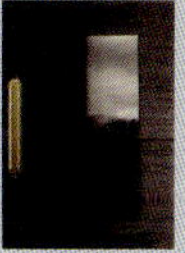
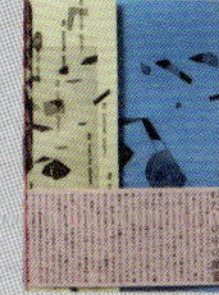
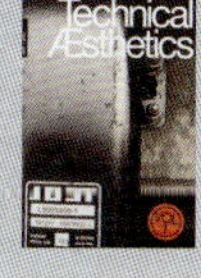
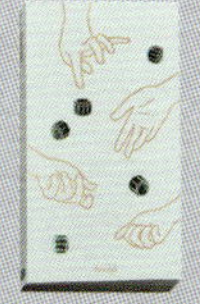
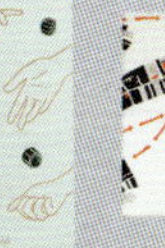
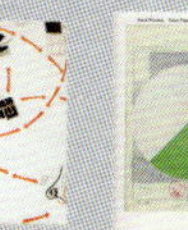
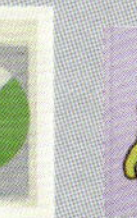
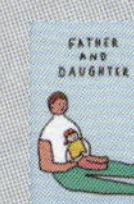
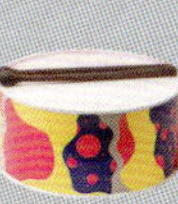
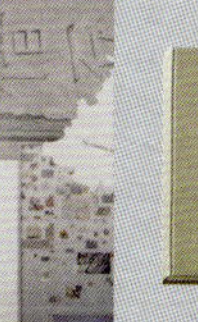
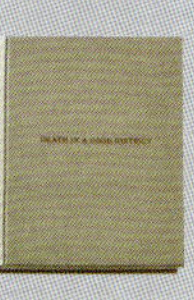

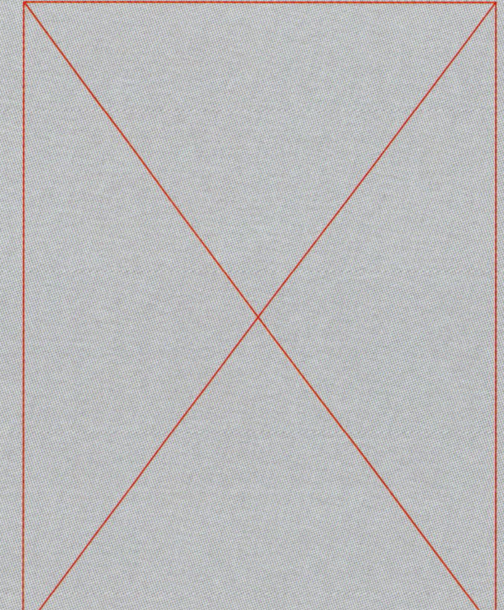

210×280mm—297×430mm

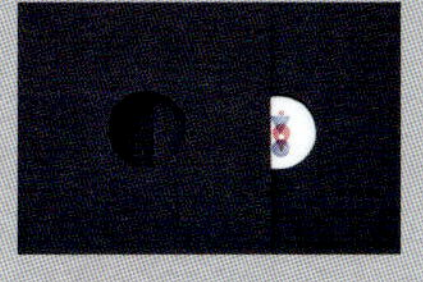
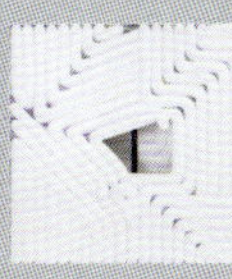
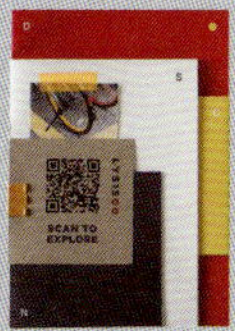
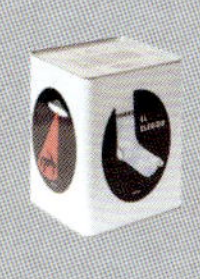

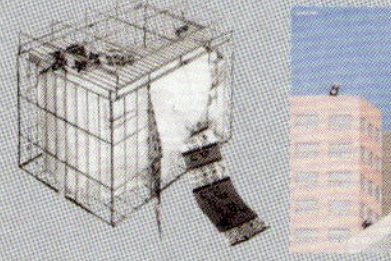
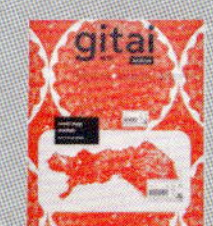
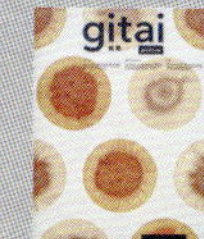
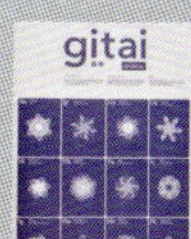
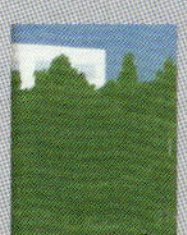
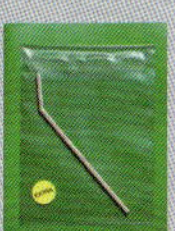
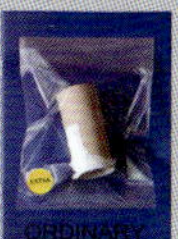
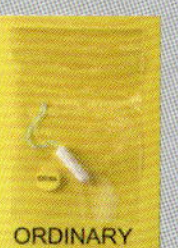
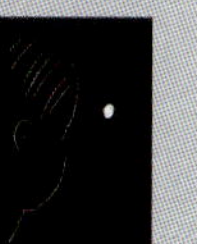
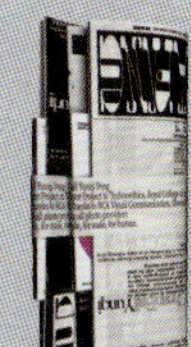
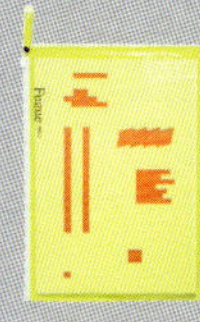
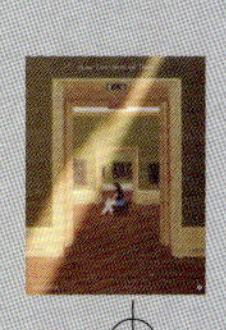
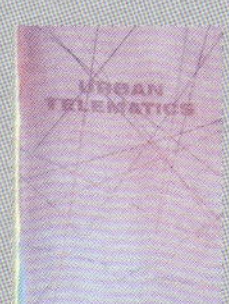
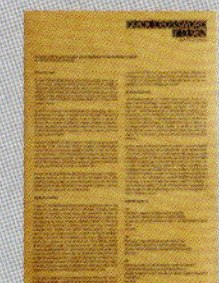
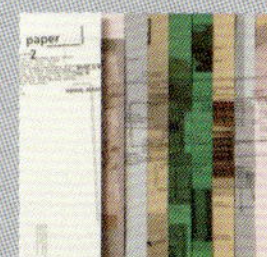

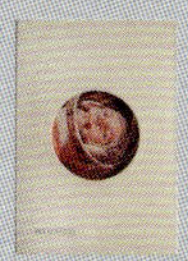

INTERVIEWS × SELF-PUBLISHING STUDIOS

MACGUFFIN

SPECTOR BOOKS

HEKICHI

TXTBOOKS

MIJEONG JEONG

DREAMER FTY

1

Editor
Gakky Luk

SELF-PUBLISHING OFFERS A NEW PERSPECTIVE

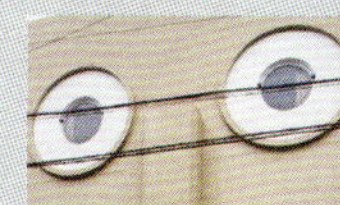

Taking advantage of the Internet, self-media has developed rapidly. The burgeoning growth of social media and the dizzying emergence of different platforms have enabled every single person to become their own "broadcaster". The power of traditional mainstream media has been decentralized, while the individual voice has been elevated to an unprecedented height. Since entering into the era of self-media, these possibilities for the individual have also opened up new opportunities for a number of industries that had been suffering significant difficulties. For example, a new model of influencer-led marketing on live streams has had a huge impact on the e-commerce industry. Customers flock to some bricks-and-mortar stores that have become instantly famous thanks to social media promotion. It has even led to a new development—self-publishing—in the publishing industry, for long regarded as a so-called sunset industry.

Instead of seeing this as a totally new phenomenon, it might be more accurate to describe self-publishing as something that has long been developing in the shadows of mainstream publishing. Thanks to the rapid advances in the related technology and equipment most notably in desktop publishing, printers, and online platforms, publishing is no longer an unattainable dream for many. Those engaged in self-publishing are typically at the heart of the whole process—from creating, typesetting, selecting materials, to printing and binding, and even to distribution and promotion. The publishers are not only responsible for the quality of the content, but also for ensuring the book design in harmony with the content, as well as selecting materials that can best convey the vision of publications from the creator's perspective. It can be said that the publishers have to consider all aspects, from the tiniest punctuation mark to the global marketing strategy.

It should be noted that people often confuse "self-publishing" with "independent publishing" in the Chinese context. Independent publishing often refers to cooperative projects between creators and independent publishing houses. The creators are only responsible for the publication itself, and the independent publishing houses take charge of the subsequent promotion and sales. No matter if it is self-publishing or independent publishing, the rights are always held by the creators, who are not restricted or controlled by any other parties. Many people choose to express their views and perspectives—serious, wacky or funny—through self-publishing because its fundamental characteristic is ideally suited to the needs of the self-media era, providing readers with a new perspective on this world.

Similar to independent studios that have become popular in recent years, self-publishing studios remain quite small scale, mainly consisting of a few team members or maybe just one person. A small-scale self-publishing studio can make quick and flexible adjustments according to the needs of actual situation, which means the work that used to be finished by the vast teams of an established publishing house, now becomes the sole burden of a handful of people or even just one person. A reasonable division of labor and overall project planning are key factors in maintaining an efficient output. Besides, self-publishing studios shoulder the responsibility of promotion. In addition to conventional online publicity, the increasingly popular art book fairs have become another way for these studios to promote their projects. Art book fairs provide a venue for like-minded publishers and readers to meet and communicate face to face. Besides, such events also help to develop and expand the self-publishing community. Self-publishing has rapidly become a rising force among the generally declining traditional publishing industry as self-publications, with their unique and idiosyncratic perspectives, continue to draw people's eyes away from the electronic screen back to the actual books people can hold in their hands.

MACGUFFIN

MacGuffin The Life of Things N° 1

The Bed

ISSN 2405-8203

US $20 UK £12

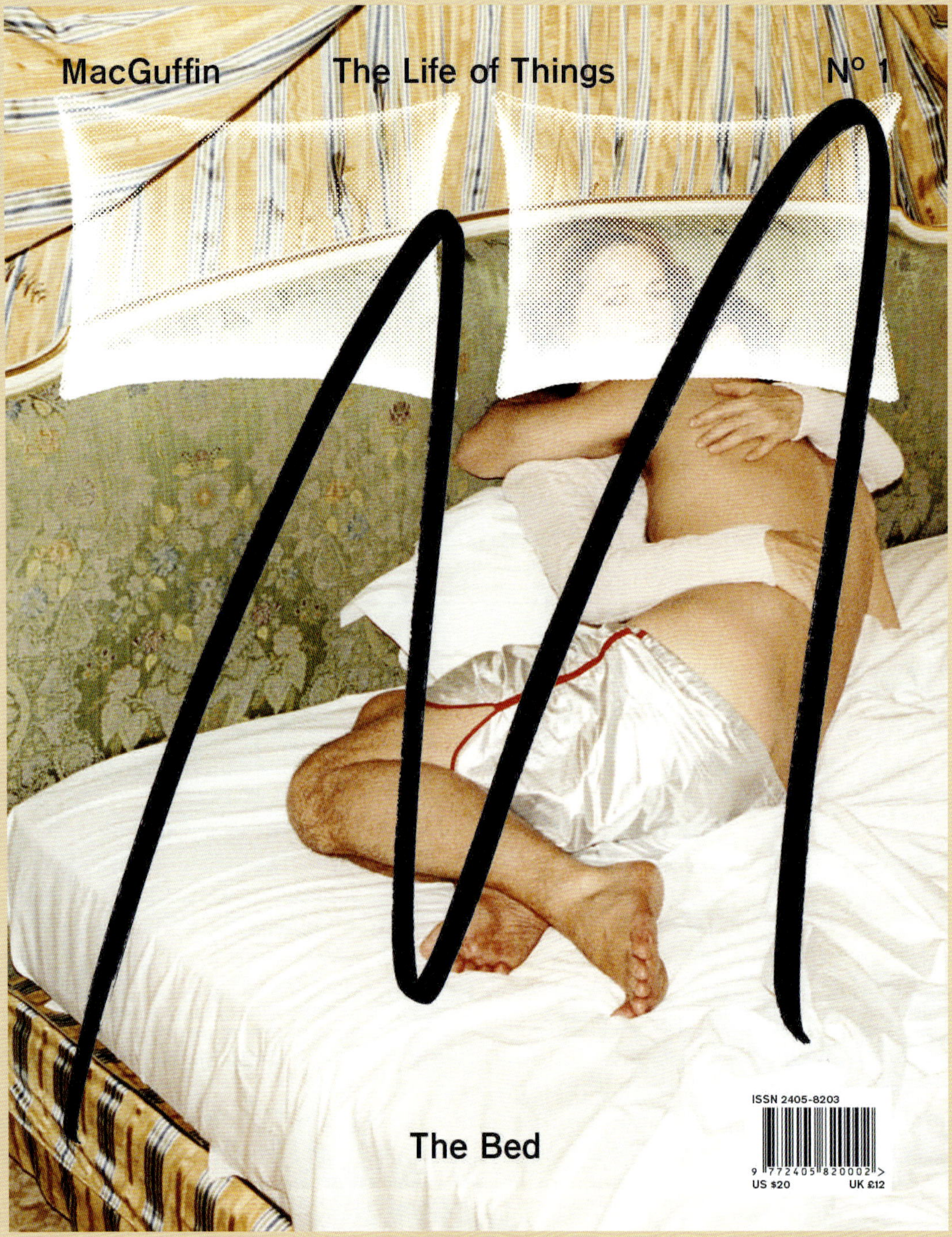

MacGuffin Issue 1 "The Bed"

MacGuffin

MacGuffin is a biannual independent design magazine. Its two founders are Kirsten Algera, a design historian, and Ernst van der Hoeven, an architectural historian. Each issue only selects and explores one object that impacts on daily life. In-depth exploration is carried out into this object from a multiplicity of perspectives—history, cultures, literature, lifestyle, and among others.

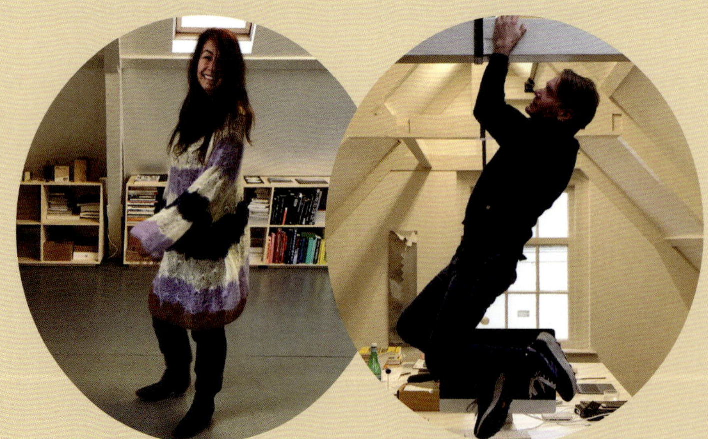

Page: 224

Dimension: 210×275mm

Weight: 650g

Paper/Material: Fedrigoni's Arcoprint Milk 1.5 80gsm; Fedrigoni's Freelife Vellum 170gsm; Igepa's Magno Star 115gsm

Binding: Perfect Binding

Interviewer
Gakky Luk

Continue the Life of Things

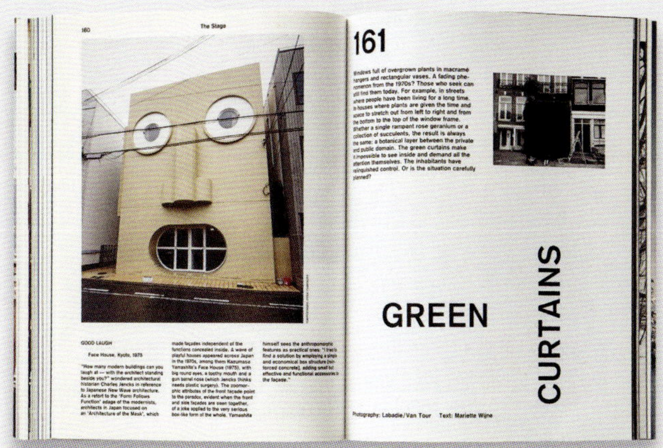

MacGuffin Issue 2 "The Window"

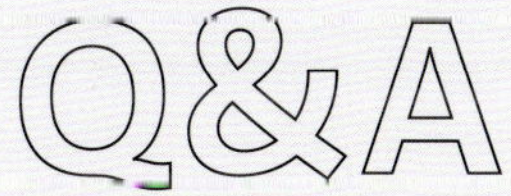

MacGuffin **explores only one object in each issue. What inspired you to create this magazine? What difficulties did you experience in going from the idea for the magazine to the actual publication?**

We were mainly inspired—or better: uninspired—by the congested design world in which we worked when we started. It felt like it was pretty much obsessed by commercial success, star designers, an overload of empty new titles and an obsession with "innovation". We were much more triggered by the "afterlife" of everyday objects. How are they used? What does the world look like when you observe it through the lens of an object? In a way, we wanted to stretch the definition of design. Our second inspiration was Hitchcock, one of the greatest storytellers ever. He invented the word "MacGuffin", the object in a movie that sets the story in motion. We borrowed the name because we wanted to create a platform that is not so much about the design of objects, but rather about the stories they generate. We thought a magazine would be the best medium for the research, the longer reads and the visual essays we had in mind.

Between the idea and the actual practice was a long process of finding funds. Eventually, we applied for a research grant for the first issue and got it and found an investor. So, we started and hoped—quite ambitiously—that a good magazine did not need to be aimed at certain readers, but rather could define a new readership. And that proved to be the case, fortunately. It reminded us of a quote by famous editor Tina Brown: "If you don't have a budget, have a point of view." Our point of view was to present another perspective on design, combining both visual and text research in as intriguing and as sustainable a way as possible. Like a portable exhibition, one that you can keep and carry with you.

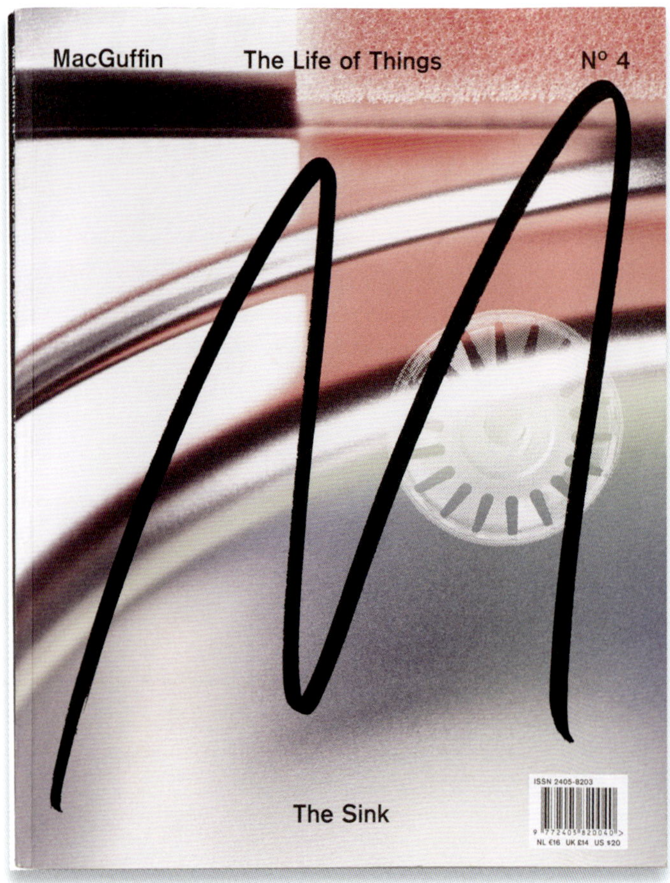

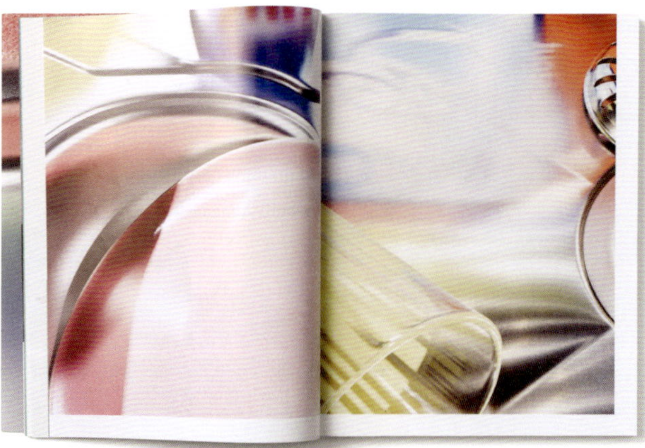

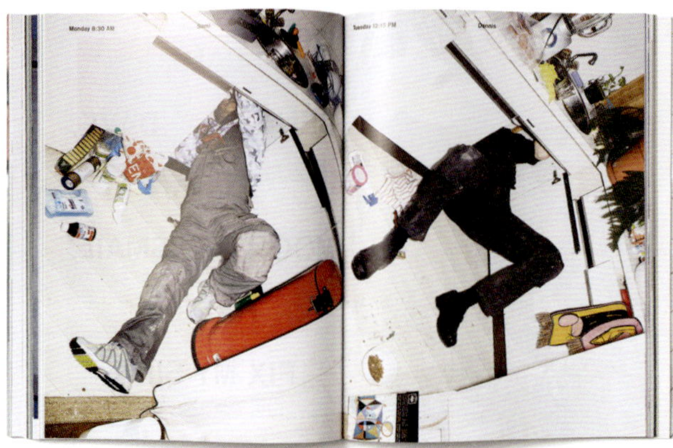

MacGuffin Issue 4 "The Sink"

The magazine reinterprets inconspicuous objects in daily life and carries out a multifaceted exploration of the object. How do you determine the theme and direction for exploration at the planning stage? Could you please introduce your working process?

Almost every issue starts with a work or a text that inspires us. Often, it leads to a sort of editorial sketching process. With "The Sink", for instance, it was based on *Invisible Cities*, a collection of stories about imaginary cities written by Italian writer Italo Calvino. He wrote about an underground city that is completely made of pipes, "a forest of pipes" as he called it. That image, and the idea that there is a world between the here and the one below, fascinated us. For "The Trousers", we read Umberto Eco's article about his tight jeans, and how it altered his behaviors. For "The Cabinet", the autobiography of Walter Benjamin gave us a wonderful peek into his parents' cabinet. He described how it was not just an object to show things off, but also to hide things and to keep things. It is both "veil" and "what is veiled". So, most of the time we start with a specific interest in the subject. Then of course, there is a lot of research to be done. Sometimes it drives you crazy, because there are so many options and interesting subtopics you can research. The danger is that you go on researching forever. We try to limit ourselves by picking a couple of subthemes as quickly as possible, and divide the theme into chapters. One thing we're strict about is dividing the magazine into three or four chapters. In "The Rug", for instance, it was clear from the beginning which subthemes we wanted to discuss: the materiality of rugs, the counter history of carpets and rugs, the way they were empowered or suppressed, and the way in which the carpet is a cultural phenomenon, a mirror of cultures.

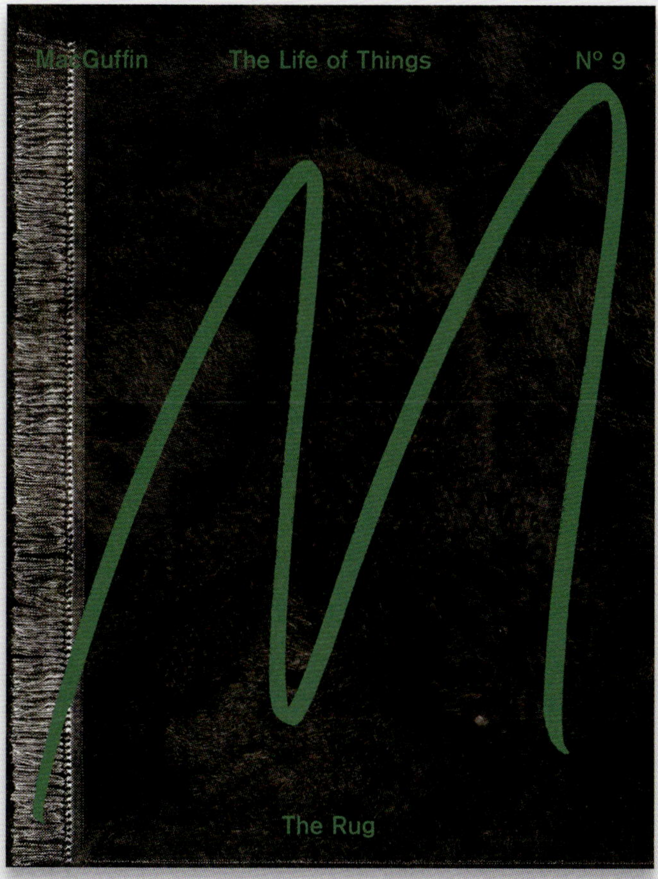

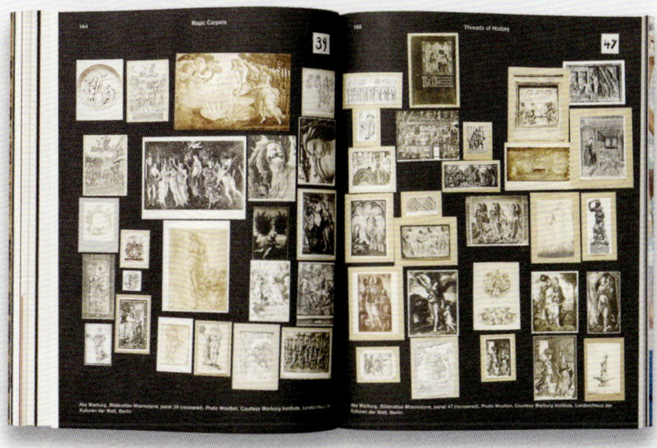

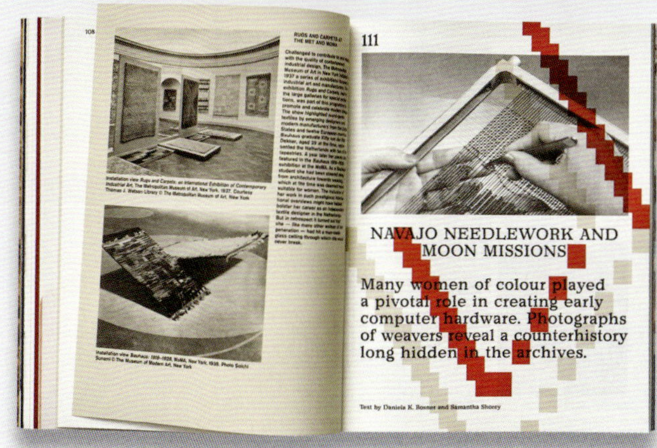

MacGuffin Issue 9 "The Rug"

The cover of the magazine is a photographic image related to the theme of the issue, together with a casual but elegant handwritten "M". Why did you choose the handwritten form? What message does it try to convey to readers?

For the identity—a visualization of our subtitle, "The Life of Things"—we were searching for a way to literally use our hands. Kirsten, who has the most pronounced handwriting, had to write the word "MacGuffin" about a thousand times. But we were still not completely happy with the logotype. The title was just too long and complicated when handwritten. So at the very last-minute we changed it (in the train on our way to the printer) to just the written letter "M". It reminded us of the *La Marque Jaune* (means "The Yellow M" in English), the sixth comic book in the Belgian comic series *Blake and Mortimer* from the 1950s. The other element that is important in the cover policy is that the idea of the magazine is an object itself. So, the cover always has a graphic layer which defines it—literally a bed or a window or a cabinet. With the abstract "M", those "objects" were easier to convey.

***MacGuffin* has published nine issues so far. Compared with the first issue, what progress do you think is represented in the newest issue? Are there any short-term goals you want to achieve?**

The editorial model hasn't really changed since the first issue, but the print run has increased from 2,000 to 15,000 copies. We're really proud that we are able to present design research—that is not always easy to understand—in such a way that we reach a substantial and young audience. The other thing we are happy with is the fact that we have been able to expand the contents of the magazine to other platforms, like exhibitions, workshops, podcasts and videos. We just curated an exhibition about "The Desk" in Design Museum Gent, worked together with Palestinian designers on a series of movies about "The Rug", and are preparing podcasts together with the Research Center for Material Cultures about "The Chain", one of our future themes.

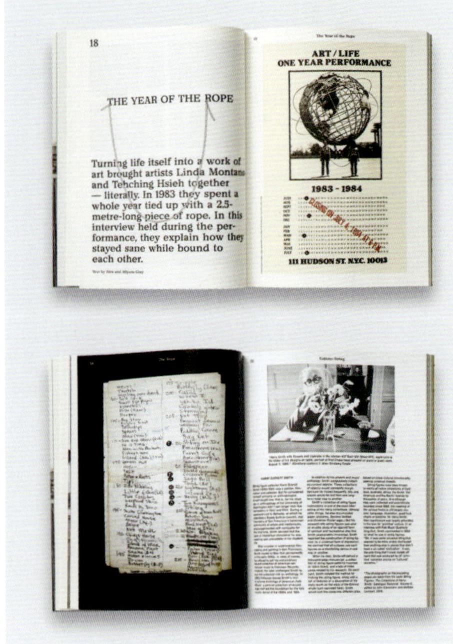

MacGuffin Issue 3 "The Rope"

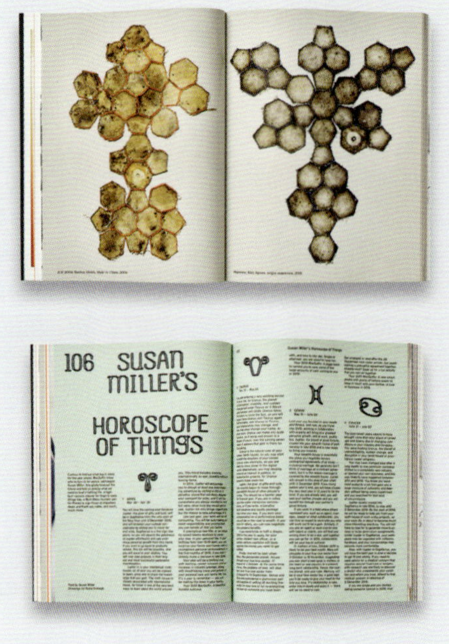

MacGuffin Issue 6 "The Ball"

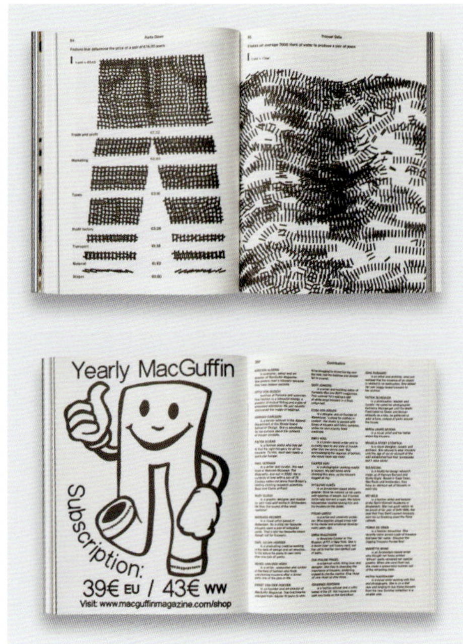

MacGuffin Issue 7 "The Trousers"

As an independent magazine, how does it present the term "independent"? What is the most difficult thing to be copied of this magazine in your opinion?

Our independence is key to the success of the magazine. It made it possible to make the portable design research exhibitions we want to make without having to compromise on issues like critical stance, time pressure, unexpected angle—also, we cannot be compelled to do product placements. The other side of the medal is of course the constant quest for financing. But that is a sacrifice that we like to take for granted.

Generally speaking, publishing doesn't bring great profits to the creators. What is your current operating model in terms of maintaining the funds for production of magazine?

The classical model of advertising in magazines is getting overshadowed by the importance of social media. It is an intriguing phenomenon that we in the beginning underestimated. Now that we have reached 16,000 followers, and we have really started liking the platform. It is a great way to reach a broader international readership, and a very direct and reciprocal platform to share *MacGuffin*-related projects and stuff we haven't been able to publish in the magazines, or specific work we like to promote of writers, artists and designers. Although we have been lucky with some generous media partners—often brands with the same design mentality and peer group—*MacGuffin* has never been really dependent on advertising. Most funding has been realized in other ways: joint ventures, events and collaborations. The magazine tends to be more and more of a flywheel for other activities. It also helps in our favor that the zeitgeist is at our hands. We also observe that luxury brands like Loewe, Saint Laurent and Hermes have developed a keen eye for existing and emerging niches in society, often represented in smaller independent magazines. And the distinctive photography of these kinds of fashion shoots plays a major role. Our visual essays series is a great way to stage more autonomous work of these creative minds.

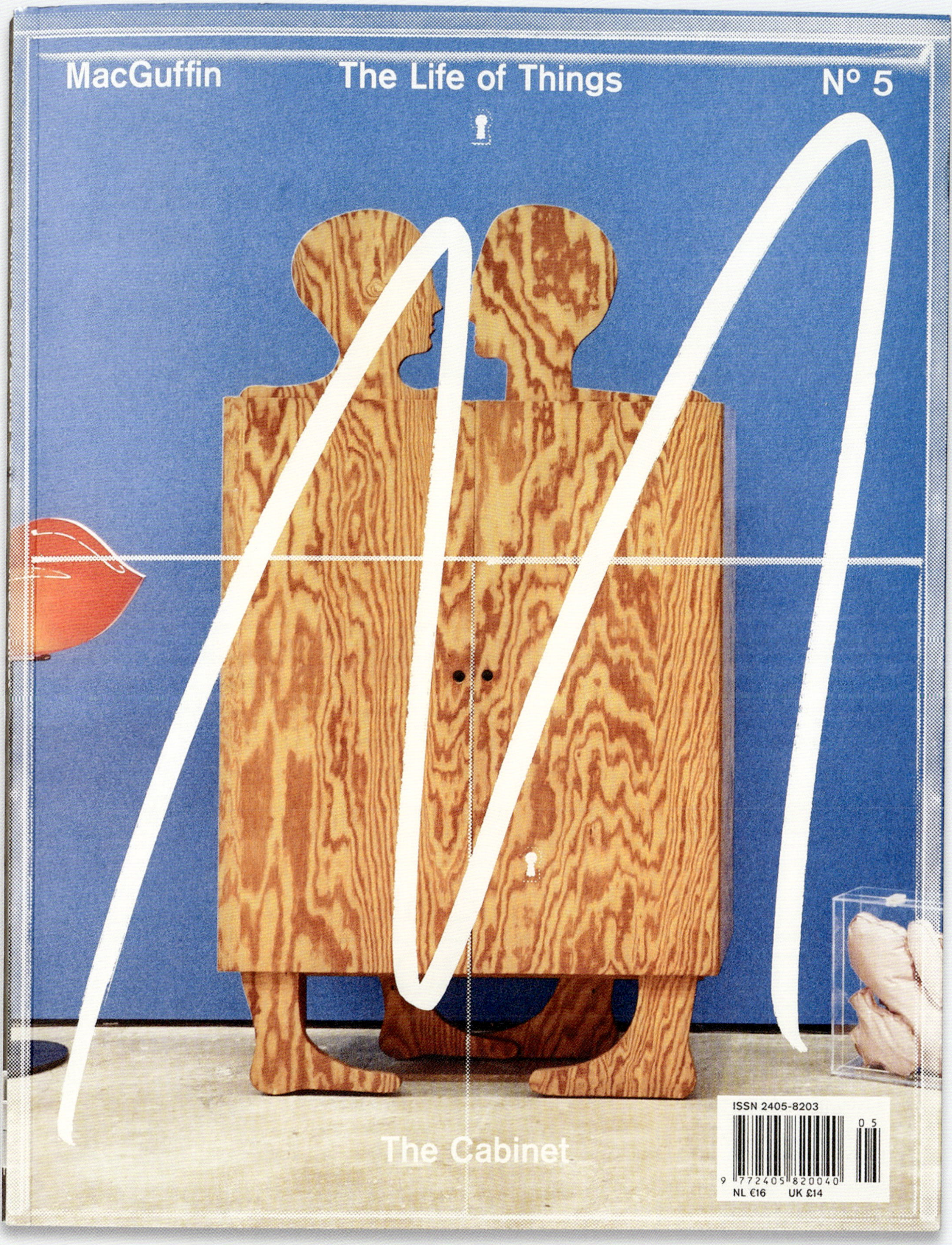

MacGuffin Issue 5 "The Cabinet"

SPECTOR BOOKS

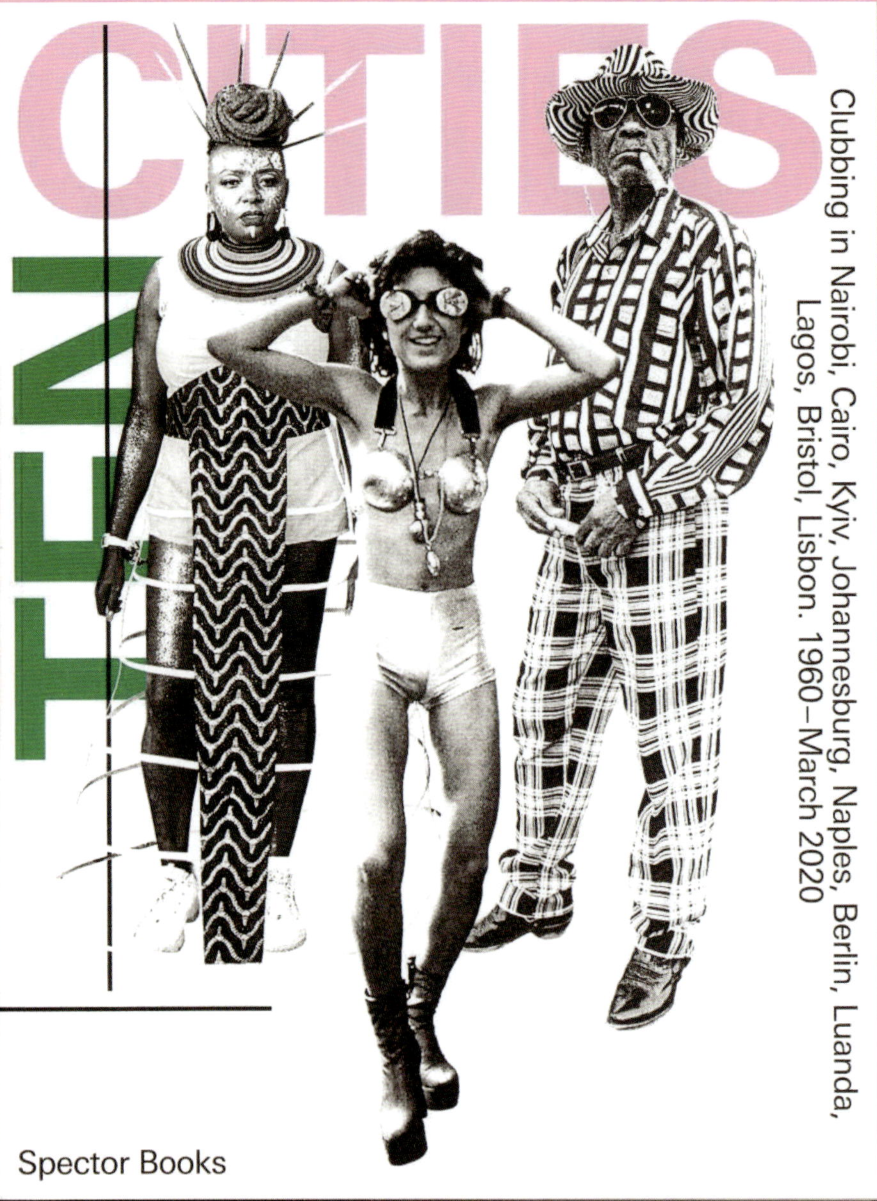

Ten Cities

Page: 560 **Dimension:** 200×270×42mm **Weight:** 1.11kg

Spector Books

Spector Books is an independent publishing house based in Leipzig, Germany. It has remained highly efficient in the field of publishing since its establishment. Spector Books believes that, in order to find innovative approaches to the medium today, it is necessary to have a well thought out interplay between the content, design, and materiality of a book.

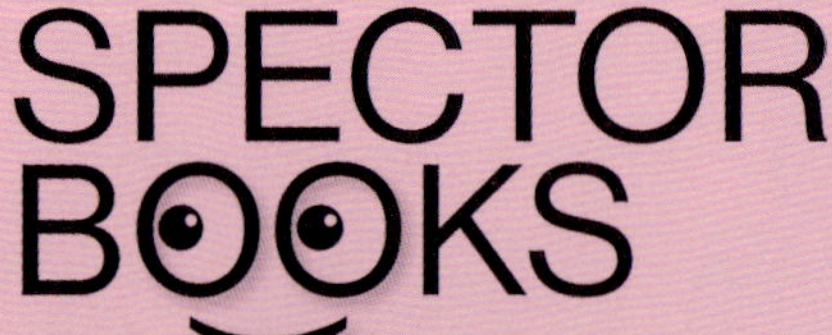

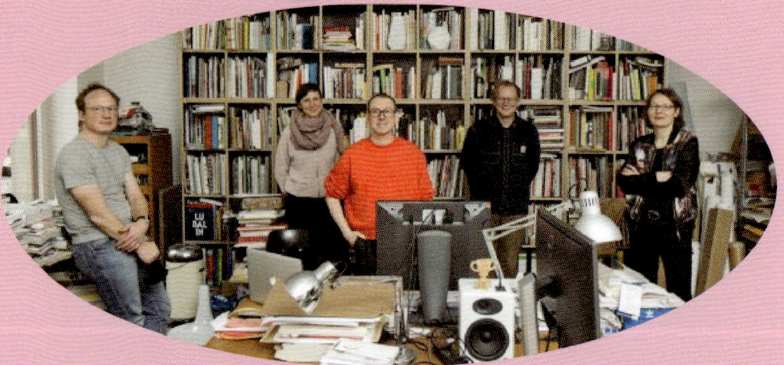

Paper/Material: Euroboard Spezial GT2 350g (Cover); Holmen TRND 2.0 70g (Inside Page) **Binding:** Sewn Binding

Interviewer
Gakky Luk

Create a Brand-New Editorial Logic

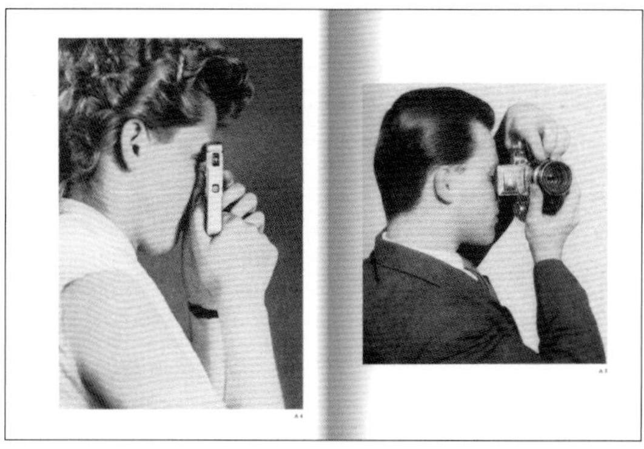

Holding the Camera

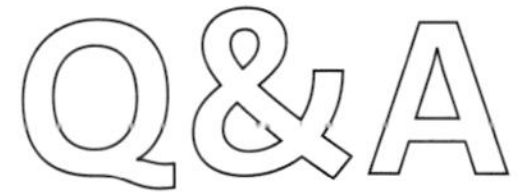

There are 10 members in the Spector Books team, but the team produces over 50 publications every year. How does the team maintain such an efficient working mode?

We publish at least one book per week, and it is only possible due to the large network of people we work with. At Spector Books we are a small team, but behind each publication there are large numbers of people and institutions with whom we cooperate. That includes of course the artists, editors, authors and graphic designers but also printers, bookbinders, translators...

As the publisher, we are the ones who connect everyone involved, and we offer a space to discuss and develop a project together.

Printing and publishing are the main industries in Leipzig. Does such an environment influence your work? How has your publishing business affected the local culture?

Leipzig has a rich history in book culture, but when we started Spector Books, most of that cultural and industrial heritage had disappeared. Nowadays it is very rare for us to actually produce a book entirely in Leipzig. We cooperate with different printers and bookbinders in Germany. Some are in Leipzig, but for most productions we travel to other parts of the country.

But still there are influences on our work because we are based in Leipzig. We often cooperate with students or teachers from the Academy of Fine Arts Leipzig, a school that is dedicated to the art of making books. We have also had cooperation with the German Institute for Literature which is a part of the Leipzig University.

I am not sure how our publishing practice affects the local culture in Leipzig. Of course, we organize book presentations, launches and readings, but sometimes I have the feeling that Spector Books is more established outside of Leipzig and even outside of Germany.

Do you have a preference when you choose the theme for publication? Content, design and material—which aspect takes up most of your energy and why?

Most books that we publish are in the fields of art, photography and design, always taking into account the history and theory of these fields. Furthermore, we edit and publish books dedicated to architecture, urbanism, film and literature. What we are interested in is to develop a contemporary practice of publishing. That means we want to publish and distribute crucial and decisive contents which question the political and economic conditions we are living in. Seeing the design and the materiality of our publications, you can see that we search for specific design solutions for each publication. In our practice, the design is always part of the content itself.

You have published publication series such as *DNA*, *Analysis & Exzess Bundle*, to name a few. How did you create the unique visual style for each series?

As an example, I can talk about the *DNA* series which started in 2021 and has been developed by Markus Dreßen, Hannes Drissner, Malin Gewinner, Olaf Nicolai and Jan Wenzel. By the end of 2022 we will publish 25 volumes in this series. DNA stands for Das Neue Alphabet (means "The New Alphabet"). For its design, the logic of the alphabet (elements, combinatorics, sequencing) was adopted. The components of the design are letters, words, colors and the materiality of the paper. These elements function according to the variation and permutation. Placed side by side, the open dust jackets form a series of posters that merge to form a color gradient which ties all 25 publications of the series together. The multi-layered visual and semantic combinations not only link the volumes to one another; they also provide options for playing with arrangements, with which alternative logic and readings can be introduced into the order of the series.

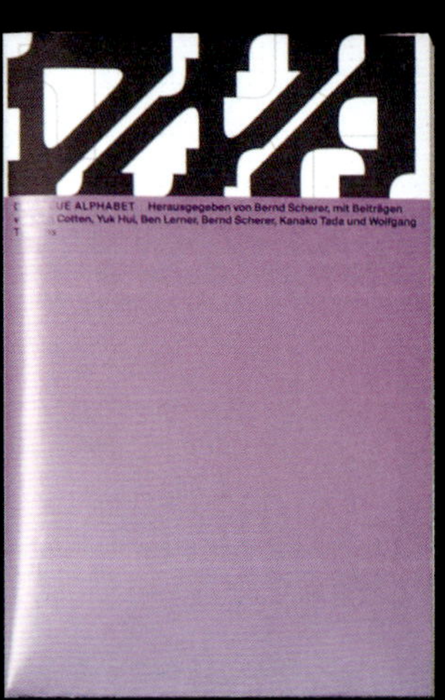
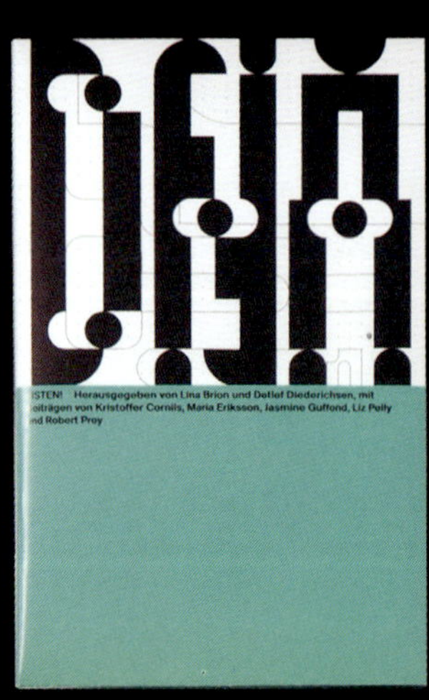

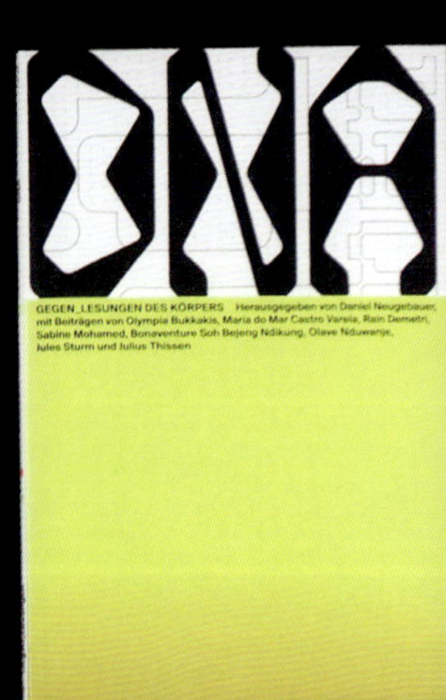

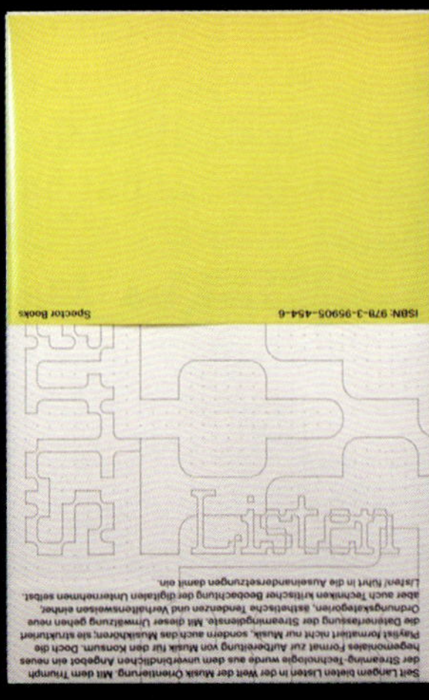

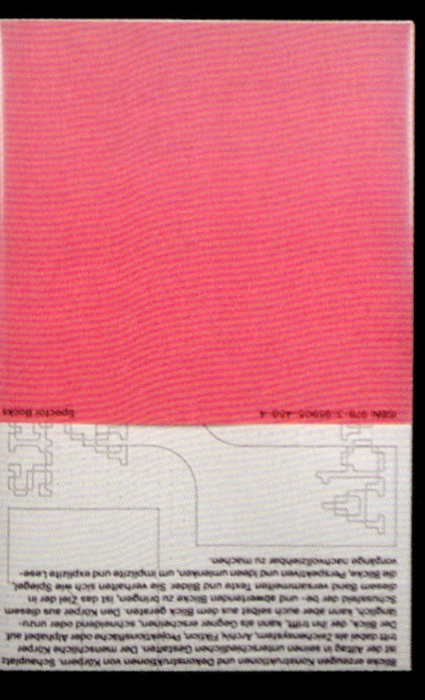

DNA

DNA

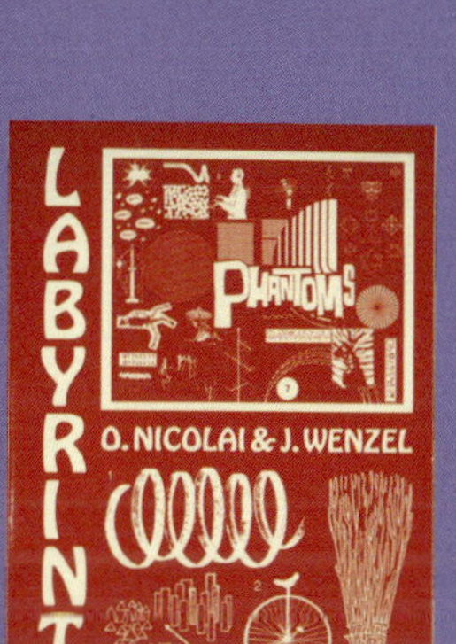

Four Times Through the Labyrinth

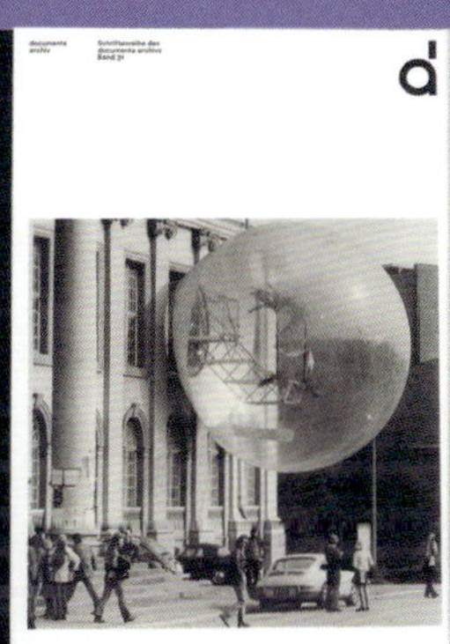

Bauhaus Documenta

You have participated in various art book fairs hosted in different countries. Due to geographical, social, cultural and other factors, the characteristics of each art book fair are different. Could you share your feelings and experiences of the different art book fairs you have participated in?

In a normal year we would visit round about 10 fairs. That includes large book fairs in Leipzig and Frankfurt and many art book fairs around the globe. One main difference we notice when comparing art book fairs in Europe and the United State to China is that the visitors in China are younger than those in Europe or the United State. That makes me very happy because it seems like there is a growing interest for printed matter in the younger generation. Many people in the publishing industry fear digitalization and forecast the decline of printed books. At the fairs we experience quite the opposite. There is a growing interest in surfaces, materiality, printing, papers and binding techniques, and it is also a huge appreciation for the printed book.

In China, self-publishing is rapidly becoming a new force that is advancing the development of the publishing industry. How about the development of self-publishing in Germany? What lessons can be learned?

Self-publishing has been around in Germany since the late 1960s and I think today it has lost some of its initial diversity and dynamic. To learn about self-publishing in Germany and Western Europe I can recommend the publication *Under the Radar–Underground Zines and Self-Publications 1965–1975*, which offers a broad overview of various projects from the very beginning.

Coming together, browsing through each other's publications and talking about books, I learn a lot when visiting international art book fairs.

Under the Radar
Underground Zines and
Self-Publications 1965–1975

Edited by
Jan-Frederik Bandel,
Annette Gilbert, Tania Prill
Spector Books

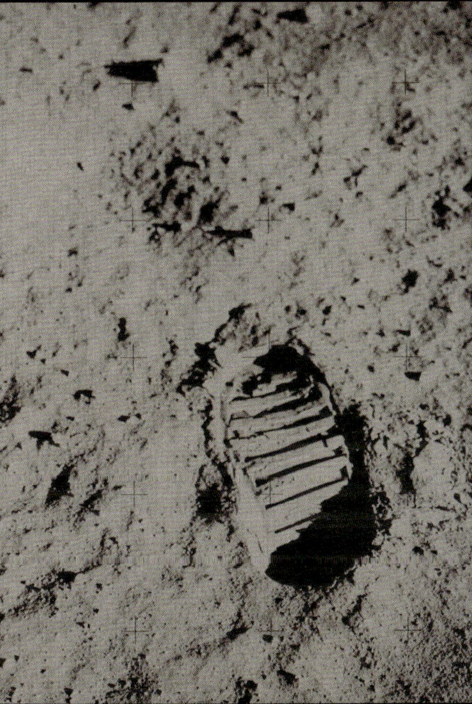

Nasa Apollo 11

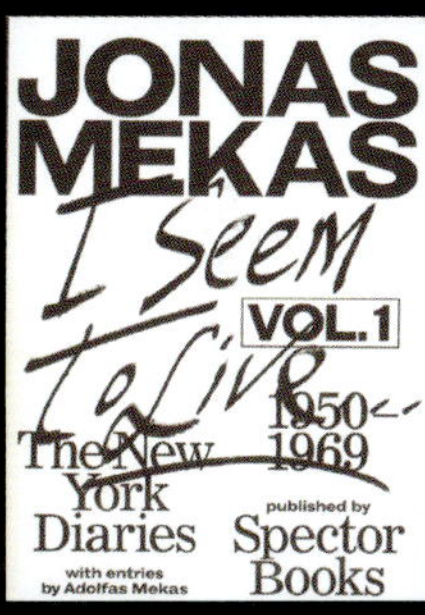

I Seem to Live

With texts by
Chowra Makaremi

Hannah
Darabi

Enghelab
Street,

a Revolution
through Books:

Iran 1979
– 1983

Spector
Books

Le Bal

Enghelab Street

design
rehearsals

conversations
about
bauhaus
lessons

EDITION BAUHAUS 57

Spector Books

Design Rehearsals

HEKICHI

HB-019

uni-curve

masatoshi tabuchi

uni-curve

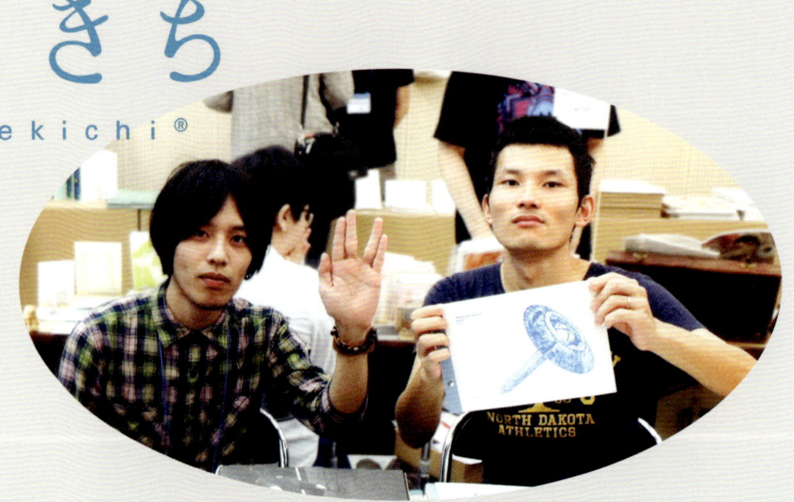

Hekichi

Hekichi is a Japan-based design studio mainly specializing in publication. It was co-founded by Masatoshi Tabuchi and Hirokazu Matsuda in 2011. It has released 55 publications since its establishment.

Page: 56 **Dimension:** 190×265mm **Paper/Material:** OK Muse Linter; GA Cotton; Tanto; Mag Plain; OK Adonisu Rough **Binding:** Case Binding

Interviewer
Gakky Luk

RECORD THE PRESENT IN A BOOK

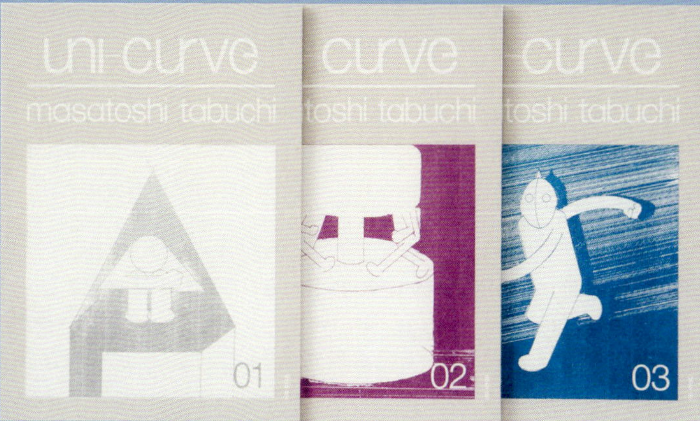

uni-curve

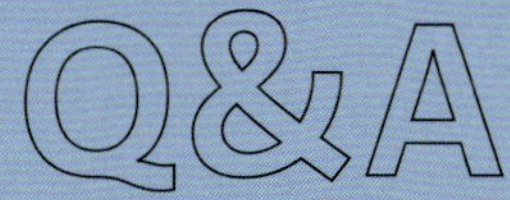

Hekichi means "isolated place". Why did you use this word to name your studio? What features of the studio did it symbolize?

The reason why we chose it as the name of our studio was because we thought it had a nice ring to it. Thinking back now, the meaning of "hekichi" is also our attitude towards publication—each book is like an isolated place. Therefore, we think it can be the representative of the activities conducted by the studio.

Hekichi is good at conveying the essence of a theme by using its unique methods. How do you "tailor" the most suitable "shell" for different contents?

In fact, our work is very simple. Tabuchi takes charge of images, and I am responsible for design. This kind of cooperation gives the shape to the design. It is a reflection of our thought at that time, and we both value the worth of our thoughts in the moment.

For example, the title of one of our publications was uni-curve, which was inspired by a drawing tool used by Tabuchi. Tabuchi challenged himself to draw freely using this limited tool, so he only used a ruler named "uni-curve" during the process. When I saw the paintings, I came up with the idea of categorizing them into three types. Therefore, we divided the paintings into three categories based on the mood they presented: ancient, medieval, and modern. Each of them was a single story in the book. These decisions were not made through our consultation as such, but rather as a result of personal feelings when we both worked on the project.

What do you think is the difference between self-publishing and traditional publishing? While many say that self-publishing provides designers with more room for creativity, what is the most challenging aspect of your creative work?

I think the biggest difference between the two is "freedom". Self-publishing enables us to decide the price, the format, the way of binding, the printing method and so on. We can fully control the whole process. In addition, there is no deadline for us, so we can work on it until both of us are satisfied with the product. It is difficult to do when it comes to traditional publishing. Also, we think it is important for us to create things that are meaningful for ourselves rather than just focusing on the public.

As for the most difficult part, I think it is the sales and promotion. Neither of us are good at increasing the sales of our publications. So, we opened an online store in an effort to overcome this problem.

Those engaged in self-publishing need to focus not only on the content, but also on design, printing, promotion, and sales. What is your current mode in the field of promotion and sales?

Originally, the purpose of our activities was to turn Tabuchi's works into books. We used to sell our publications in a limited number of places such as art book fairs, but many of these events have been cancelled due to the COVID-19 pandemic.

Now we have an online store. Recently, we have also started to present our books and show the making process through Instagram Live.

Self-publishing requires a vast investment of time and energy. Are both of you engaged full-time in this work? How do you maintain a balance between the investment and the return?

Neither of us are full-time publishers. Tabuchi is an illustrator, and I am a graphic designer. As you say, making books requires a lot of energy, but it also is something that delights us at the same time. We believe that the return we get is not only in terms of money, but also in other things. It is meaningful for us to invest money and time to create something we really want to make.

There are only two members in Hekichi. How do you divide labor among the two members effectively?

Our way of working is very simple. We talk about many things in daily life, but we don't talk about the books before we start making. We often talk about things that are not related to the creation process, but just our normal, everyday thoughts. If I have to specify about the labor division between us, it is probably the preparation stage before production.

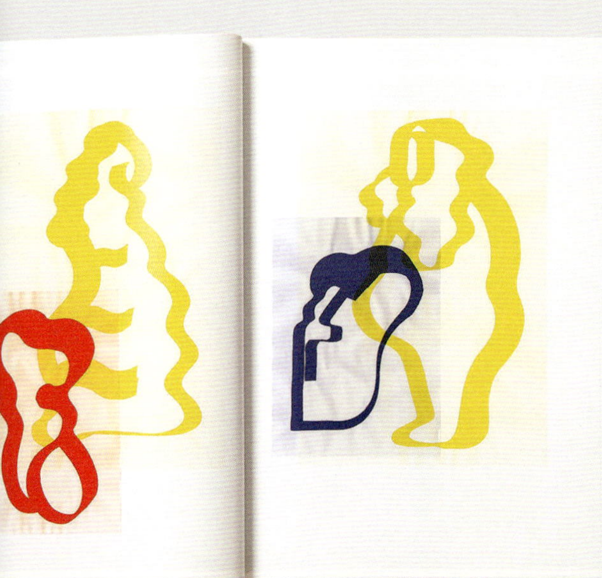

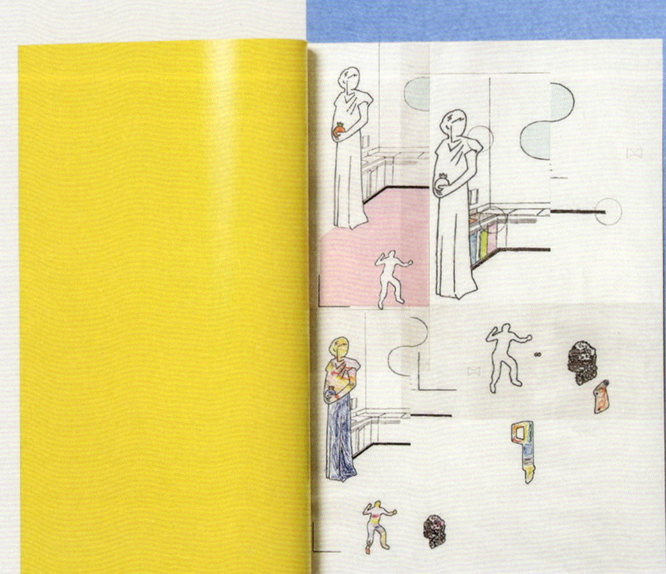

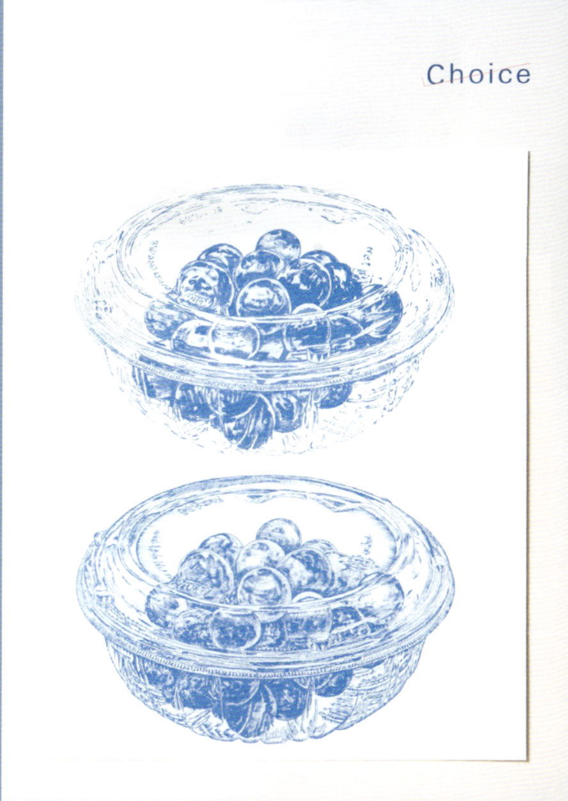

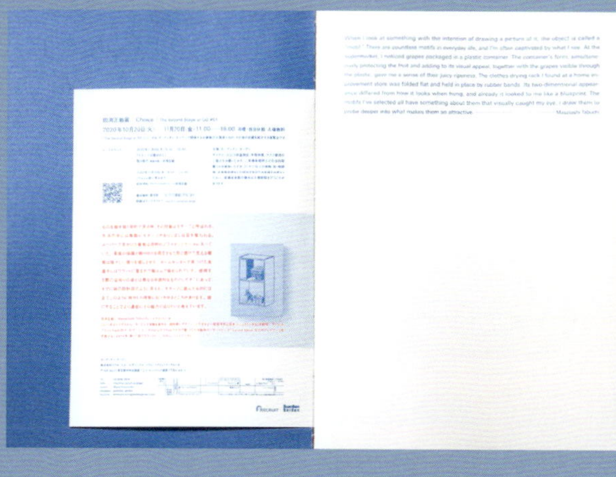

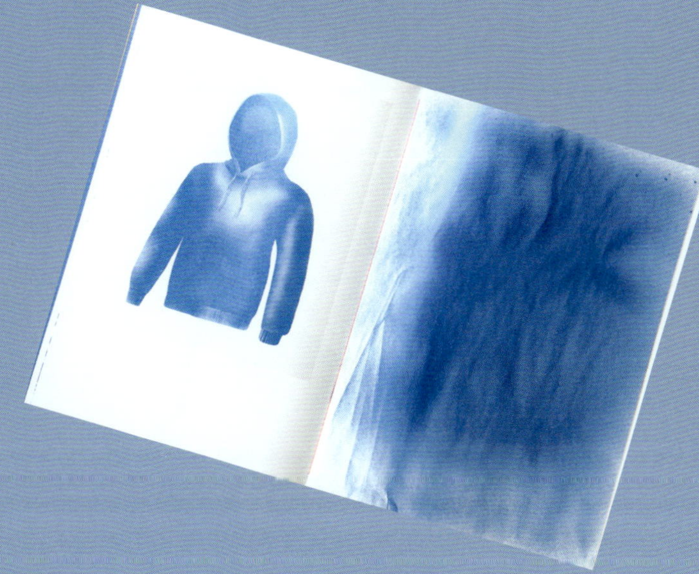

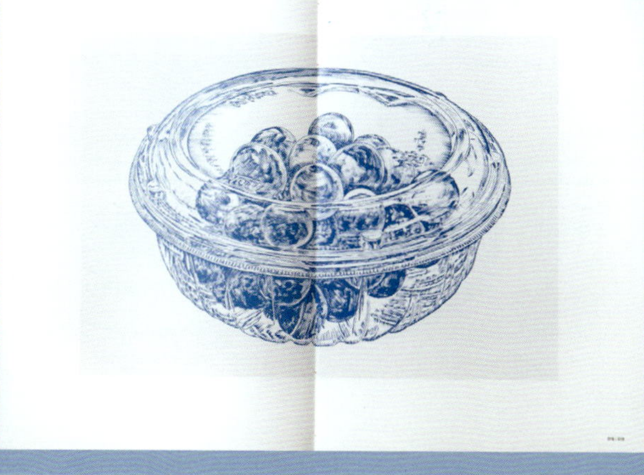

When I look at something with the intention of drawing a picture of it, the object is called a "motif." There are countless motifs in everyday life, and I'm often captivated by what I see. At the supermarket, I noticed grapes packaged in a plastic container. The container's form, simultaneously protecting the fruit and adding to its visual appeal, together with the grapes visible through the plastic, gave me a sense of their juicy ripeness. The clothes drying rack I found at a home improvement store was folded flat and held in place by rubber bands. Its two-dimensional appear-
blueprint. The
I draw them to
Masatoshi Tabuchi

Choice

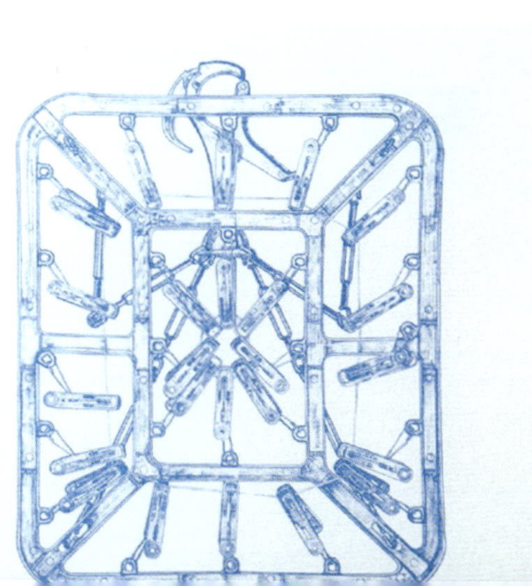

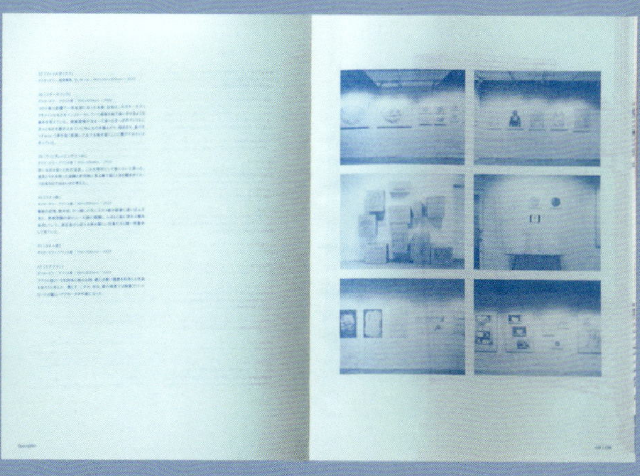

Choice

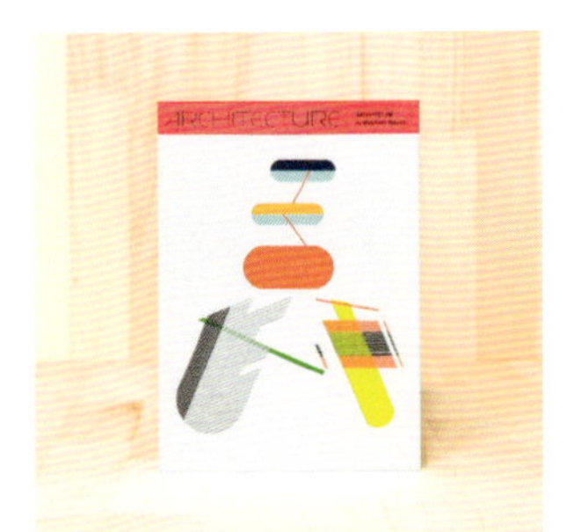

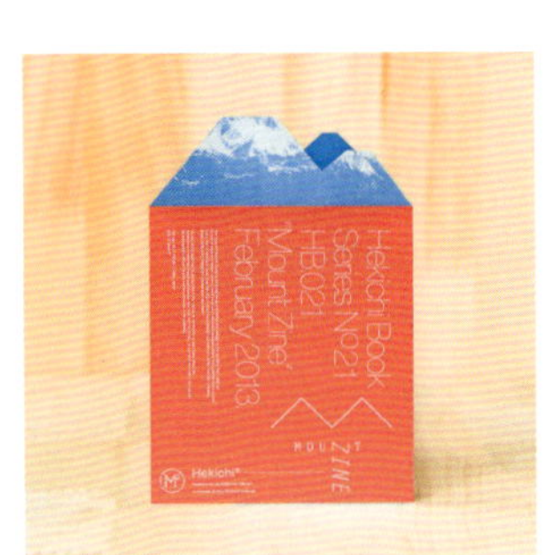
Hekichi Book
Series №21
HB021
Mount Zine
February 2013

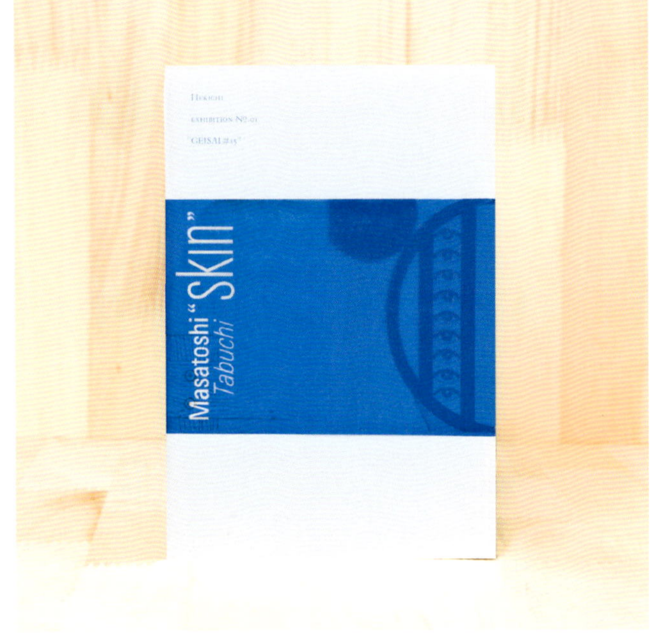
Masatoshi "skin"
Tabuchi

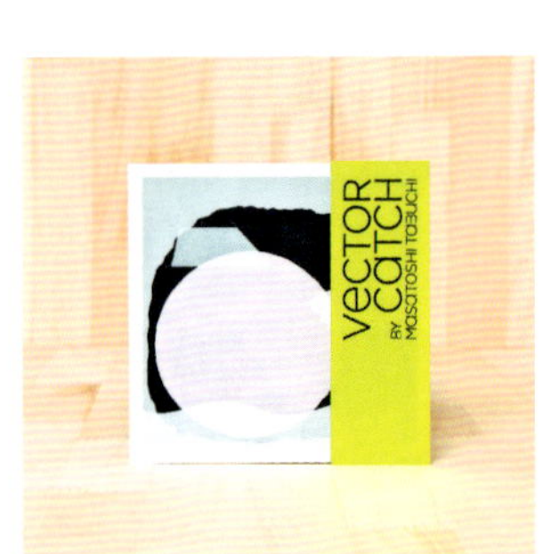
vector catch
BY MASATOSHI TABUCHI

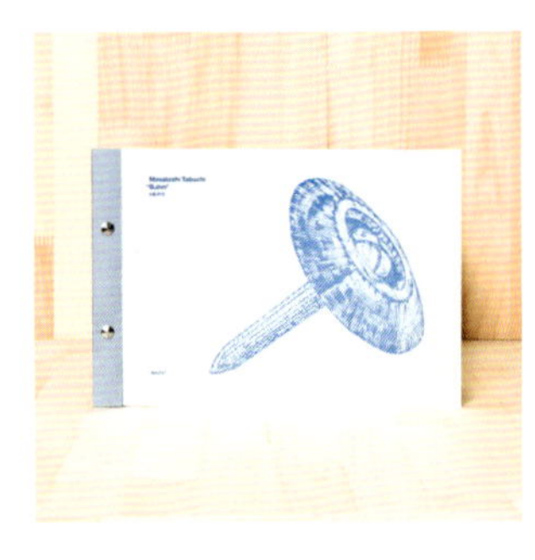

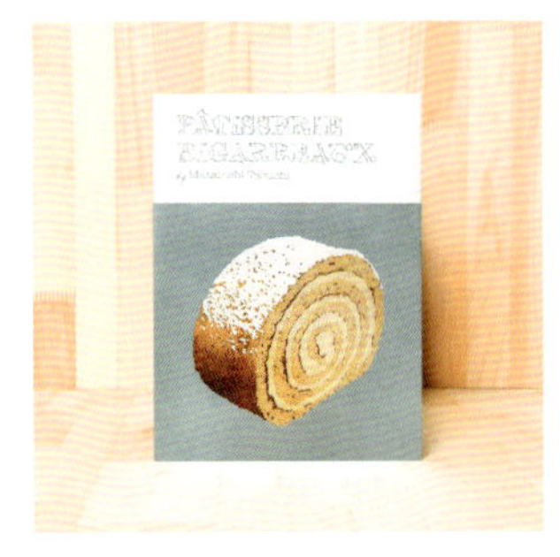

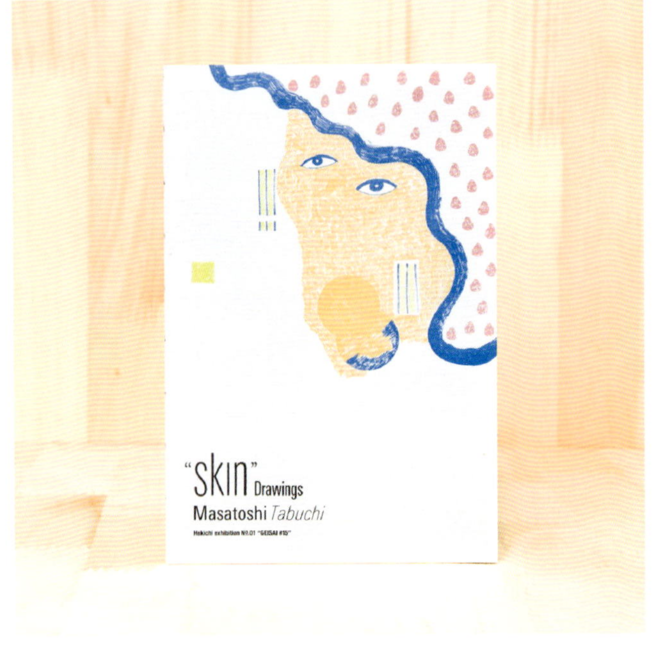
"skin" Drawings
Masatoshi Tabuchi

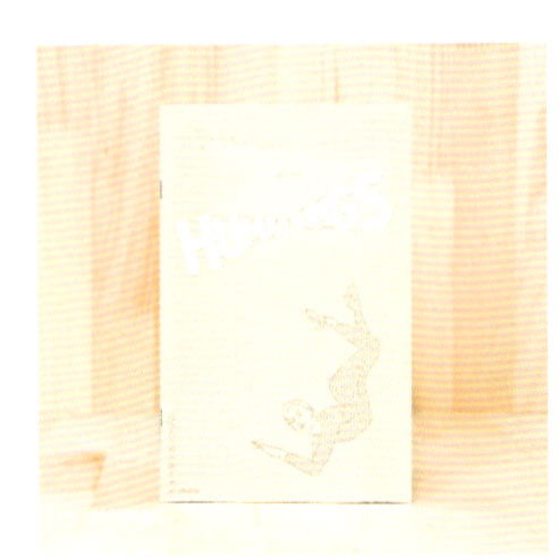

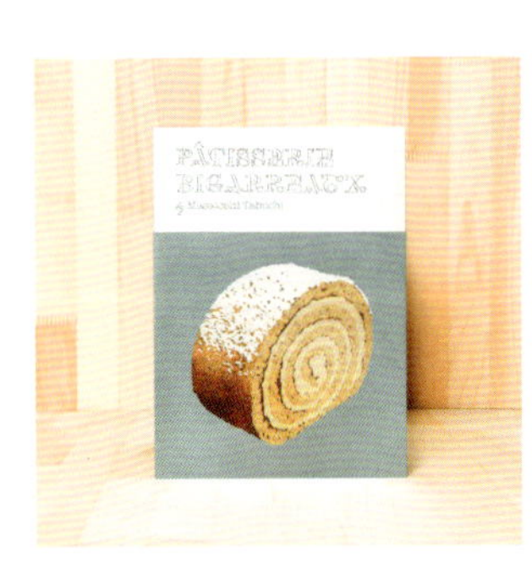

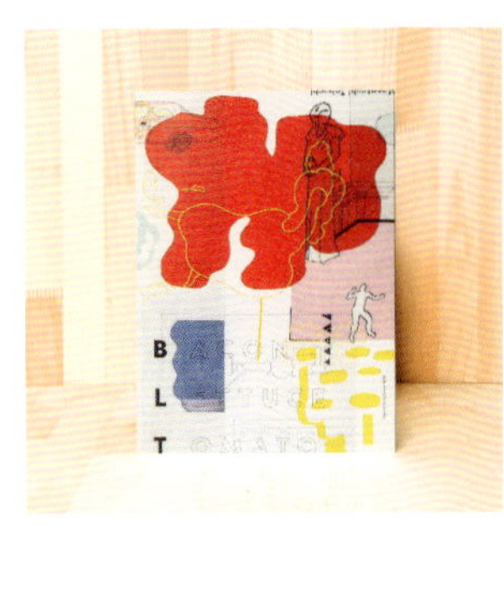

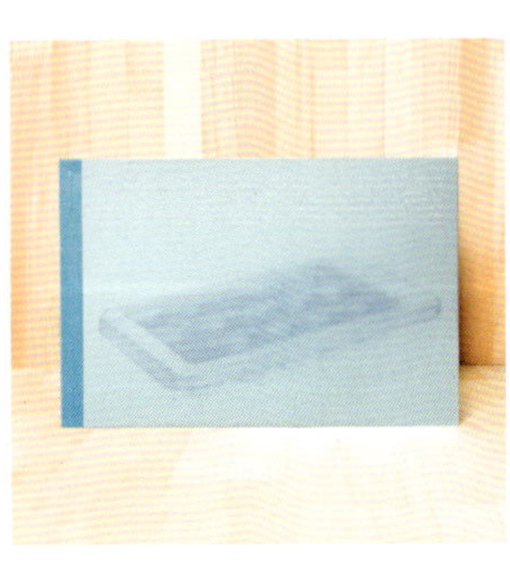

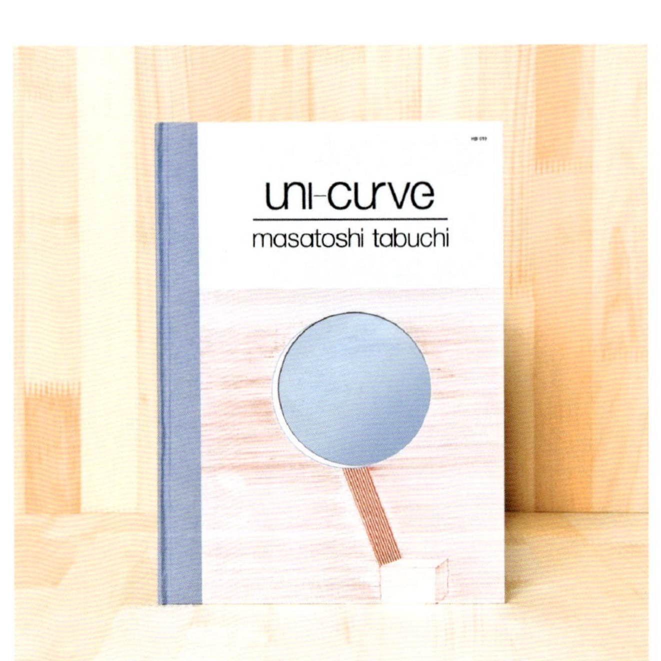
uni-curve
masatoshi tabuchi

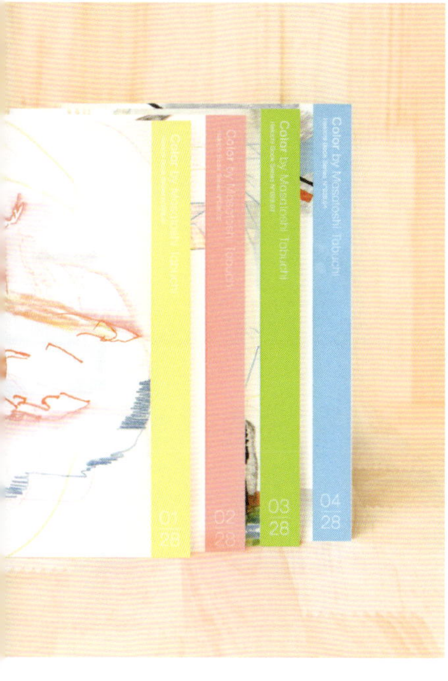

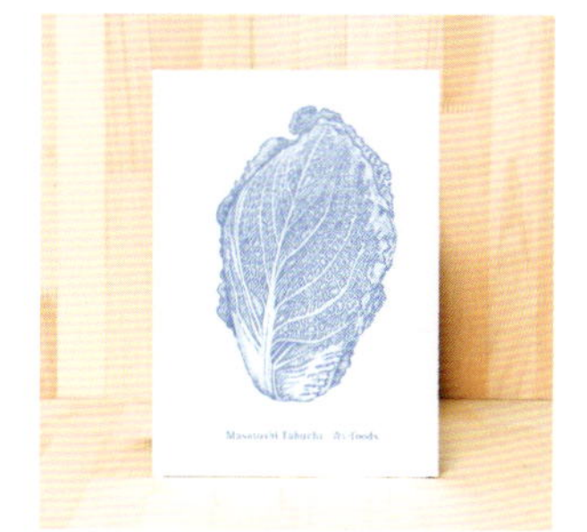

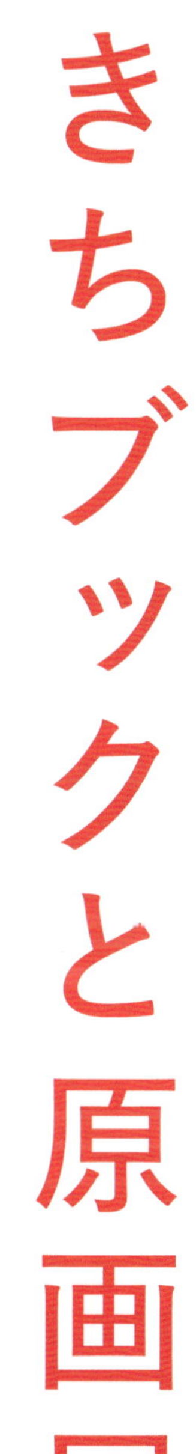

at AOYAMA BOOK CENTER

5/18 sat

6/4 tue

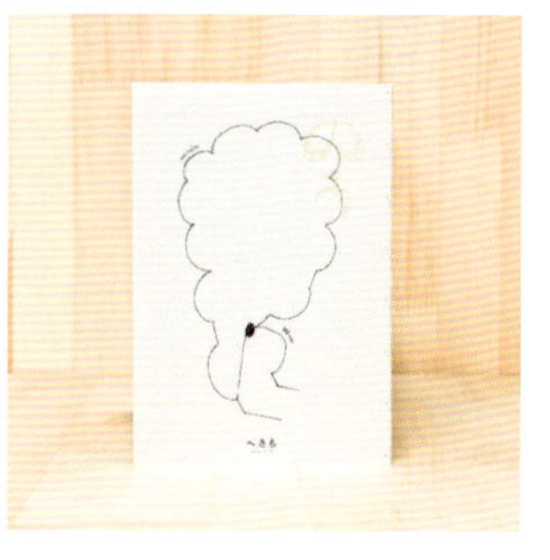

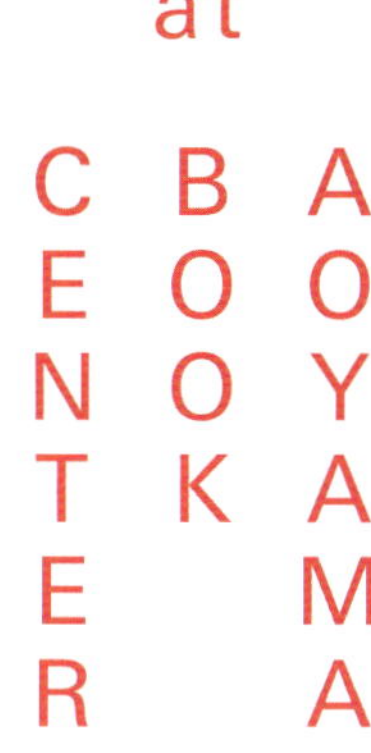

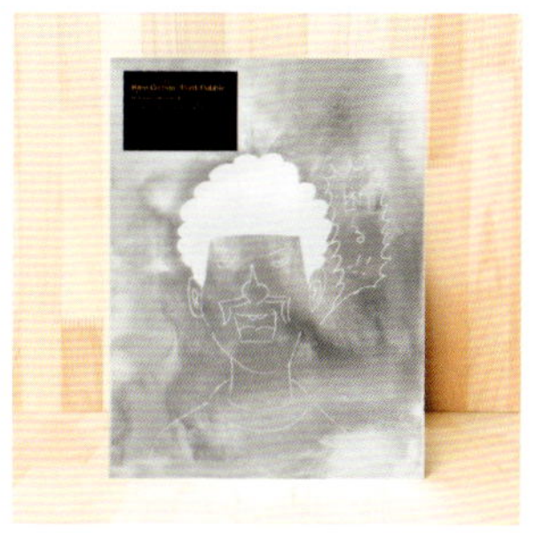

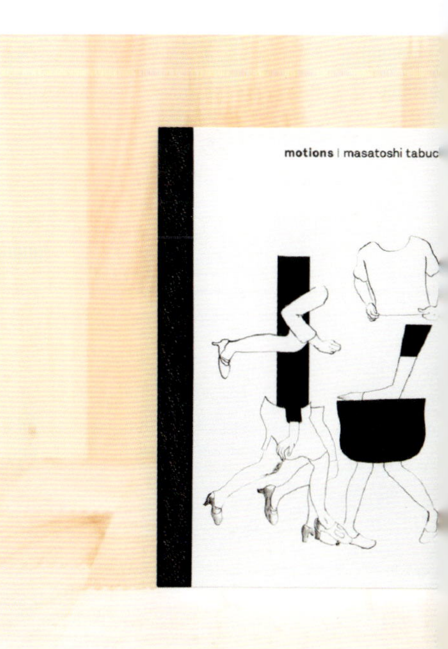

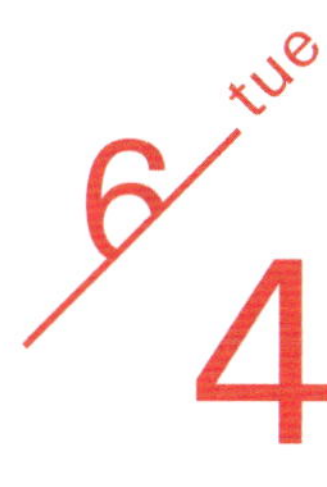

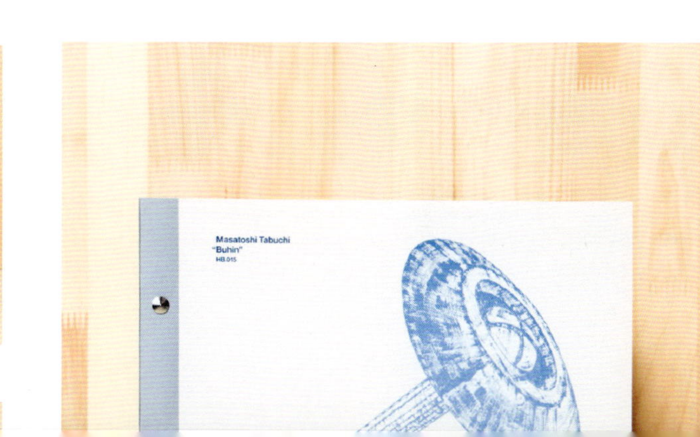

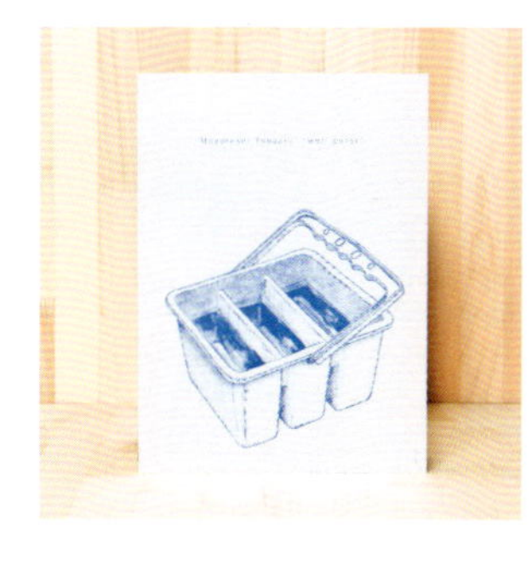

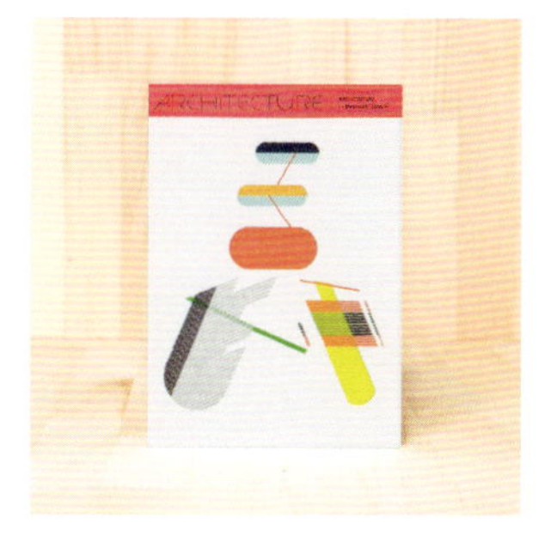

TXTBOOKS

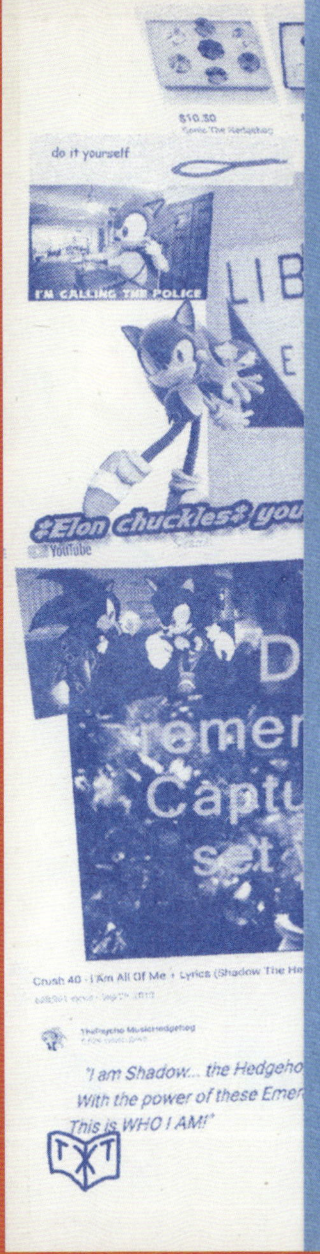

NinTXTdo b.k.a. TXTbooks

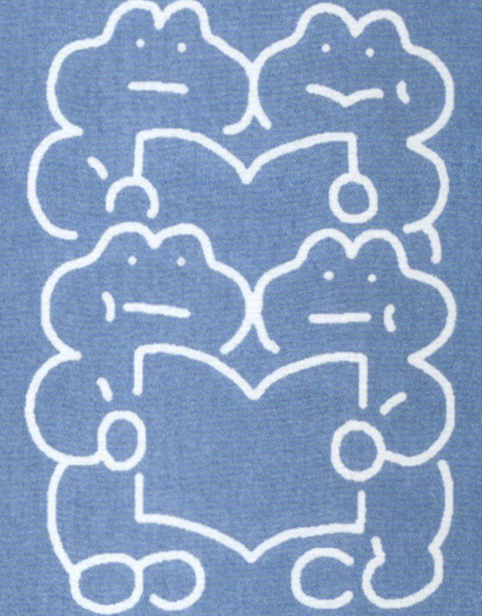

TXTbooks is an artist-run independent publishing initiative and risograph print studio based in Brooklyn, NY.

Since 2014 we have worked with artists and writers across many disciplines to create publications both serious and silly, working to highlight those who do not consider publishing as their "main practice."

Each zine's rights go to their respective artists.

"Finally... I Can Game In Peace."

Edition of 300
Winter 20/21

TXTbooks.us
@txtbooks

TXTreader Issue 3

TXTbooks

TXTbooks is a New York-based independent publishing house founded in 2014. It mainly applies Riso printing in the production of its publications. Its best scenario is to publish zines that have not yet considered to be produced. TXTbooks's ultimate goal is to create passionate projects with as many people as possible.

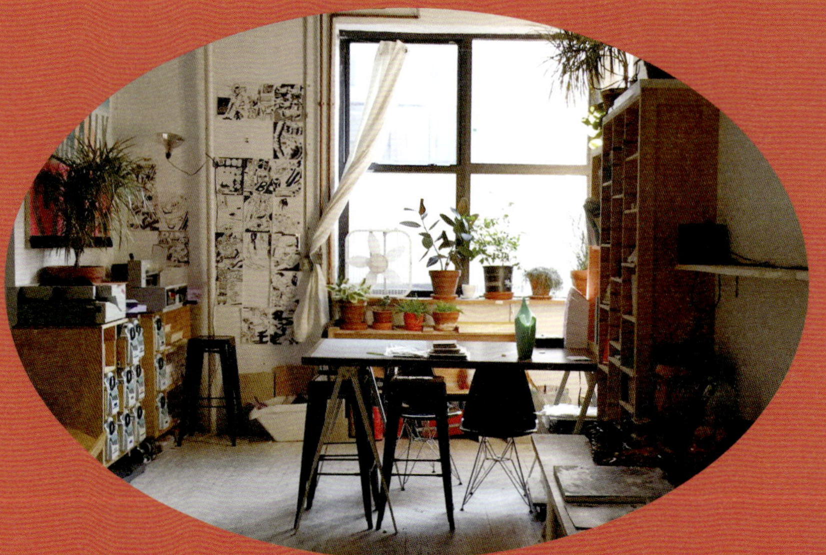

Page: 206 **Dimension:** 127×190×25.4mm

Weight: 230g **Paper/Material:** Mixed Paper Stock **Binding:** Saddle Stitching; Perfect Binding

Interviewer
Gakky Luk

No Judging on the Publishing Ideas

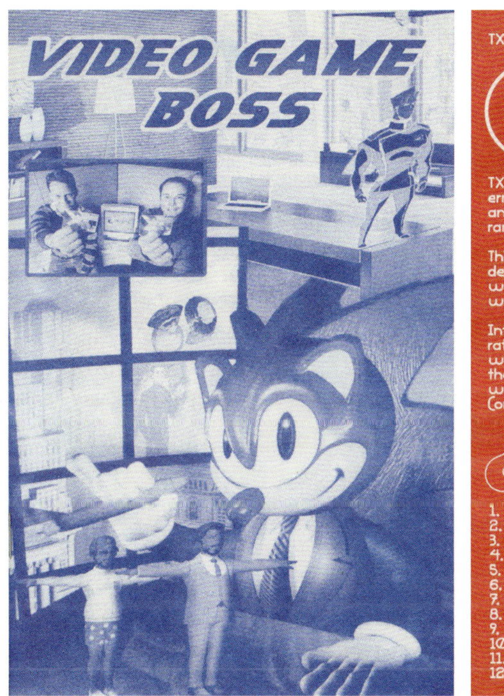

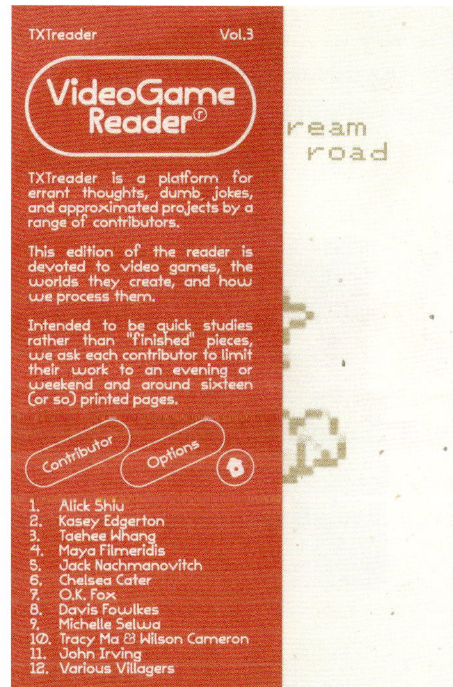

TXTreader Issue 3

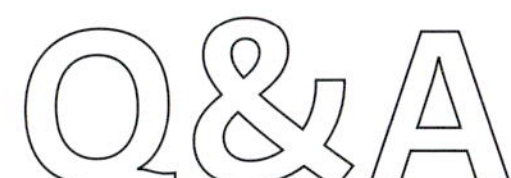

Why do you insist on Riso printing as the main printing method? Does it somehow limit the content of publications in terms of technology or presentation? Would you consider other printing methods?

We use Riso because it has the perfect amount of customization and consideration built into its process. It situates easily between more bespoke "special printing", high-production offset, and desktop at-home printers. We are of course never going to buy an offset printer due to size and operating costs. Special printing methods like litho or silkscreen are either impossible or really annoying if you don't have a good setup. And at-home laser printers don't really produce that beautiful or special feeling you look for in artistic output. So, it's kind of perfect for now. In another regard, by limiting our production method to a single source, we've been able to find an easy way to do what we want. Through the natural constraints of Riso, we create a visual harmony with each project. We believe this has a benefit overall to the visual output. It definitely limits in terms of presentation because it never produces the real image, but only a facsimile. But if we wanted a HD image we would just produce a JPG. In the future we might branch out, but for now we are happy with where we are.

There are 12 zines in *TXTreader*, the self-publication of TXTbooks. How did you plan and coordinate these zines? How long did it take? What feedback do you expect to get from readers about the zines?

We usually plan these books over around 6 months from invitation to production. However, the last *TXTreader* was delayed by around a year due to the COVID-19 pandemic. To start, we send an email to gauge the artist's interest, after which we send them a prompt to spark their thoughts. For example, our most recent zine series was on video games and how we relate to them. In developing their projects, some artists like to work closely with us, and others prefer to work more privately and send a PDF when ready. Either way we generally give artists the opportunity to make whatever it is they want to make without restriction from us.

As for feedback...we are producing a variety pack with the hopes that there is at least "something" for everyone. Readers might enjoy some contributions more than others based on their personal backgrounds and that's okay. Hopefully at least something sparks a thought or reflection.

Why did you choose self-publishing as the way to share your projects? What are the advantages and disadvantages of self-publishing for your creative output?

We have always loved the idea of multiples. In art, there is so much pressure put on one finished project, and in the end if you sell it—that's that. Multiples give us a way to make a lot of things and give them to a lot of people. When you have an edition run of 200 books, you don't feel bad about giving a copy to a friend, which I think is key.

Self-publishing is also a reclamation of an artist's autonomy. In fine art you can become so weighted down by the infrastructure of the systems in place that make that world function financially. But with self-publishing, you can make anything you want, press print, then sell it online or in a fair. No idea is too big or too small—it all sits on a level playing field on the table.

I think most artists would place people seeing their work and engaging with it at a higher priority than making a ton of money off it—and self-publishing does just that. People come together from all over the world to fairs to buy and sell books. There are so many people you meet by doing this than you ever would by having 2-3 gallery shows a year. It builds community quicker and makes the community stronger.

Foamy

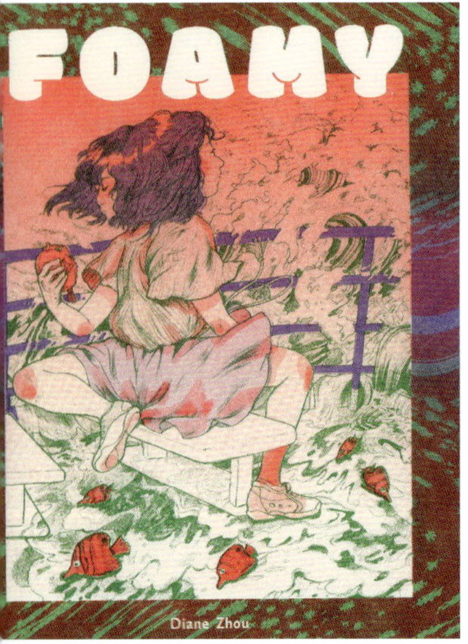

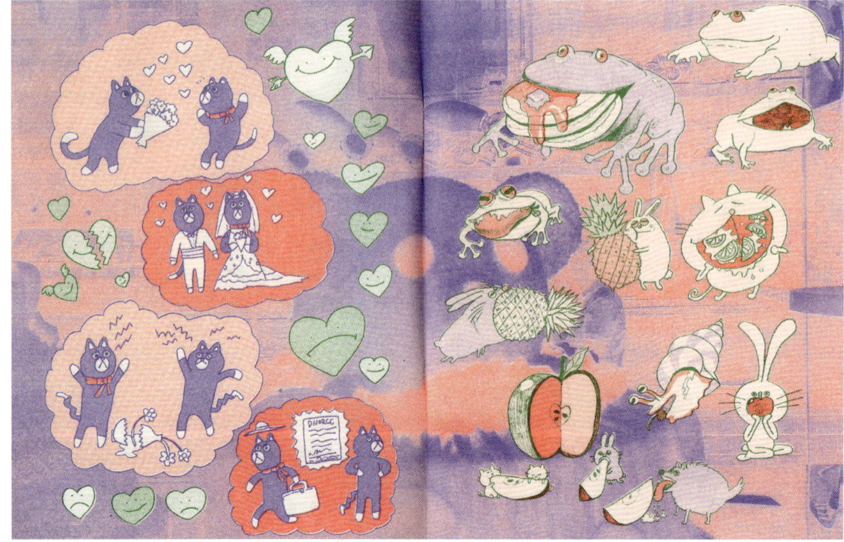

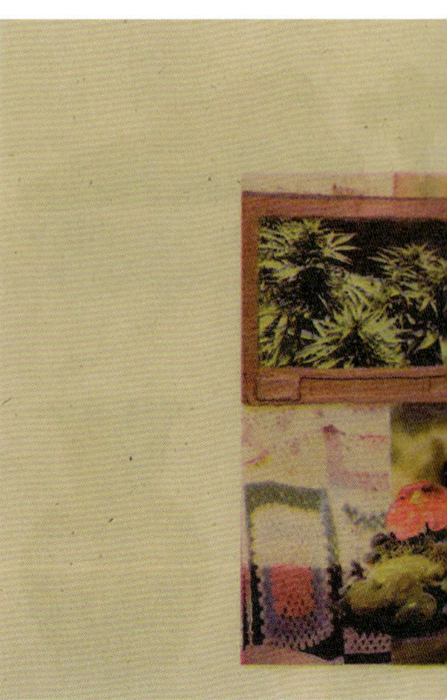

What standards do you apply to price your self-publications? What considerations are involved in pricing?

Pricing your own stuff is hard. You have to battle a lot of conflicting narratives in your own head. "Would anyone even want to buy this?" or "Would anyone ever want to spend 20 bucks on this thing I made?" can be a tough thought cycle to get out of. There is a lot of pressure you can put on yourself when you've made something completely of your own volition and asked people to buy it. For the most part, we try to keep everything attainable price-wise. We factor in things like time, cost of paper, amount of colors used and the labor that went into finishing it. But in the end, it can also become a bit more gestural. Something we thought would be a 25-dollar book can end up feeling like a 15-dollar book in the end, and vice versa.

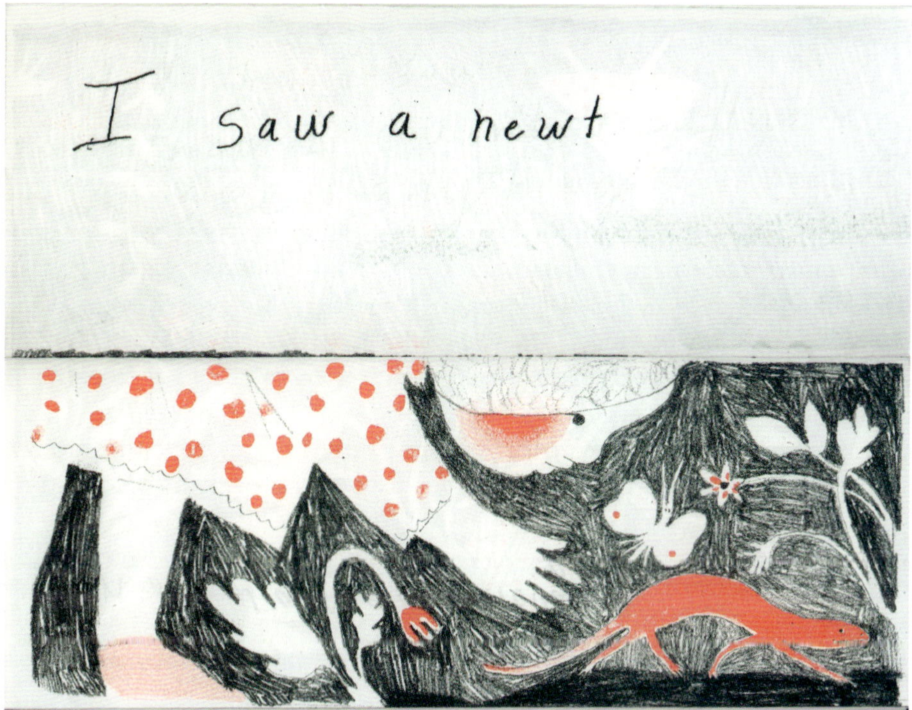

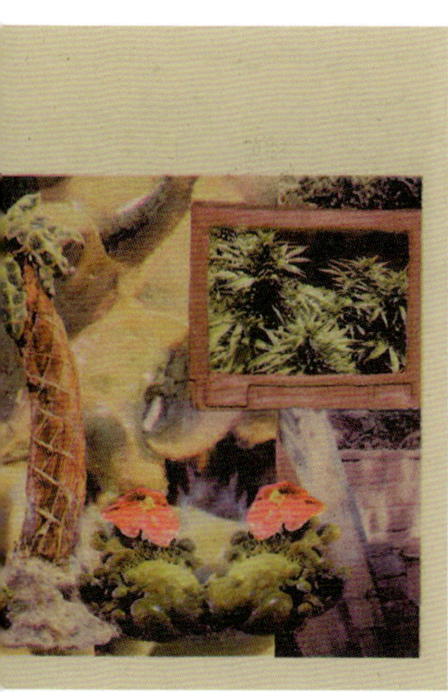

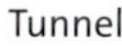

Tunnel

Sleep

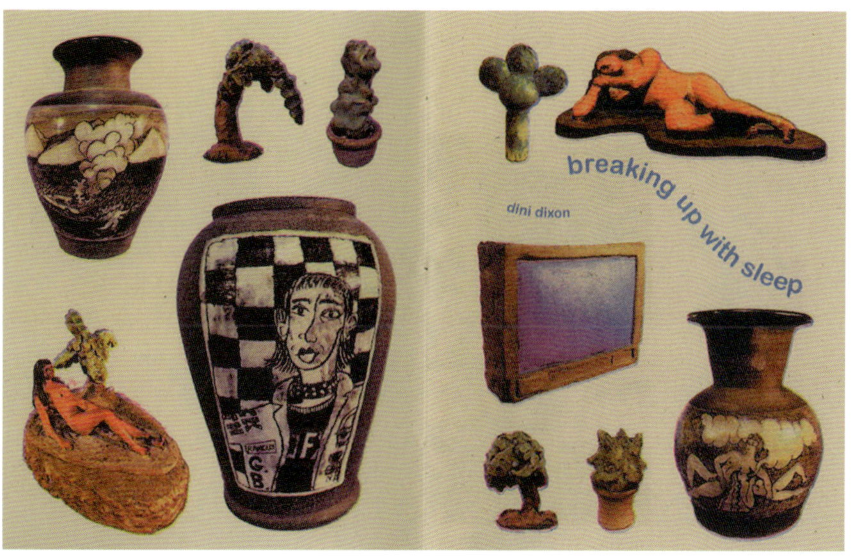

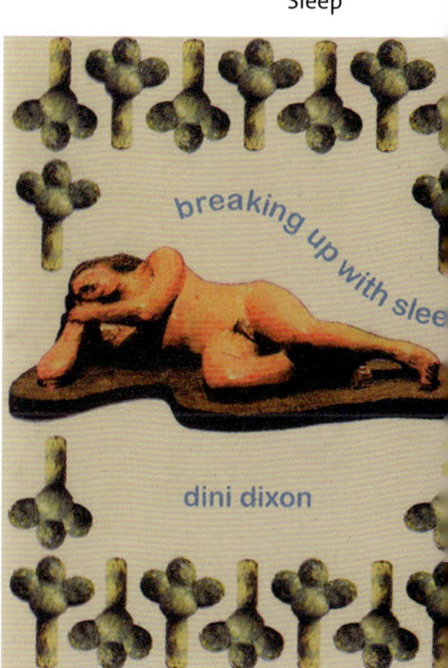

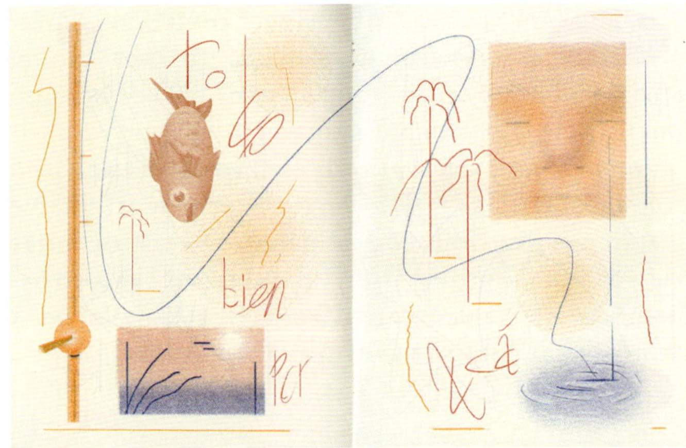

Flojo

As some studios cannot afford operating funds solely from publications, they fill in the gaps by holding workshops and selling products. Do you have similar problems? Can you tell us something about the developing situation of self-publishing in Brooklyn?

We definitely have problems between managing operating costs and overall goals. However, we are somewhere between a side-project and a part-time job, and never expected this project to make money, which, as a result, is more reasonable as we navigate those pressures. We each maintain full-time jobs or rigorous freelance schedules, so we can make our personal income from other sources. This grounds us in a way, so we are never trying to turn a huge profit through TXTbooks specifically. Rather we try to produce work we are interested in through this avenue. In the past we have led workshops, held artist-tutorial hours, produced small art shows, and more. But in that regard, we don't really "set" a schedule to work to, and instead throw these events on spontaneously based on need in any given season. We also do a range of printing services for a small group of clients and independent artists. With all this, in recent years we have become more financially stable.

Regarding self-publishing in Brooklyn, we are so lucky to be surrounded by so many amazing presses and individuals who inspire us. It's been an amazing community to grow with and become a part of. We want to do a quick shout out to Endless Editions who along with a number of dedicated volunteers to organize the Brooklyn Art Book Fair have done so much to bring the community together. We are also, of course, grateful to Printed Matter and the New York Art Book Fair which is what got us interested in this field to begin with.

TXTbooks has participated in art book fairs in Brooklyn, New York, Los Angeles, and other cities. What do you think are the characteristics of readers in different regions?

People seem to view the fairs as homologous events where vendors bring books and hope to sell them the same way each time. But after having been to many fairs, we can tell you they each have their quirks. The New York Art Book Fair is the most frenetic. It's the sweatiest and the most raucous, and probably by far the most energetic. The Los Angeles iteration of Printed Matter's fair feels similar but with 3 times the space. No one is competing to get to a table or squeezing through a pathway. It also feels like LA has a big interest in what's going on at the fair, everyone is asking questions about "what this is" or "why do you want to do this" in an earnest way, and it feels good to wax poetic for a bit in the 70-degree weather. The Brooklyn Art Book Fair put on by Endless Editions feels like a nice in between. Its close quarters set up leads to a lot of socializing, and it only held on one day. Low stress and a great hang out place. All the European fairs we have done have been incredibly fun.

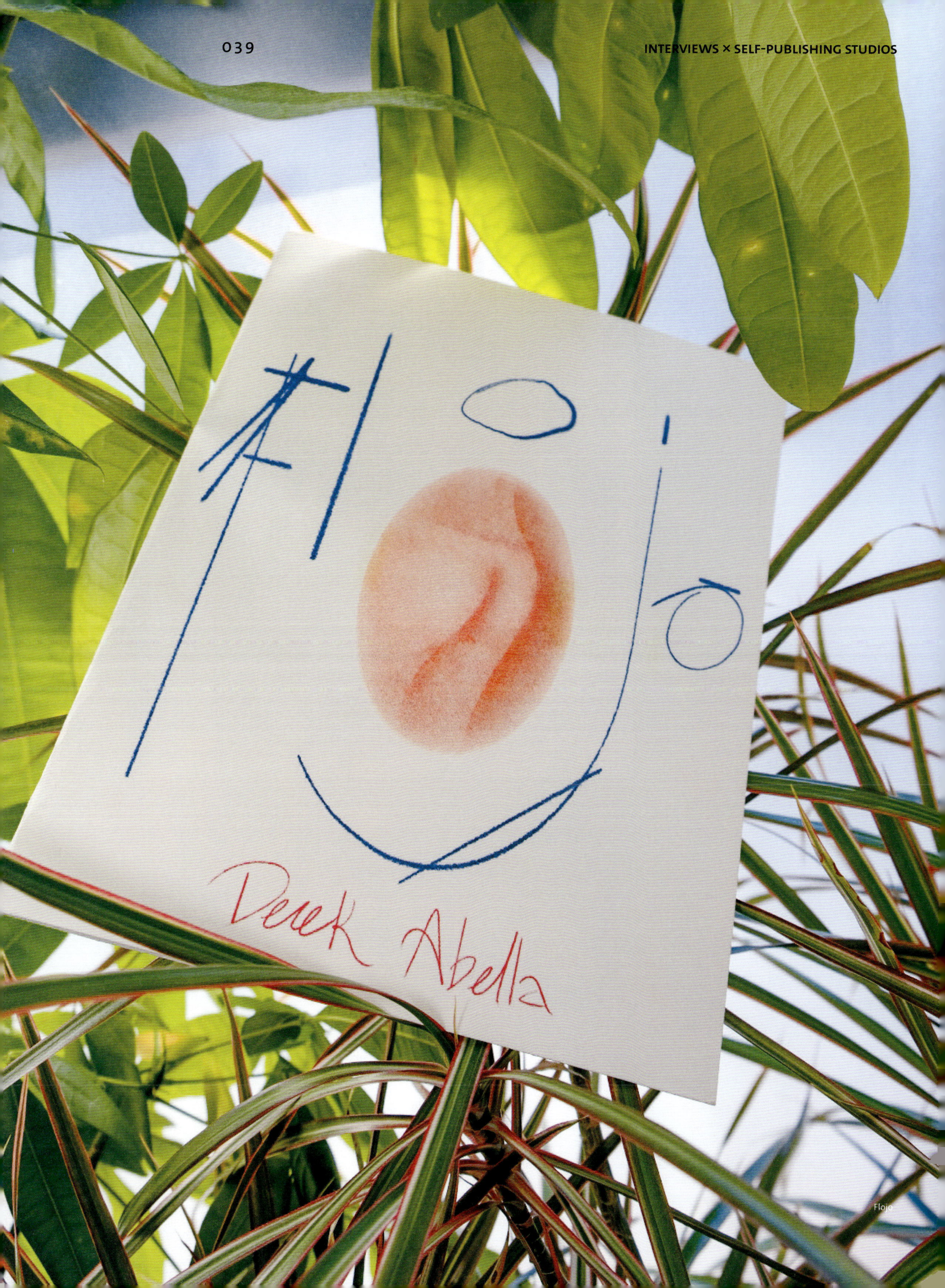

Flojo

MIJEONG JEONG

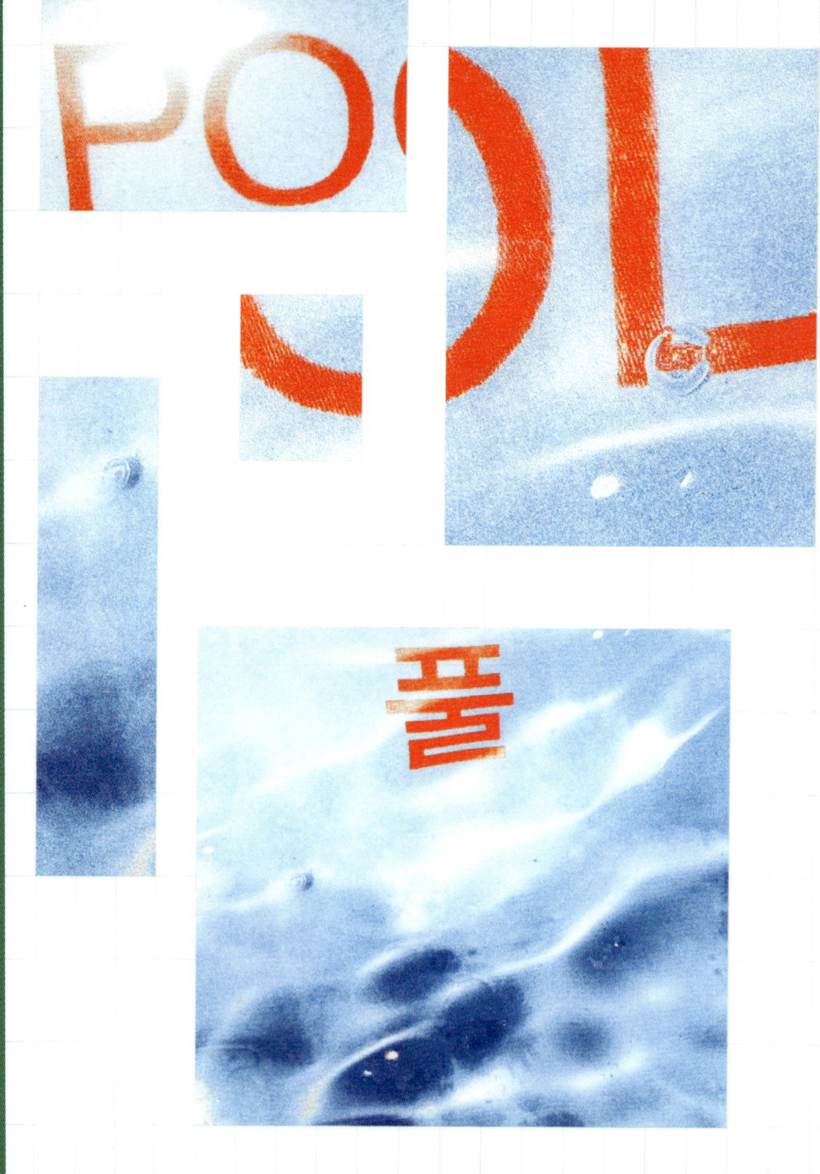

POOL

Mijeong Jeong

A South Korea-based designer. Jeong received her master's degree from the Basel School of Design in Switzerland. In 2019, Jeong set up her own design studio in South Korea, and officially joined the self-publishing industry with her first graphic design collection *693+41*.

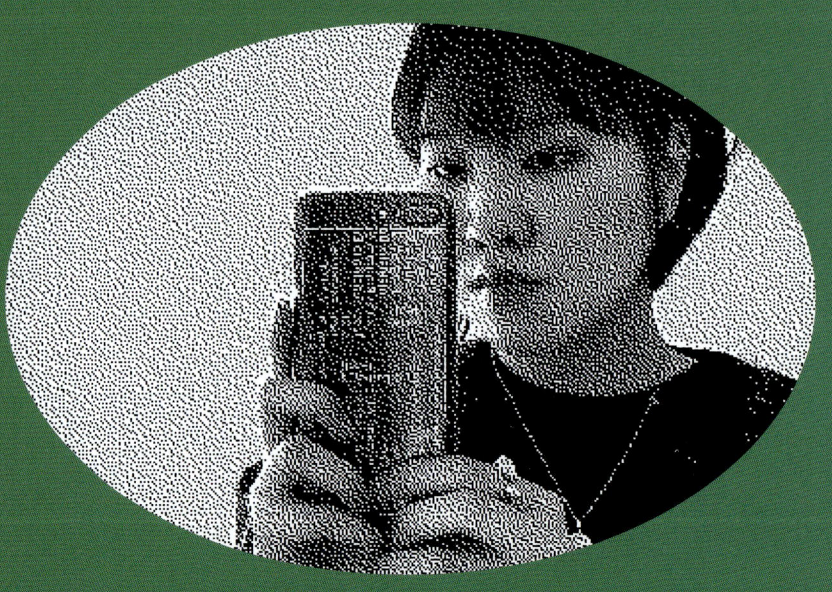

Page: 92 **Dimension:** 180×258mm **Weight:** 434g **Paper/Material:** Partly Epoxy Coated Paper (Cover); Gloss Coated Paper (Inside Page) **Binding:** Perfect Binding

Interviewer
Gakky Luk

Make a Personal Style with Fragmented Elements

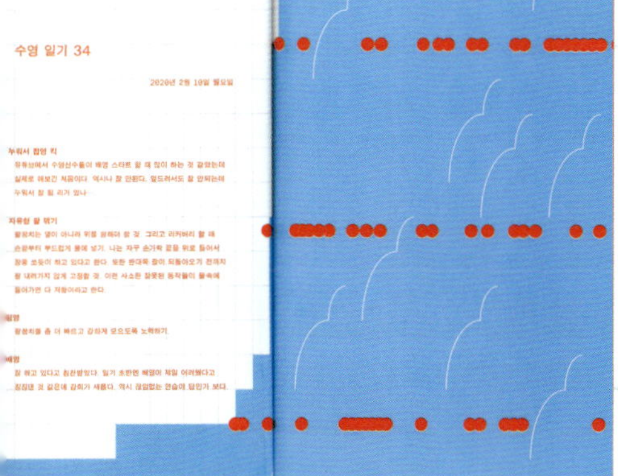

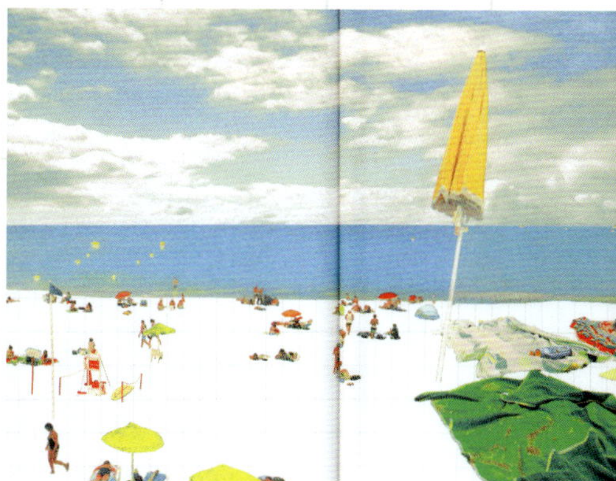

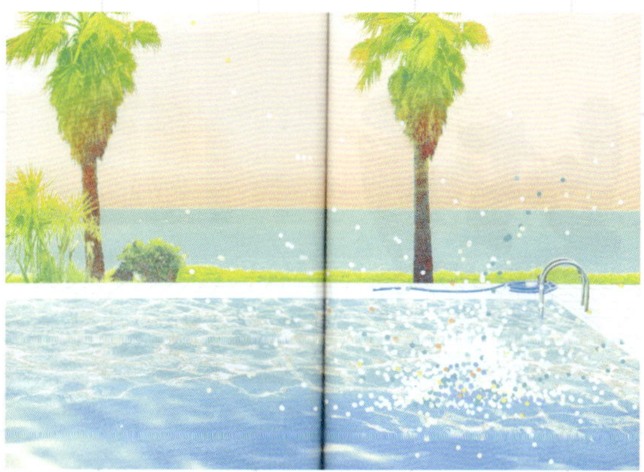

POOL

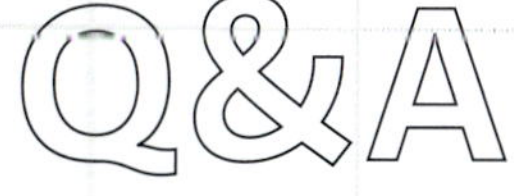

Your work is full of highly saturated and strongly contrasting colors. What explorations have you made in developing such a highly personal style? What have been your influences?

Images are the main materials of my work, and they are basically taken by myself in my daily life. These images from daily life are deconstructed following concepts such as shape, object, texture, light and movement. Then I reconstruct all the images together with certain ideas—for example, creating a new way of seeing an object or restructuring a space, in order to compose a unique visual rhythm. In this process of deconstruction and reconstruction, each image can be a really small part of the original figure, or can have the sense of a minute taken from videos. Consequently, the quality of every image is inevitably different; and the images do not harmonize with each other. Therefore, I reinterpret the color and texture of the whole composition so that each fragment of the images holds the others more tightly. Thus the composition finally appears not as a shattered image, but as a structural image. I usually get inspiration from paintings, especially impressionism art. Reproducing a sense of light is also an important aspect of my work. I often use complementary color combinations to represent the brighter feeling of color on printed matter.

What design techniques did you use to better present the content and convey the emotion when making publications like *693+41* and *POOL*?

Firstly, I observe the images closely before I start to make a composition. I literally try to inspect every single part of the images so I can pick a proper shape or object which can be expanded by the combination with part of other images and a diverse mix of colors. Secondly, I carefully arrange

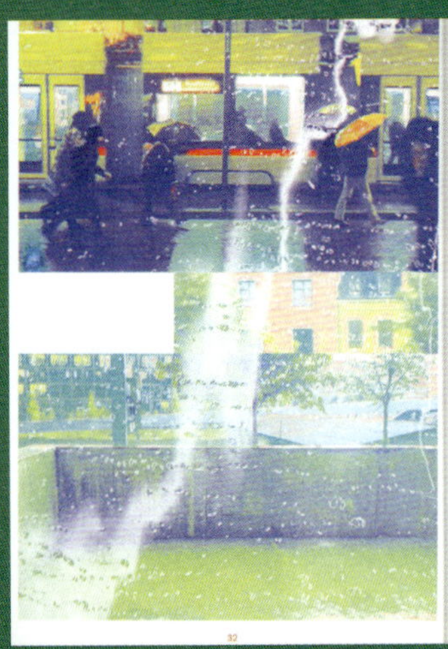
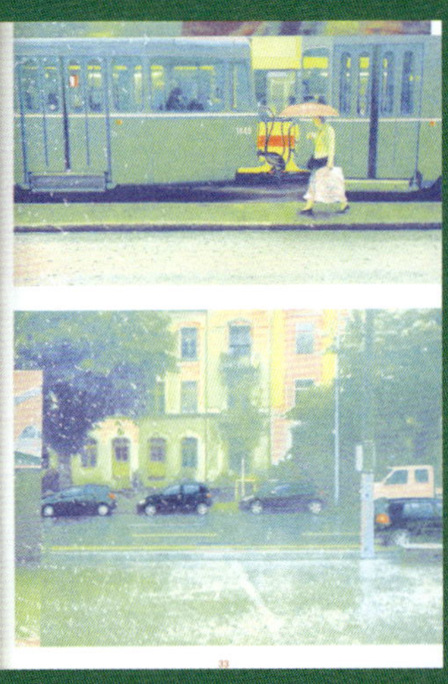
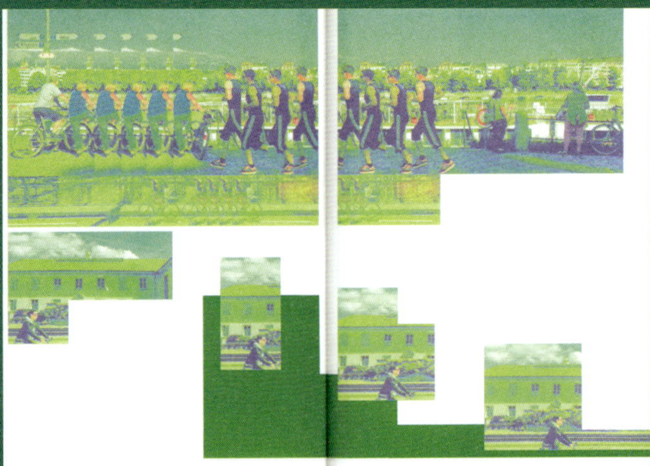

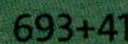
693+41

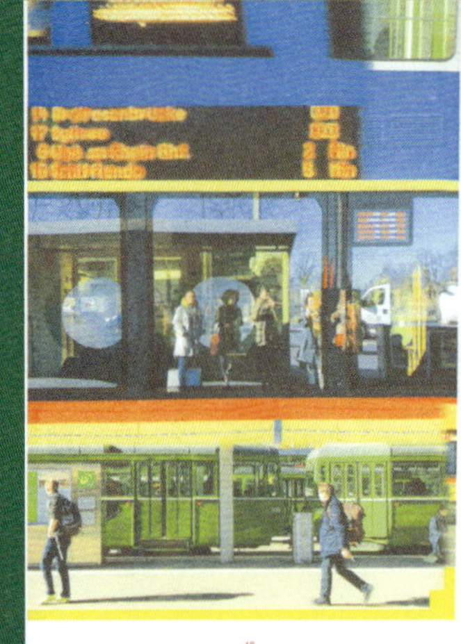
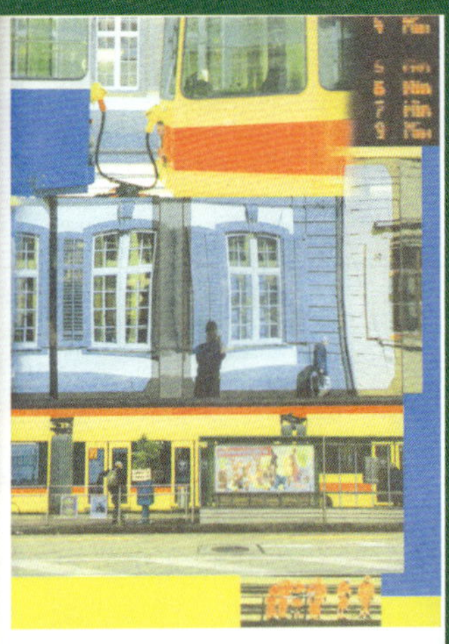
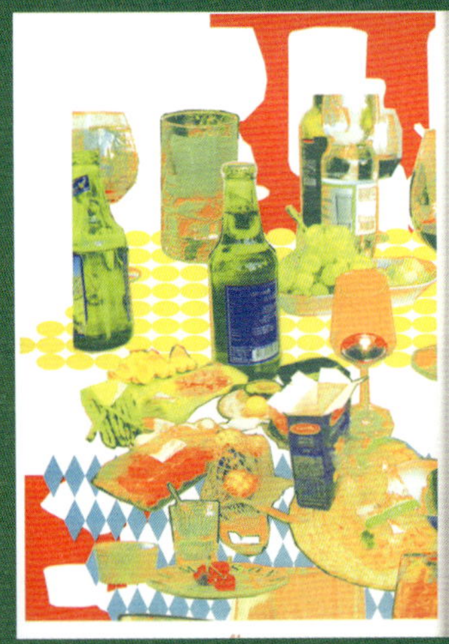
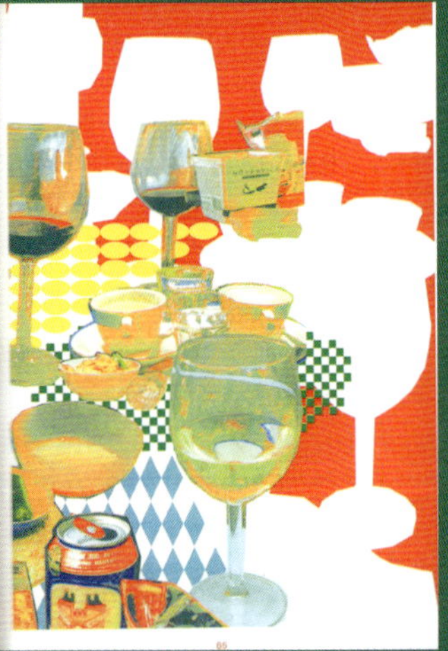
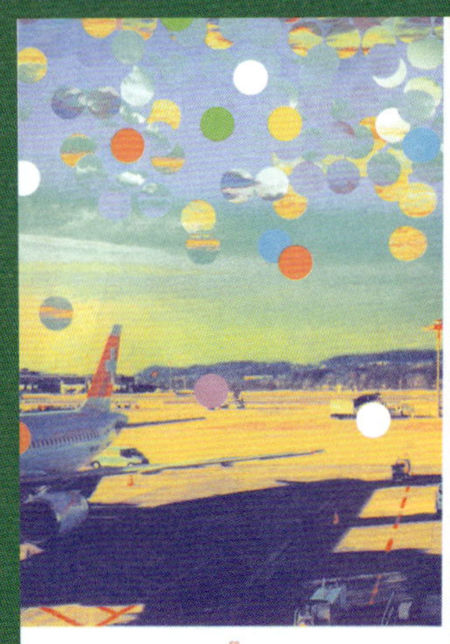
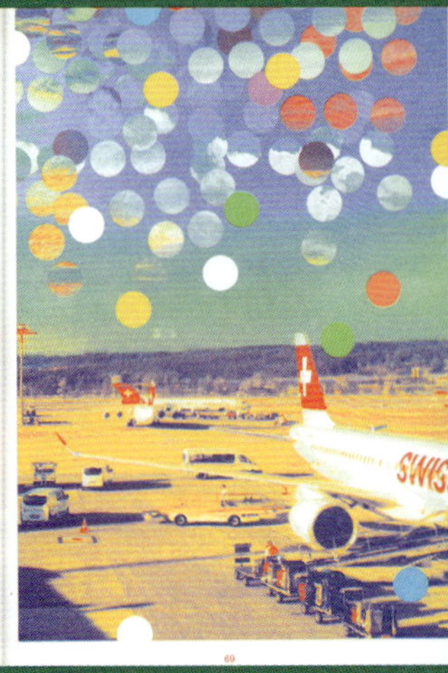
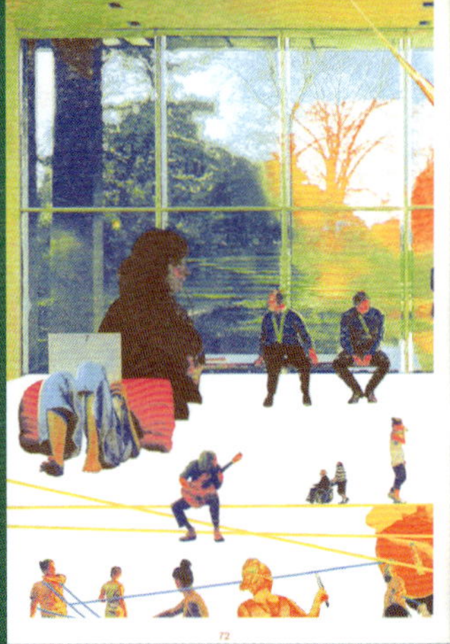
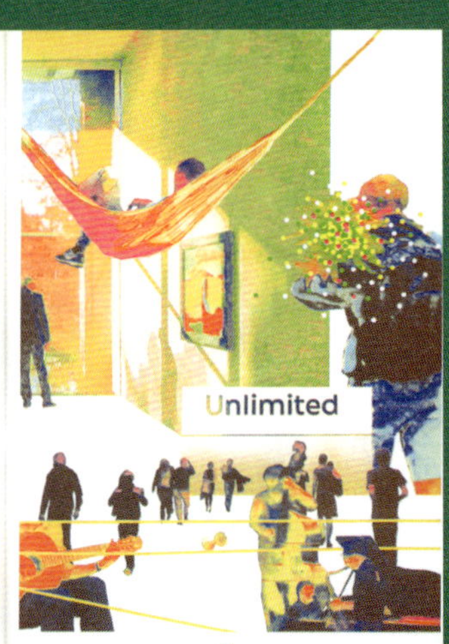

the images by taking into consideration the flow of sight—in other words, create visual tension by controlling space through the way of placing and combining the images as well as handling contrasts of scale, complexity and color. Lastly, I often make an effort to represent the atmosphere that I experienced when I took the picture, and this appears to maximize the sense of light and textures by blending lots of tiny color dots.

Before you became a self-publisher, you did the design work for other publishing projects. How did these experiences help and influence your personal projects?

My past experience of producing books helps me a lot in various aspects, and one of the most helpful points is how to achieve a consistent rhythm within the whole book. Designing a book is really different from making a single image like a poster in terms of presenting images. A book has a much slower tempo in comparison with the flash and explosive tempo which appears in a single image, so I try to discover the right tempo to deliver the images—not too relaxed, but also not too aggressive.

What do you think is an effective way to increase the exposure of your work? How can you expand the audience of your work?

Consistency is the most important issue for me, not only the style of work, but also the amount of work. I try to keep participating in the art book fair annually. Therefore, I constantly have the motivation to continue to produce self-inspired work besides other more commercial work.

In China, the development of self-publishing is on the rise. What is the current state of self-publishing in South Korea? What factors do you think have made it so popular?

Self-publishing is really a live culture in South Korea, and I guess that this great interest and growth in self-publishing have been made possibly because of lots of online and offline platforms where both self-publishers and readers can easily access and interact with each other.

You have participated in exhibitions such as Unlimited Edition, Seoul Art Book Fair, etc. How do you choose exhibitions that are suitable for your work? How can exhibitors and book fairs benefit each other in your opinion?

Unlimited Edition is one of the most inspiring and representative fairs in the self-publishing scene, and I have always had a desire to participate in the fair as an independent publisher for a very long time. So it is meaningful for me that I can present my first self-publishing project at the fair. It is also a great opportunity for me not only to directly hear feedback on my books at the venue, but also to see lots of inspiring self-publishing projects. At the same time I can exchange advice and tips with other self-publishers.

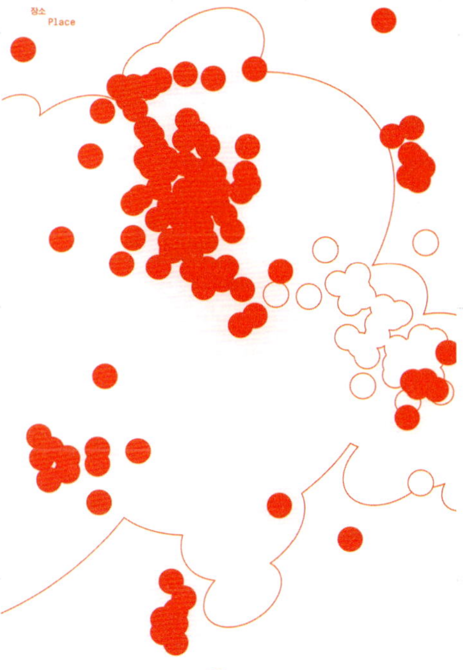

693+41

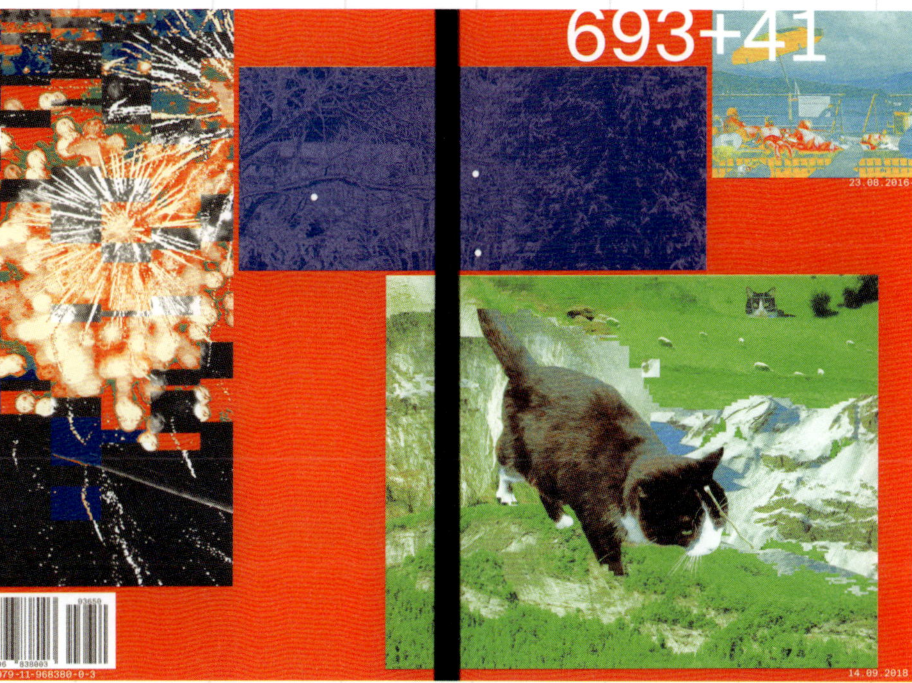

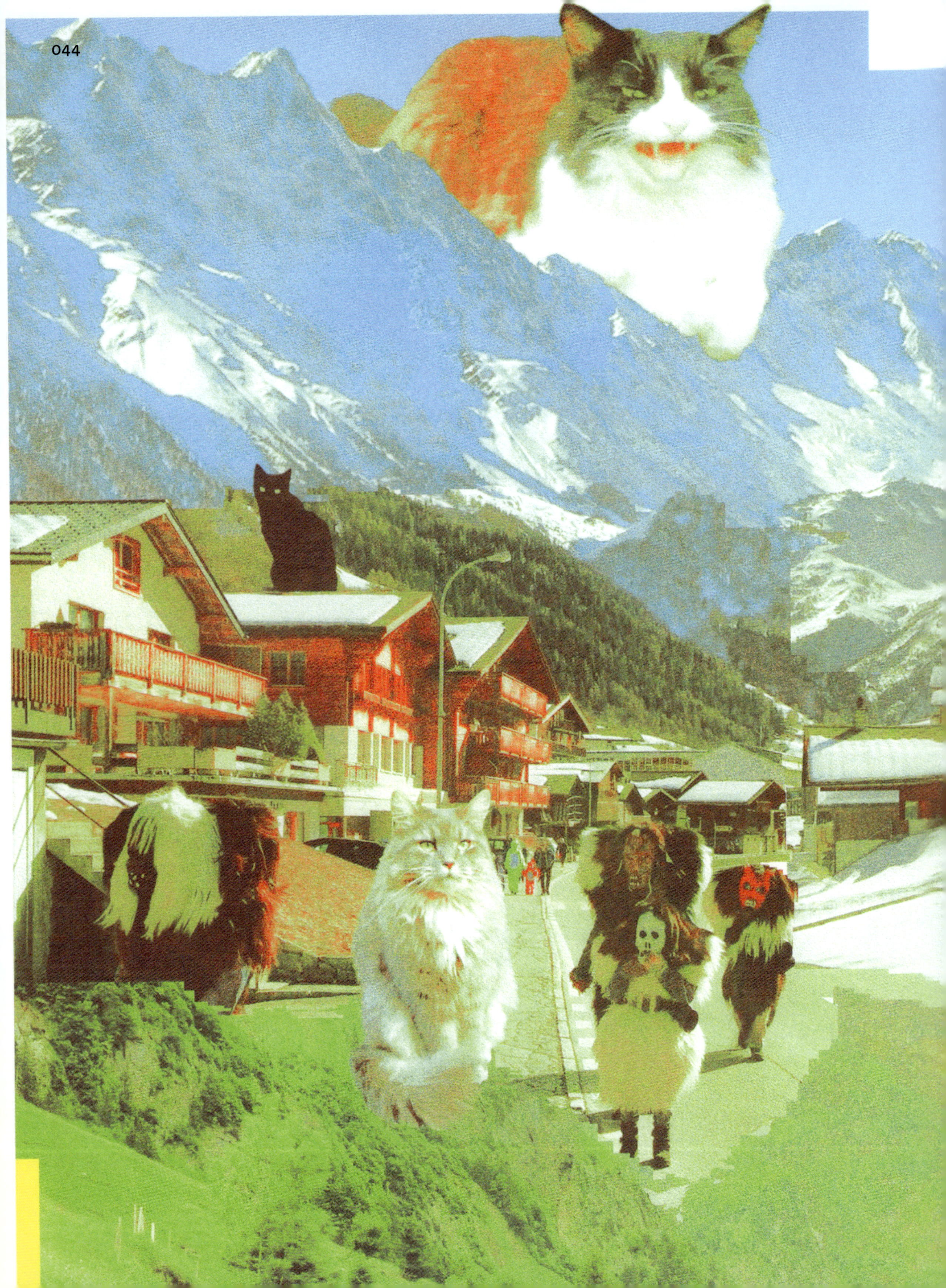

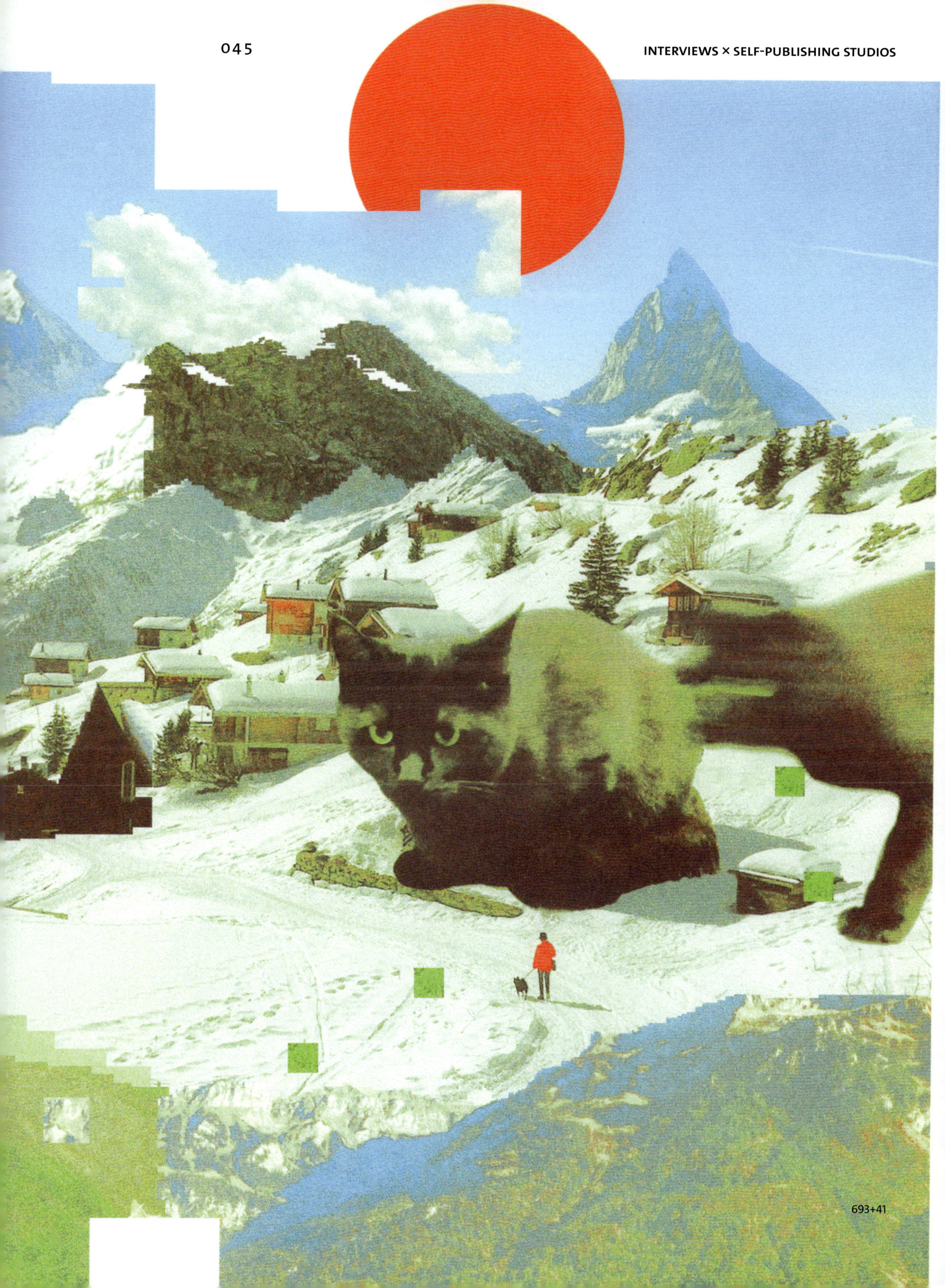

693+41

DREAMER FTY

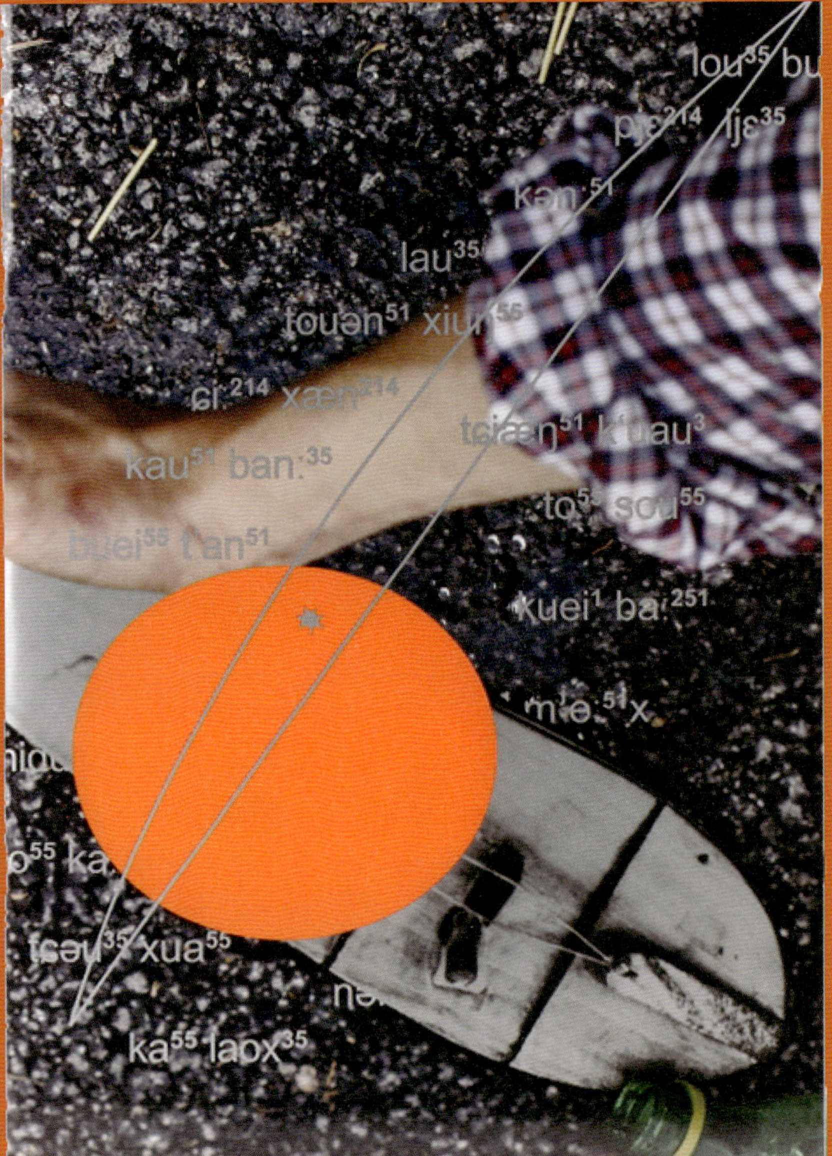

Dòng

DREAMER FTY

DREAMER FTY is a self-publishing project started in 2007 by Qindi Hu and Yue Zhou. They regard book as the communicative medium of their project, and self-publishing as their expression of artistic creation. At the same time, they promote cooperation among creatives. DREAMER FTY has become a key art book publishing project of the institute—art book in China.

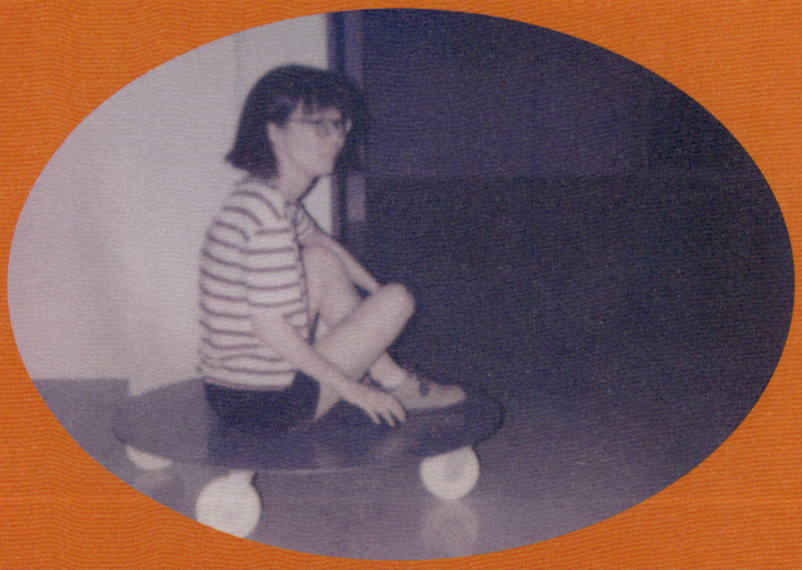

Page: 66

Dimension: 240×340mm

Binding: Saddle Stitching

Interviewer
Gakky Luk

Blur the Boundary Between Five Senses with Self-Publishing

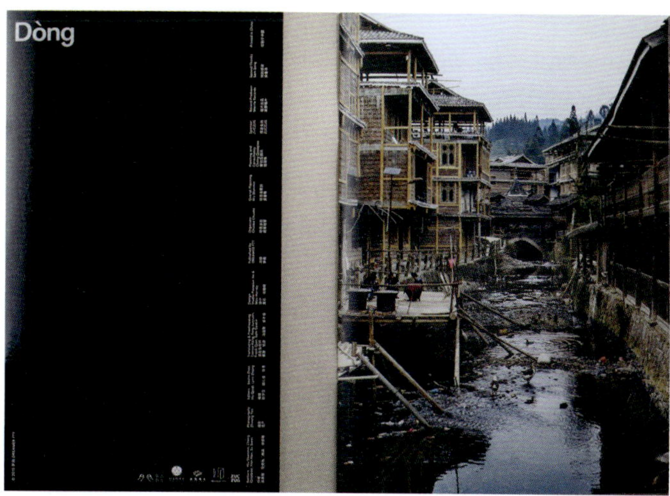

Dòng

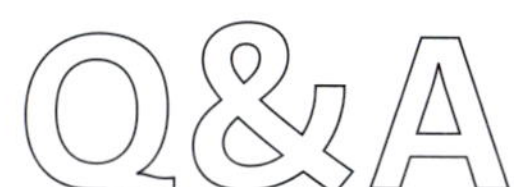

DREAMER FTY has published a lot of self-publications. What is your creative process when you are given the content of the book? Which publication has impressed you the most?

We often start the project by brainstorming around a word which comes out naturally based on our current situation and thoughts. Then we discuss together. I will invite some artists to create based on the theme after the content and the structure are decided.

The most impressive one is The Rose series, which is a project we worked on from 2013 to 2015. It is a collection of lithographic art books, a pocket book and a hardcover. The Rose series was a turning point for us. It took me half a year to complete the whole process from lithographic printing to binding. There are 35 volumes in the lithographic art book series. The making process included stone dressing, drawing, corroding, color mixing, inking and printing on newsprint. Afterwards, I published a pocket book named *P.s: under the rose*. It recorded the printing process, some interesting things and a postscript. Later, these two publications were made into a hardcover collection named *Rose is a rose is a rose is a rose*. They together formed the "rose" for the time given by DREAMER FTY.

You have collaborated with artists from various fields. What have been the most interesting or impressive artistic collision?

Launched in 2019, the publication named *Dòng* was closely related to a three-year project centered on the culture of the Gam people, which is officially known as the Dong people in China. The project was jointly initiated by Chuoke Chuoke and Walking Ear Radio. The publication documented the recognition, exploration and imagination of the Gam Grand Choir of creators such as 33EMYBW, Gooooose, Qiaoqiao Cheng, Siwei Xu and the photographer Yan Zhuang. I really like the perspective offered by Pianpian He and the designer of this publication Max Harvey, which allows us to go to a quiet place hid deep in Southwest China as we read and listen.

DREAMER FTY has been established for 14 years. How would you describe your current development stage? What have you learned from the process of founding, exploring and growing? What difficulties have you experienced?

DREAMER FTY now averagely publishes an exhibition collection that regards art book as a medium, as well as 1 to 3 volumes of zines in cooperation with the creators every year. Although DREAMER FTY still has a long way to go, it is in a stage of steady and lively development, and we hope that we can always collaborate with others with an experimental and open mind. What we make and what we aim for is book. We are fortunate enough to be able to meet the book makers and readers who are always with us.

As for one of the difficulties encountered, the publications are so heavy after being packed in a box, so it is better to rent a studio or a house with an elevator.

What would be an ideal publishing environment for you? Is there any improvement needed to make in your opinion?

For me, an ideal environment is pure, where there are books and zines with great content as well as loving readers. I think all aspects still need to improve—we can read more, then learn more. Also, I hope that there are more "effective" books in the publishing industry, rather than those that just waste paper.

It is important for creators to increase the public reach of their works. Does it cause any pressure for you?

There is no pressure to increase our publicity for us because we are relatively lazy in this field—maybe it is related to our original publishing intention.

Do you think the self-publishing industry is just a fad or it can develop into a large-scale industry?

Self-publishing exists in each era. It is always full of vigor and vitality as a spontaneous force.

Rose is a rose is a rose is a rose

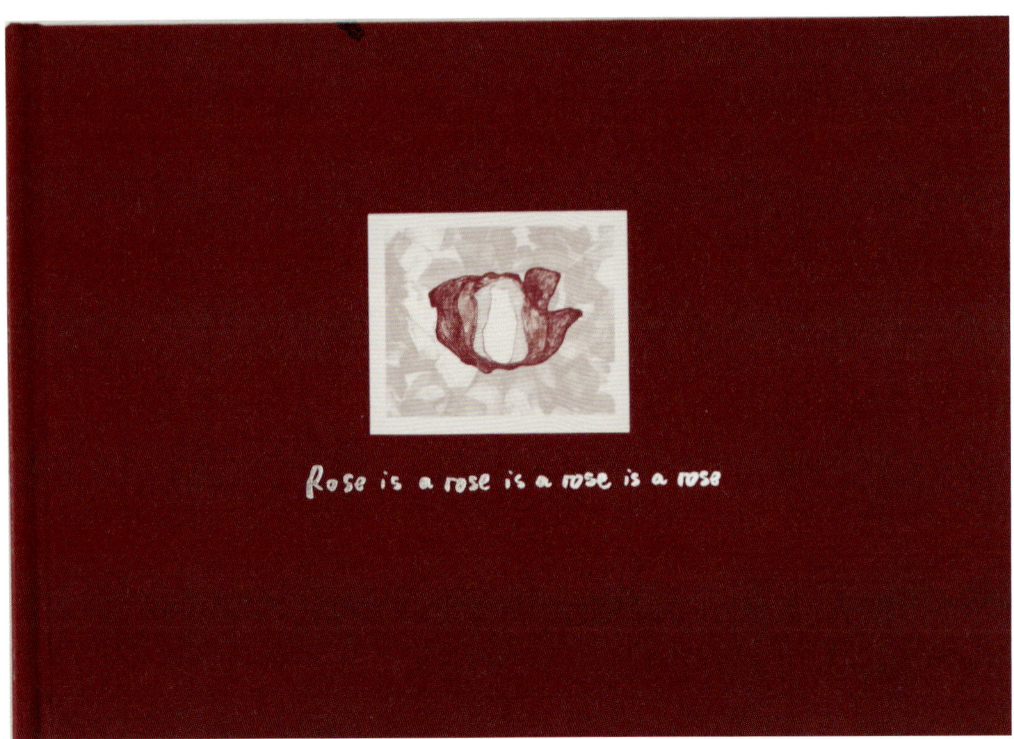

P.s: under the rose

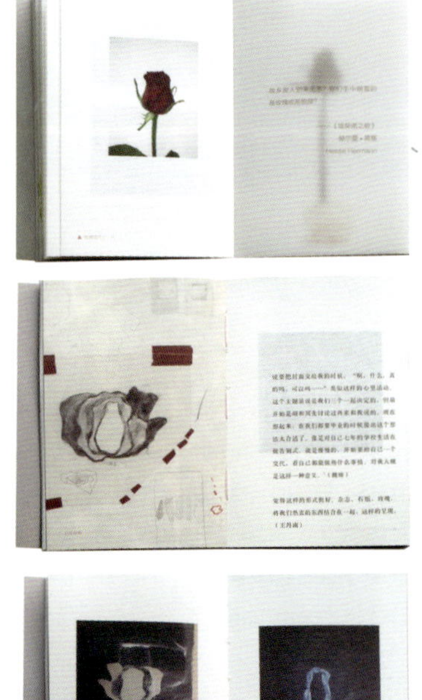

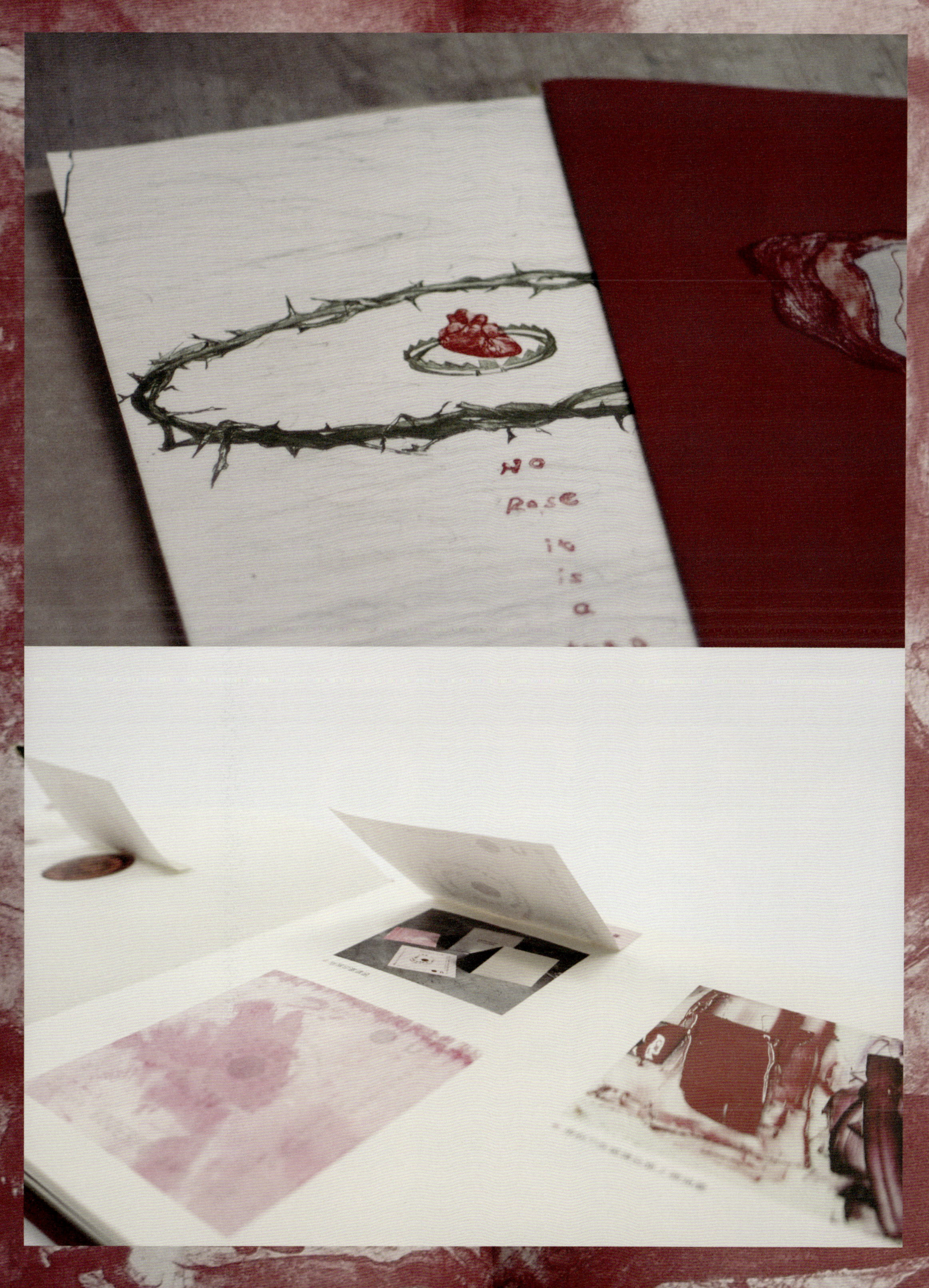
No
Rose

CHRONOLOGY OF SELF-PUBLISHING OF INDEPENDENT MUSIC IN CHINA

Editors
Yue Zhou & Sasha Zhao

1992 1992, *Music Heaven* was founded by Liangping Deng and some others in Sun Yat-sen University.

1994, founded in Beijing, *Rock* magazine is one of the earliest underground culture magazines in China. Mengjin Sun is the chief editor.

1996, *Sound* magazine was founded in Guangzhou, edited by Dali Qiu.

1997, Tina, an Italian student from Beijing Language and Culture University, printed and distributed *Construction* to introduce the most avant-garde underground punk bands in Beijing.

1997, *The Comprehensive Voice*, founded in Guangzhou, is of pioneering significance. It focused on industrial music, which had been rarely seen in China. It introduced pioneering experimental music.

1998, *Punk Era*, a special issue of *Music Heaven*, was founded. For the first time, the content in music magazines touched upon the resistance consciousness of reality. At the same time, the special issue *The Era of Rock* was launched to introduce the hippie culture in western countries in the 1960s and 1970s. In October of the next year, Bo Yang, the editor-in-chief, merged the two magazines and founded *Music of Freedom*, which was a pioneering experiment in the world of Chinese music magazines. In addition to those rock classics that were already widely accepted, it also took the lead in introducing a series of music genres such as European industrial music, extreme metal music, and German avant-garde electronic music.

1998, in December, the magazine *Music Worms* was founded in Hangzhou by Music Worms Club in Zhejiang University.

1999 1999, the experimental book *New Sound of Beijing*, which was jointly written by Ning Ou, Jun Yan and Zheng Nie, was supported and published by Hunan Literature and Art Publishing House. The preliminary planning was done by the authors independently. This book introduced the music culture of the new generation of Beijing in the 1990s.

1999, in December, *The Undertones* magazine was founded in Changsha.

2000, Jun Yan founded the music label Sub Jam and began releasing independent music, films and literature.

2002, after leaving *Tongsugequ Rock* magazine, Hongwu Peng, a music critic, founded the independent music magazine *Not Only Music* in Guilin, Guangxi.

2002, *Di Huo 2002* and *Manifesto of the Fei Generation* were founded in Lanzhou.

2003, the leading magazine in Wuhan's punk movement *Chaos* was founded by Dian Mai, but it was suspended due to a lack of funds after the publication of the fourth issue.

2003, *Sound of Freedom* magazine was founded in Shenyang by Sound of Freedom Records.

2004, the sound magazine *The Small Ecosystem* was jointly edited by three female college students in Tianjin. It focused on song reviews of metal, neoclassical darkwave, and medieval folk songs.

2004,*Wuya Music* was born in Shijiazhuang with the theme of "Darkwave". In the second issue a year later, the team came to Beijing and got a legal ISBN for their magazine
2004 from an audio-visual publishing house in Northeast China.

2006

2004, *Extreme Music* magazine compiled gothic and darkwave content into an independent special issue *Gothic Age*.

2006, *Unite!* from Beijing was a magazine focused on punk music.

2006, Changsha's *Free Status* magazine was an independent audio-visual magazine, with half the content consisting of rock music and the other half of independent film reviews.

2007, *Under FM* was founded in Beijing by Dying Art Productions.

2008, *SD! Zine* was founded in Beijing. It was given away for free to rock fans at live houses in nearly 30 Chinese cities in the form of a monthly issued magazine. In addition to band interviews, it reported on the rock scene, and had equipment recommendations as well as *Cult Youth*, a manga series by Ca Zhuxi. The manga had the exclusive support of Sina Rock website, and the previously published content is still available online.

2009, in December, *Noise* magazine published its first issue. It was produced by Beijing underground experimental label NOJIJI and was given away for free.

Along with the innovation of social media on the Internet, self-publishing has sprouted among cartoonists and photographers in China since 2004. Many independent music labels that are now active in the public experienced rapid growth in this period as well.

2013

A band called yourboyfriendsucks! which was formed by members of Full Label, the predecessor of Guangzhou's Qiii Snacks Records, started publishing *MAN MAN THINK* with some friends in 2013. Later in 2016, Qiii Snacks Records was founded and began to release music and zines as part of their label. They published a total of 7 issues of *MAN MAN THINK*.

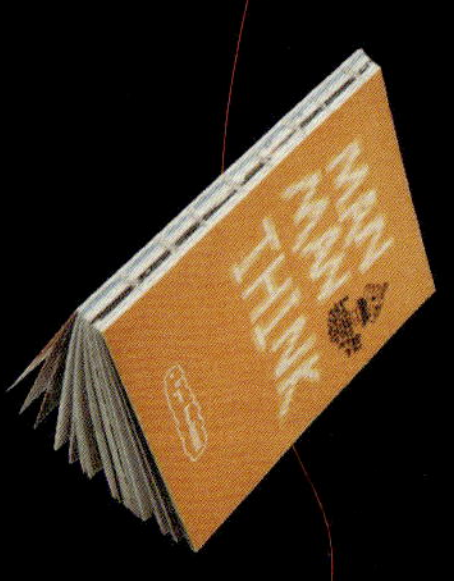

Born in 2007, VOX is the live house with the longest history in Wuhan. *Voice* magazine was founded in 2013 and given away for free. It showed the venue's concert listings, and subsequently, it started to be published as a monthly magazine in 2014. Wild records, founded in 2015, is VOX's music label.

2014

In 2014, FunkeeCookee and Endy founded the Daily Vinyl studio in Shanghai. The two founders also have their own independent labels: Eating Music and Groove Bunny Records. In April 2015, Daily Vinyl and Uptown, a physical record store based in Shanghai, jointly produced the *Daily Vinyl* newspaper. It is released approximately every 2-3 months and is available for free at major performance venues, activity spaces, record stores and other places in China. It covers a wide range of content from music at home and abroad, performance recommendations to cultural trends. Chief editor FunkeeCookee is responsible for topic selection, typography, printing, and distribution, while Endy, Uptown and other members of the team are in charge of interviews and writing. Daily Vinyl has had its own physical space since 2017.

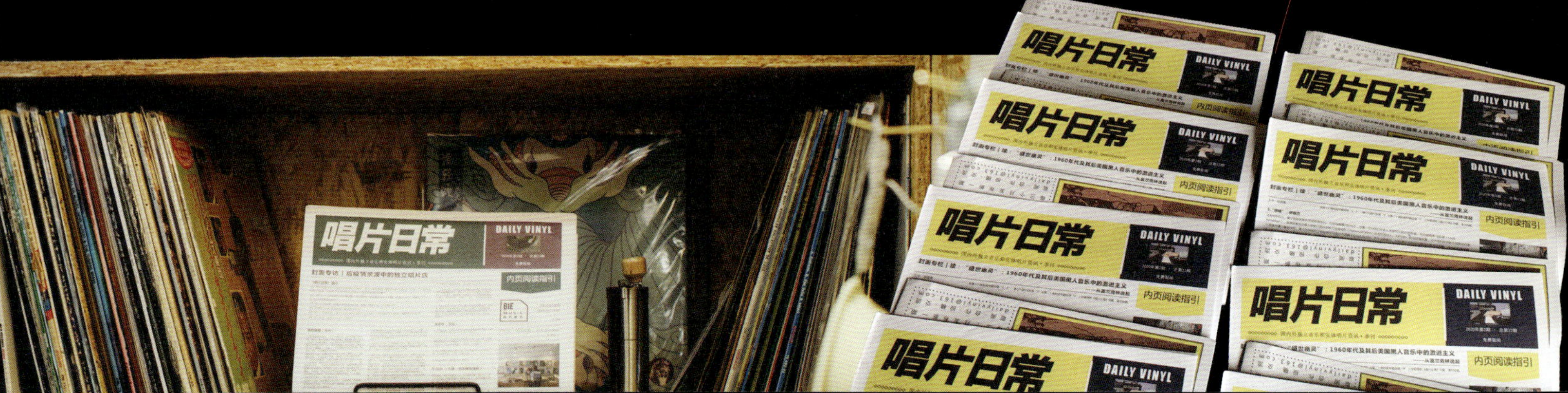

In 2015, another group of musicians based in Shanghai spontaneously created the independent music culture magazine *JUZHEN* edited by Olivia. Based on the background of alternative music and art culture, it reports on the lives of contemporary artists at home and abroad. The collaborators include Howell, director of VBKVLT label, Gooooose, 33 from the band Duck Fight Goose, independent musicians Chacha, J-Fever, and others. *JUZHEN* usually announces its new issues with release parties in different cities to connect with the local youth culture.

2016

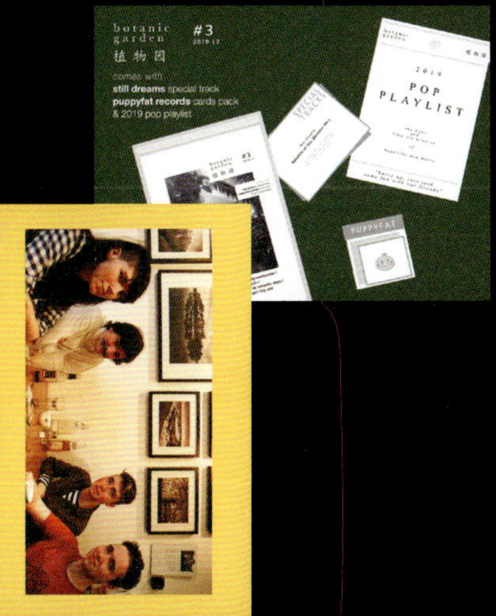

In February 2016, Shi Yu, Shika, and a few friends produced the first Zine + CD *Botanical Garden* in China, introducing indie-pop from all over the world. It was suspended after the 2nd issue but re-emerged and published its 3rd issue in December 2019, when Shi Yu bought a home printer. The production team for this zine are still active in the independent music industry. Shika established Puppy Fat Records, a label focused on indie-pop. In 2017, he held the Up A Tree Indiepop Festival, and Shi Yu also participated as a staff member. In 2019, the physical space of Puppy Fat Records was open to the public in Shenzhen, selling albums, art books, and hosting performances.

In April 2016, Maybe Mars released a music criticism newspaper *Maybe Mars Rugs*. It had an academic focus, which had rarely been seen in similar magazines, as well as a very unique design, typography, and packaging. In its first issue, independent musicians such as Yulong Yan, Misan, Jun Yan, Wenbo Zhu offered record recommendations, observation about the industry, and other new perspectives.

2018

In March 2016, Beijing's fRUITYSPACE was open to the public. In 2017, the Space Fruity Records music label came into being. In April 2018, a side project, fRUITYPRESS publishing project, was launched. It has published 9 artists' books so far.

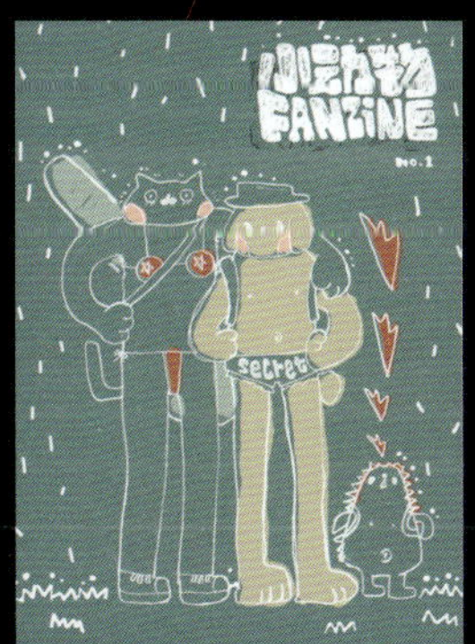

In 2018, Little Animals Record, a Changsha D.I.Y. music label, was founded. The first issue of *Little Animals Fanzine* was released in July, and the second issue was released in March 2019.

Beyond the Billboard 2018 magazine was released by Merrie Records in February 2019. With a fusion of auditory and gustatory senses, it tells the stories of people from different urban music scenes. The Pelican Music Academy is another new project of Merrie Records which started in late 2019, bringing a series of forum presentations and *The Ultimate Guide for Beginners* magazine, which aims to search for new musical voices.

The two members of the new-born label Letter Records established in 2019 come from Shanghai and Guangzhou. Both of them have backgrounds in band and music label operations as well as design. In addition to record production and distribution, the team also has a publishing direction of textual content. Meanwhile, the visual design of the record tends to cooperate with graphic designers and illustrators.

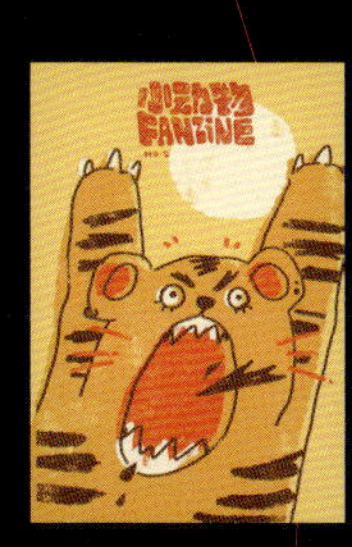

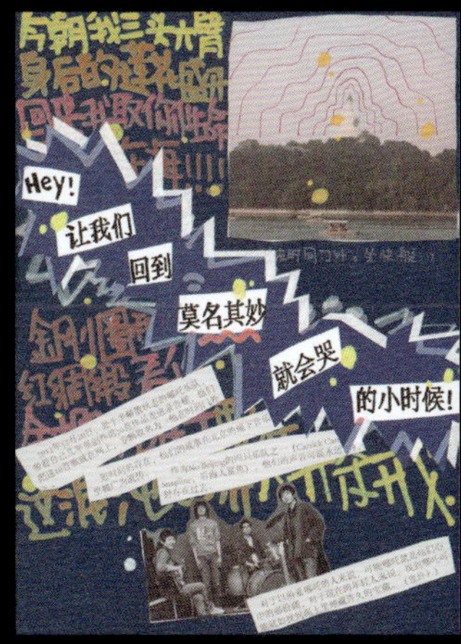

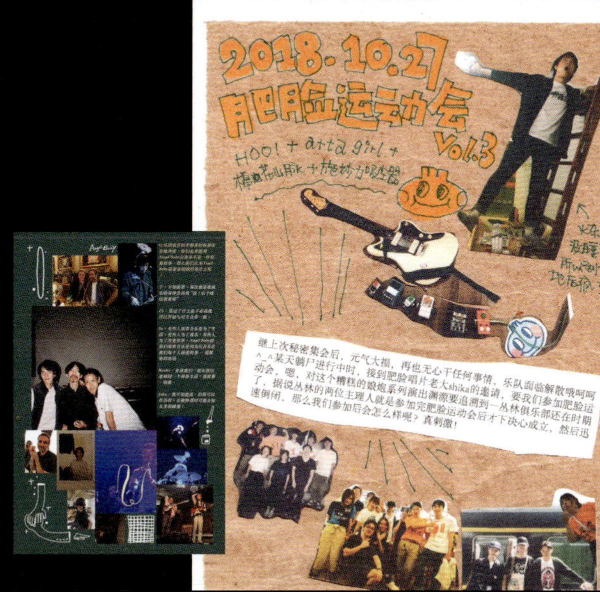

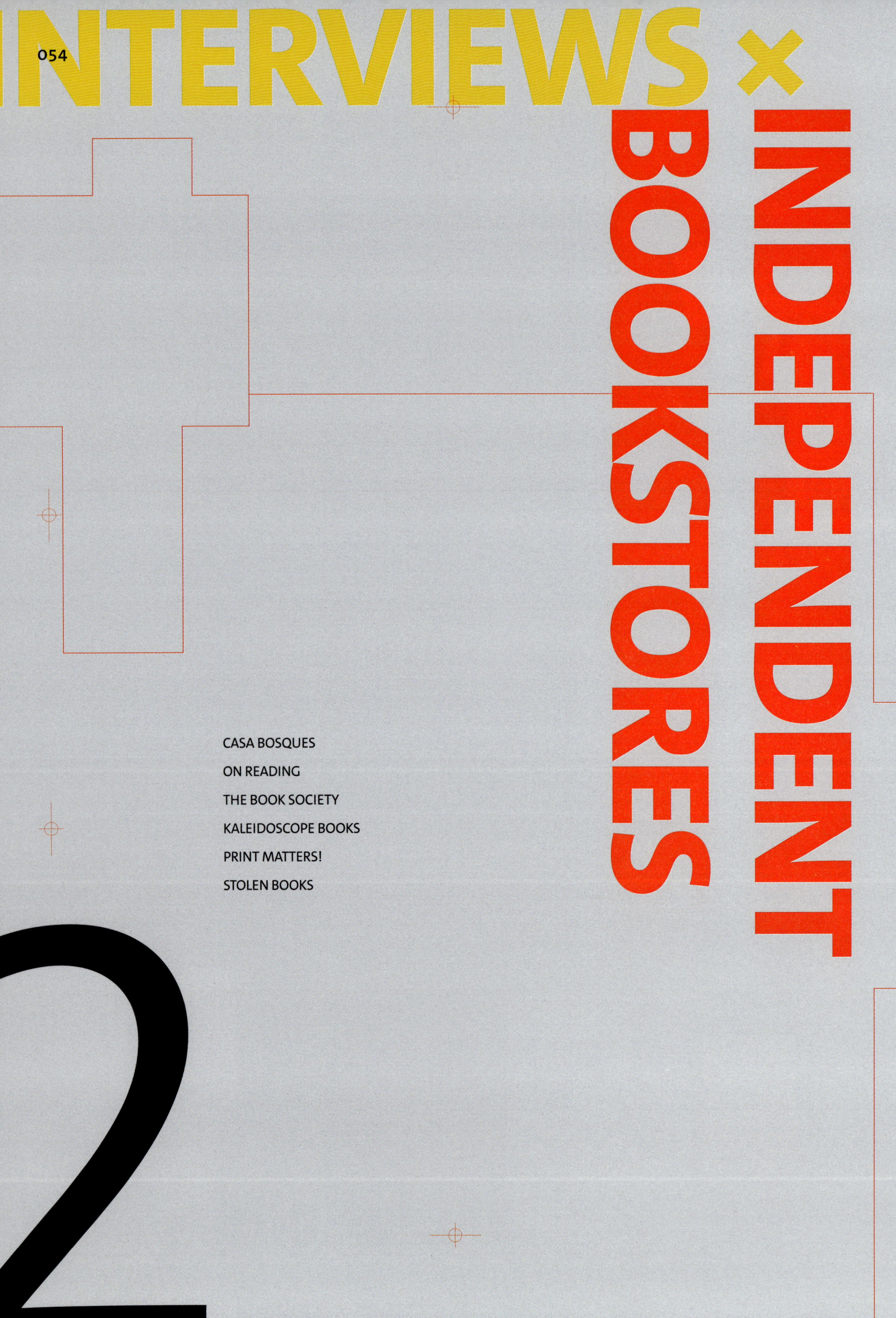

INTERVIEWS × INDEPENDENT BOOKSTORES

2

Editor
Gakky Luk

YES! WE ARE OPEN TODAY

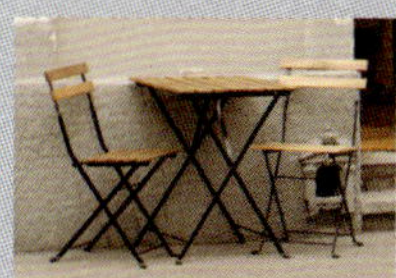

Many industries underwent a reshuffle due to the COVID-19 pandemic that began in early 2020 and continues to this day. In the field of bricks-and-mortar bookstores, many large chain bookstores had to close reluctantly as a result of the pandemic and the lockdowns that followed in many countries. The economic strength of independent bookstores seems miniscule when compared with bookstore chains that seem to have such a solid economic foundation. But why is there such a determination to keep these independent bookstores going? Maybe it is because the world needs their voices.

Most people get to know various publications through traditional bricks-and-mortar bookstores, as this is the most convenient way for them. Most of the books circulating in the mainstream market are characterized by a certain homogeneity both in terms of content and design. It seems like the more bookstores follow marketing trends, the more they confine readers within an limited range of choices. Surely, if these bookstores want to escape this increasingly vicious circle, it might be a better idea to shift their focus away from saturated areas of the market to the less explored aspects of publishing. Even in this era of big data, independent bookstores are pursuing an individual and idiosyncratic approach to book selection and are ignoring the conventional "reading guide".

The defining characteristic of independent bookstores lies in the fact that they each represent the particular viewpoints and thoughts of their respective owners, highlighting their respective personalities and tastes. Unlike traditional bookstores that try to attract customers with as wide a range of product as possible, independent bookstores do not blindly follow the mainstream marketing trends and insist on following their own criteria for selecting books. The books displayed and sold in the bookstores are screened and filtered by their owners. In other words, the owners can express their personal preferences through these books, which sets, at the same time, a certain expectation for readers who come to the bookstores. In fact, it is a process of mutual screening between independent bookstores and readers. With the development of self-publishing, independent bookstores have become one of the most important channels for self-publishers to promote their projects. It is increasingly common to find in independent bookstores some self-published products of various sizes, which often feature bold colors and a distinctive style and voice. They stimulate readers' interest in a niche area through their book selections, and motivate them to explore further.

"It was the best of times; it was the worst of times." These words open Charles Dickens's great novel *A Tale of Two Cites*. The bookstore industry, which has been struggling for so long, has come under attack as a result of lockdowns and self-isolation measures during the pandemic period. However, the owners of independent bookstores have opened up a new path toward sustainable development through actions like discount sales and transferring to online platforms. Having experienced desperate times and managed to survive, they kept the light of the bookstores.

CASA BOSQUES

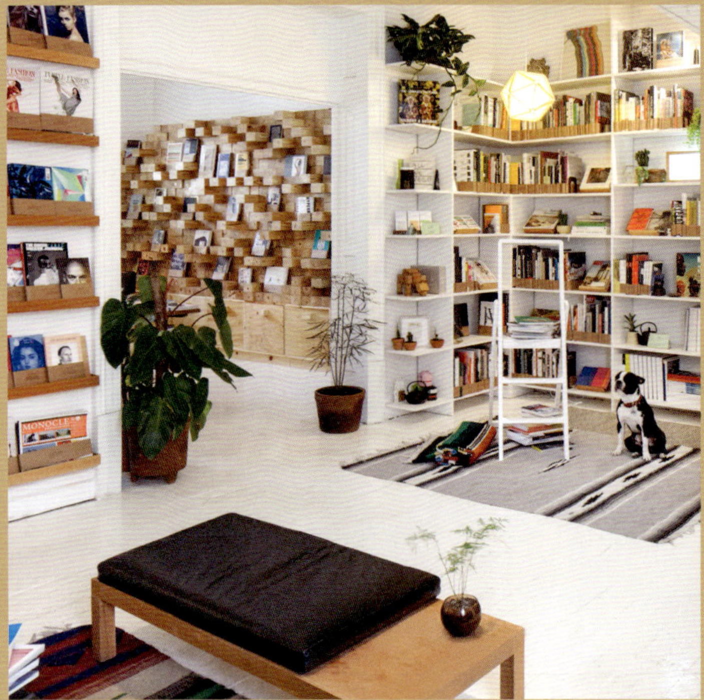

Casa Bosques

Founded in 2012, Casa Bosques is the first bookstore in Mexico that focuses on independent publishers. Through a careful selection process, the store can offer what it considers the most relevant titles from local and international independent scene.

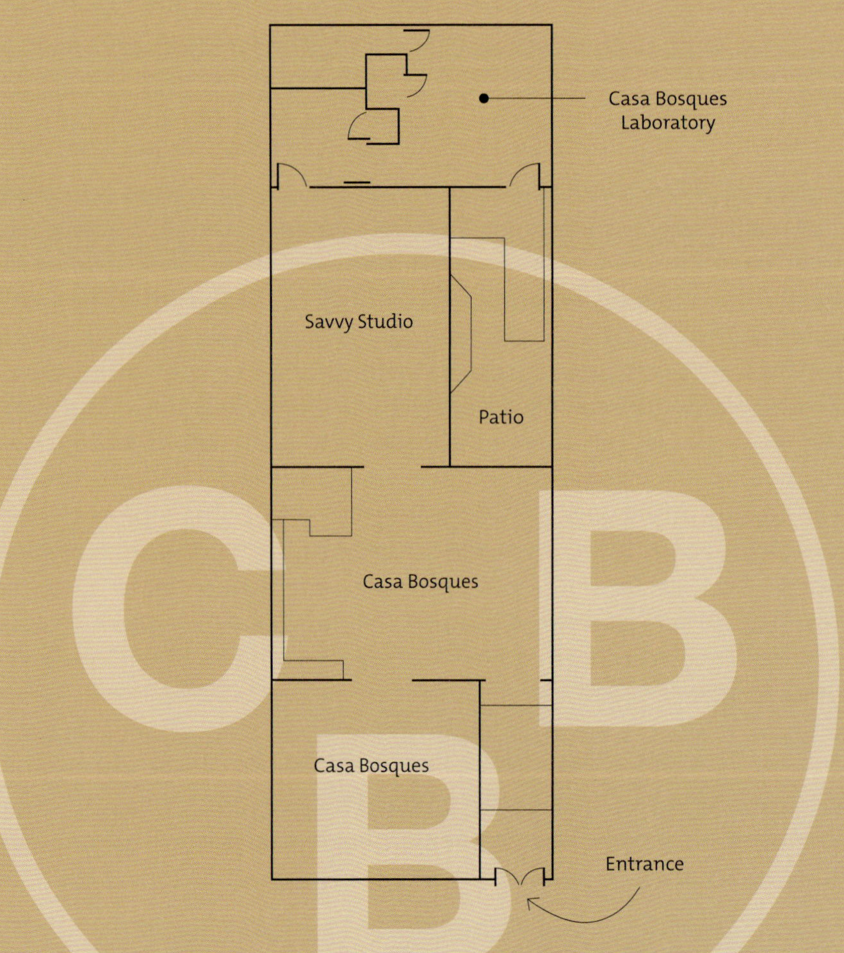

Interviewer
Gakky Luk

RESTART COMMUNITY CULTURE

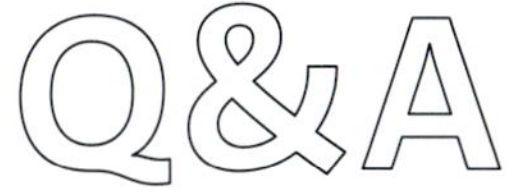

The furnishing and decoration of a bookstore can always tell people a lot about its spirit. Why Casa Bosques chose to use logs as bookshelves? What information do you think the logs communicate?

Because Casa Bosques is housed in an early 20th Century mansion, we decided to maintain the cozy atmosphere that came from the house's original use and architecture. Using wood conveyed these properties well, and paper is made from wood pulp, so it all made sense. With this in mind, a modular bookshelf system was developed that allowed us to not only highlight publications but also store them, and it has become an expressive and striking feature of the bookstore in itself. Since the wood wall is modular, it can be periodically rearranged to suit different needs.

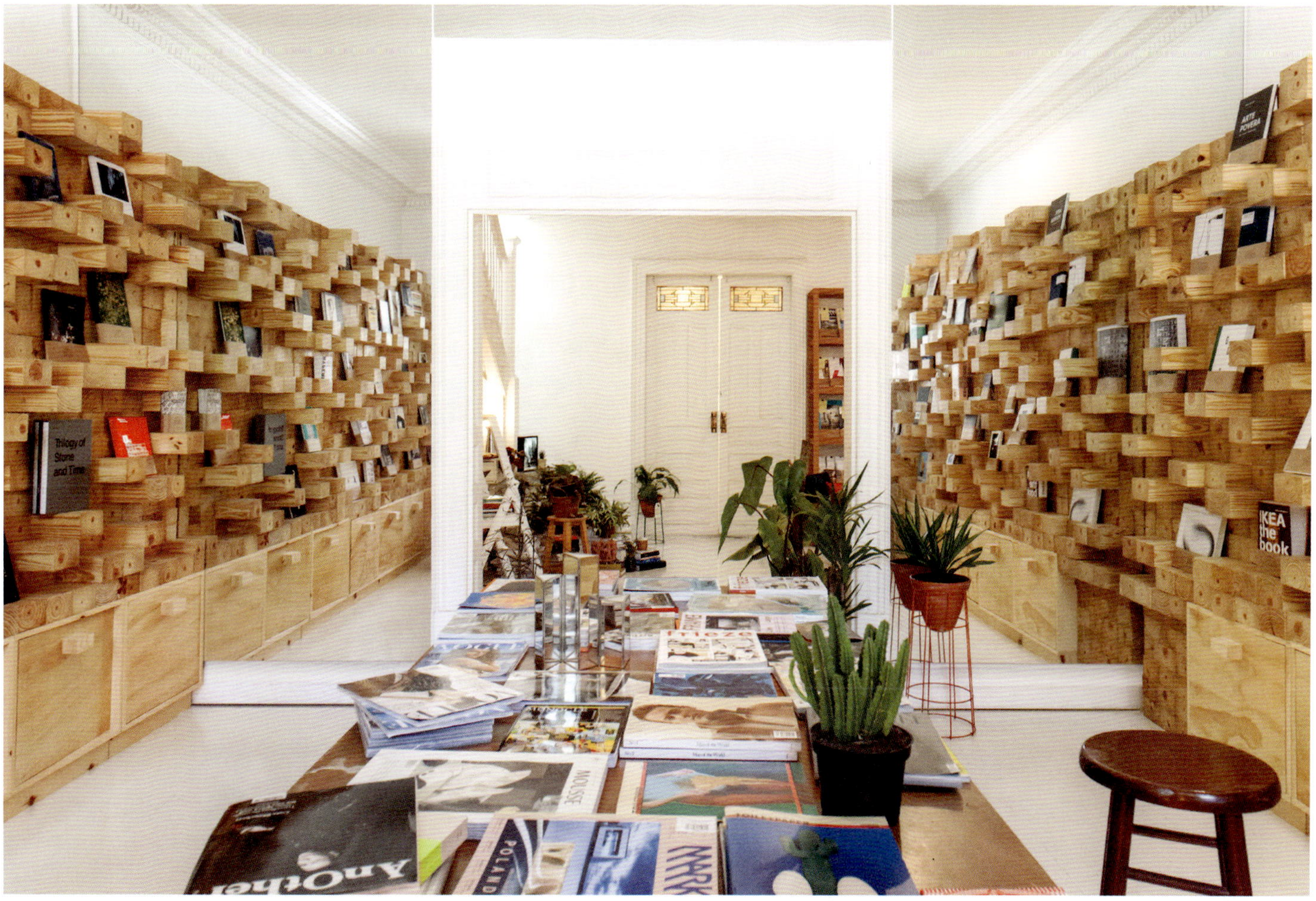

Independent bookstores are not always influenced by the market trends in the way they choose books. Do you have a preference for a certain kind of book? What kinds of books are typically displayed and sold in Casa Bosques?

My personal preference for books is that consider all the fundamental aspects of a publication: content, layout, material, navigation, rhythm, etc., uniting them into a coherent whole. I'm also always excited to see books that follow the legacy of Ulises Carrión, challenging our assumptions of what books are or should be. Casa Bosques stocks art and design titles from independent publishers mainly. We offer a diverse mix of publications from Latin America, Europe, the US, and other parts of the world, as well as a range of printed matter (fanzines, photo books, artist books, multiples, and so on). Mainstay categories include Community and Resistance, Feminism(s), Queer Studies, Latin American Art and Photography, among others.

Casa Bosques communicates directly with readers through lectures, workshops and other activities. What is the purpose of these activities? What do you hope readers can gain from these events?

Books are inert objects. Humans activate them. Events facilitate this process. The activities we organize link authors and publishers directly with our customers and audiences. They are special occasions where readers get to discover new publications, as explained directly by their creators, who expand and illuminate on what is to be found in them. It is also an opportunity to meet like-minded people and to facilitate discussion and dialogue. Bookstores need to be alive, and events and activities are the most direct way of engaging and sharing with the community that has developed in and around Casa Bosques for the last nine years.

As an independent bookstore, how does Casa Bosques integrate with the surrounding community? What role does it play in the local community?

I believe we have integrated quite well to Roma, the neighborhood where we are located. Casa Bosques shares the same spirit that animates a lot of the other independent shops, galleries, restaurants and cafes that have sprung up in the area in the last 20 years or so. We are guided more by passion and principles than commerce. We have come to foster a very diverse community that is composed of people in the arts and culture sector mostly, who find in Casa Bosques a safe haven from what can sometimes feel like a chaotic city. If anything, independent bookstores have become spaces for dialogue and dissent that allow for genuine encounters and exchanges, promoting content that is not necessarily a part of the online conversation, and advocating for complexity in what has rapidly become in many ways a binary world.

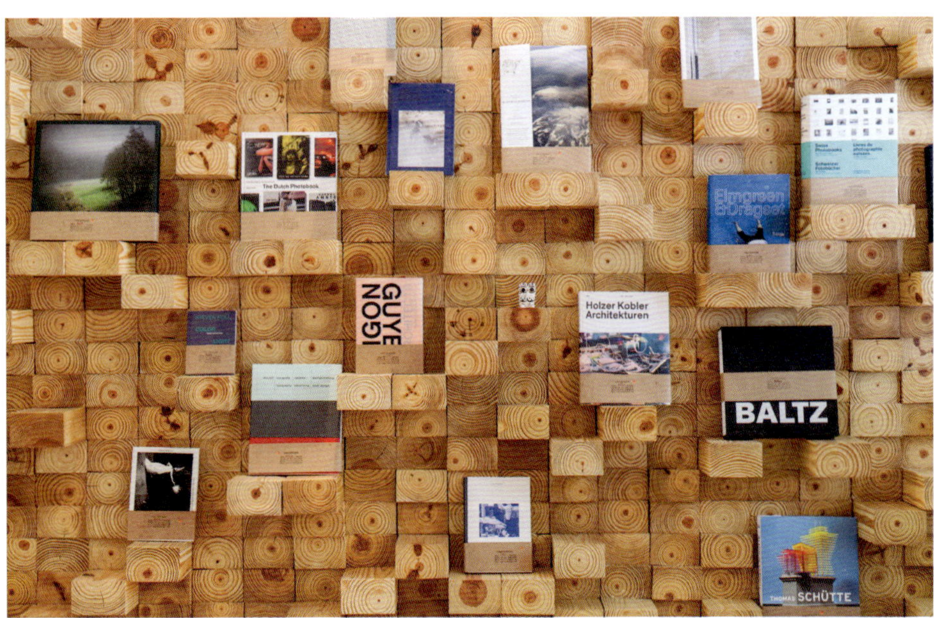

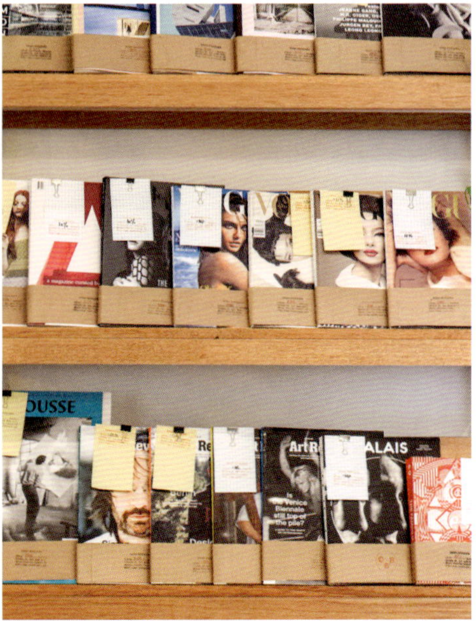

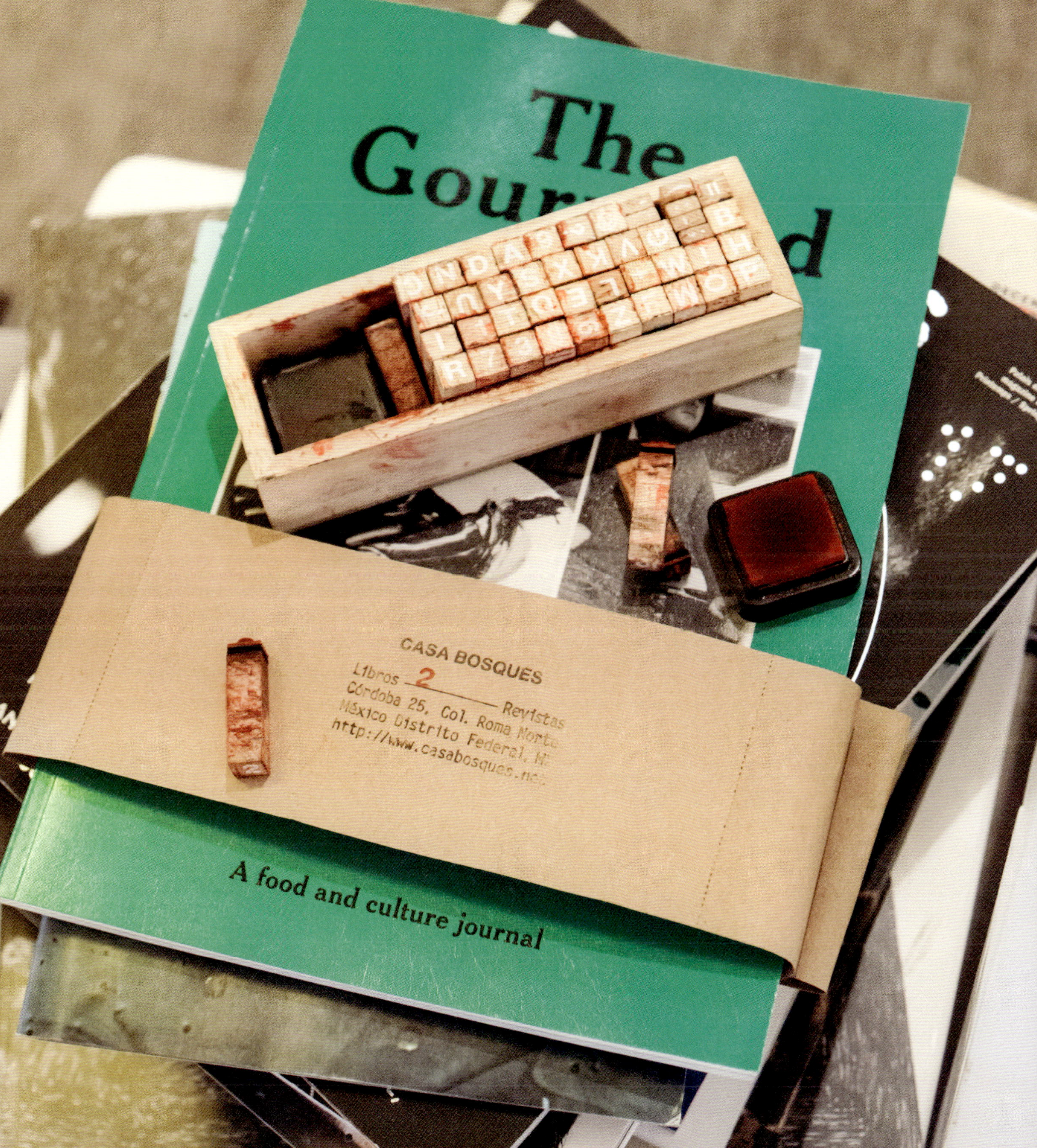
The Gour d
CASA BOSQUES
Libros 2 Revistas
Córdoba 25, Col. Roma Norte
México Distrito Federal, MX
http://www.casabosques.net
A food and culture journal

ON READING

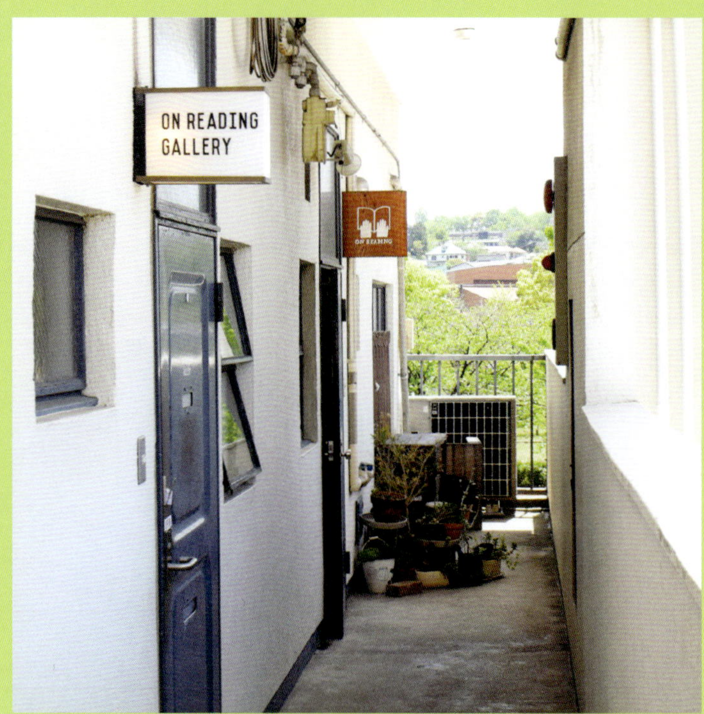

On Reading

Established in 2011, On Reading is an independent bookstore located in Nagoya, Japan. It is a bookstore for "people who feel and think", and it is committed to stimulating people's curiosity through various kinds of publications. Besides, On Reading is also a gallery that provides exhibition space for emerging artists. It also holds activities such as seminars and live concerts from time to time.

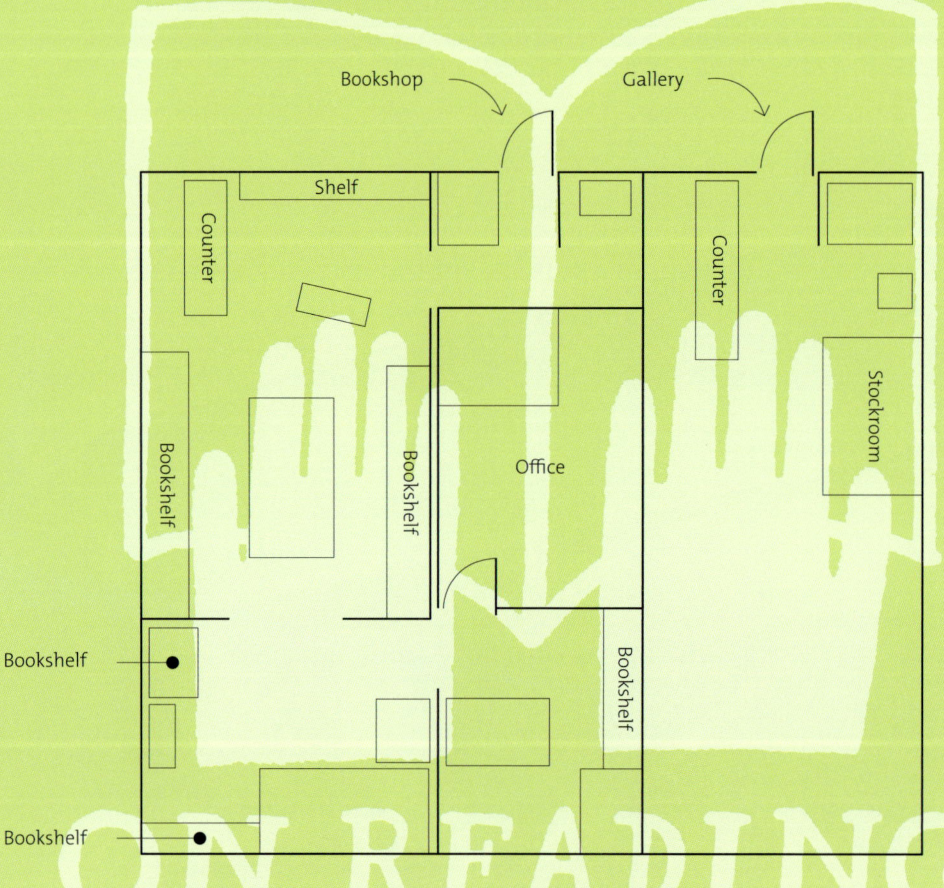

Interviewer
Gakky Luk

Stimulate Curiosity by the Selected Books

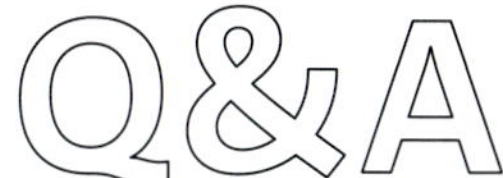

On Reading is located on the second floor of an apartment block, and the shop front is very similar to an ordinary house. Why did you choose this location? What kind of reading atmosphere do you want to create for readers?

The current location of the bookstore used to be an imported goods store ran by my friend. We moved in and took over this place after we heard that the store was moving. My decision to choose this location was because of its size, rent, and the proximity to the subway station.

It's a comfortable space for me, as I can see some greeneries from the window, and the sunlight comes in. I didn't particularly want to make it a hidden space although it is located in an apartment building. It is not noisy because it is far from the downtown area, which endows the bookstore with a peaceful atmosphere.

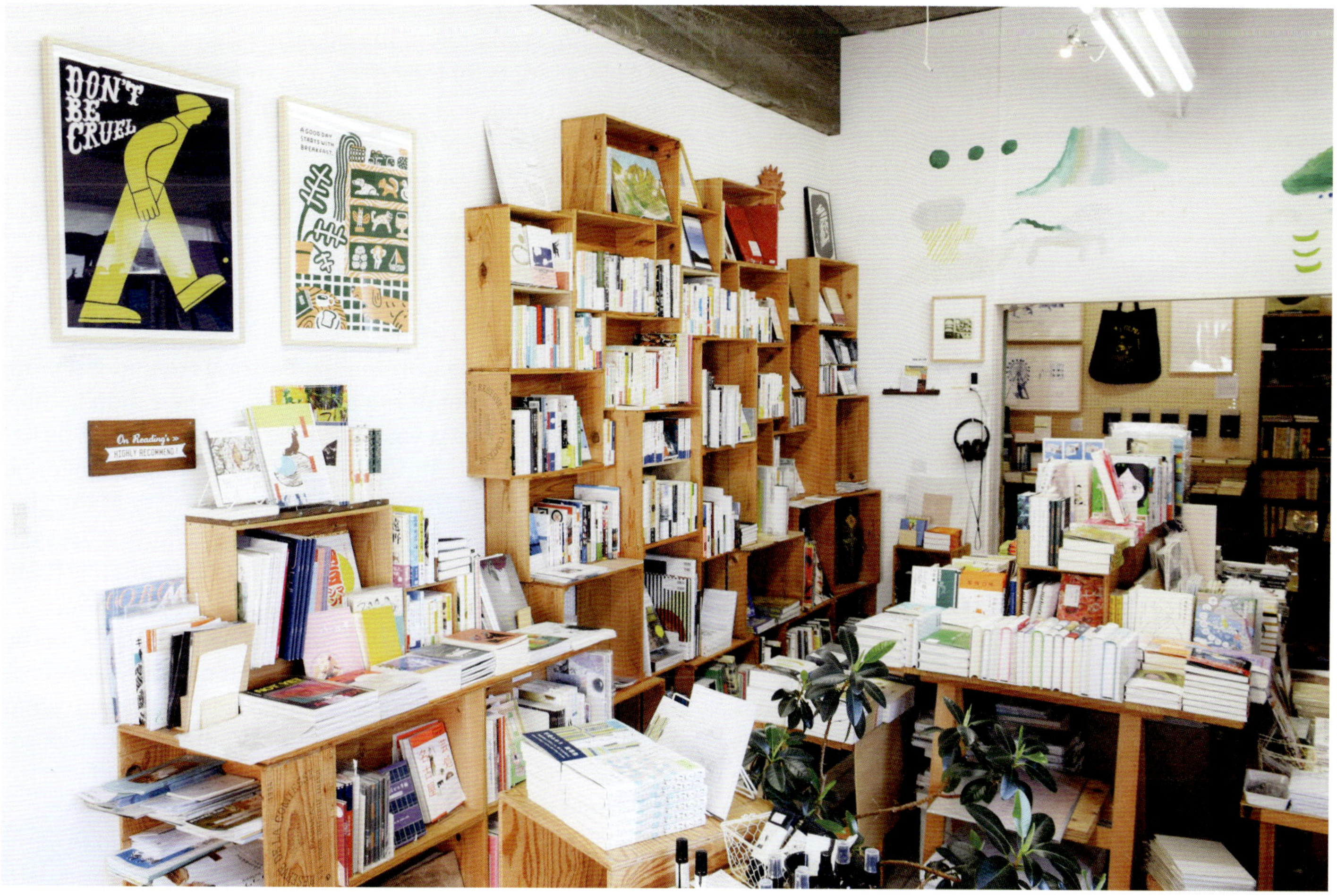

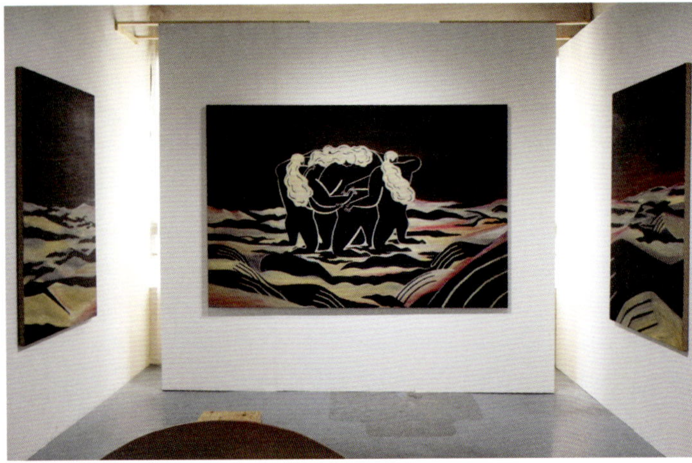

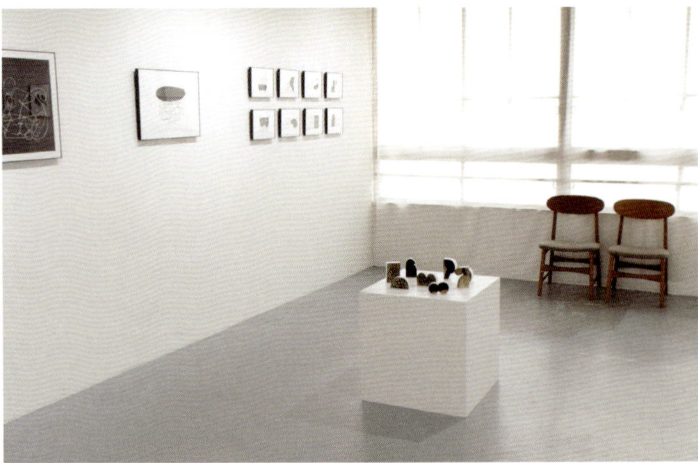

There are piles of self-publications from all over the world in the bookstore. What platforms do you pay attention to or what activities do you take part in to get the latest publishing information?

For the past few years, I have been getting information mainly from social networking sites such as Instagram and Twitter. We run a publishing label called ELVIS PRESS. Apart from the art book fairs held in Japan, we also attend the fairs in Seoul, Taipei, Shanghai, and so on. That's where we often meet artists and publishers from all over the world and get information from them. It's a pity that I can't go to foreign book fairs now because of COVID-19 pandemic.

On Reading is not only a compound art space, but you also select books for certain shops as Book Director. There are only 2 members in the team—how do you manage to maintain such an efficient output? Could you tell us about your working schedule?

Some people often say that I look busy, but actually I don't feel that busy. My daily routine is to put the newly arrived books on the shelves after arriving at the store in the morning. I can browse the publishers' websites and social networking sites and place orders for the new publications as I serve customers. In my leisure time, I can work on book selection and write introductions for books. I run the bookstore with my wife, so we can still talk a lot about our work after we go home. However, it is not troublesome for us because we enjoy what we do. In fact, I hired a new member of staff this year. Now that I have more time on my hands. I'd like to work on book design, and I'm currently studying for that.

On Reading celebrates its 10th anniversary this year. Has there ever been a moment when it was almost impossible to continue operating? What do you see as your main challenge in the next 10 years?

We opened our store just before the 2011 Tōhoku earthquake and tsunami. We were far away from the epicenter of the earthquake, so we didn't suffer any direct damages. However, the first year was the most difficult for us because the whole country was thrown into a period of self-restraint due to the nuclear accident that resulted from the earthquake (I was angry at the government for still wanting to continue with nuclear power plants after such an accident). After that, the business got back on track and fortunately there were no difficulties that made it impossible to continue our operations.

Over the past 10 years, I think our thinking has gradually changed. In the beginning, we were just selling the books we wanted, but now we have come to think deeply about the meaning of running a bookstore in our town. What kind of impact will the books we sell have on society? What is the kind of society where everyone can live in peace? We now sell many books on various social issues, and also hold talks, events and workshops.

I don't have any big plans for the future, but I would like to continue introducing great books and wonderful authors and artists as I have did in the past.

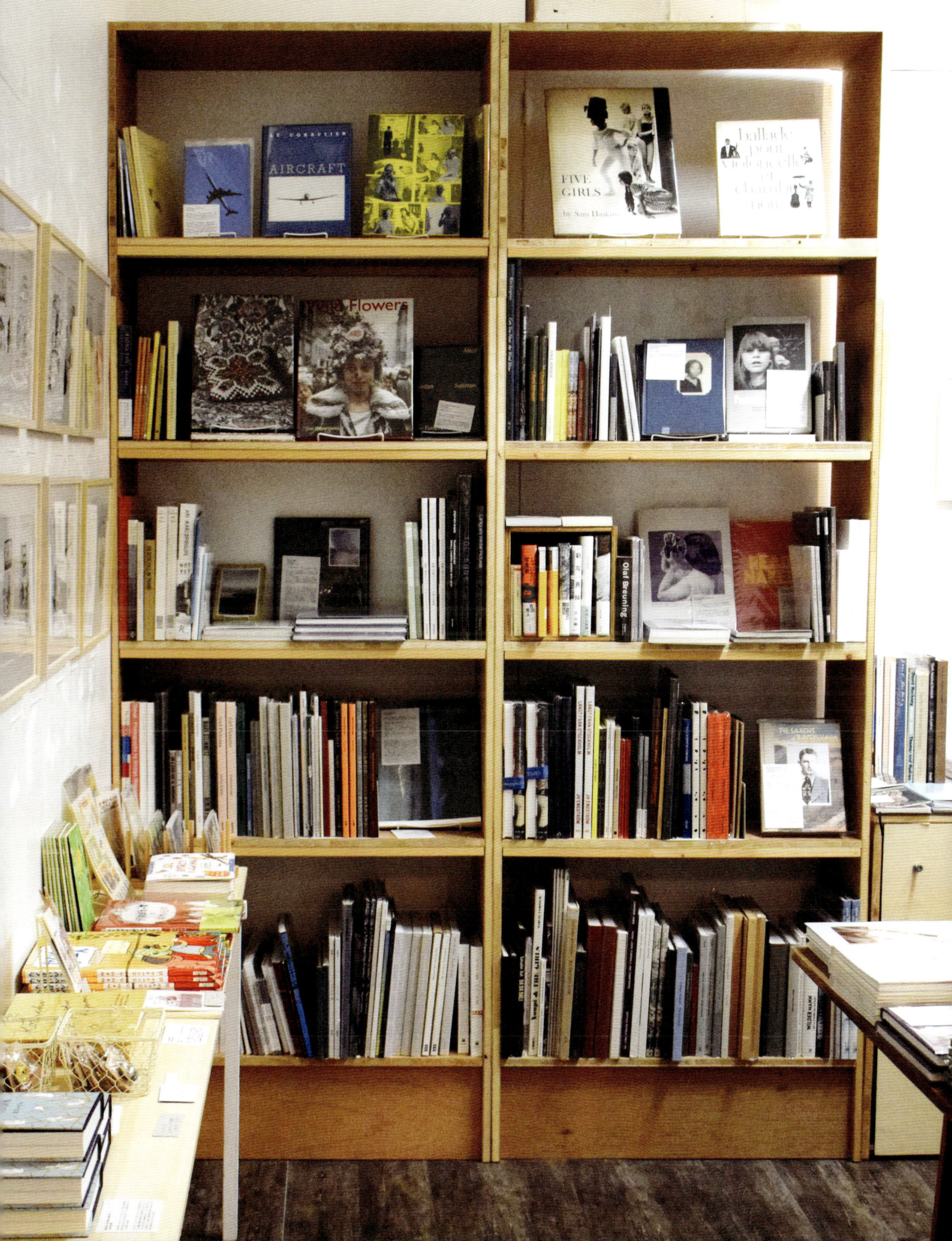
AIRCRAFT
FIVE GIRLS
Flowers
Olaf Breuning

THE BOOK SOCIETY

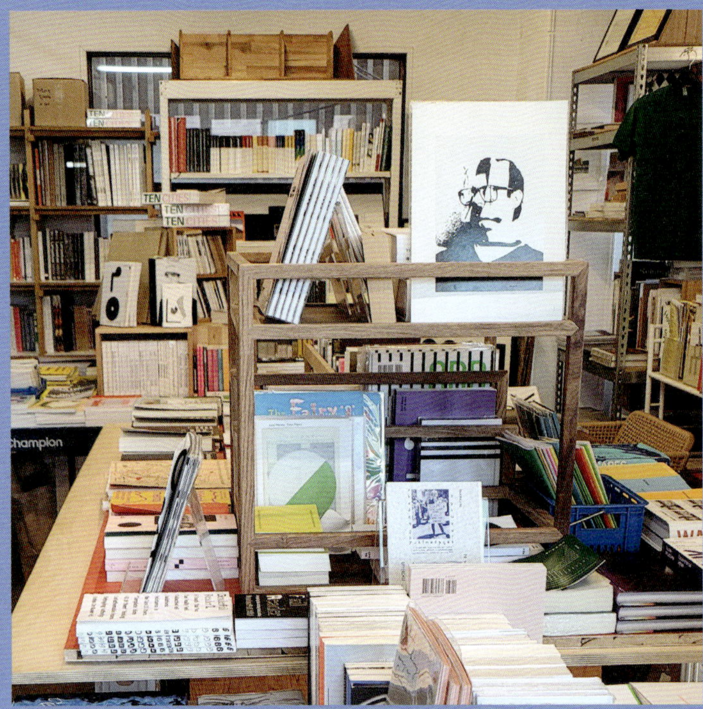

The Book Society

The Book Society is a collective bookstore located in Seoul, South Korea. It was curated by a publishing house named mediabus in 2011. The Book Society regards book as a way to bring people together for events like talks and reading groups. A study session called "reading room" was conducted in this space to translate and discuss essays by various artists.

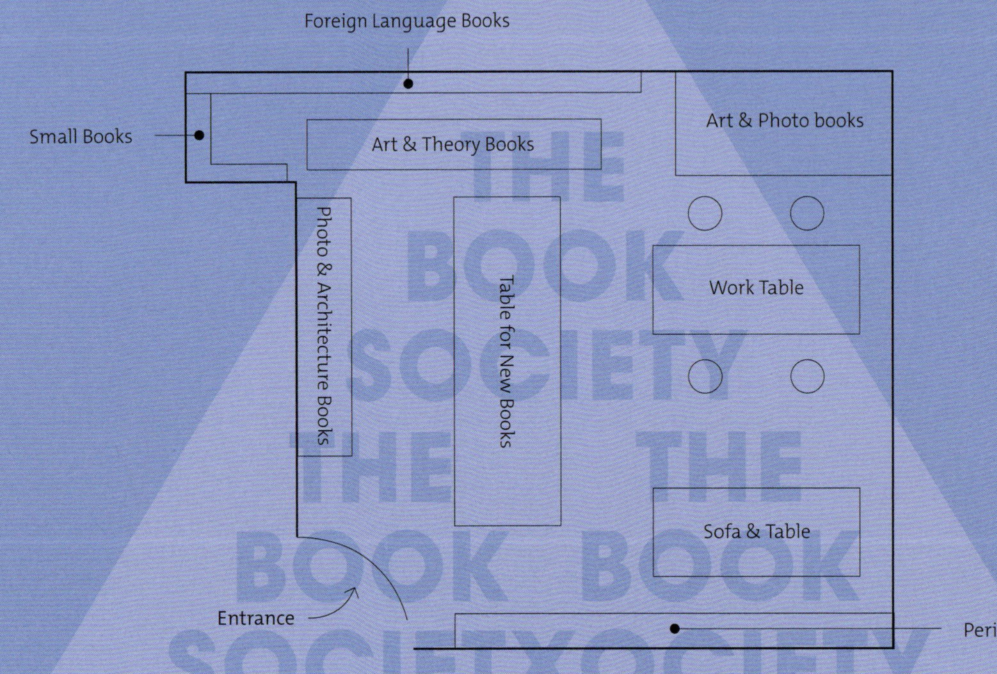

Interviewer
Gakky Luk

Disable the Search Functionality of Bookstore

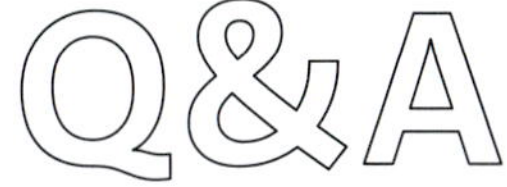

The Book Society often holds exhibitions and activities. How do you decide on the theme of activities that best align with the spirit of the bookstore? What are the criteria?

Our projects are often curated for the specific needs. In 2020, we held an exhibition and publication on small-scale publishing culture in Asia named "Publishing as a Method". Prior to that, we worked on projects related to the graphic design scene and small-scale publishing. In an architecture exhibition we held, we made the library and bookstore through the concept of "common", and also joint curated an exhibition with a fashion brand COS. Most of the activities are about how knowledge and information are produced and distributed in our time. We have focused on this issue through various activities such as publications, exhibitions and workshops.

There are some display bookshelves in the store. How do you select books for special display?

In fact, our bookstore is very small and has been in operation for more than 10 years, so many books that are not sold just pile up. Therefore, sometimes rare book seekers can find their own treasures in this space. In some cases, books are intentionally placed, but most of them just happen to be placed where they are. It's not particularly intentional to put Raymond Queneau's book next to Georges Perec's, but with the book which seems to have nothing to do with Perec, people try to read something into that relationship. In fact, there are thousands of ways to categorize books, but I don't think any of them are absolutely correct. What's interesting is that book sales are influenced by the arrangement of the books. That's why we always subtly change the position of the books every day. There are quite a number of factors to consider, such as the size, shape, color, paper, language, and theme of the book.

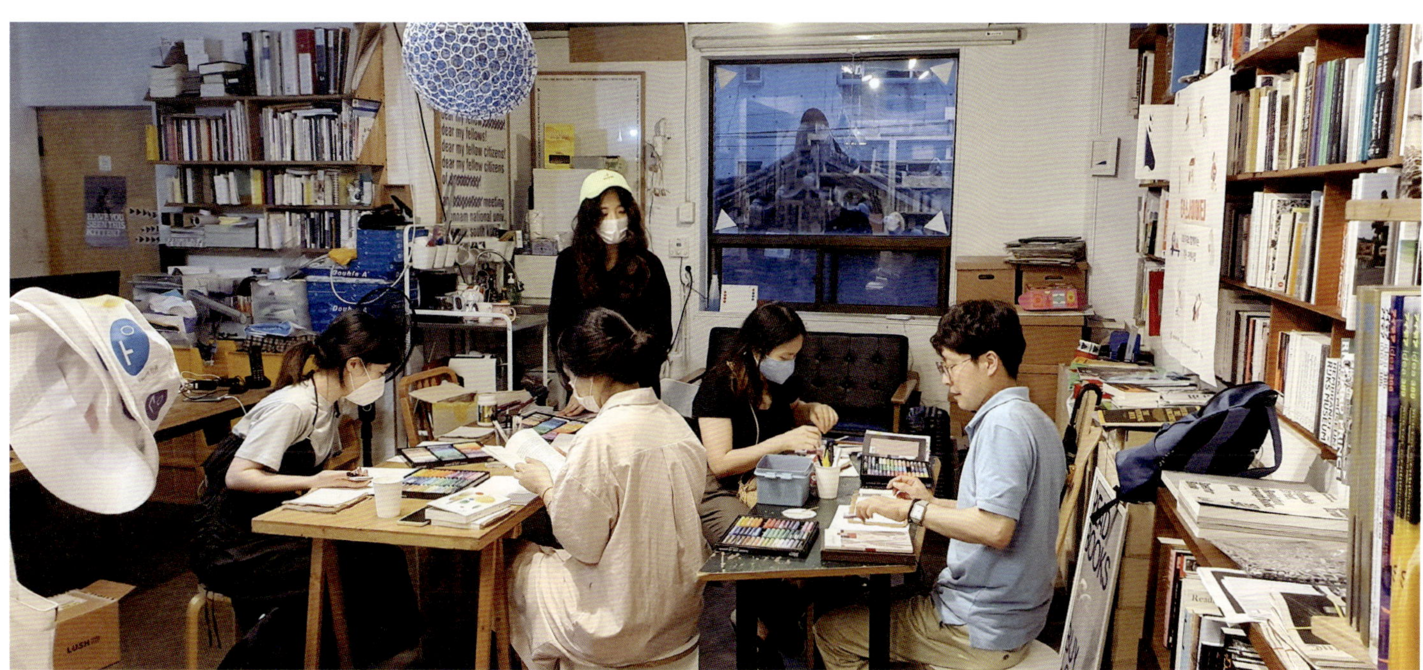

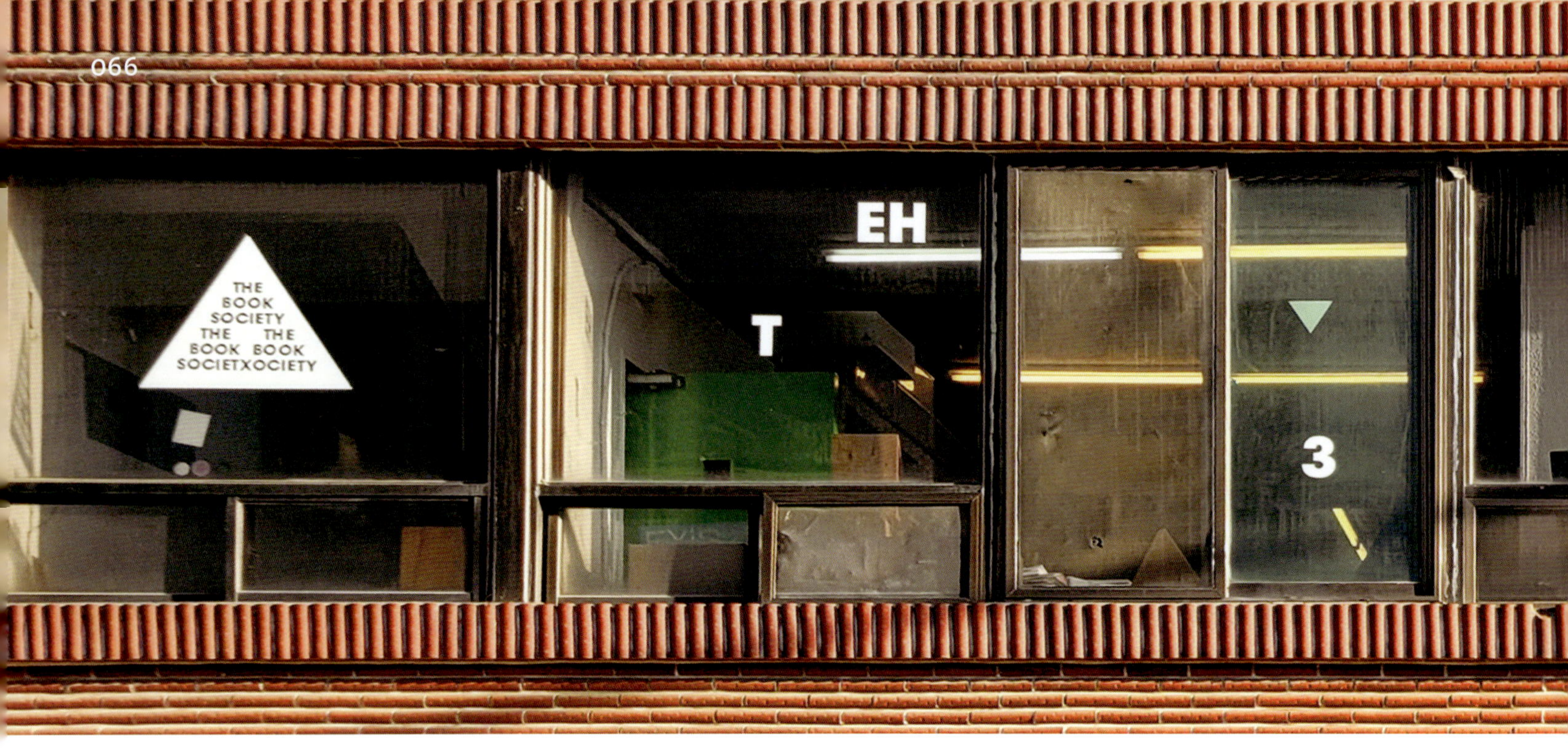

At the beginning of 2021, you reorganized the space of the bookstore. What messages do you want to convey to the readers through the space?

I think a bookstore is a unique space. There are countless spaces for books around us, such as libraries, which are tightly organized by decimal classification. Everyone would have created a space for books in their home, and they choose and place the books in their own way. When you go to a clothing store, you sometimes see things like small sofas and tables, with magazines placed on them. I think this is also an interesting book space. Anyway, every book space has its own identity through the relationship between the users and the books. Bookstores, especially The Book Society, aspire to be a book space where the past and the present are mixed up. Here, books published 20 to 30 years ago are placed next to those being published yesterday. And next to a zine printed with a photocopier, a beautiful book made by a European book craftsman can be placed. I sometimes want The Book Society to function like the Internet without search windows. For example, we usually go to bookstore to get knowledge of a certain field, but in fact, The Book Society does not offer a solution in that sense. We rarely deal with textbooks or practical books because I think it is more efficient for the Internet to offer such a solution. I think books can play their own role as a medium rather than just being a source of practical information. Of course, the role will emerge based on the relationship between books, not just on the character of one individual book.

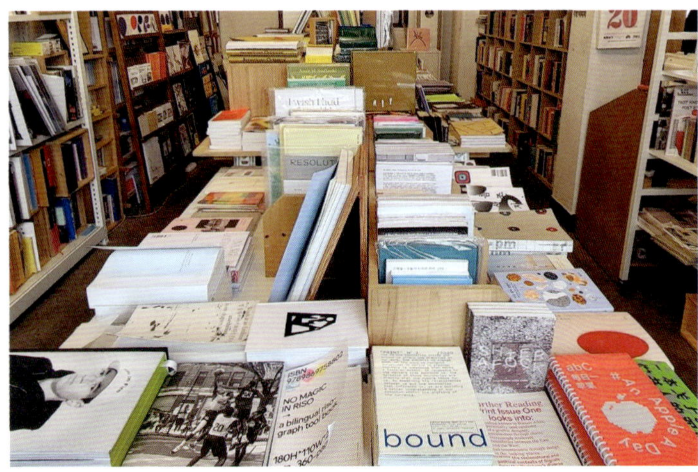

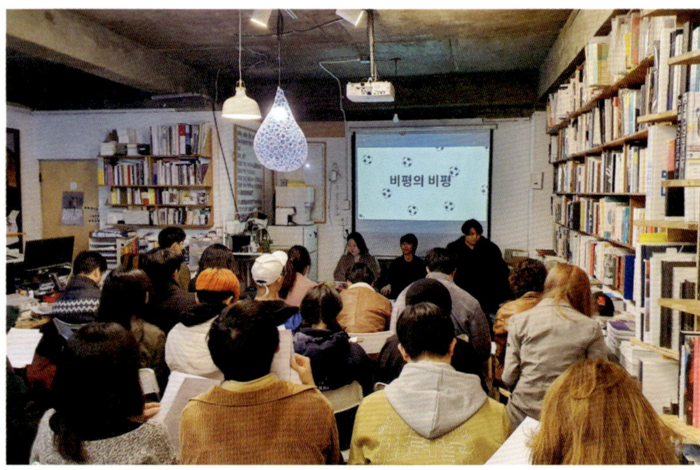

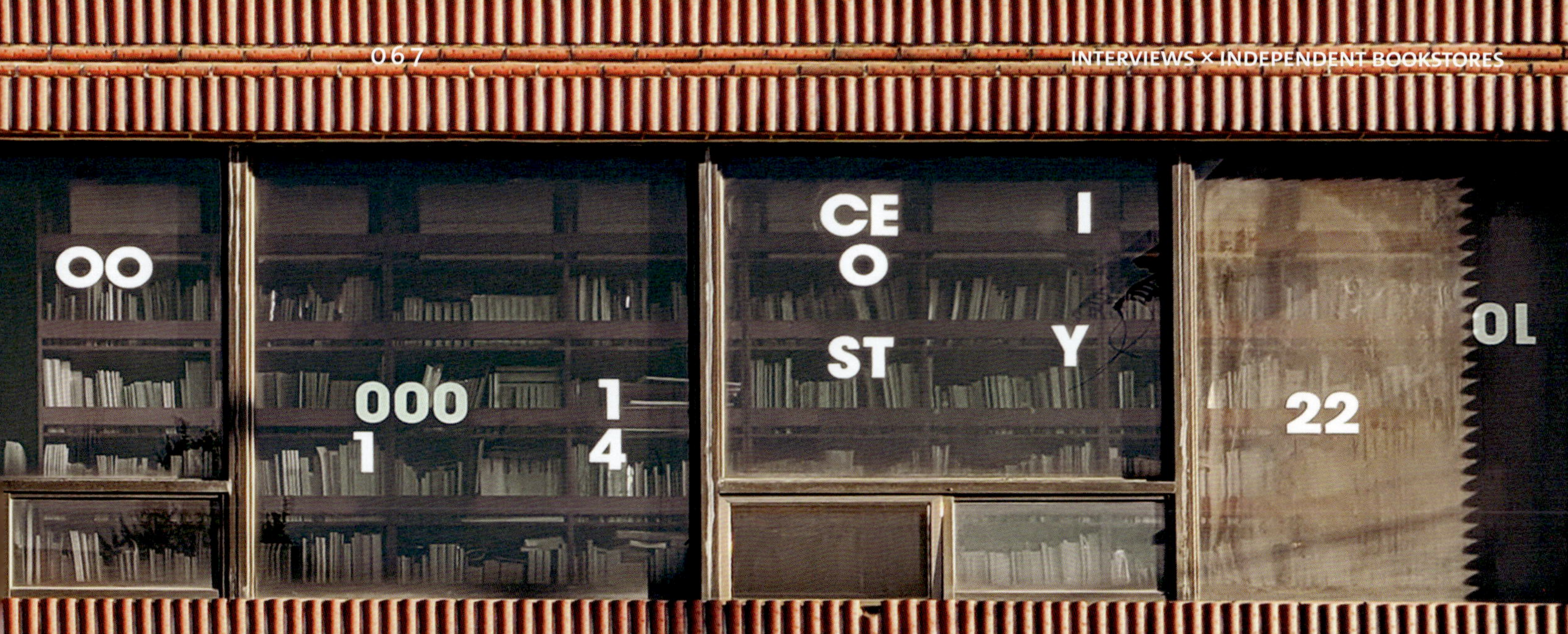

The COVID-19 pandemic has forced people to slow down. What has The Book Society faced during this period? Have you thought about the future development of the bookstore?

Due to the COVID-19 pandemic, many changes are being detected in our society. Bookstores have been struggling before the pandemic, but online distribution seems to have greatly accelerated since the COVID-19 pandemic outbreak. In fact, in these circumstances, there do not seem to be many options for us to choose from. Before the COVID-19 pandemic, we held many events in the bookstore, but we haven't been able to host a single event since last year. This is unfortunate, but I think that new conditions for book distribution have been created. Next year we will be working on a project to explore new possibilities for online publishing. This will be something in the middle of paper books and e-books, and fortunately, the whole process can be done over the Internet.

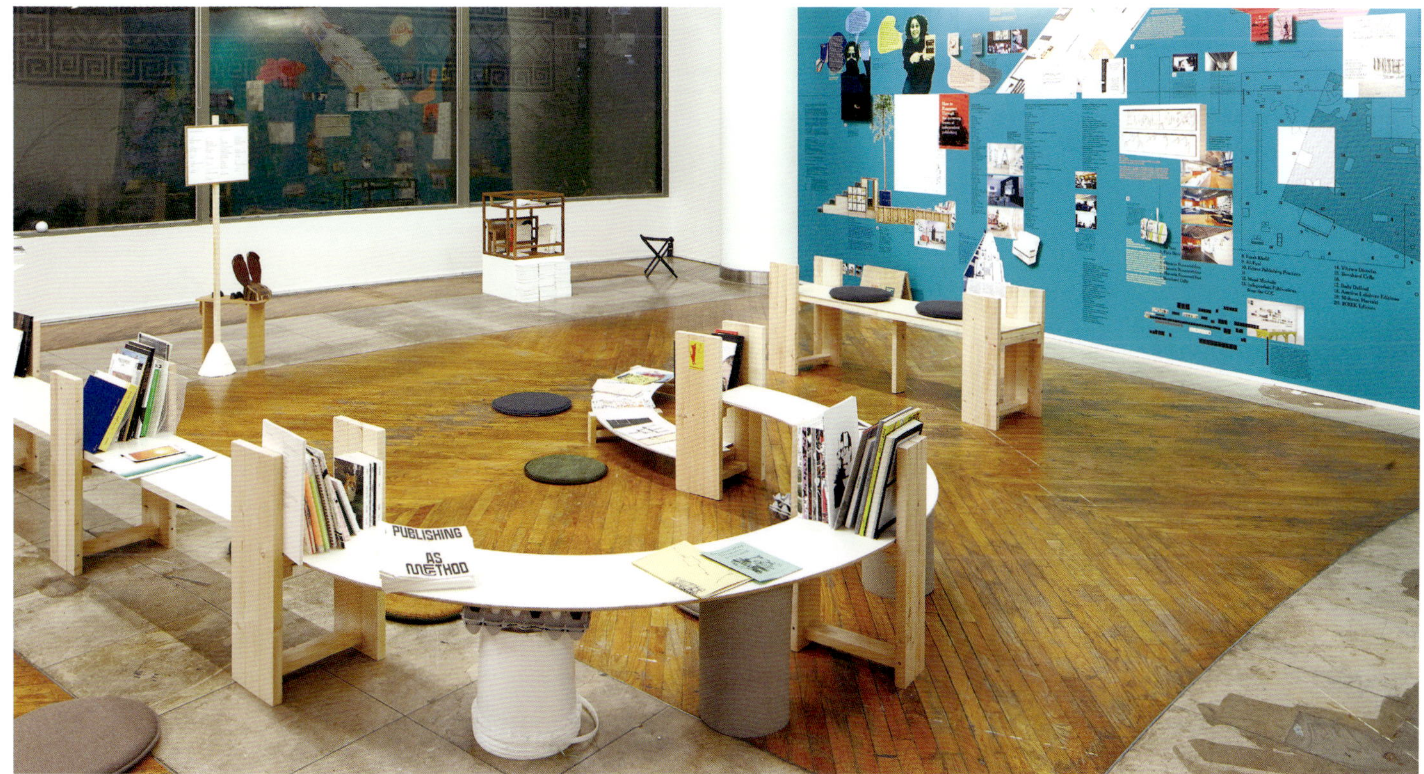

KALEIDOSCOPE BOOKS

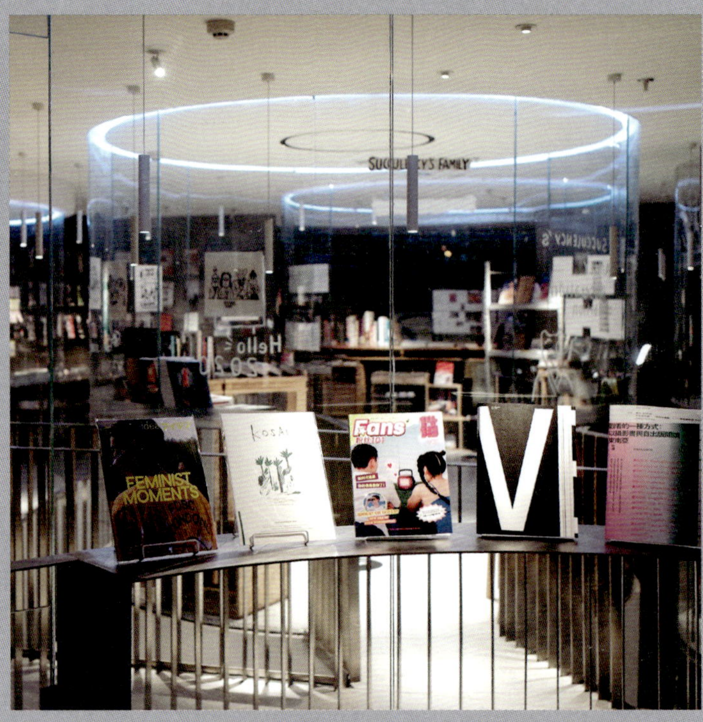

Kaleidoscope Books

Kaleidoscope Books is a Shenyang based bookstore founded in 2019. It mainly engages in the fields of art, design and lifestyle. Kaleidoscope Books is also a platform for sharing information. It also regularly holds small-scale talks, workshops and other art-related activities.

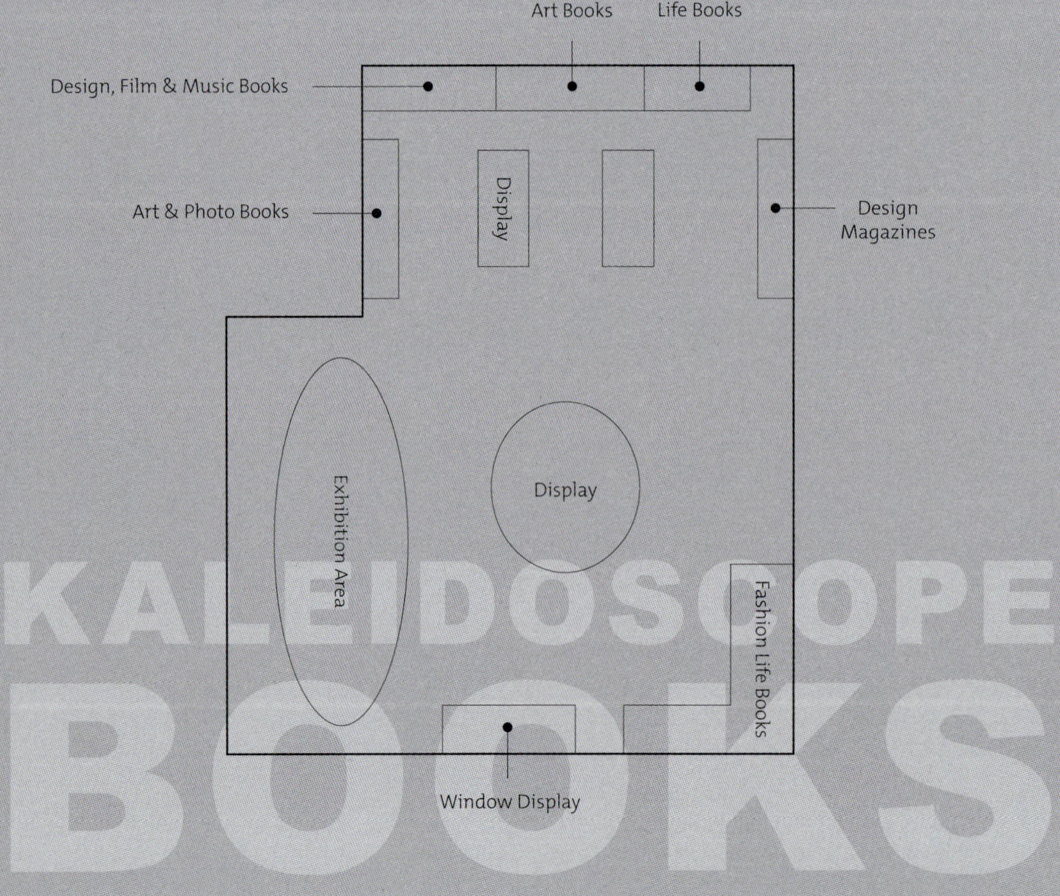

Interviewer
Gakky Luk

SEE THE WORLD WITH A KALEIDOSCOPE

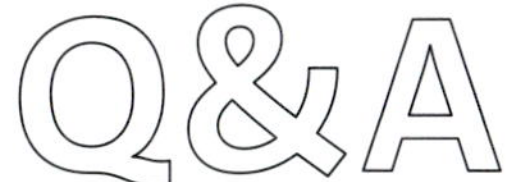

There is an occupation named "Book Director" in Japan. As the Book Director of Kaleidoscope Books, what are your criteria when selecting books?

I once thought about how to balance between running a bookstore and keeping my own personal preferences at the beginning when I established the bookstore. However, one of the characteristics of an independent bookstore is that it's comparatively free when it comes to book selection, so I would like to choose the books I like. I don't want to compromise my aesthetics and preferences in order to cater to the mass market. A bookstore with attitude is what people truly like.

You can communicate with readers directly when you participate in offline activities. How can these experiences help you in terms of product selection, operation and event planning?

Readers often come up with some unexpected questions and suggestions when you take part in the activities in different cities, which is one of the driving forces for us to make continuous progress. Pop-up bookstore is one of the ideas that emerged from these kinds of conversations. We have cross-industry collaboration both in China and other countries from time to time, and we set up a special section for each activity. Some seemingly unrealistic suggestions and ideas can be made possible if we work together and put them into practice.

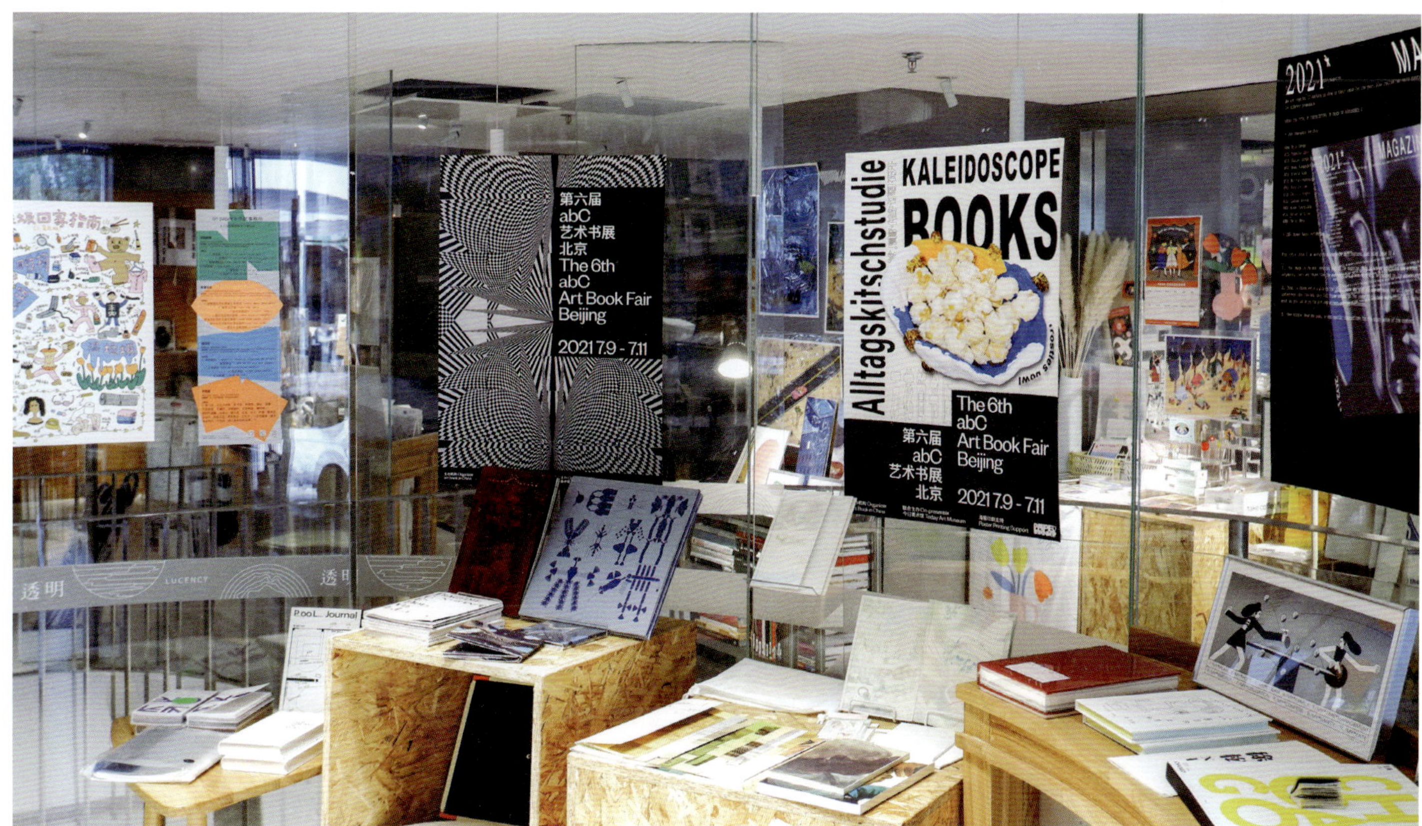

Why did you locate the bookstore in Shenyang, Liaoning? What influences do you think Kaleidoscope Books have brought to the surrounding area and the city?

There are two main reasons. The first reason is that I have lived in this city for a long time, and at the same time, my family supports me to establish a bookstore. I also found a suitable space for it. The second reason is that there are many people in Shenyang who are interested in art books. The majority of this group of people engage in the creative arts—design and illustration, just to name two—and they need a space for communication. Since the establishment of the bookstore, we have been committed to promoting art books and industry-related trends on social media platforms and in the bookstore. We gradually found that there are many people in Shenyang and the surrounding areas who are interested in art books. They are willing to discover some bookstores that are new to them through our promotions, which presents a new growth model.

There are more and more independent bookstores emerging in China. What is the characteristic that made Kaleidoscope Books different from other bookstores? What are the challenges you want to take on in the next period?

The increasing number of bookstores is a tremendous thing in the overall environment, which shows that there are still many people willing to enjoy the unique charm of books in brick-and-mortar bookstores. Kaleidoscope Books is an inclusive bookstore because it is not limited to being just an art bookstore. I have been trying to broaden its relationship with art in different aspects. I am going to try to have crossover cooperation with some artists to create something new in the next period.

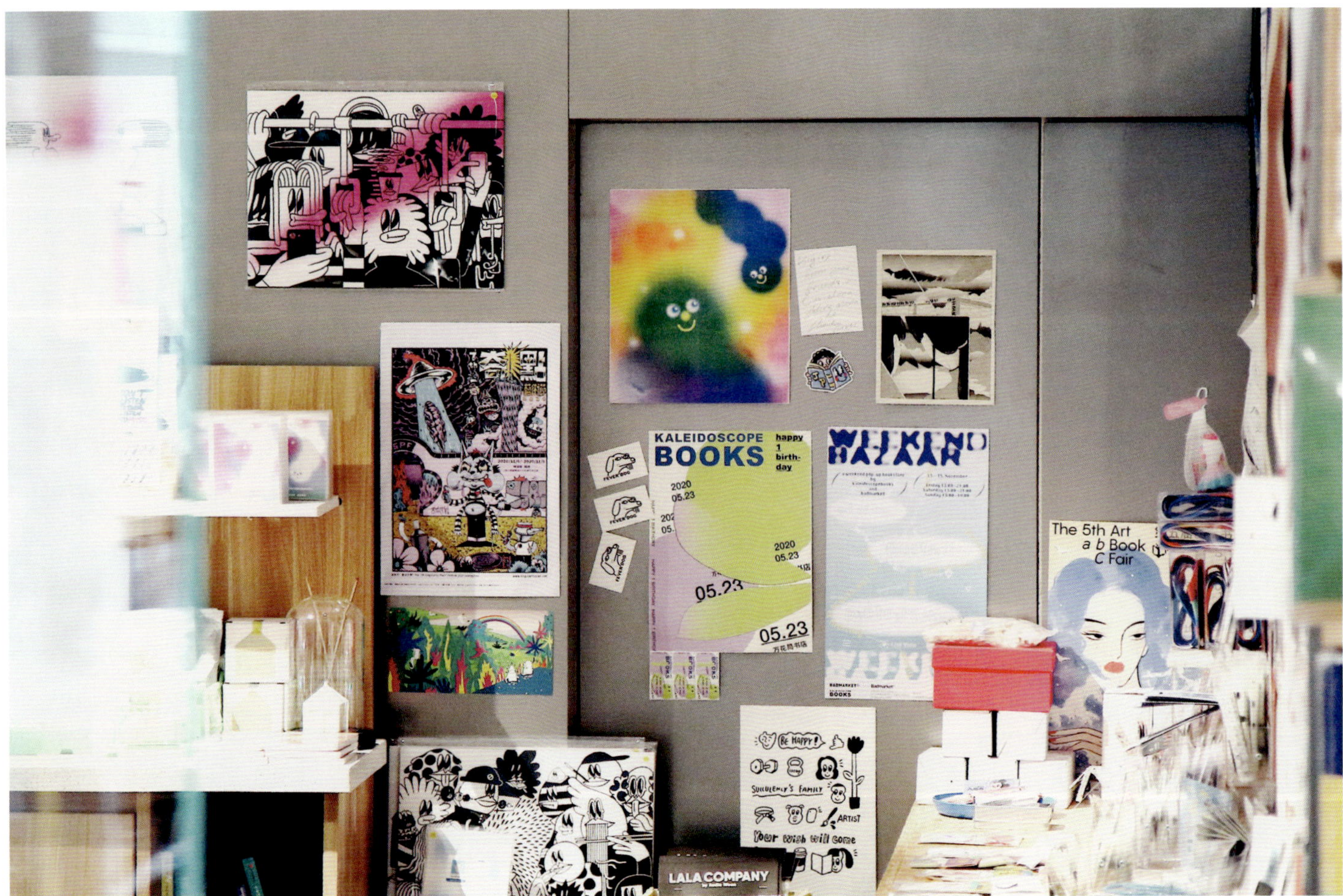

一家书店可以折射的无限可能

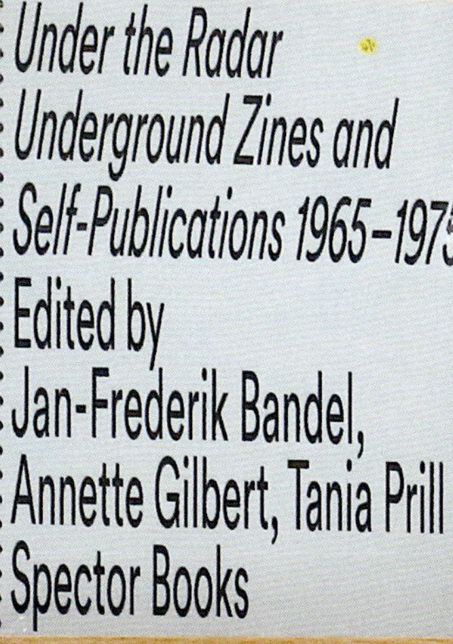

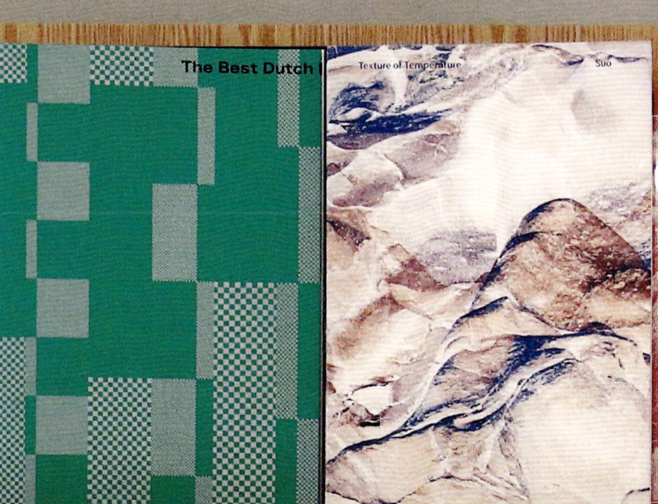

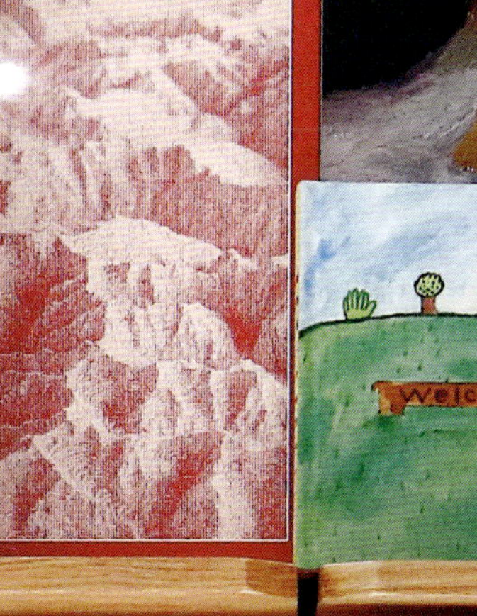

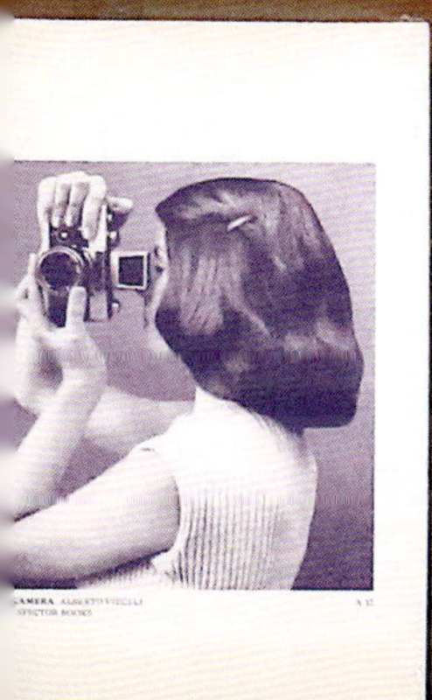

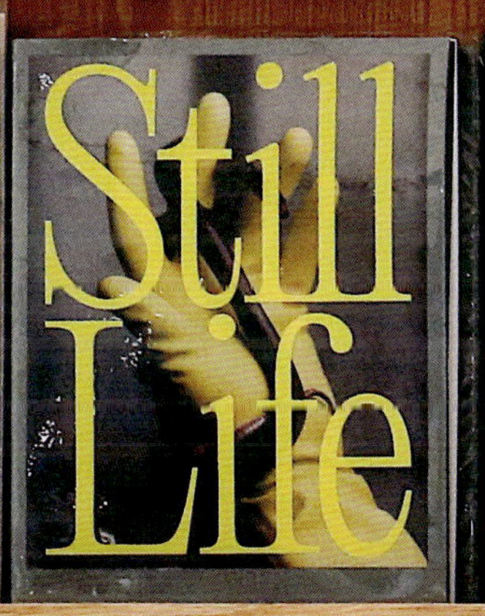

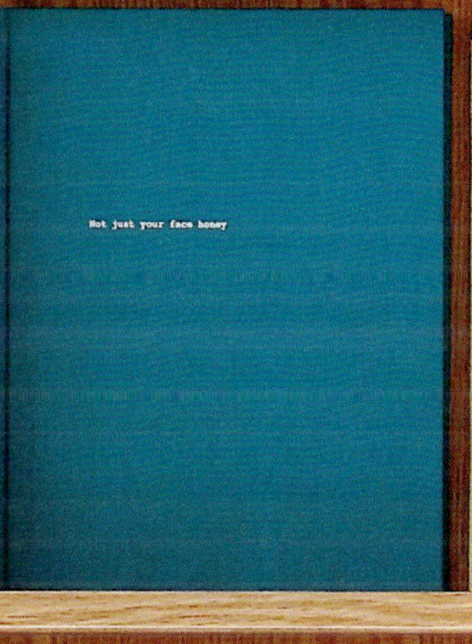

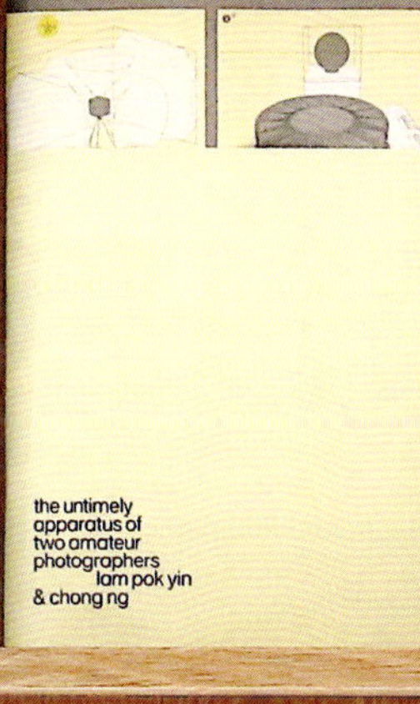

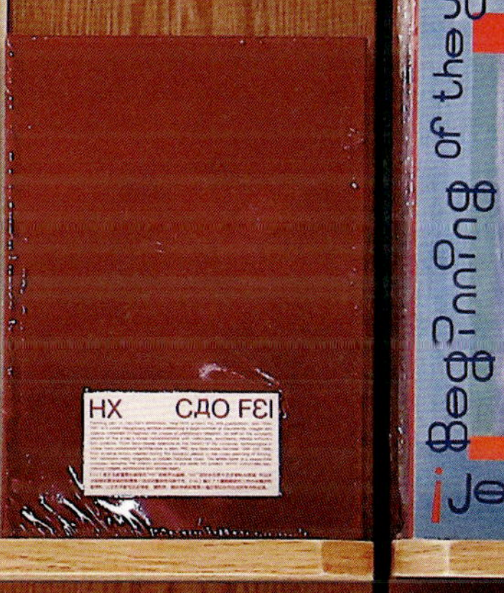

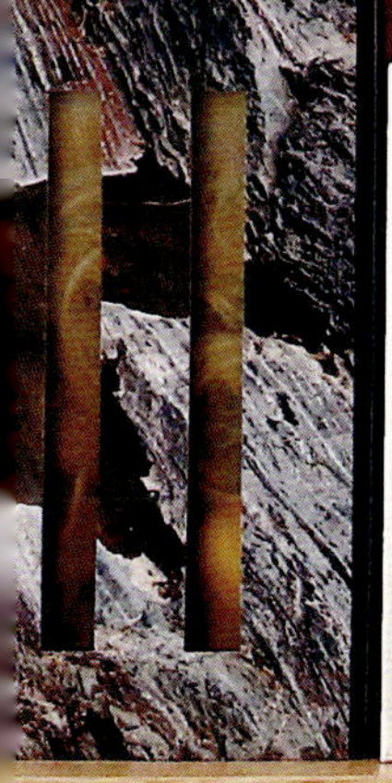

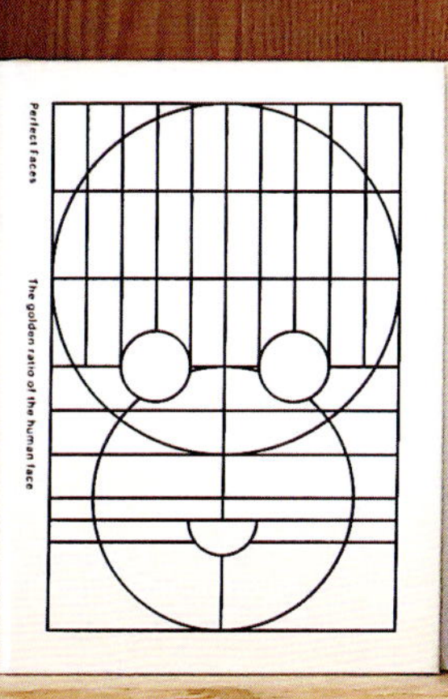

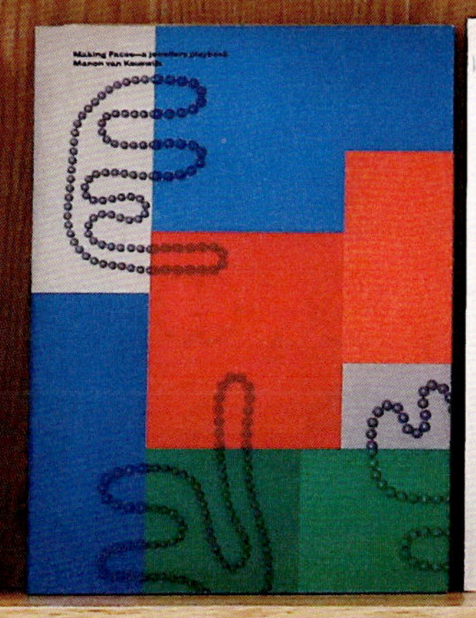

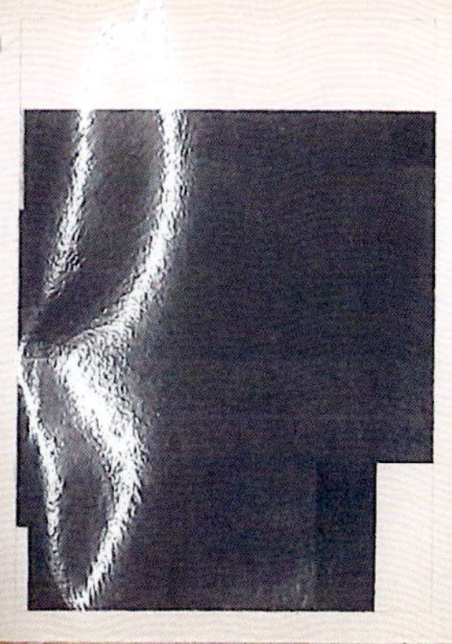

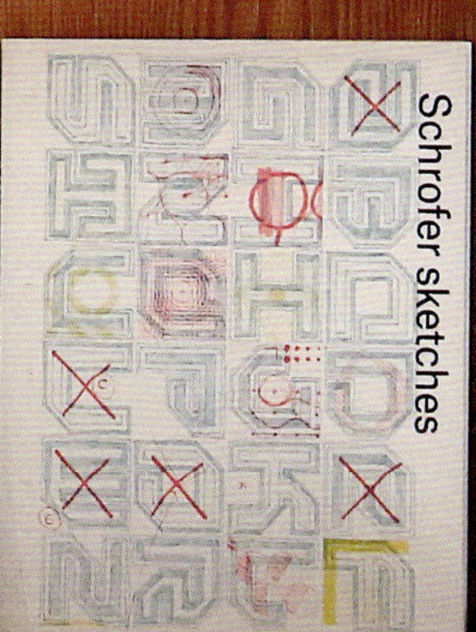

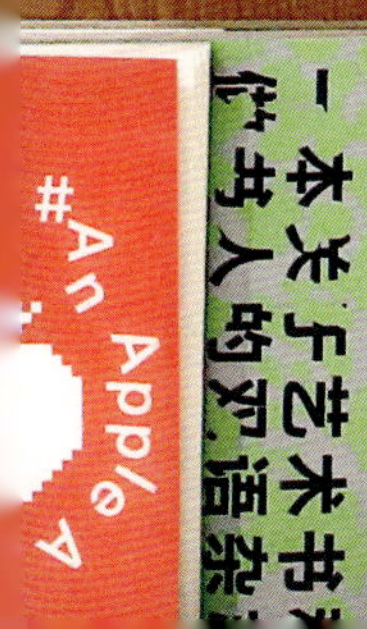

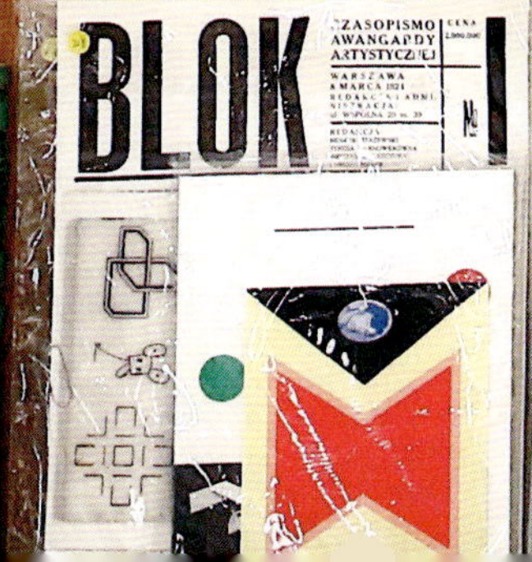

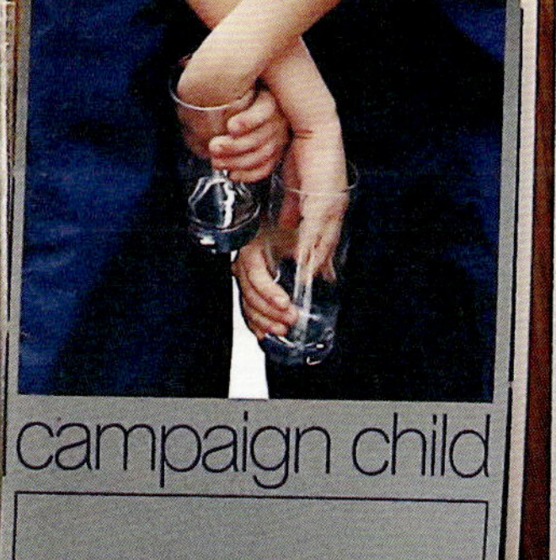

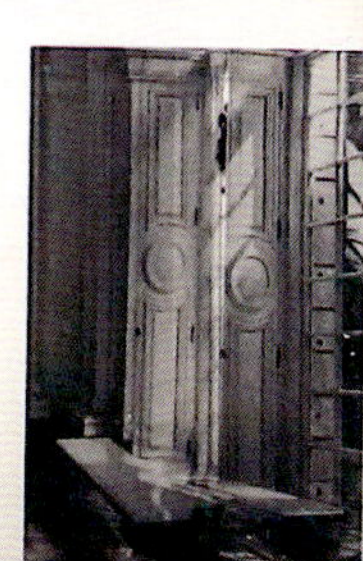

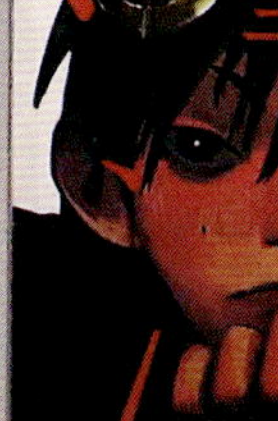

PRINT MATTERS!

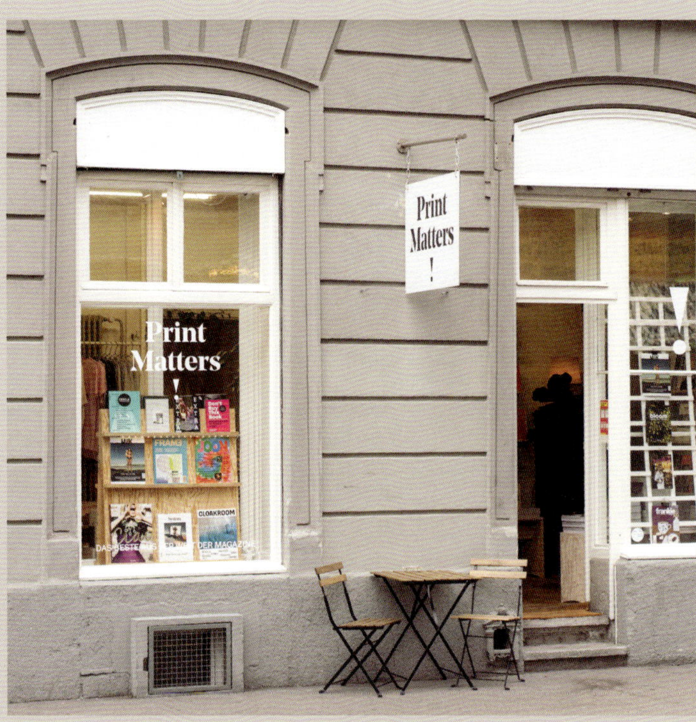

Print Matters!

Print Matters! is an independent bookstore located in Zurich, Switzerland. It is committed to inspiring readers with independent magazines, books and artworks.

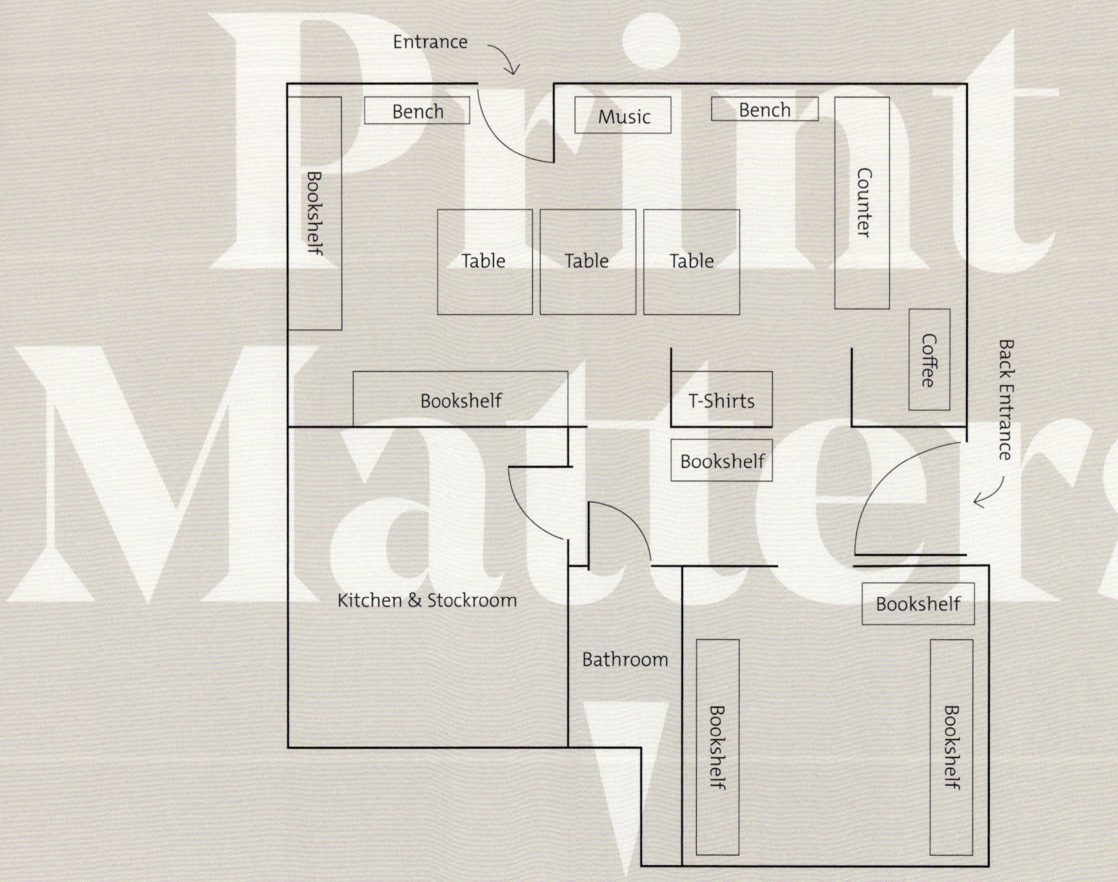

Interviewer
Gakky Luk

Why Not Niche Magazines?

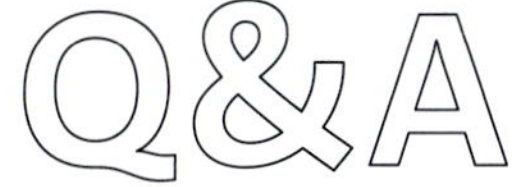

Independent bookstores often represent the values of their owners. What do you think the values of your bookstore are? What influences have these values had on the local culture and readers?

Print Matters! is a place where you can find magazines which are not available at the regular kiosks anymore. While the space previously reserved for print publications is being replaced with food, cigarettes and lottery tickets in these kiosks, my goal was to bring back the kind of stores where magazines are still the center of attention. I guess you could say that my value is that I want to sell magazines that are worth the price. Many of the titles in my store are more expensive than the usual magazine you'll find in a kiosk. This is due to the fact that most of them are independent and published without advertisements. You will also notice that many are made with much higher quality paper. These magazines are made to keep and collect—not to be just thrown away after one quick read. Since we are the only store of this kind in Zurich, we have had quite an influence. Most of our customers didn't even know these titles existed before and to be able to let them know about these magazines and appreciate them is so rewarding.

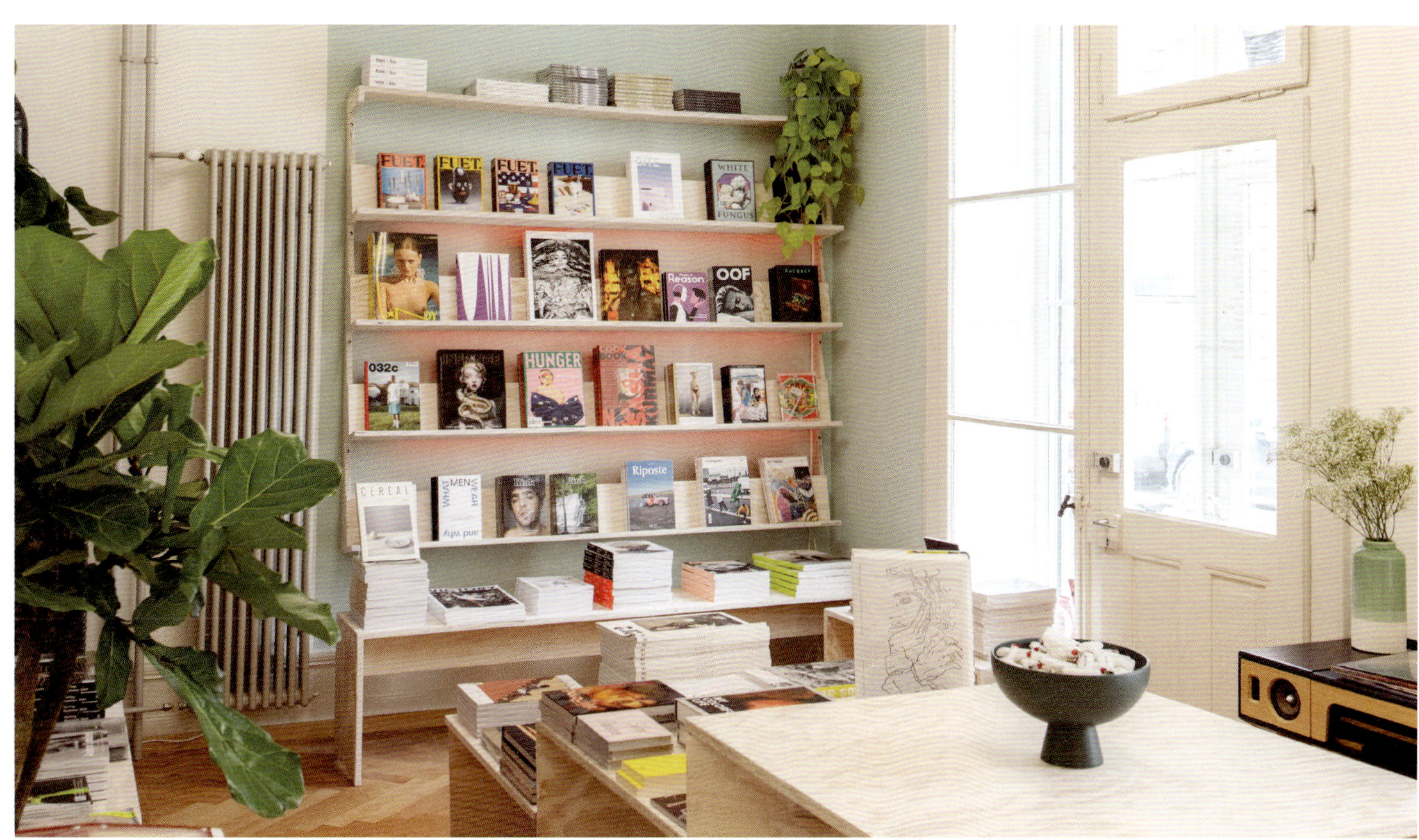

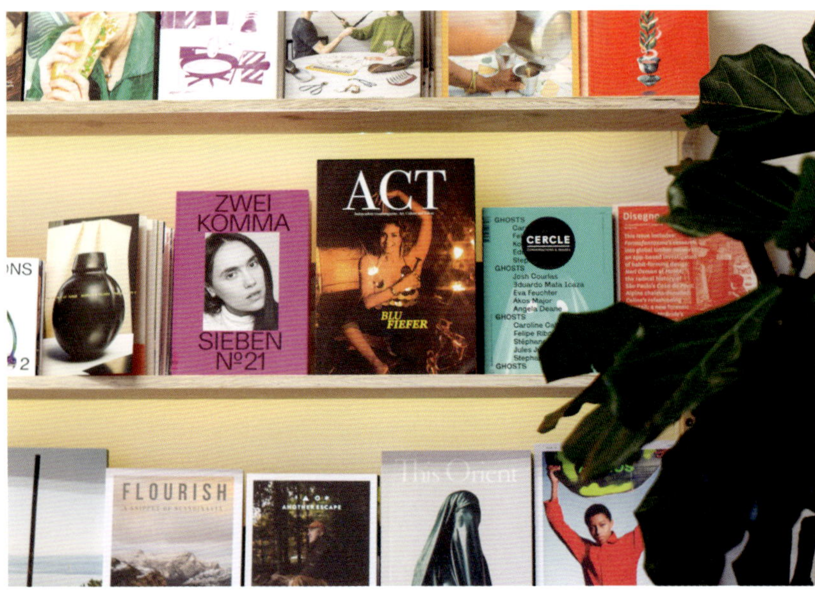

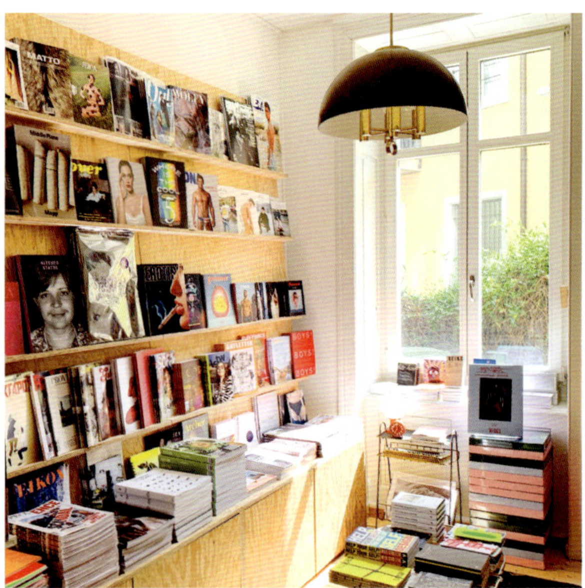

Print Matters! holds activities like concerts in the bookstore from time to time. How did you decide on the themes of this type of events? How did these themes relate to the bookstore? What information was conveyed through these activities?

When I started planning to open the store, I knew that events were going to be a big part of it. I love when people come together to talk about what they have seen or experienced. Most of the events were magazine launches. I invited magazine creators and artists to present their new works here and to use the location as a place to celebrate it. We have also had two in-store concerts so far. Both were super nice and I think they were like a thank you to our customers: free live music from bands or solo artists that they didn't know before.

No matter if it's a magazine launch or a concert, we always invite small, independent names and I think this is the big connection they all have with our store and the magazines we are selling.

What is your standard for selecting the books and magazines that are sold in the bookstore?

Many of the bigger titles and bestsellers have a saved space for every issue because these are the titles that will always sell. For the smaller ones, it is a mixture of customers' recommendations and my own taste. Selecting magazines is actually really hard since there are so many that I could fill up five times the space I have. When I select, I try to find out which topic is not well represented yet and then I'll try to find titles to fill up that part of the selection. From the experience I gathered in the last two years, I know now that the cover images are sometimes much more important than the content, which might be frustrating sometimes, but this is just what people see. Especially when the magazines are surrounded by so many other titles—to sell they have to stand out.

The Swiss Style emphasizes minimalism and cleanness. Based in Zurich, Switzerland, were you influenced by the Swiss Style in planning, interior design and other aspects?

The Swiss Style as you call it has been a huge influence, maybe even subconsciously. Studying at the University of the Arts in Zurich—it is what you learn and your taste in terms of interiors will be informed by whether you like it or not. Don't get me wrong, I am proud to have studied design here and I like the Swiss Style—well most of the time. When I designed the space I wanted it to look clean and tidy with lots of white, which was hard to achieve since the building we're in is super old. I will let readers be the judge if I made the store look like the Swiss Style.

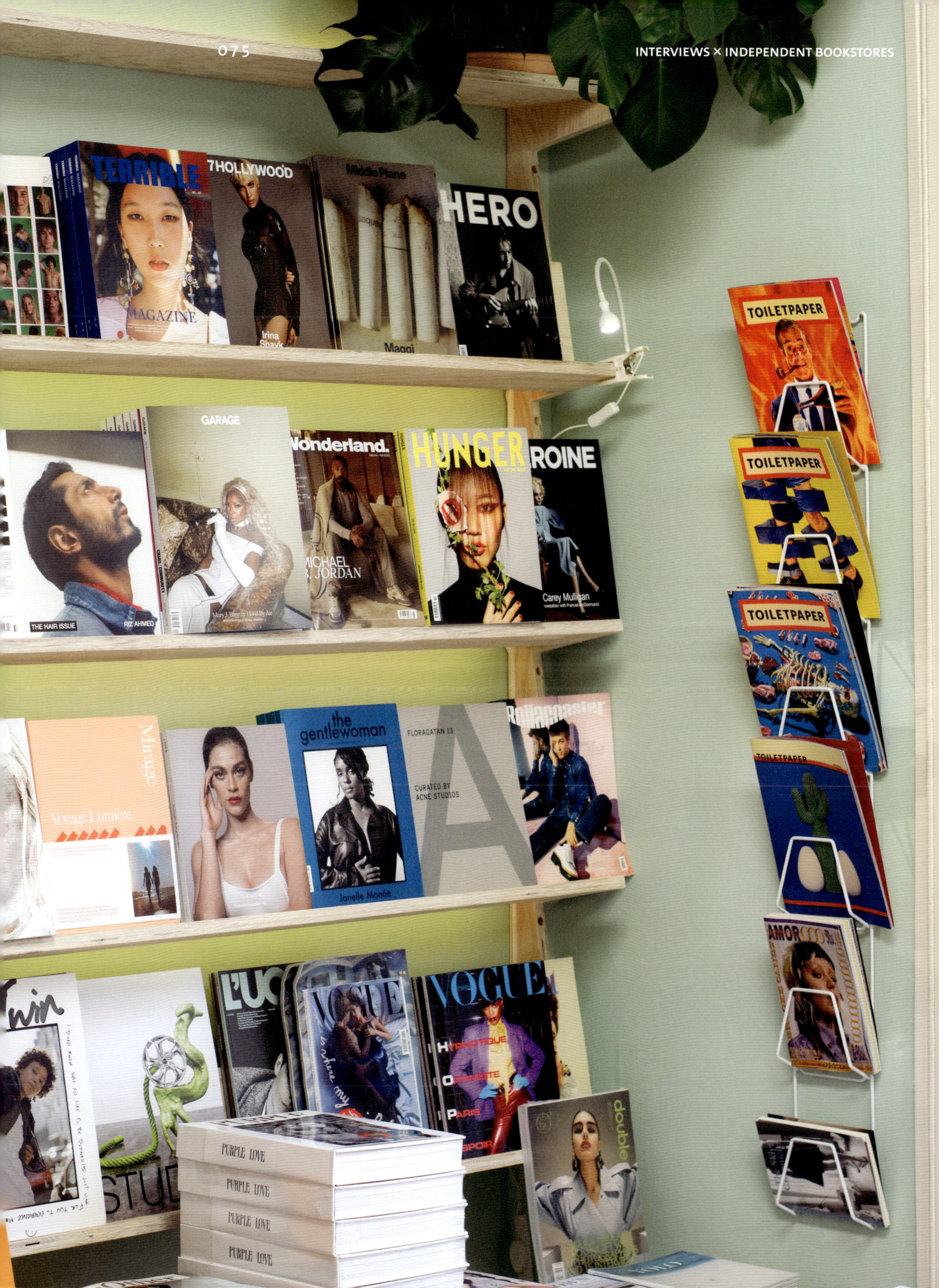
TERRIBLE
MAGAZINE
7HOLLYWOOD
Irina Shayk
Middle Plane
HERO
TOILETPAPER
GARAGE
Wonderland.
MICHAEL B. JORDAN
HUNGER
ROINE
Carey Mulligan
THE HAIR ISSUE
RIZ AHMED
TOILETPAPER
TOILETPAPER
Mirage
Voyage Lumière
the gentlewoman
Janelle Monáe
FLORAGATAN 13
CURATED BY ACNE STUDIOS
TOILETPAPER
VOGUE
VOGUE
PURPLE LOVE
PURPLE LOVE
PURPLE LOVE
PURPLE LOVE
double

STOLEN BOOKS

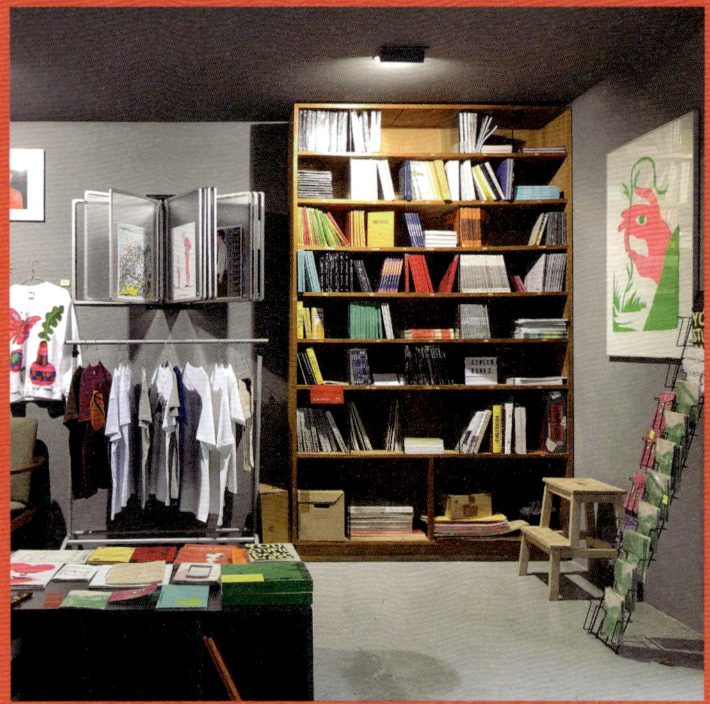

Stolen Books

Stolen Books is an independent bookstore and publisher based in Lisbon, Portugal. Since its establishment, Stolen Books has been inspired by the idea that "To steal a book is an elegant offense." It has participated in art book fairs in Berlin, Los Angeles, Shanghai, Taipei, Tokyo and other places.

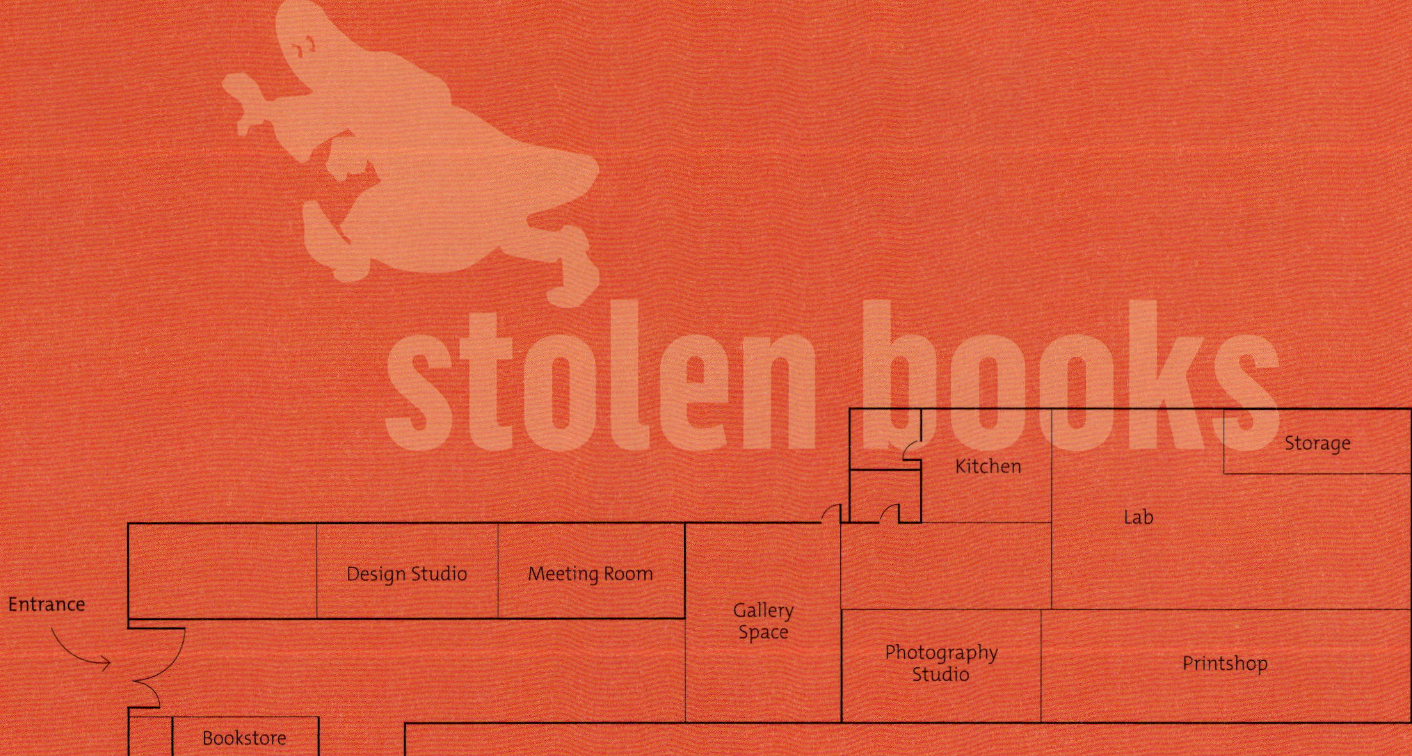

Interviewer
Gakky Luk

Injecting the Personality into the Bookstore

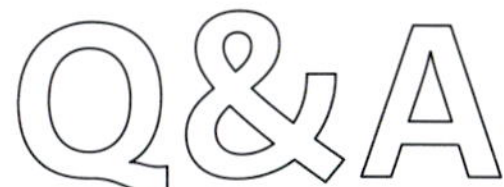

The name of the bookstore is "Stolen Books", and the logo is a dark shadow with the implied meaning of "thief". Why did you choose it as the name? How does it represent the characteristics of the bookstore?

The whole concept of publishing and distributing books is a form of appropriation of the artists' or authors' works. In other words, a form of "consented theft" that ultimately benefits everyone involved, since it makes possible the existence of the books and the consequent visibility of the works. Increasing availability is a big part of our mission: to democratize the art book. Our logo is a ghost that acts in the shadows, stealing from the rich to the poor, and this metaphorically represents the philosophy on which Stolen Books is based.

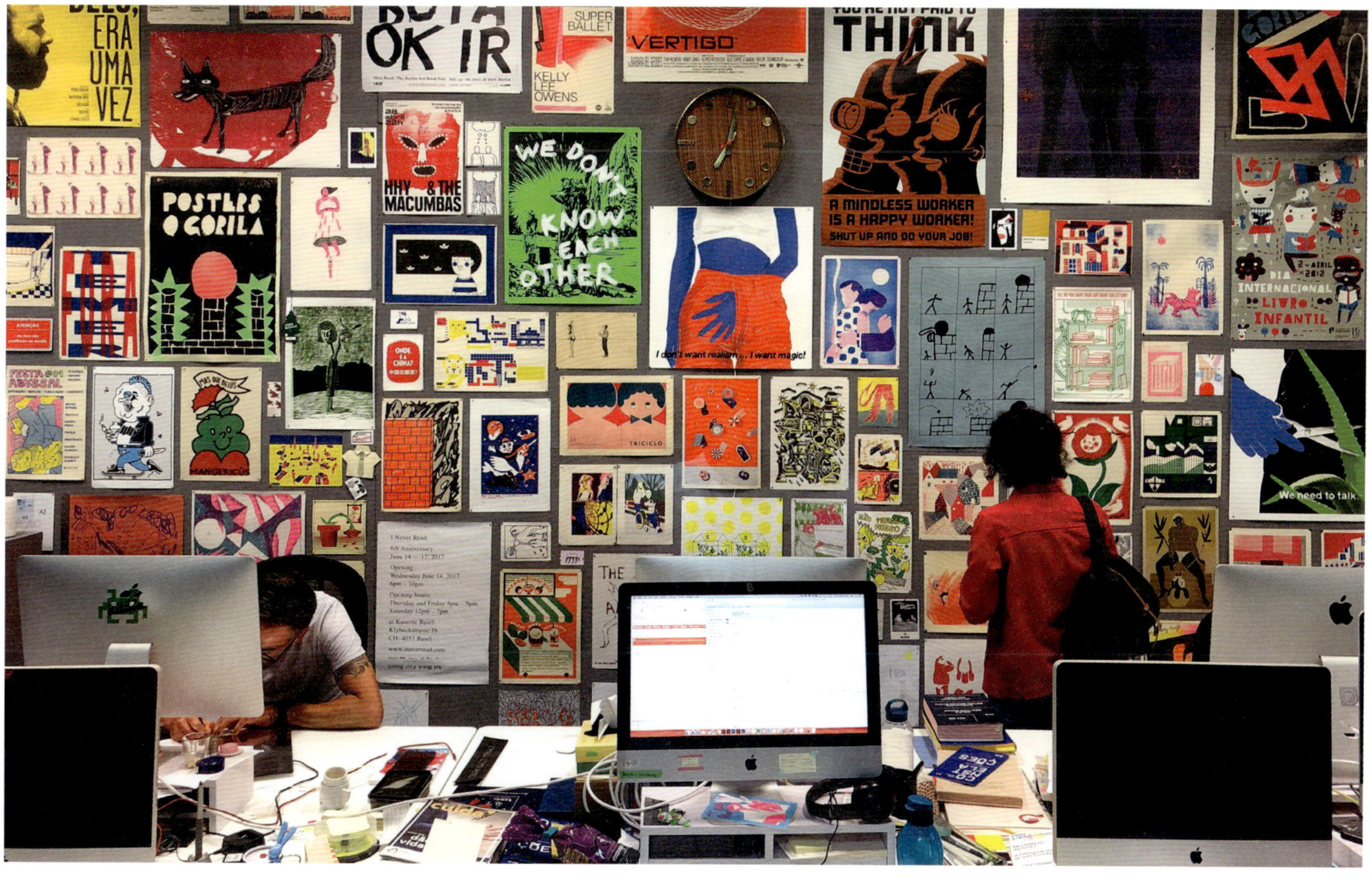

Independent bookstores could represent the personalities of their owners. What do you think is the personality of Stolen Books? What's the difference between it and a traditional bookstore?

It is true—our store is a kind of reflection of our personalities and therefore of our tastes and interests, which in this case result from a very broad vision of art and the world. Besides this, Stolen Books is mainly a bookstore and an art book publisher. At the same time, it is also a print shop and a gallery, and that distinguishes us from most projects in our field, which is not only because we bet on publishing books (which is a considerable risk), but also because of the way we choose to approach the art book market. It is a very challenging adventure that reveals itself as we get deeper into it.

You have participated in art book fairs in Japan, China, France and many other countries. What are the distinctive characteristics of readers in different countries? Can you share some interesting experiences during the activities?

Our experience in participating in trade fairs is indeed vast and practically covers countries from almost every continent. It is true that the audience is very diverse and you do find specific behaviors in each country or city. The Japanese, for example, are very thoughtful. They analyze books with all their senses before buying them. The Chinese are more enthusiastic and intuitive, and show great interest in new visual cultures. Americans and Europeans, on the other hand, are more guided by the names and trends of the moment and current agendas. It is interesting to see how in New York we probably sell more of one specific title, and in Shanghai the interest and sales are much more diversified. There are many interesting stories from fairs, but one of the most interesting was that of a customer who bought practically all of our books in San Francisco, thinking they really were stolen items.

But across all countries and cultures we find the art book cosmos to be characterized by solidarity, friendship, warmth and welcome. It is one of the best features of our job.

What is the current development status of independent bookstores in Portugal? If you had advice for someone who wants to open an independent bookstore, what would you say?

Portugal is a very small country with only 10 million inhabitants, and therefore it is a very fragile publishing market, not allowing for great survival expectations in this activity. The vast majority of Portuguese bookstores and publishers only bet on the national market and therefore they are always struggling. We are one of the few bookstores and publishers that have invested in the international market and this has made it possible for us to carry out deeper and more sustainable work. It has been a very challenging task, requiring a lot of creativity and permanent strategic actions. For example, since the first lockdown caused by the COVID-19 pandemic in March, 2020, we have not been able to be physically present in fairs around the world and this, obviously, has had an impact on book sales. But actually this circumstance has led us to engage with the online market with greater dynamism and engagement. The effects have been felt quickly, because our sales grew about 400%, surpassing by far all our expectations.

Of course this growth is amazing, but we are eager to get back to the real world, to travel and be in direct contact with the public, artists and event organizers around the world. The tangibility of the books only makes sense with that physical and face to face contact with people.

Giving advice on this activity is always an act of great responsibility, because many complex personal and business relationships are at stake. But perhaps a wise piece of advice would be to take a good look at what has already been done in this area and take a chance on a different perspective that genuinely shows passion for what you are doing.

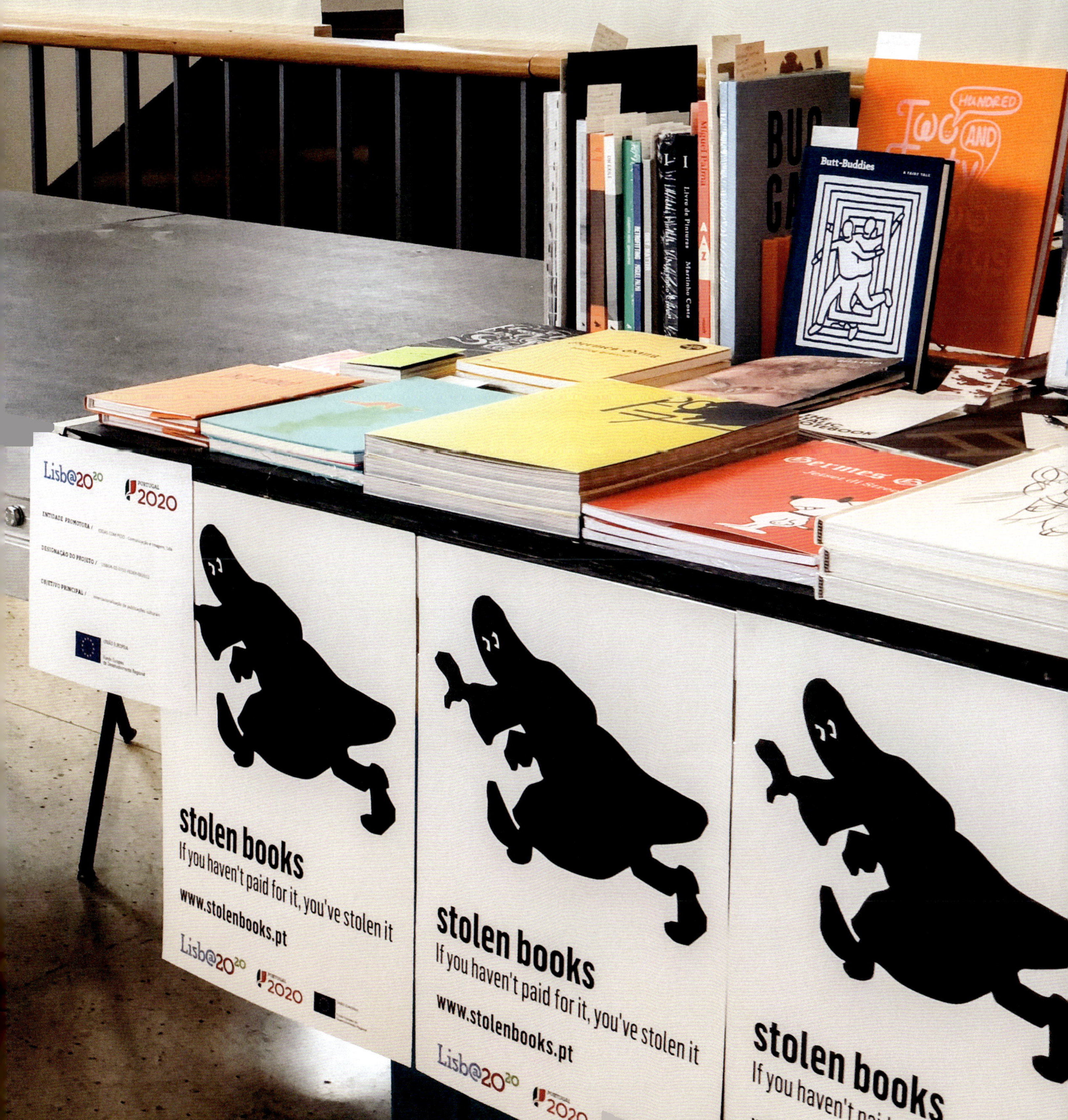

Brassaï
Victor Brauner
Claude Cahun &
Marcel Moore
Joseph Cornell
Germaine Dulac
Mobilisierung
C37 Konversion
in den Kampf:
Spanischer
Bürgerkrieg
–9. Juli 2018
LLUNG
the Present
B17 Neolithic
Childhood
Joseph Cornell
Germaine Dulac
The Spanish
Civil War
April 13–July 9, 2018
EXHIBITION
Butt-Buddies
stolen books
If you haven't paid for it, you've stolen it
www.stolenbooks.pt
Lisb@20[20]
PORTUGAL 2020
stolen books
If you haven't paid for it, you've stolen it
www.stolenbooks.pt
Lisb@20[20]
PORTUGAL 2020
stolen books

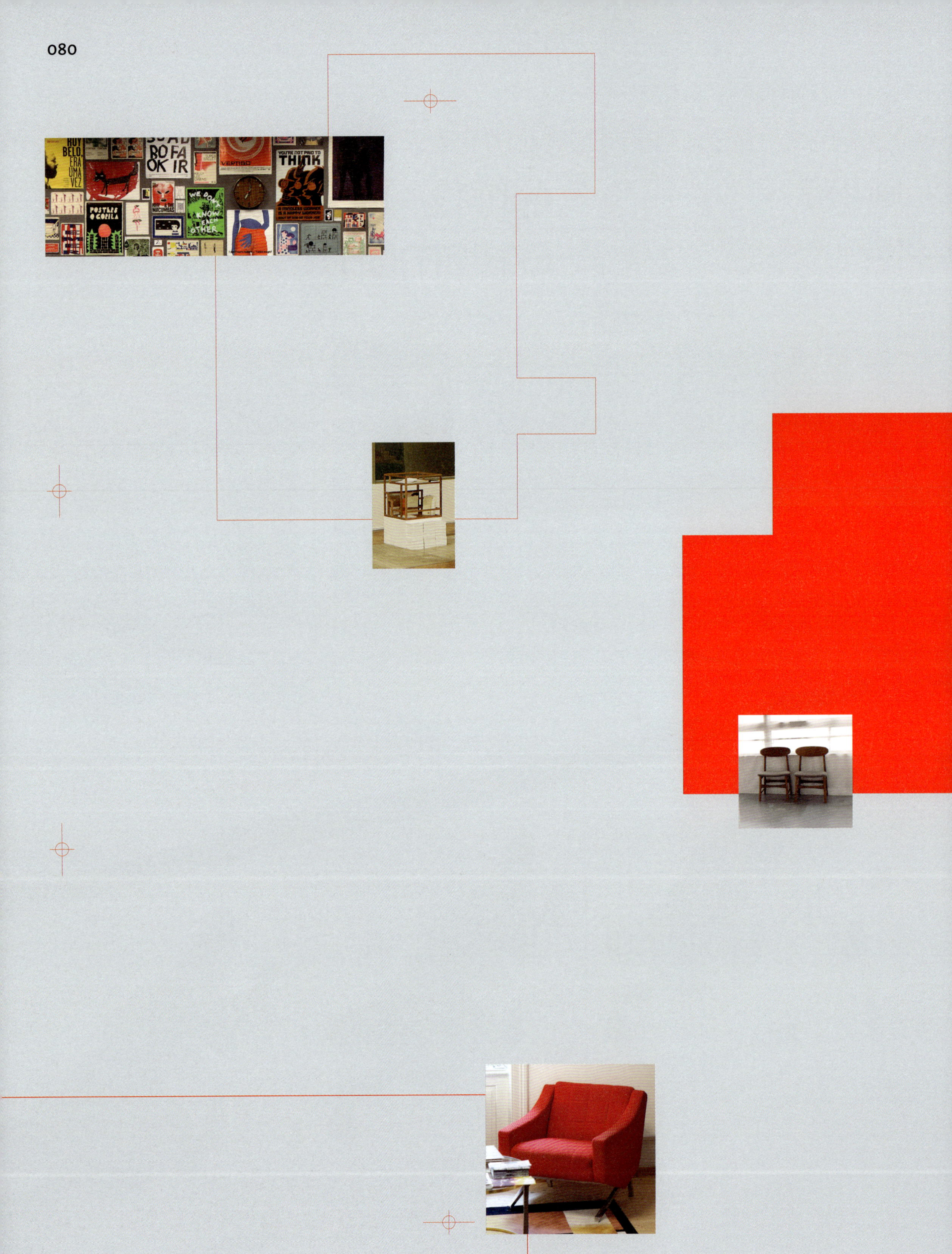
THINK

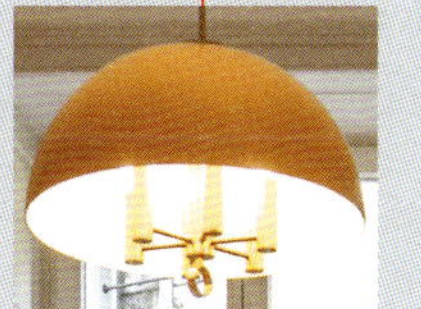

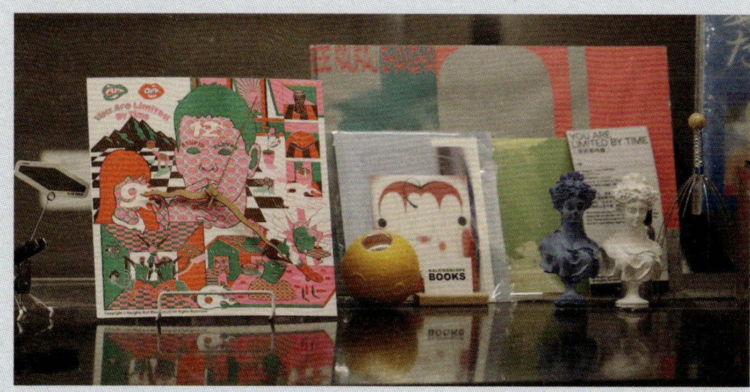
BOOKS
YOU ARE
LIMITED BY TIME

NEW YOUTH TEA PARTY

Youth with a Cup, Come and Enjoy Tea!

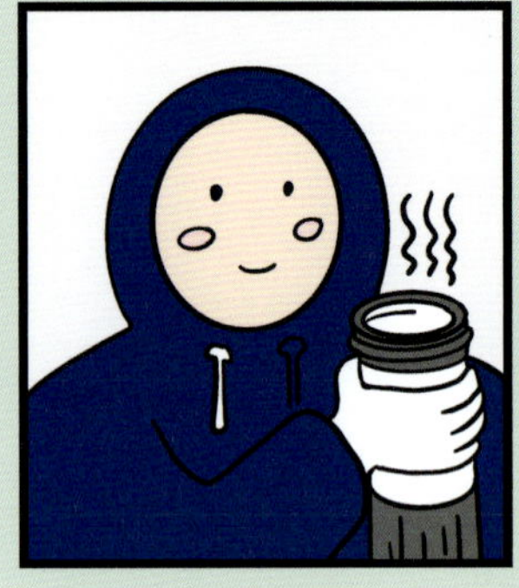

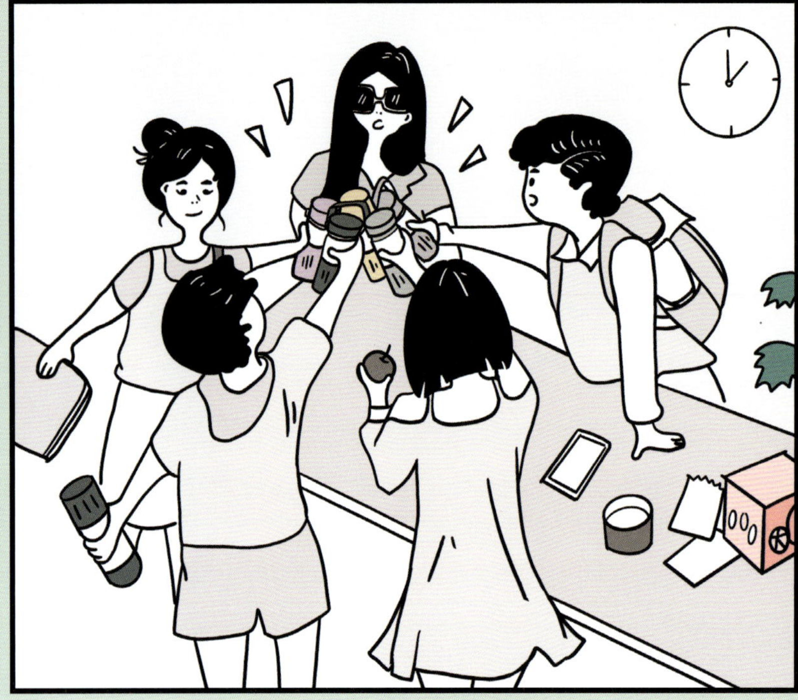

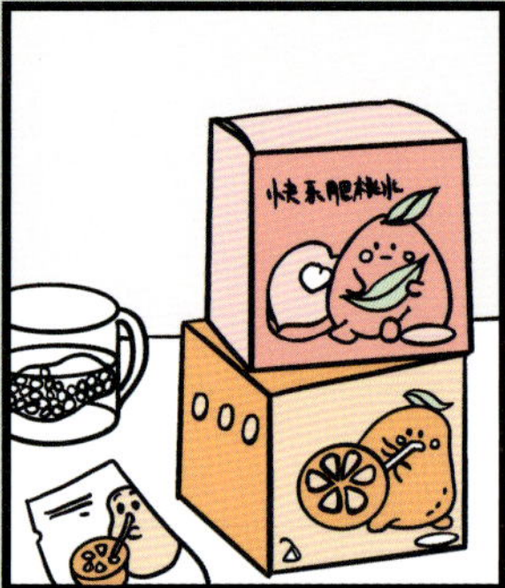

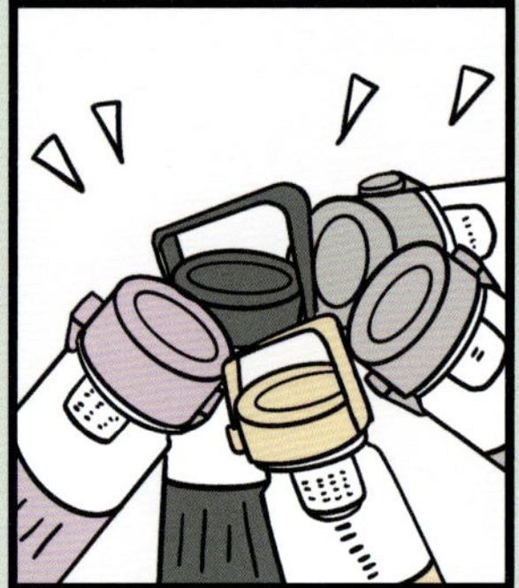

China is the homeland of tea, and tea culture has been long-standing and profound. There are many types of tea, which can meet the varied needs of tea drinkers. Every Chinese is supposed to enjoy drinking tea, but it seems that only the constantly launched new tea drinks are more able to capture the hearts of young people and gradually become the latest social language, while the traditional Chinese tea culture seems to be left behind.

Traditionally, to taste kung fu tea, you need to go through multiple processes, from the beginning of smelling the tea, warming the pot, filling the tea, moistening the tea, then brewing, pouring around the pot, warming the cup, moving the pot, and finally pouring and tasting the tea. These rituals seem to be out of place in modern times, as the young generation is always concerned about efficiency, and the complicated process would only wear down their enjoyment of leisure time. But tea on the other hand is rather a philosophy, and different ages will give rise to different tea cultures, which should not be subject to any fetters. Although the pace of contemporary life is fast and the interpersonal relationships are complex, there is no important thing that a sip of fragrant tea cannot solve. It is true for tea, and it is also true for the cups. If it is necessary to innovate the tea culture, the design and function of the cups will be the central focus. Some young people have gradually realized it. They take a fashionable tea cup as a fulcrum, aspiring to create a tea culture belonging to the contemporary youth.

What should a cup that can represent the Chinese youth tea culture be like? This question has been pondered repeatedly. In order to enable more young people to change their tea drinking habits through the cup and derive a tea culture belonging to the new era, a brand-new tea cup has been developed by BUYDEEM. The first to welcome this new product is the five initiators of the new youth tea culture—the "Youth with a Cup" group. People can carry a cup everywhere to simplify the procedures of drinking tea, so as to enjoy tea whenever and wherever they want. These five young people came together because they hope to "resist the current busy life by a cup", and through their avant-garde concept of life, they break the stereotypes of tea culture. Here are their stories.

Resist the Bottleneck of Being the Cutting-Edge, All in One Step!

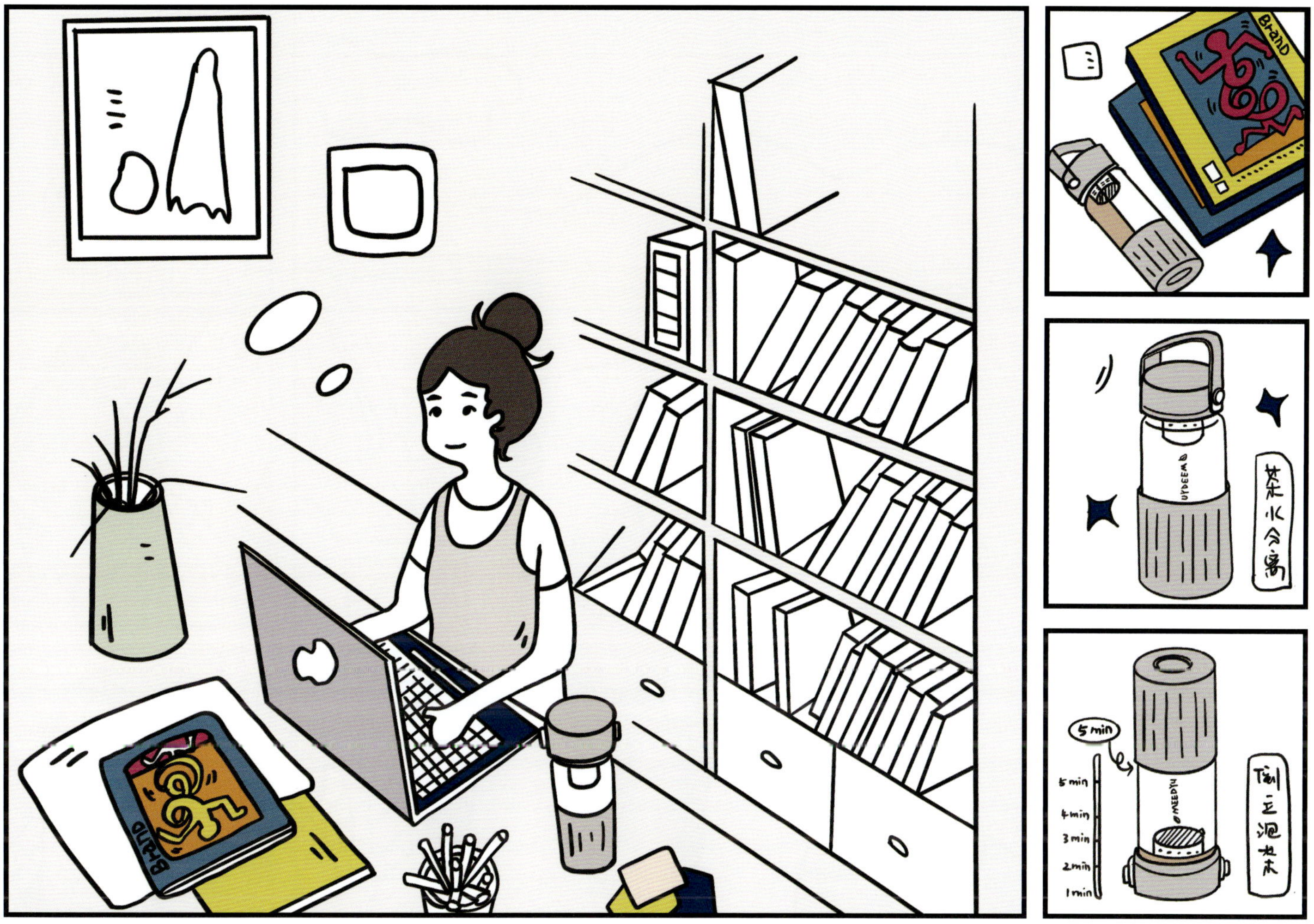

Youth with a Cup No. 1

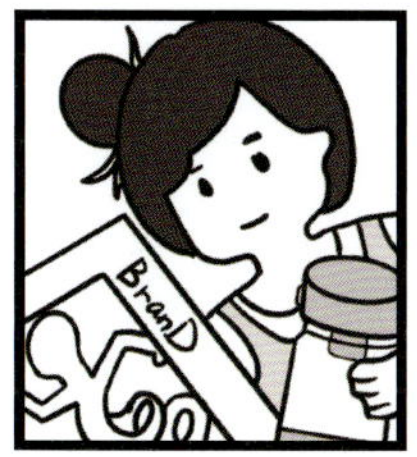

Name: Sam
Profession: Editor-in-chief of a cutting-edge lifestyle magazine
Personality traits: not settling for anything less, unconventional and very picky

"It is not complicated to make tea, and there is no need to compromise when the work is full of difficulties."

Sam's Culture of "Carrying a Cup"

A good tea cup = Design + Easy to make tea

Resist the Loneliness of the Outdoor Travel

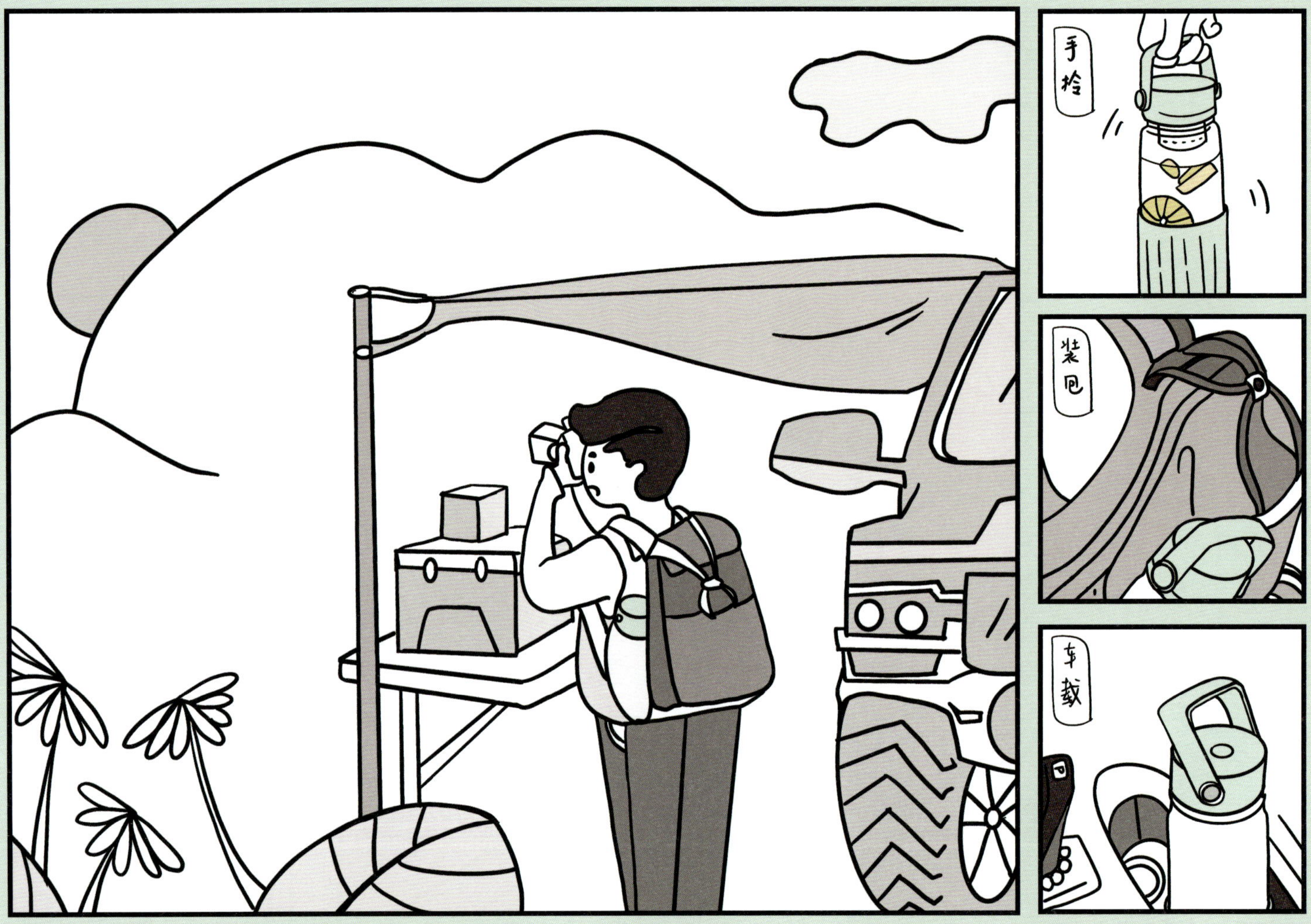

Youth with a Cup No. 2

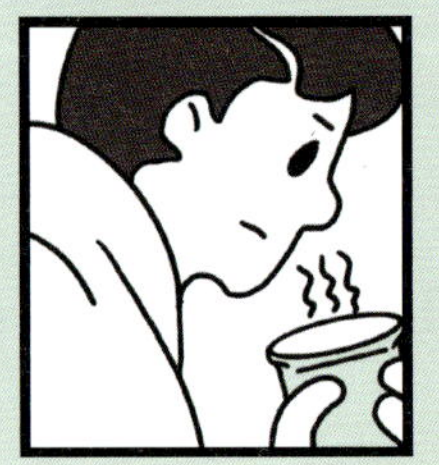

Name: Justin
Profession: Outdoor travel blogger
Personality traits: having a wide range of hobbies, adventurous and outdoor tea drinking genius

"I am always ready to taste the local famous tea with a portable cup."

Justin's Culture of "Carrying a Cup"

Loneliness during the journey can be dispelled by a cup of hot tea.

Resist the Absence of Inspiration for Homemade Tea

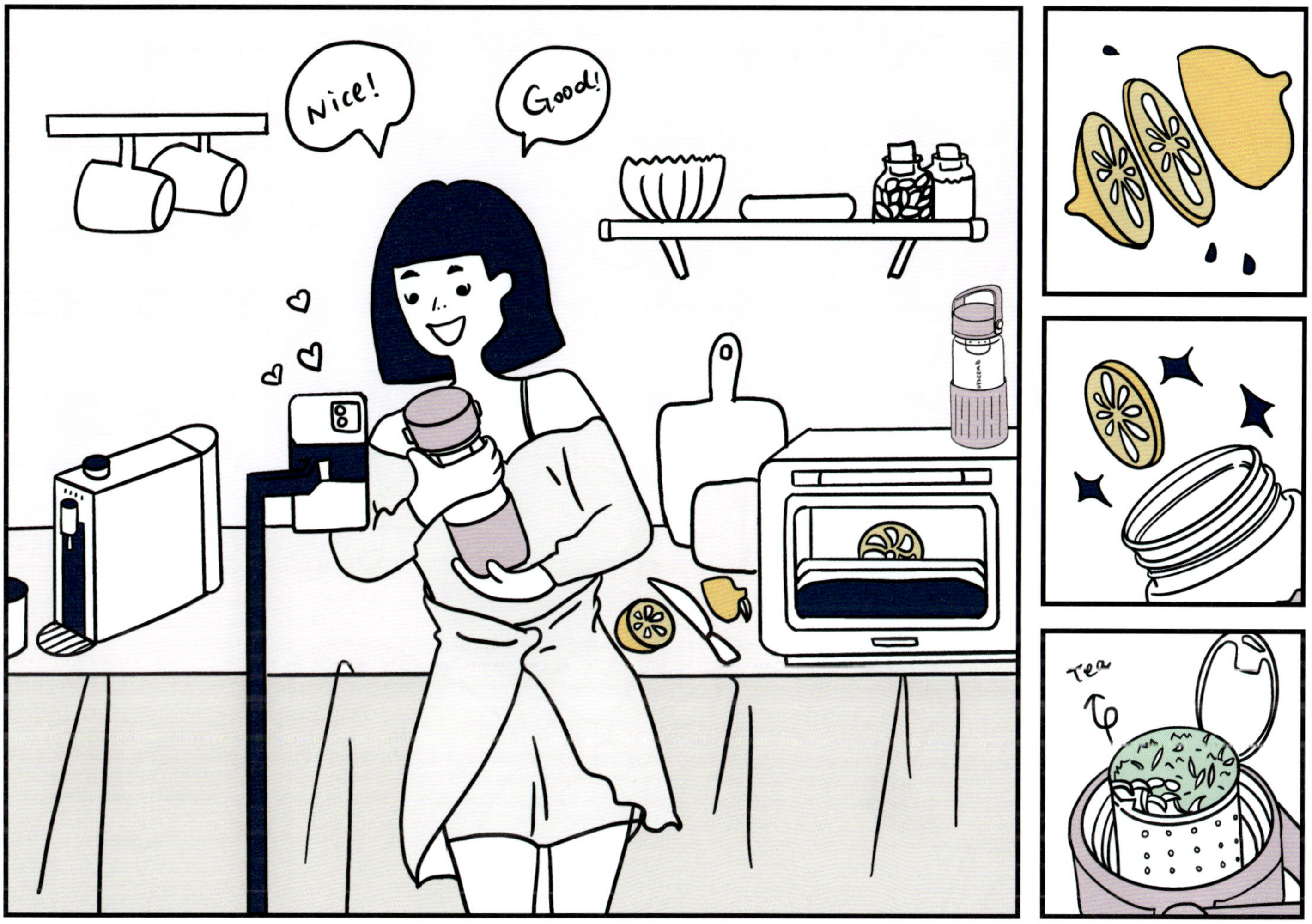

Youth with a Cup No. 3

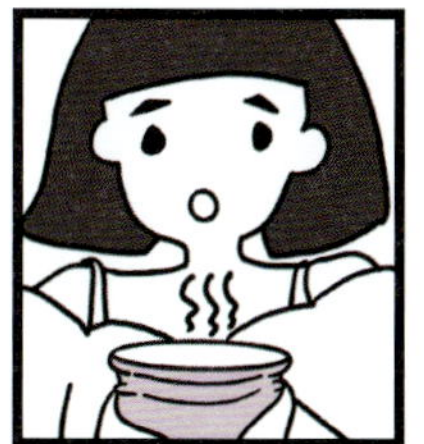

Name: Hedy
Profession: Foodie
Personality traits: trend follower, vlogger, strong practical skills

"Making a tasty homemade grapefruit oolong tea for everyone."

Hedy's Culture of "Carrying a Cup"

To make homemade healthy tea, the new Chinese tea drink is defined by me.

Resist the Outfit that is Not Cool

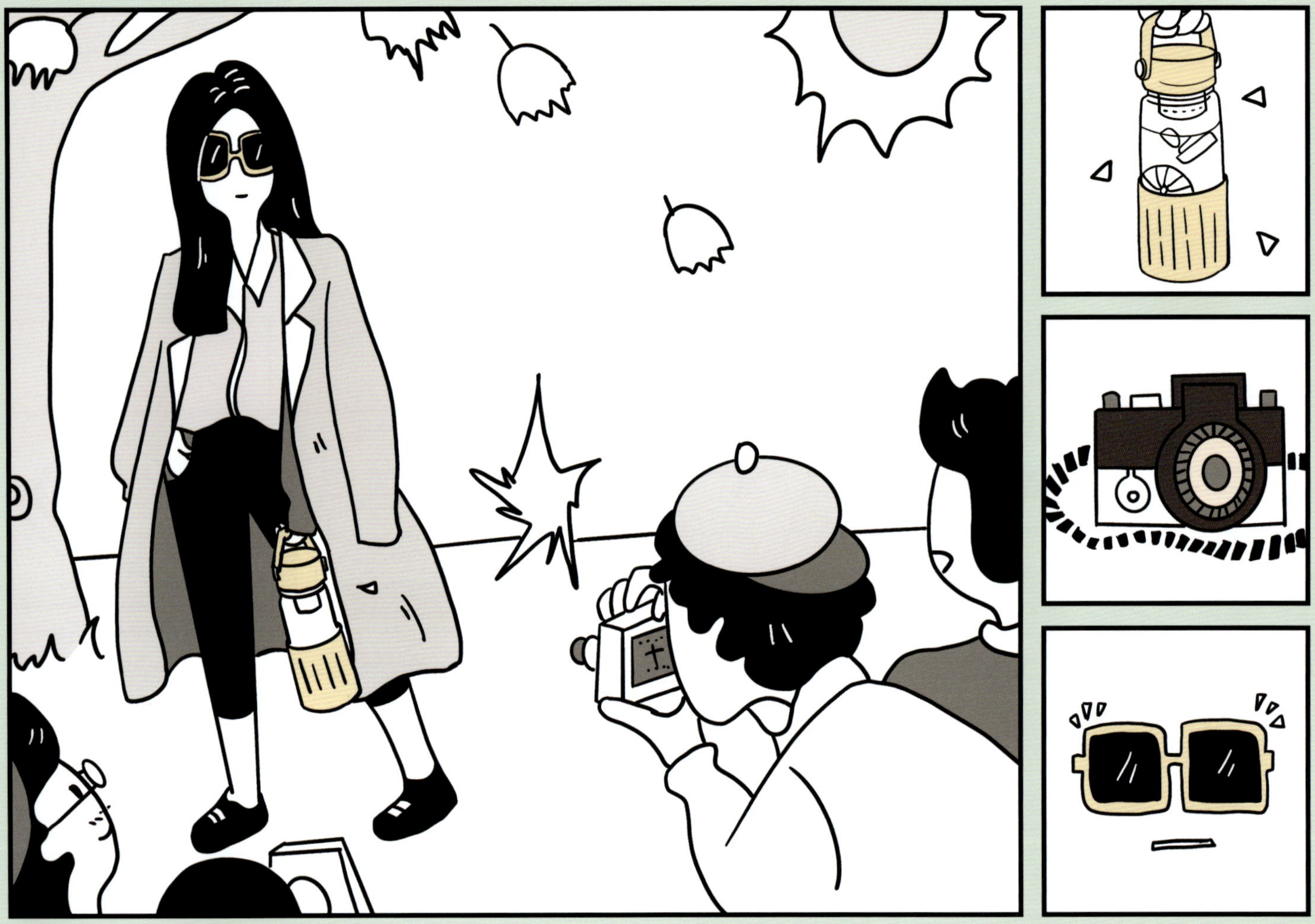

Youth with a Cup No. 4

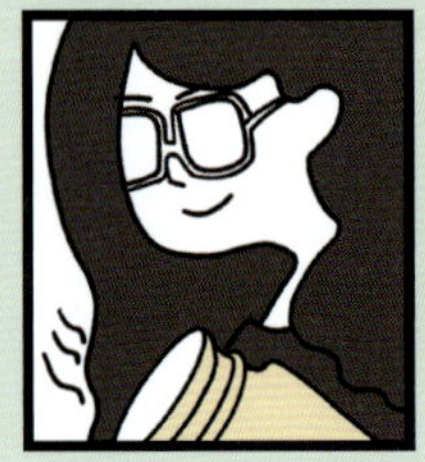

Name: Apple
Profession: Model
Personality traits: environmentalist, being passionate about photography and beautiful things

"The season's hottest fashion item is the cup in my hand!"

Apple's Culture of "Carrying a Cup"

A good-looking cup will make the tea drinking trendy.

Resist the Incoming Pressure

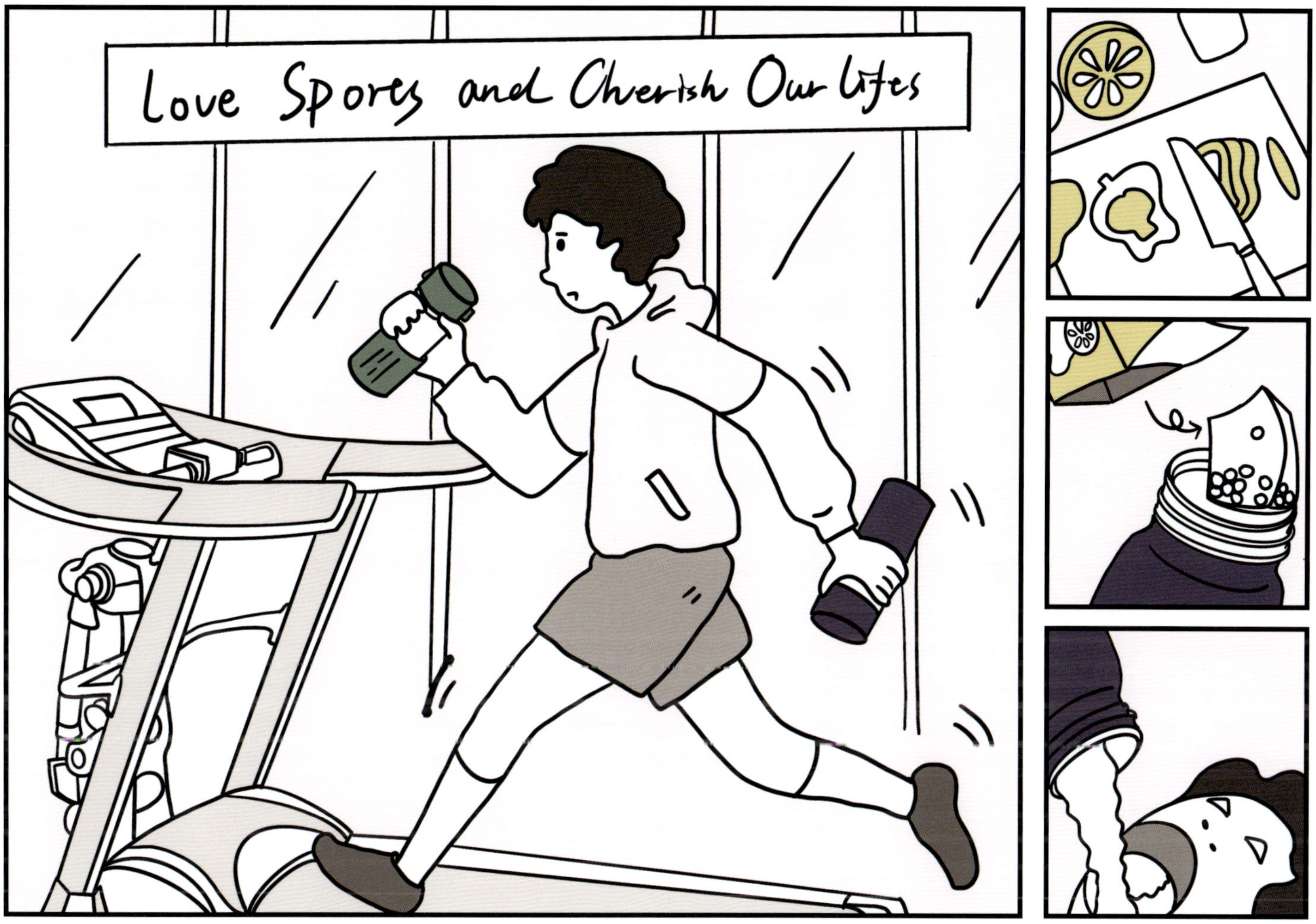

Youth with a Cup No. 5

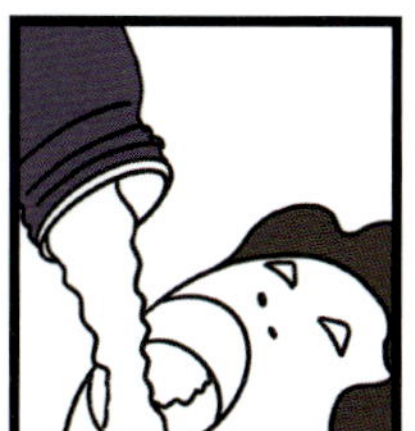

Name: John
Profession: Designer
Personality traits: health enthusiast, fitness expert

"Fitness cannot stop, so does drinking tea. I carry a handy cup in summer, and a vacuum cup in winter. I would not give up keeping fit and drinking tea."

John's Culture of "Carrying a Cup"

All year round, you can't keep your hands off your cup.

Resist the Flood of Life by a Cup

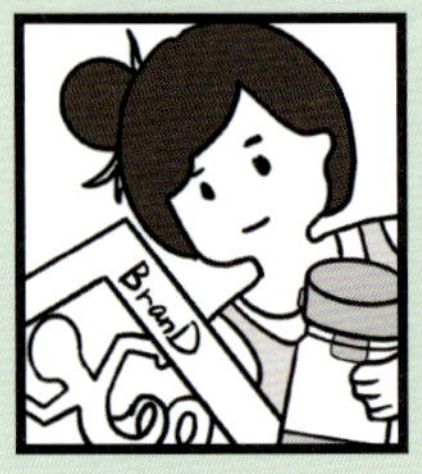

Sam

"The young people in our studio start to make tea at 3 p.m. every afternoon. It seems that there is no such thing as young people do not like drinking tea."

"Life is not easy. However, you can drink tea anytime and anywhere."

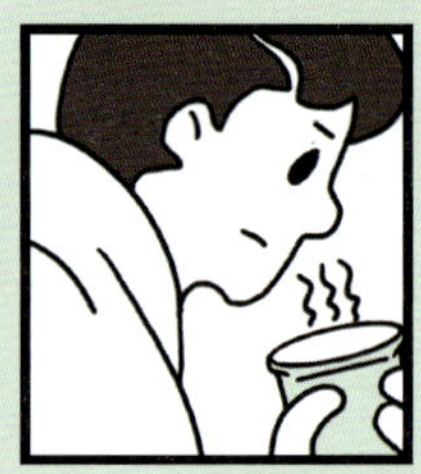

Justin

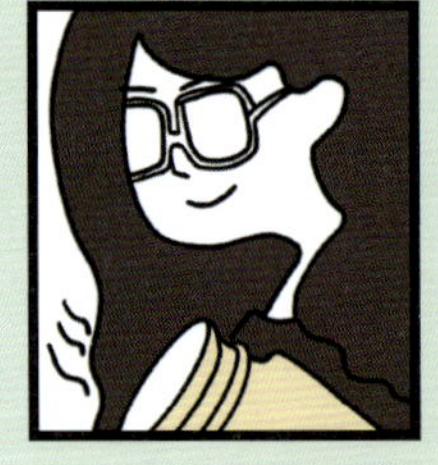

Apple

"The matter of drinking tea has to meet the aesthetics of the young generation."

"Yes, a good tea cup can motivate us to make tea every day."

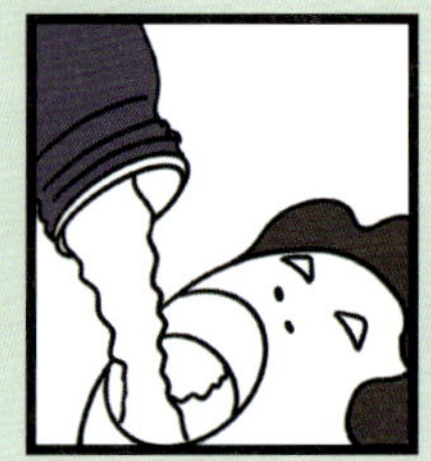

John

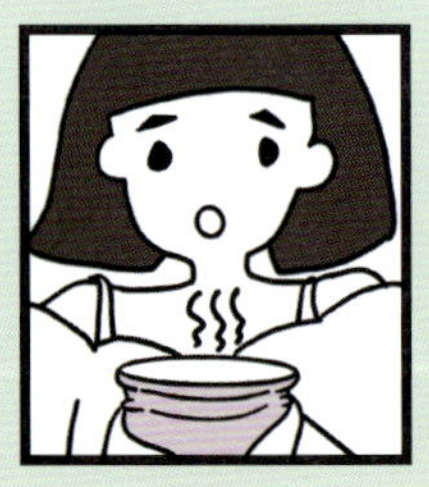

Hedy

"All in all, I am inspired by this cup to cook every day. The 'New Youth Tea Party' comes to a successful end! "

YOUTH WITH A CUP

The trend of “Youth with a Cup” allows more young people to pursue the comfort and ease of tea making, and young people can choose their favorite way of drinking tea. Through this series of illustrations, we hope that more and more readers could pick up their tea cups, lead a new trend of carrying cups, and enjoy the fragrance of the new Chinese tea drink.

BUYDEEM makes food with love, brings light to life. GOOD TASTE FOR LIFE!

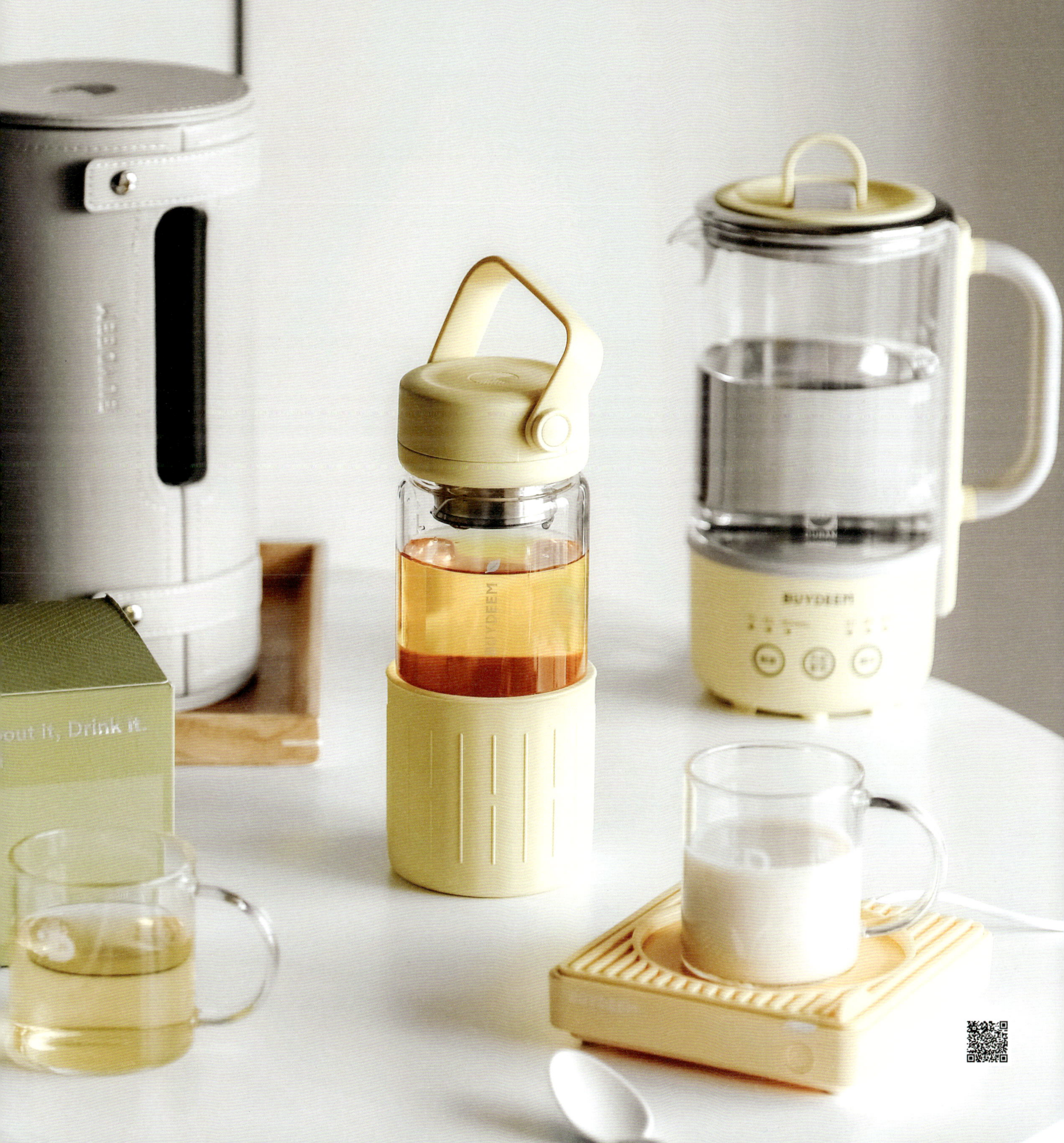

DESIGN ×

SELF-PUBLISHING PROJECTS

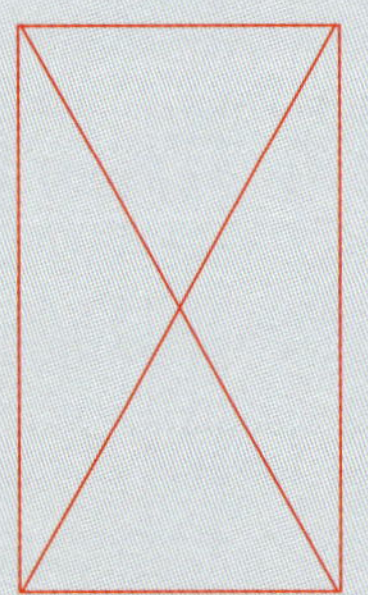

34×60mm—140×205mm

170×170mm—100×500mm

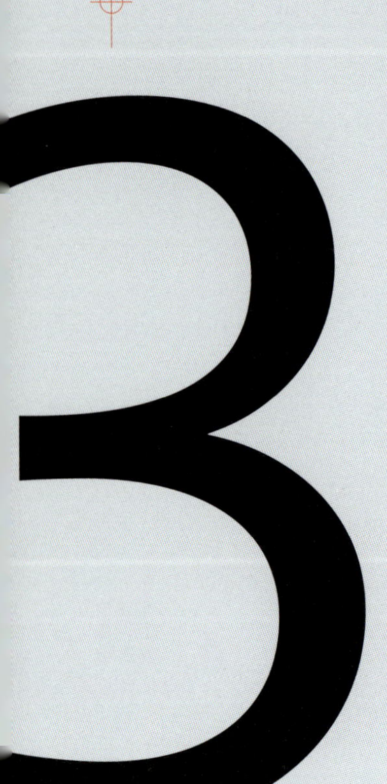

210×280mm—297×430mm

I FEEL A LITTLE SHIT

AD, CD, D & P
Ke Xu

2018

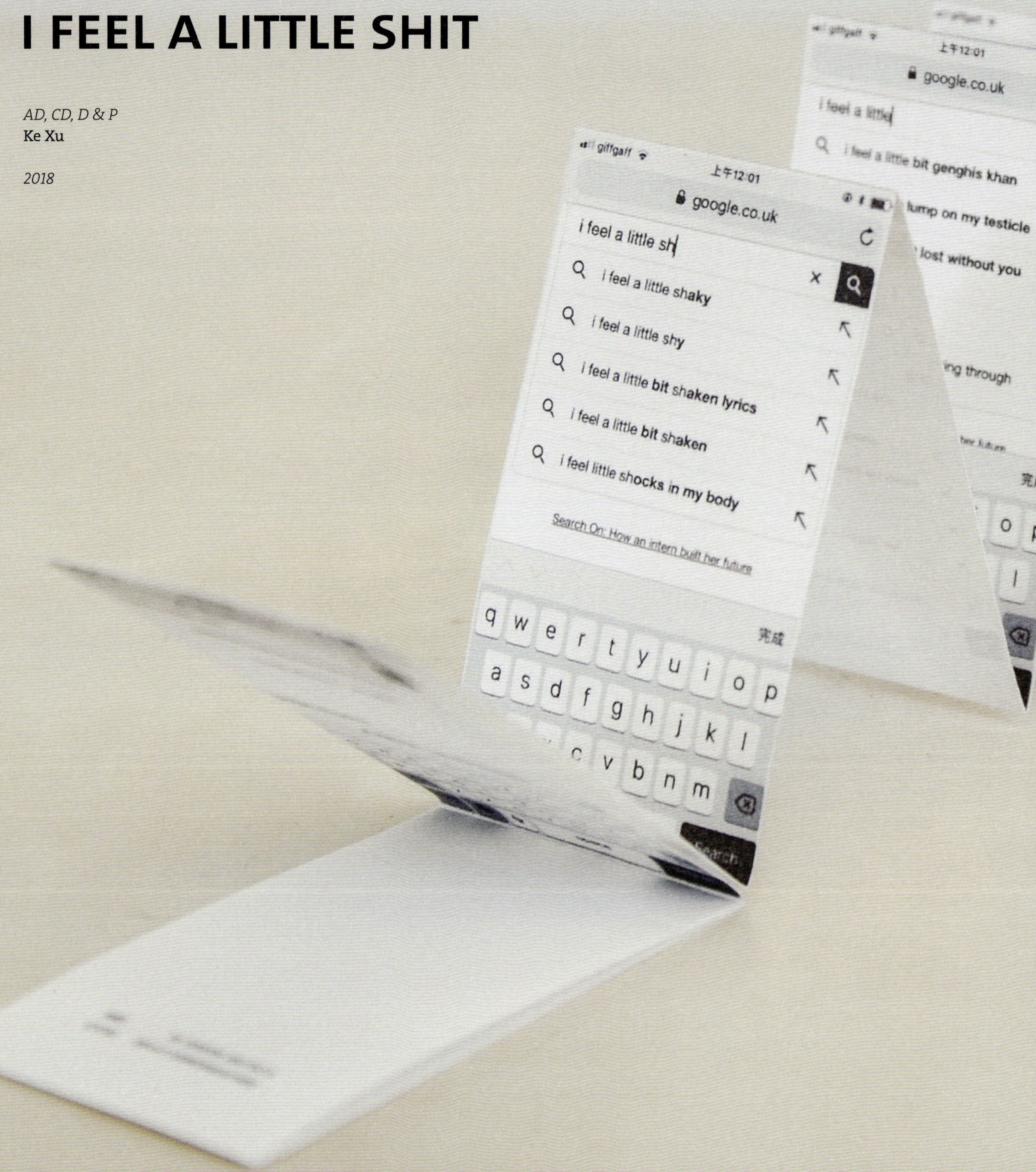

The content of this publication is the search result when searching the phrase "I feel a little shit" on Google. Accordion fold was applied to the structure, echoing the continuity of typing. The search results differ as each letter is entered. This publication presents the results as they appear when "I feel a little shit" is typed in letter by letter. Readers can see the consistency between the content and structure, which also provides readers with an immersive reading experience.

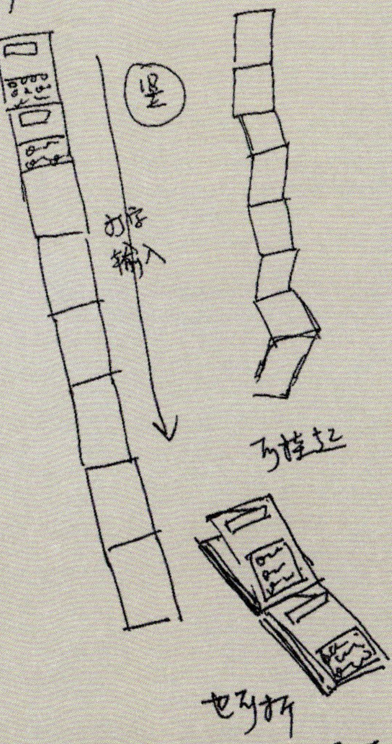

Paper/Material: Wove Paper Binding: Accordion Fold

Page: 20 Dimension: 34×60×5mm Weight: 5g

DO YOU FANCY A POEM?

AD, CD, D & P
Ke Xu

2018

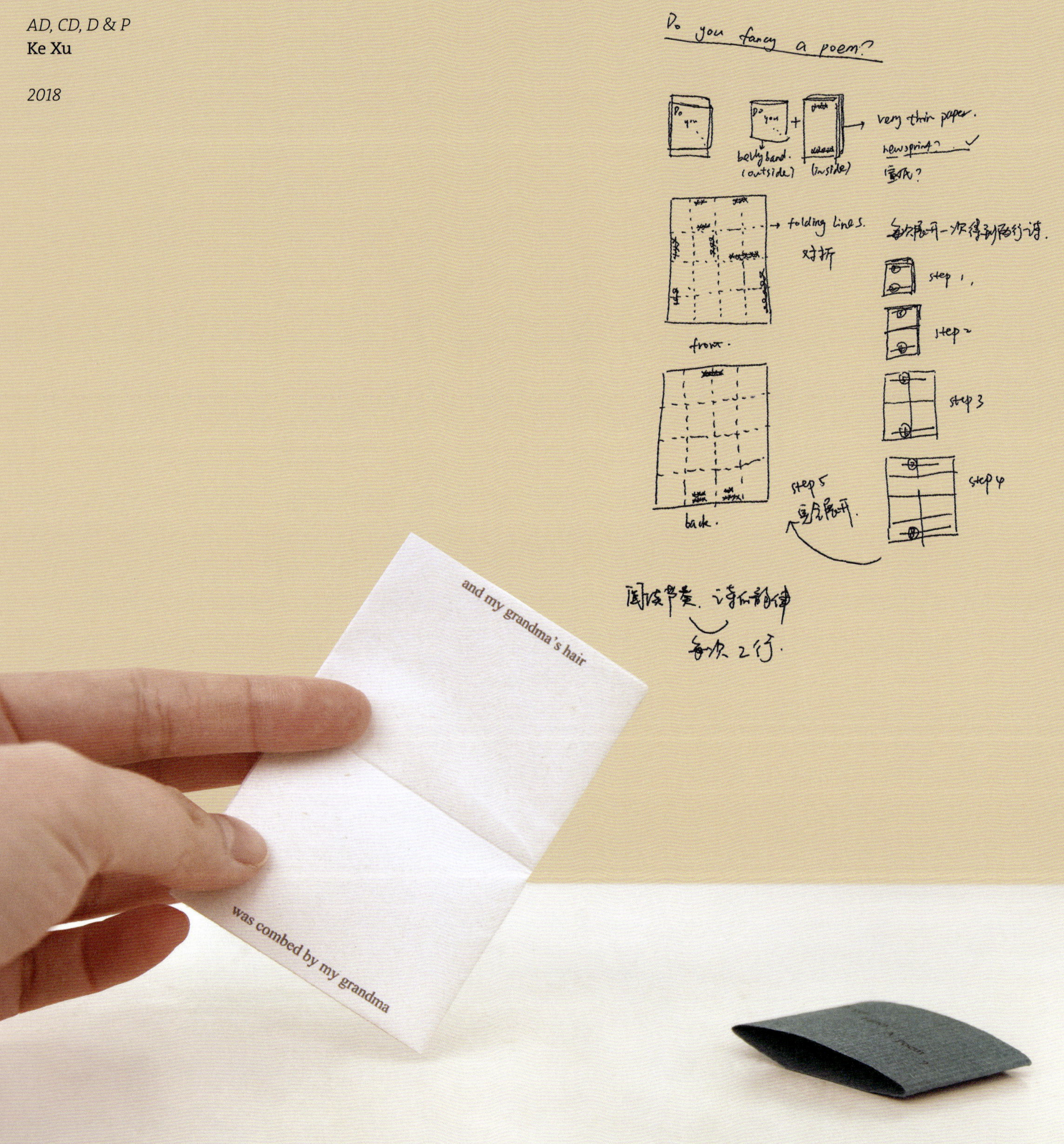

This publication is a product of the collaboration between the designer and the British artist Rob Heppell. Based on Heppell's poetry, the designer attempts to provide readers with a new reading experience through the binding design. The structure of the folding provides readers with a sense of pause and progression as they read. The intentional pauses echo the rhythm of the poem itself, and readers are also involved in the process of unfolding the publication.

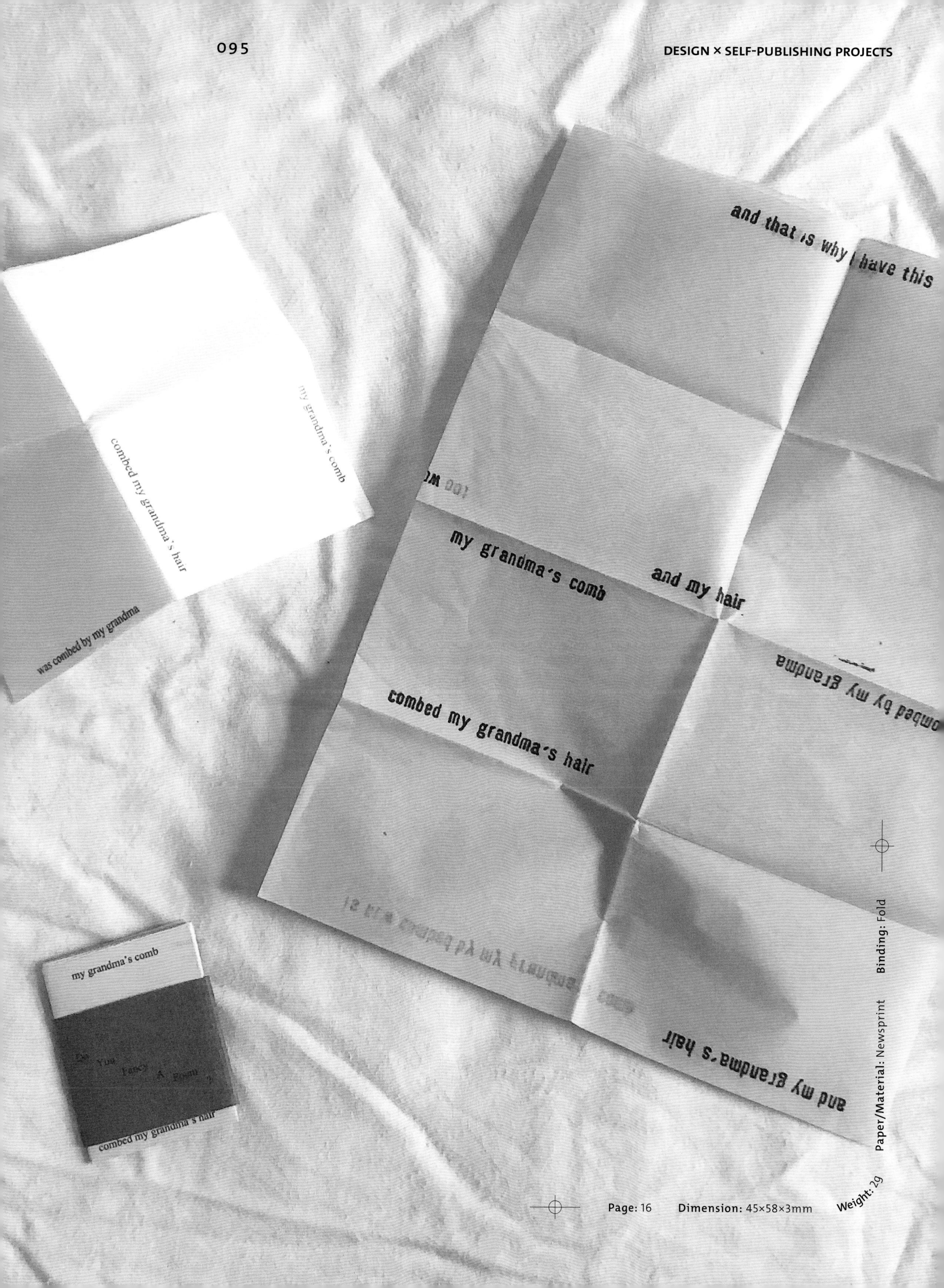

Page: 16 Dimension: 45×58×3mm Weight: 29

Paper/Material: Newsprint Binding: Fold

HAKKEN

D
Wuthipol Ujathammarat

2019

Hakken attempts to capture the essence of something small, compact and crafty that can be found on the streets of Tokyo. It also comes with a traditional Japanese hand-drawn map that details the locality within a neighbourhood, where the photographs were taken. It is a conceptual gimmick to add a playful element that reflects on the designer's journey through the streets of Tokyo—amazing things can be found, even when one gets lost.

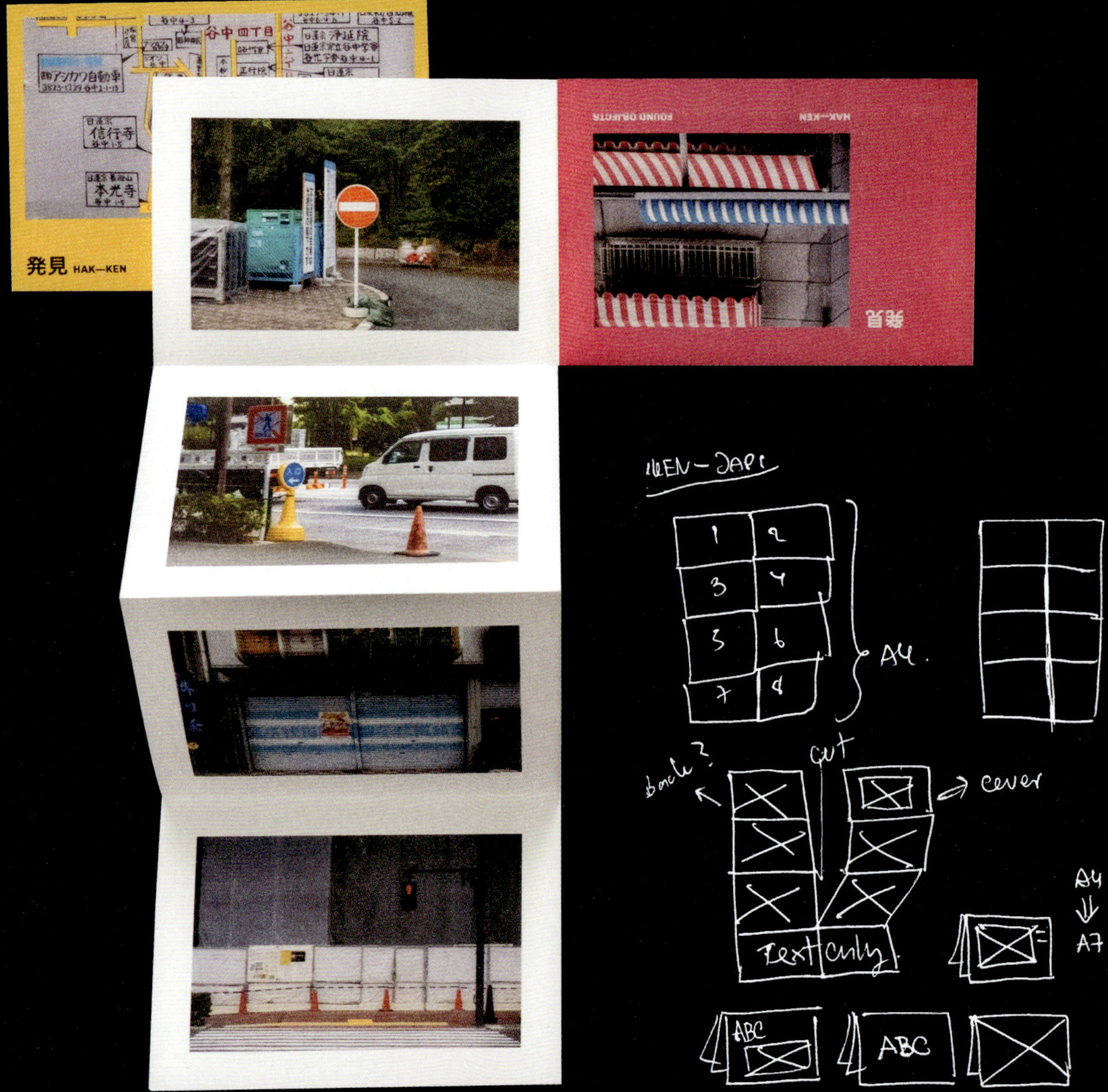

Page: 16 Dimension: 105×74mm Weight: 12g

Paper/Material: Matte White 120g Binding: Accordion Fold

D
Wuthipol Ujathammarat

2019

COVER UP

Cover Up highlights the overlooked charm and danger that are part of the beauty of Taipei with a disconsolate aesthetics of exterior tilework upon its urban buildings' structures. These outdated tiles, which are believed to help to protect buildings from the excessive moisture and high humidity that result from the prevailing wet climate, have gradually suffered damage and begun to fall off buildings and present a potential hazard to pedestrians.

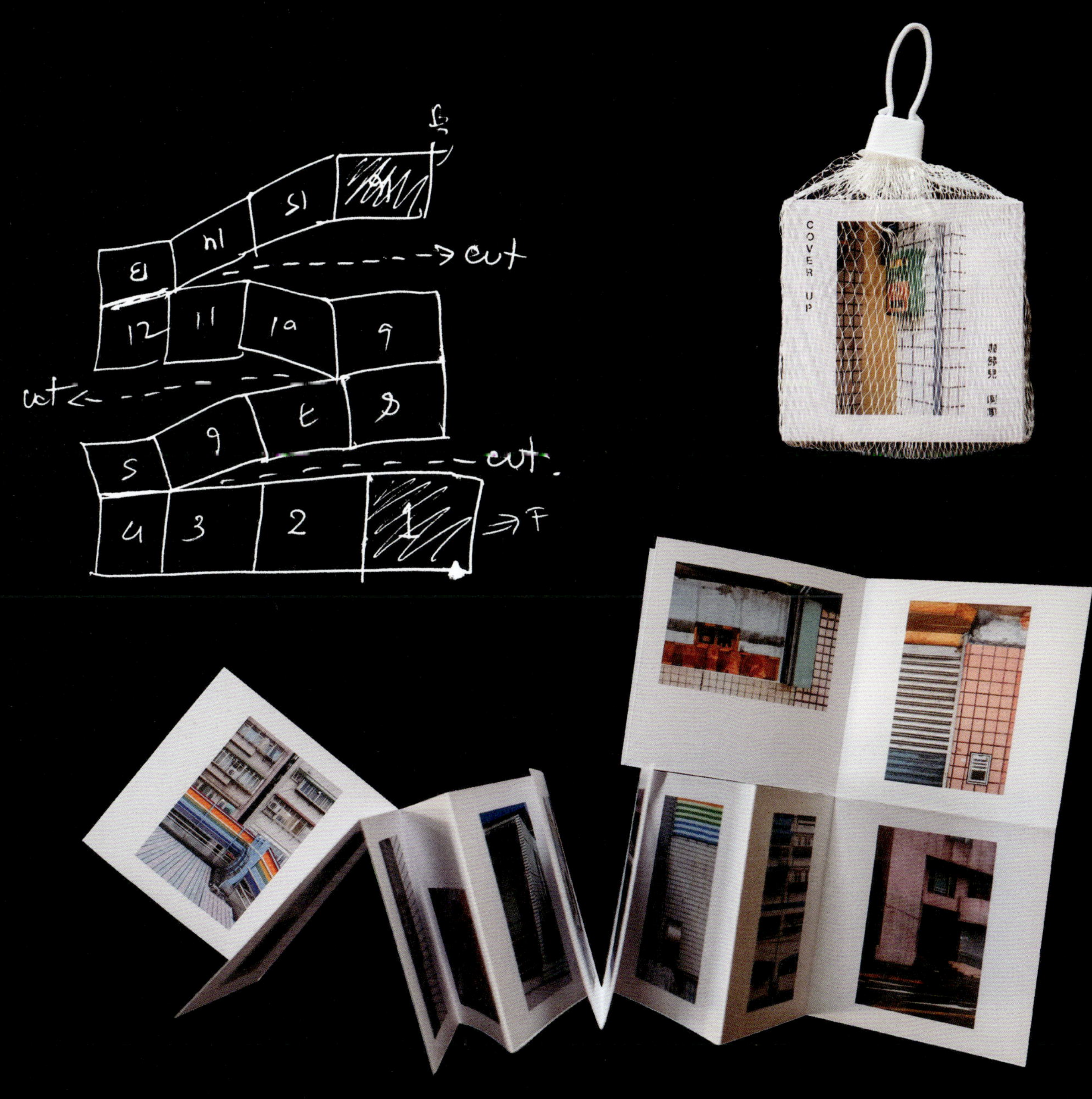

Page: 30 **Dimension:** 100×100mm **Weight:** 30g **Paper/Material:** White Card 150g **Binding:** Accordion Fold

LALATA NO. 19

AD, CD & D
Manuela Martínez & Carmen G. Palacios
P
Ramón Peco Muñoz

2015-2018

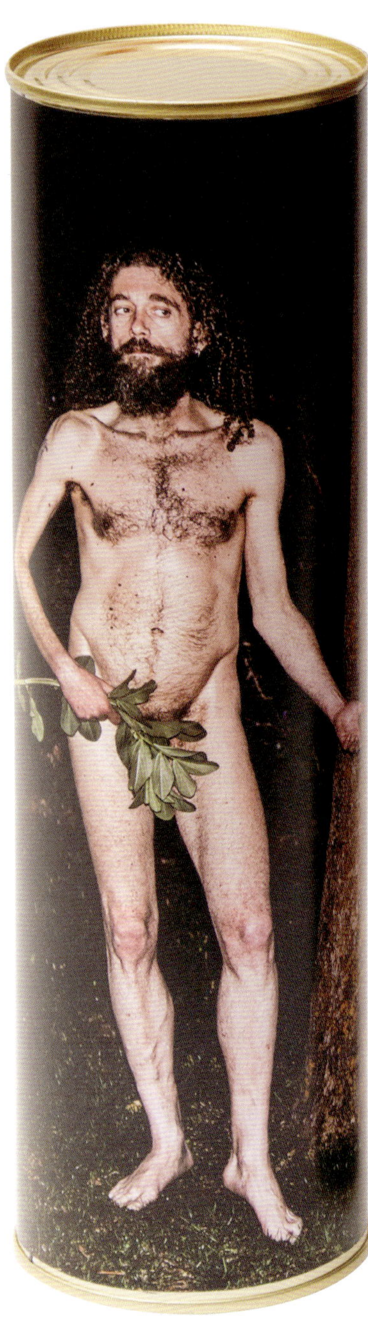

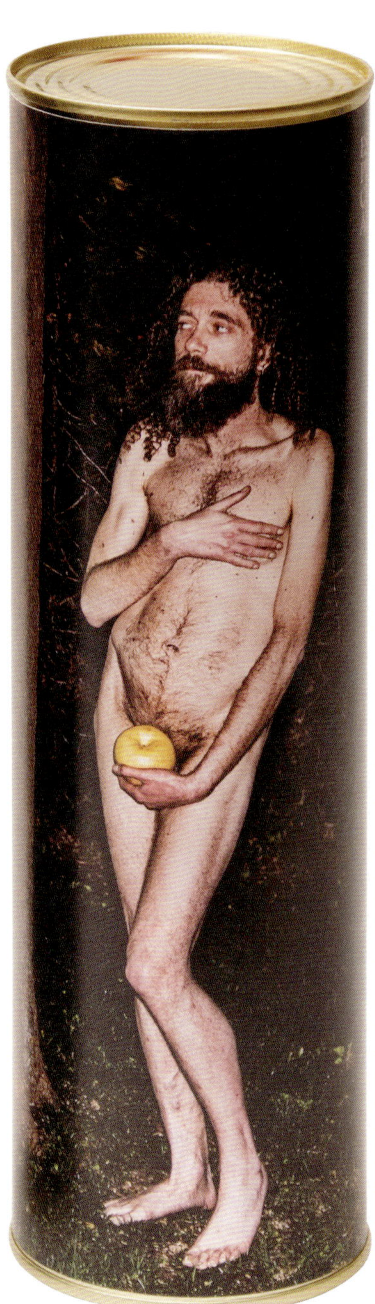

LALATA is an assembled magazine with a 3D format. Its container is a hermetically sealed can which contains artistic objects created in accordance with the different subjects that are addressed in each issue.

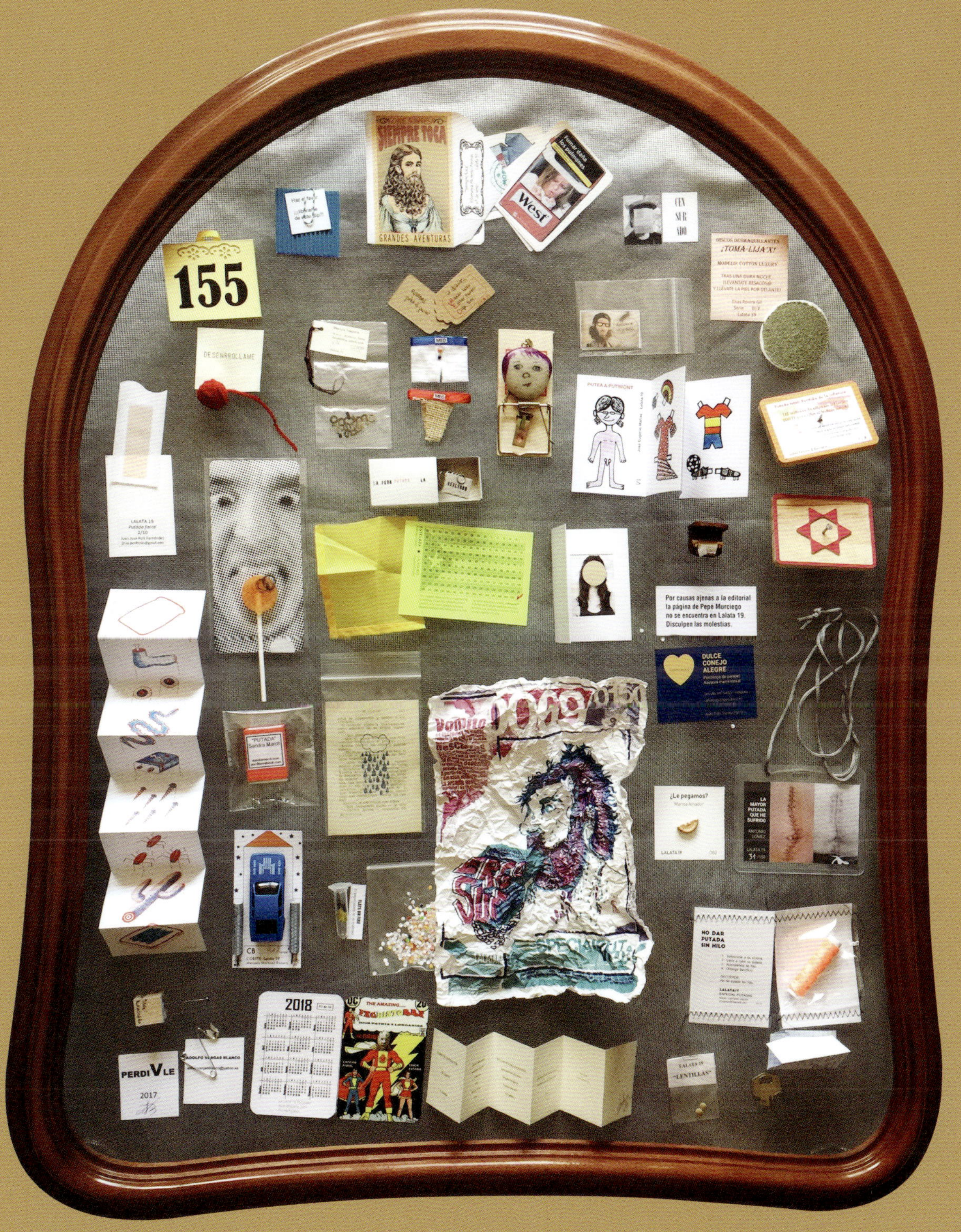

Dimension: 80×130mm

Weight: 400g

Paper/Material: Can

SELF-PORTRAITS | AT THE SINGAPORE BOTANIC GARDENS

CD
XiangYun Loh
D
XiangYun Loh & Michele Rodda
DS
Plant Press

2021

Rodda started to collect postcards of the Singapore Botanic Gardens 10 years ago, and has amassed a collection of more than 250 postcards. Loh was intrigued by a selection of postcards from the late 1800s to about the 1920s that were not typical photographs of iconic areas of the gardens, but portraits of plants, such as palms or aroids.

Although the landscape photographs allow for a comparison between the past and present views of the garden, these plant portraits are somewhat disconnected from the landscape, shifting the attention to the individual plants that may have long since disappeared. The origami folded albums encourage the act of unfolding to reveal the full image of the postcard.

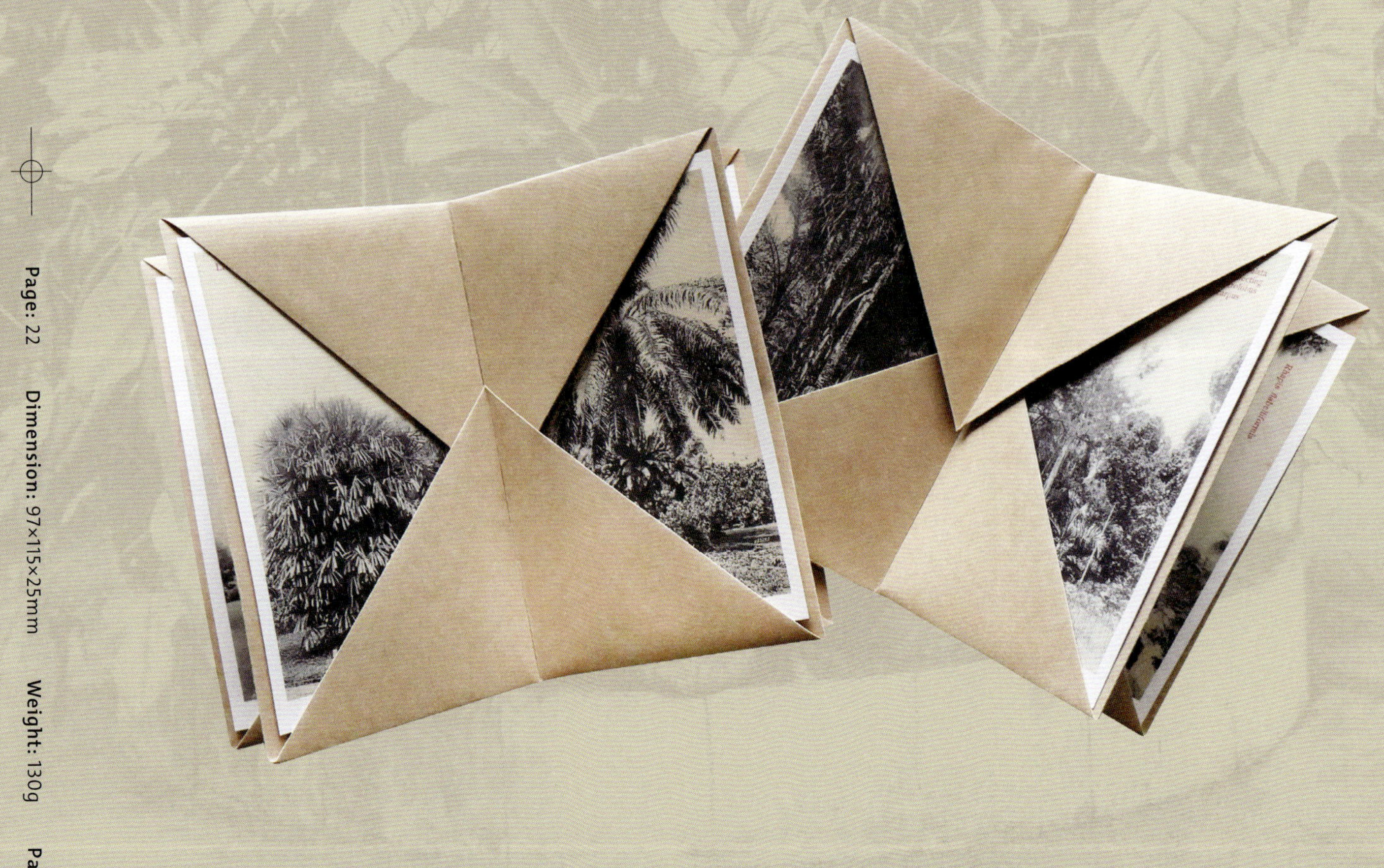

Page: 22 **Dimension:** 97×115×25mm **Weight:** 130g **Paper/Material:** Kraft Paper; Matt Art Card; Excel Satin **Binding:** Blizzard Fold

SOMEONE ELSE'S LIFE

AD, CD, D & P
Ke Xu

2017

This publication has 16 individual folding papers with a partially die cut cover. Each folding paper corresponds to an individual stranger, symbolizing a part of his or her life. Readers can take out each of them and unfold to read. They can also use their imagination based on the printed text and images to create a more personal connection with the strangers.

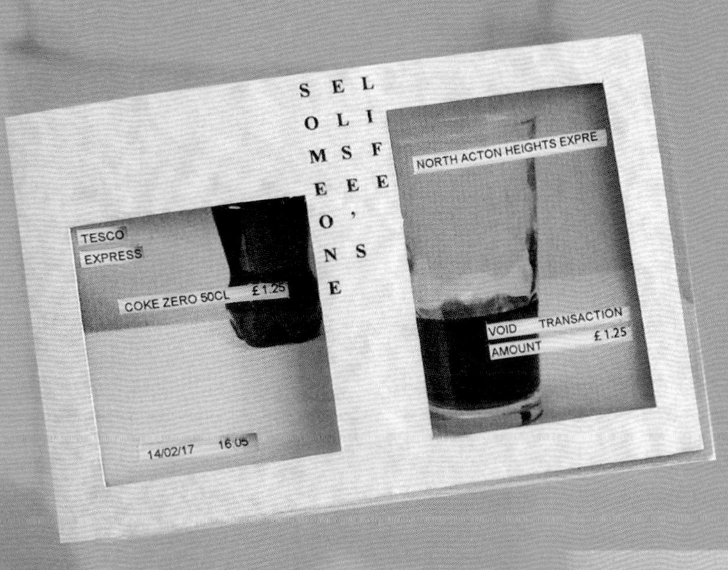

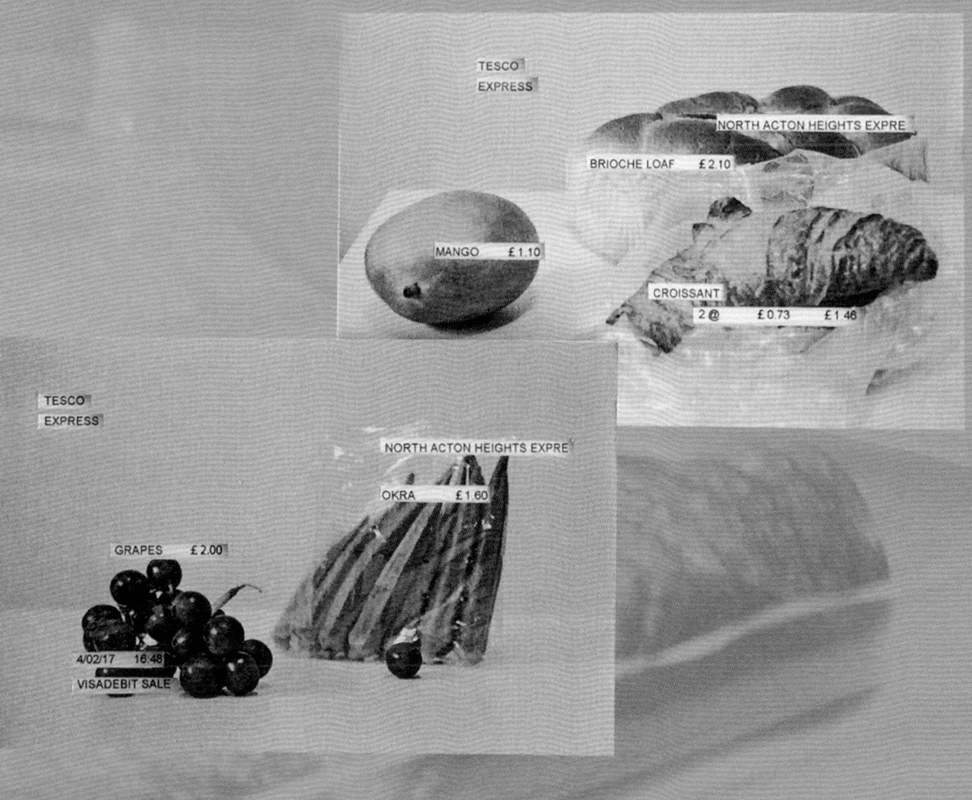

Paper/Material: Wove Paper Binding: Fold

Page: 16 Dimension: 136×91×7mm Weight: 58g

VACUUM WORDS BRICK

D
Yunqi Peng

2021

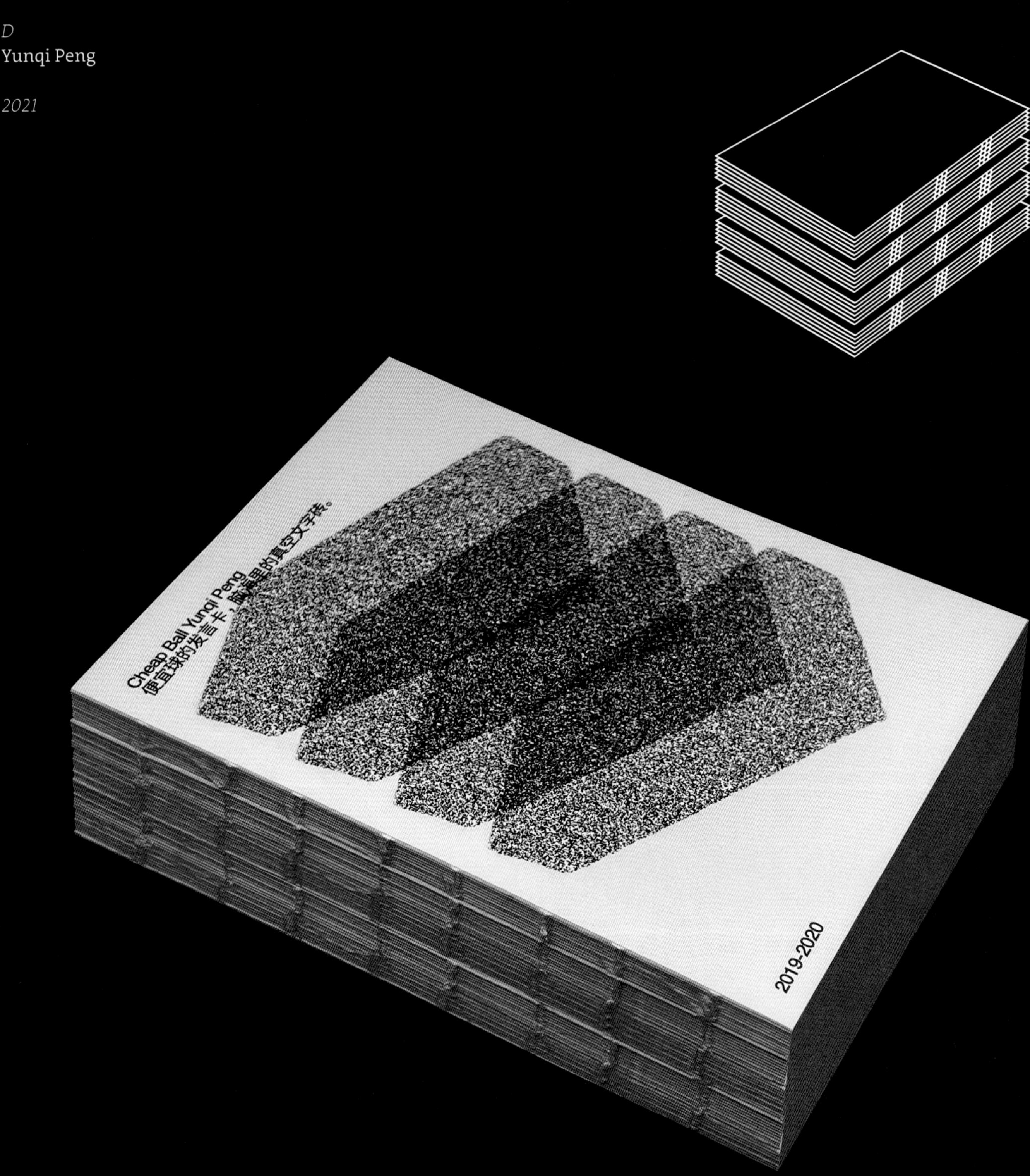

The designer made a book based on the sentences gathered from social media and that can't be read in the traditional order. She tried to create an interesting and experimental experience through the random collision of emotion and text. She firstly considered the portability and the readability of this publication during the design process. Therefore, she chose a small folio that can be put in the pocket, light paper, as well as Coptic binding.

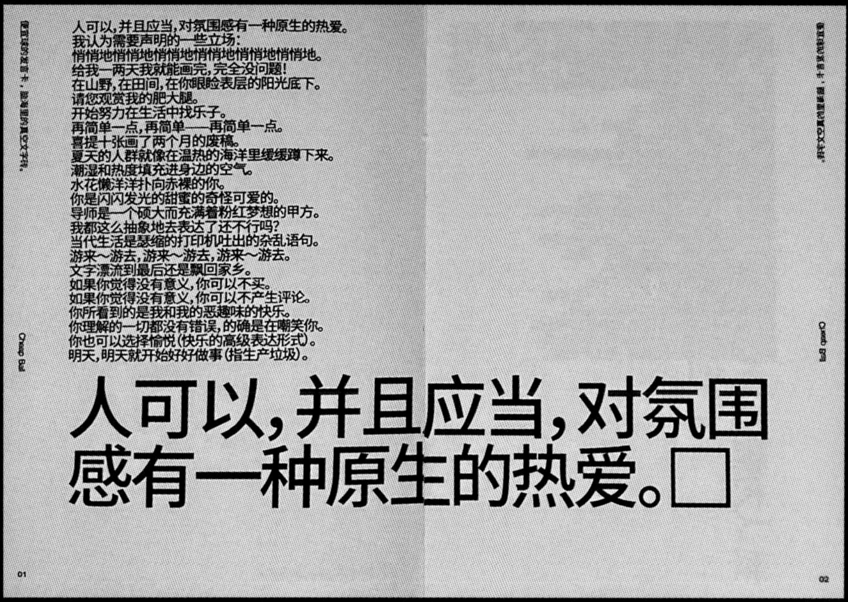

人可以，并且应当，对氛围感有一种原生的热爱。
我认为需要声明的一些立场：
悄悄地悄悄地悄悄地悄悄地悄悄地悄悄地。
给我一两天我就能画完，完全没问题！
在山野，在田间，在你眼睑表层的阳光底下。
请您观赏我的肥大腿。
开始努力在生活中找乐子。
再简单一点，再简单——再简单一点。
喜提十张画了两个月的废稿。
夏天的人群就像在温热的海洋里缓缓蹲下来。
潮湿和热度填充进身边的空气。
水花懒洋洋扑向赤裸的你。
你是闪闪发光的甜蜜的奇怪可爱的。
导师是一个硕大而充满着粉红梦想的甲方。
我都这么抽象地去表达了还不行吗？
当代生活是瑟缩的打印机吐出的杂乱语句。
游来～游去，游来～游去，游来～游去。
文字漂流到最后还是飘回家乡。
如果你觉得没有意义，你可以不买。
如果你觉得没有意义，你可以不产生评论。
你所看到的是我和我的恶趣味的快乐。
你理解的一切都没有错误，的确是在嘲笑你。
你也可以选择愉悦（快乐的高级表达形式）。
明天，明天就开始好好做事（指生产垃圾）。

人可以，并且应当，对氛围感有一种原生的热爱。□

01 02

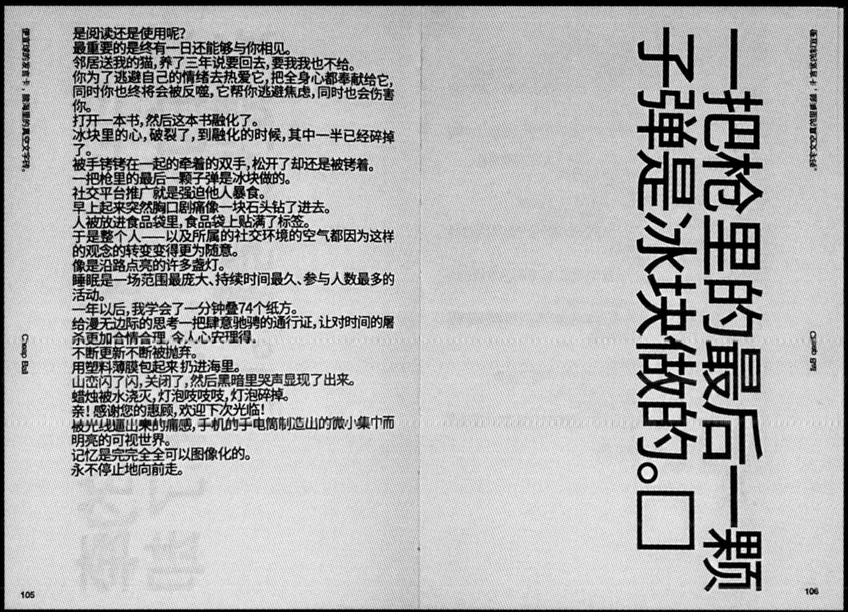

是阅读还是使用呢？
最重要的是终有一日还能够与你相见。
邻居送我的猫，养了三年说要回去，要我我也不给。
你为了逃避自己的情绪去热爱它，把全身心都奉献给它，同时你也终将会被反噬，它帮你逃避焦虑，同时也会伤害你。
打开一本书，然后这本书融化了。
冰块里的心，破裂了，到融化的时候，其中一半已经碎掉了。
被手铐铐在一起的牵着的双手，松开了却还是被铐着。
一把枪里的最后一颗子弹是冰块做的。
社交平台推广就是强迫他人暴食。
早上起来突然胸口剧痛像一块石头钻了进去。
人被放进食品袋里，食品袋上贴满了标签。
于是整个人——以及所属的社交环境的空气都因为这样的观念的转变变得更为随意。
像是沿路点亮的许多盏灯。
睡眠是一场范围最庞大、持续时间最久、参与人数最多的活动。
一年以后，我学会了一分钟叠74个纸方。
给漫无边际的思考一把肆意驰骋的通行证，让对时间的屠杀更加合情合理，令人心安理得。
不断更新不断被抛弃。
用塑料薄膜包起来扔进海里。
山峦闪了闪，关闭了，然后黑暗里哭声显现了出来。
蜡烛被水浇灭，灯泡吱吱吱，灯泡碎掉。
亲！感谢您的惠顾，欢迎下次光临！
被光线逼出来的痛感，手机的手电筒制造出的微小集中而明亮的可视世界。
记忆是完完全全可以图像化的。
永不停止地向前走。

一把枪里的最后一颗子弹是冰块做的。□

105 106

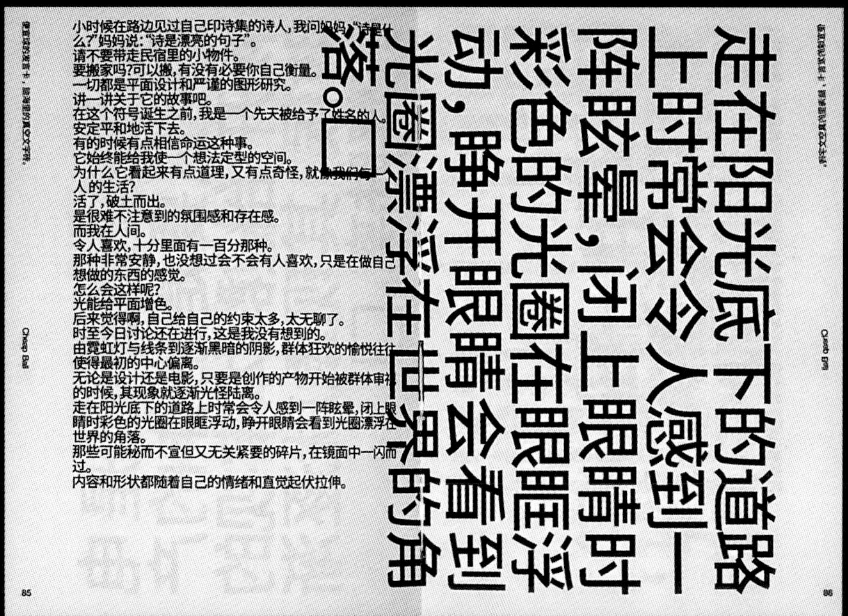

小时候在路边见过自己印诗集的诗人，我问妈妈："诗是什么？"妈妈说："诗是漂亮的句子"。
请不要带走民宿里的小物件。
要搬家吗？可以搬，有没有必要你自己衡量。
一切都是平面设计和严谨的图形研究。
讲一讲关于它的故事吧。
在这个符号诞生之前，我是一个先天被给予了姓名的人。
安定平和地活下去。
有的时候有点相信命运这种事。
它始终能给我使一个想法定型的空间。
为什么它看起来有点道理，又有点奇怪，就像我们每一人的生活？
活了，破土而出。
是很难不注意到的氛围感和存在感。
而我在人间。
令人喜欢，十分里面有一百分那种。
那种非常安静，也没想过会不会有人喜欢，只是在做自己想做的东西的感觉。
怎么会这样呢？
光能给平面增色。
后来觉得啊，自己给自己的约束太多，太无聊了。
时至今日讨论还在进行，这是我没有想到的。
由霓虹灯与线条到逐渐黑暗的阴影，群体狂欢的愉悦往往使得最初的中心偏离。
无论是设计还是电影，只要是创作的产物开始被群体审视的时候，其现象就逐渐光怪陆离。
走在阳光底下的道路上时常会令人感到一阵眩晕，闭上眼睛时彩色的光圈在眼眶浮动，睁开眼睛会看到光圈漂浮在世界的角落。
那些可能秘而不宣但又无关紧要的碎片，在镜面中一闪而过。
内容和形状都随着自己的情绪和直觉起伏拉伸。

走在阳光底下的道路上时常会令人感到一阵眩晕，闭上眼睛时彩色的光圈在眼眶浮动，睁开眼睛会看到光圈漂浮在世界的角落。□

85 86

al: Coated Paper 120g Binding: Coptic Binding

ASIAN LUNCH BOX

D
Takako Masuki
DS
Asian Food Design

2019

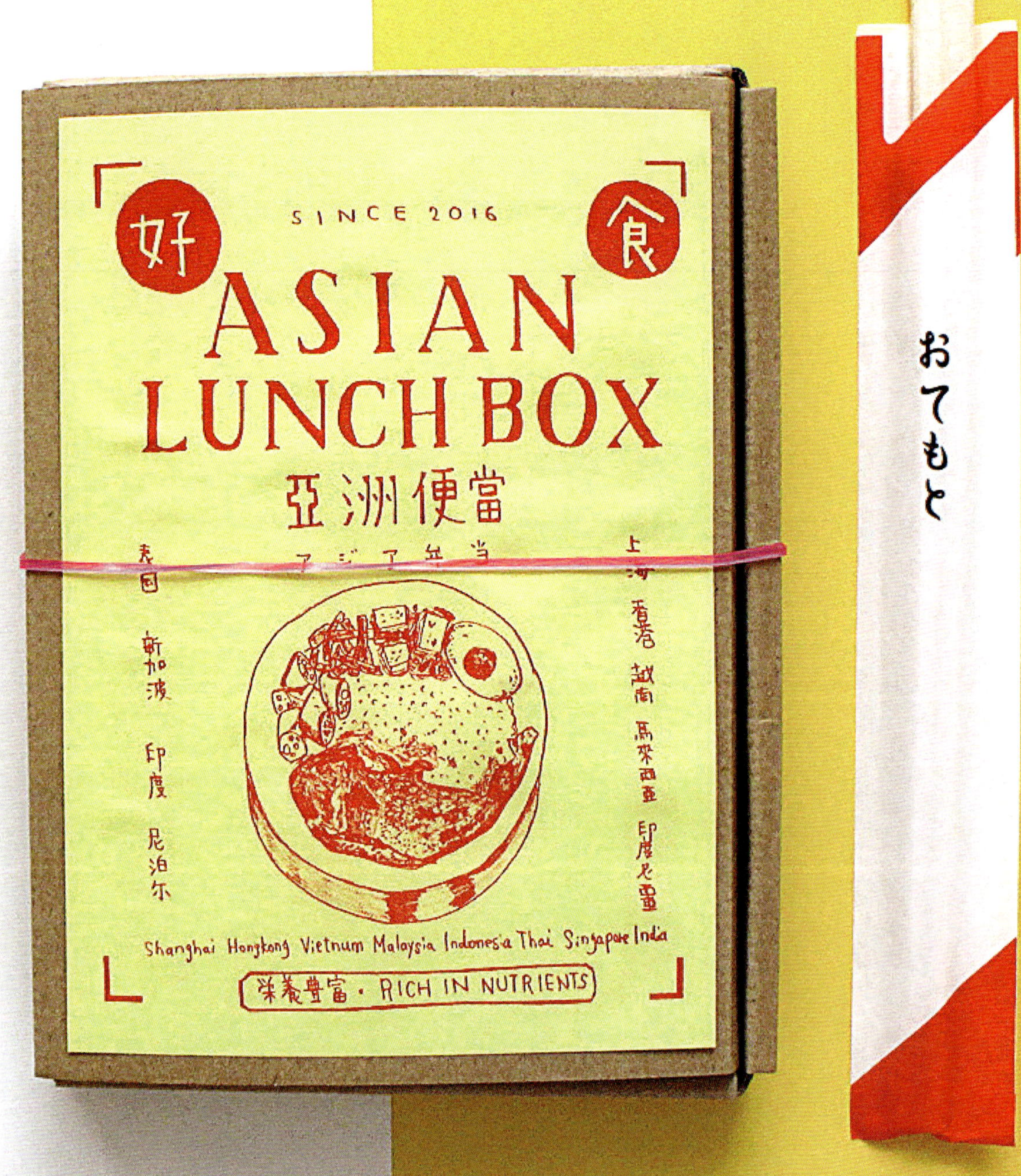

This lunch box includes five small zines featuring drawings of popular dishes from Singapore, Thailand, China, India, Nepal, Malaysia, Indonesia, and Vietnam. The designer combined the small books like a lunch box completing with chopsticks after she had drawn enough illustrations for each zine.

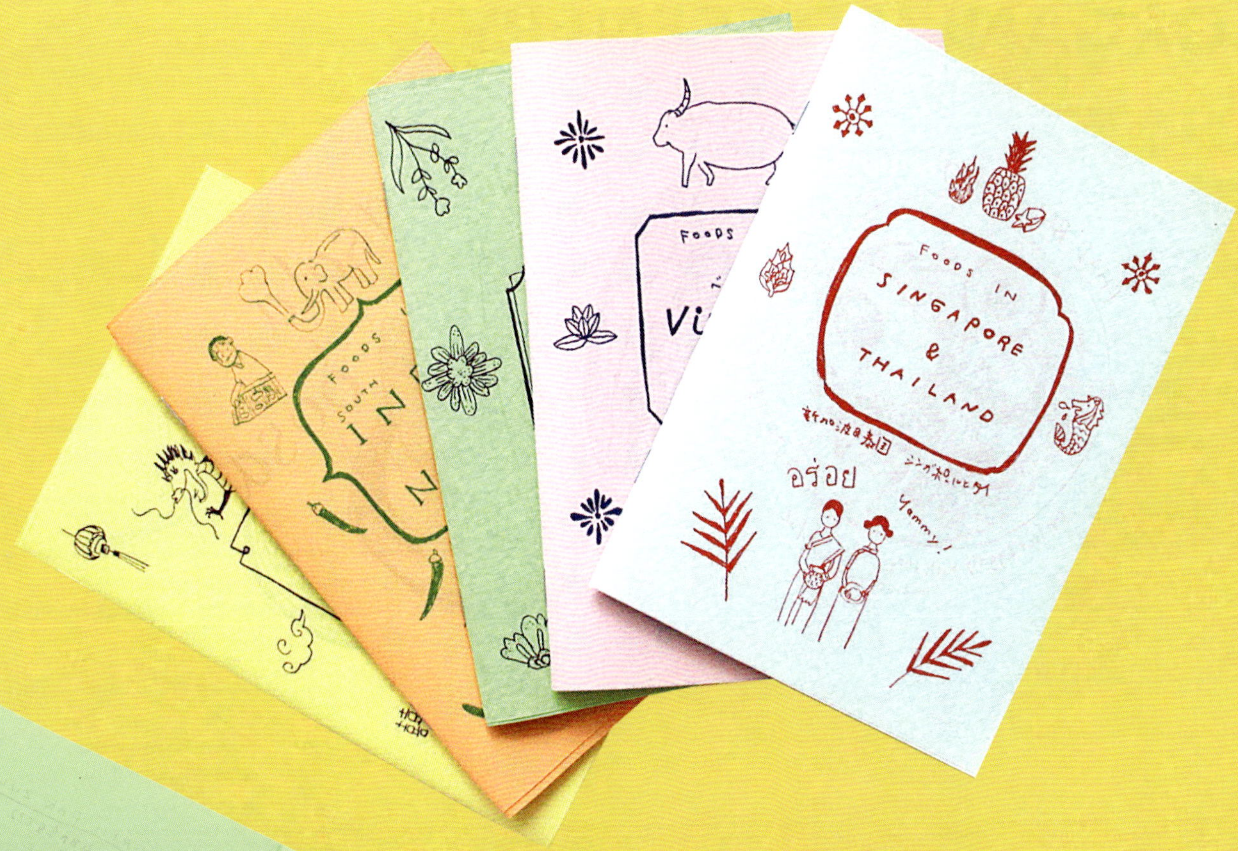

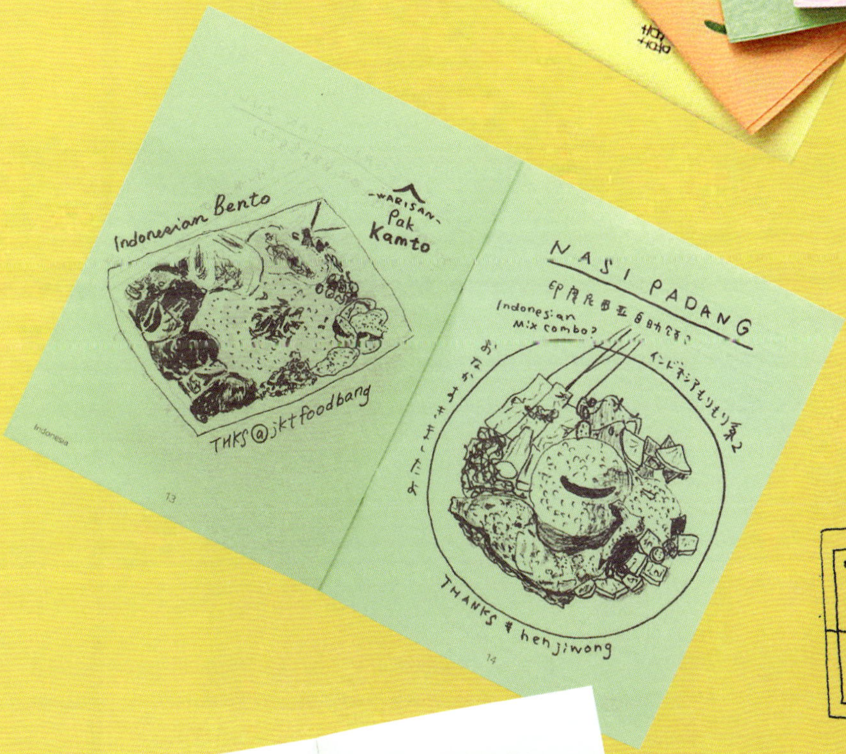

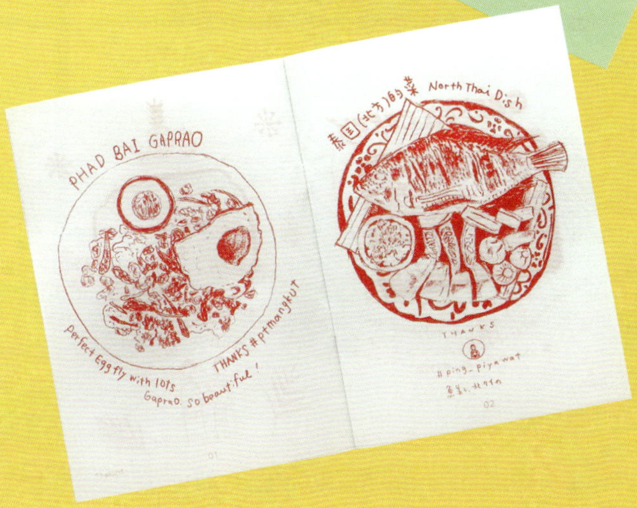

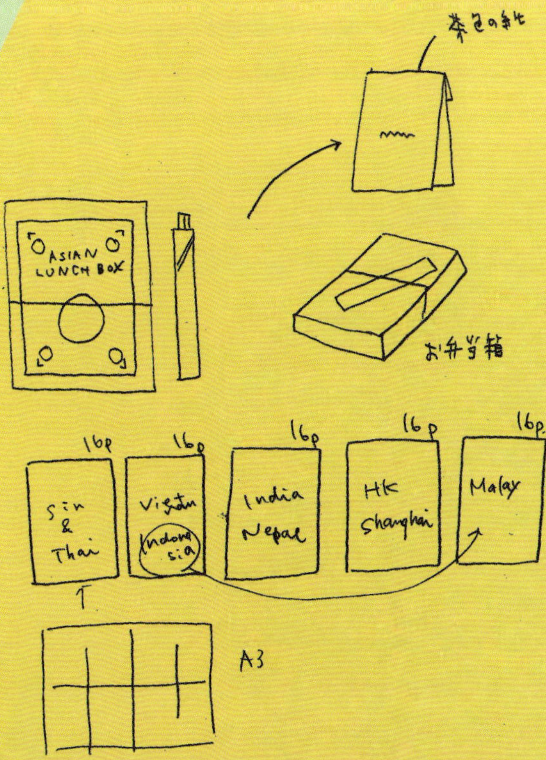

Page: 80 **Dimension:** 120×150mm **Weight:** 70g **Paper/Material:** Hardback Board (Cover); Paperback (Inside Page) **Binding:** Saddle Stitching

ORGANIZED SCENERY

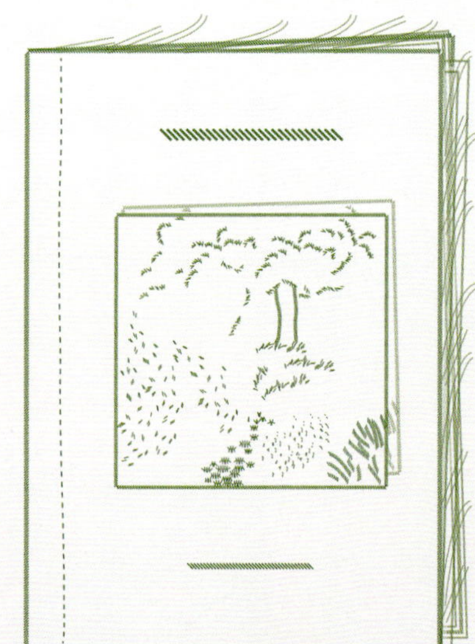

CD & D
XiangYun Loh
DS
Plant Press

2019

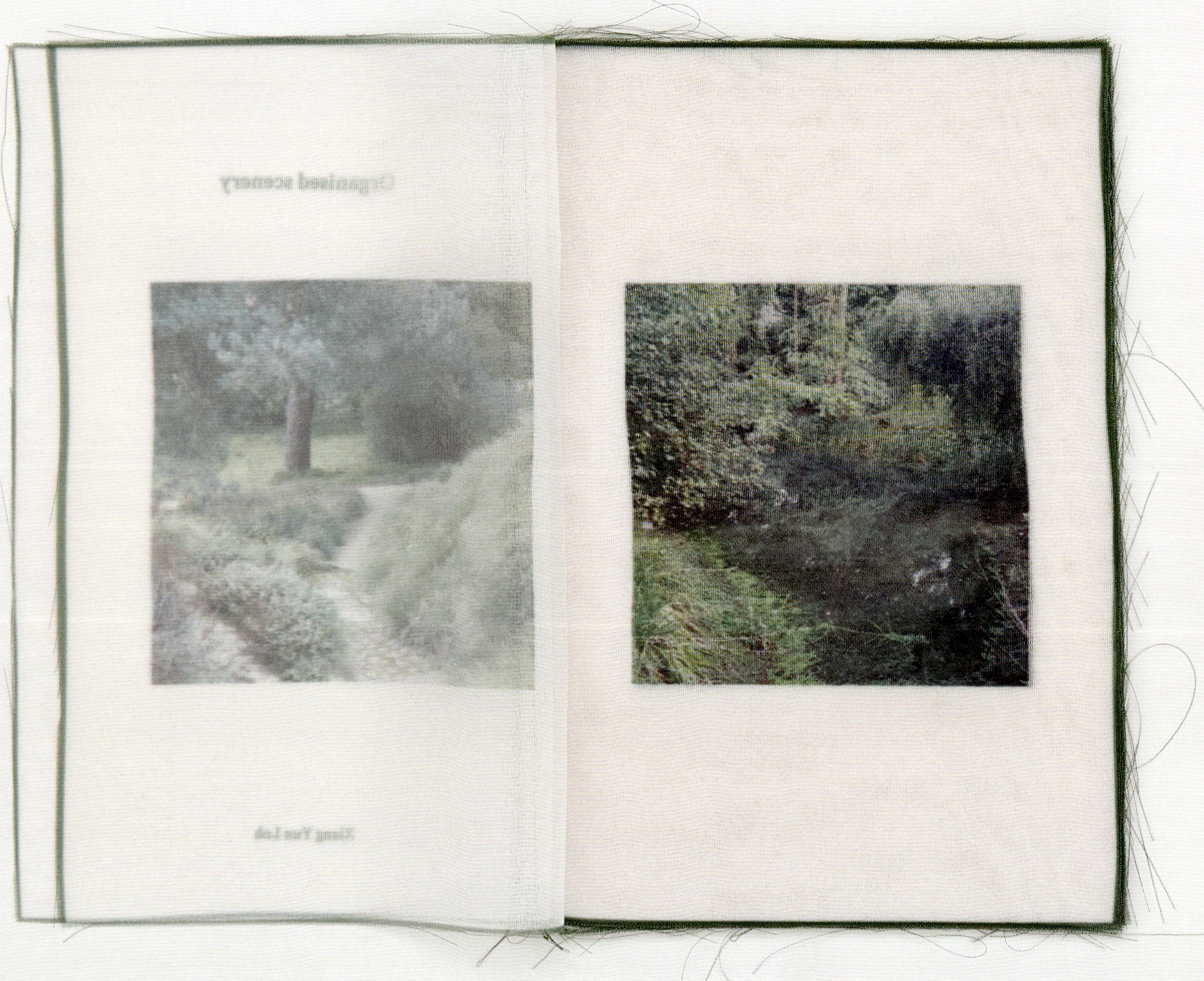

Organized Scenery is a photographic composite of picturesque scenes found in man-made parks. The designer's experience with nature is captured through a collection of these 12 photographs. Natural and man-made textures are organized together to form these "natural" recreation spaces.

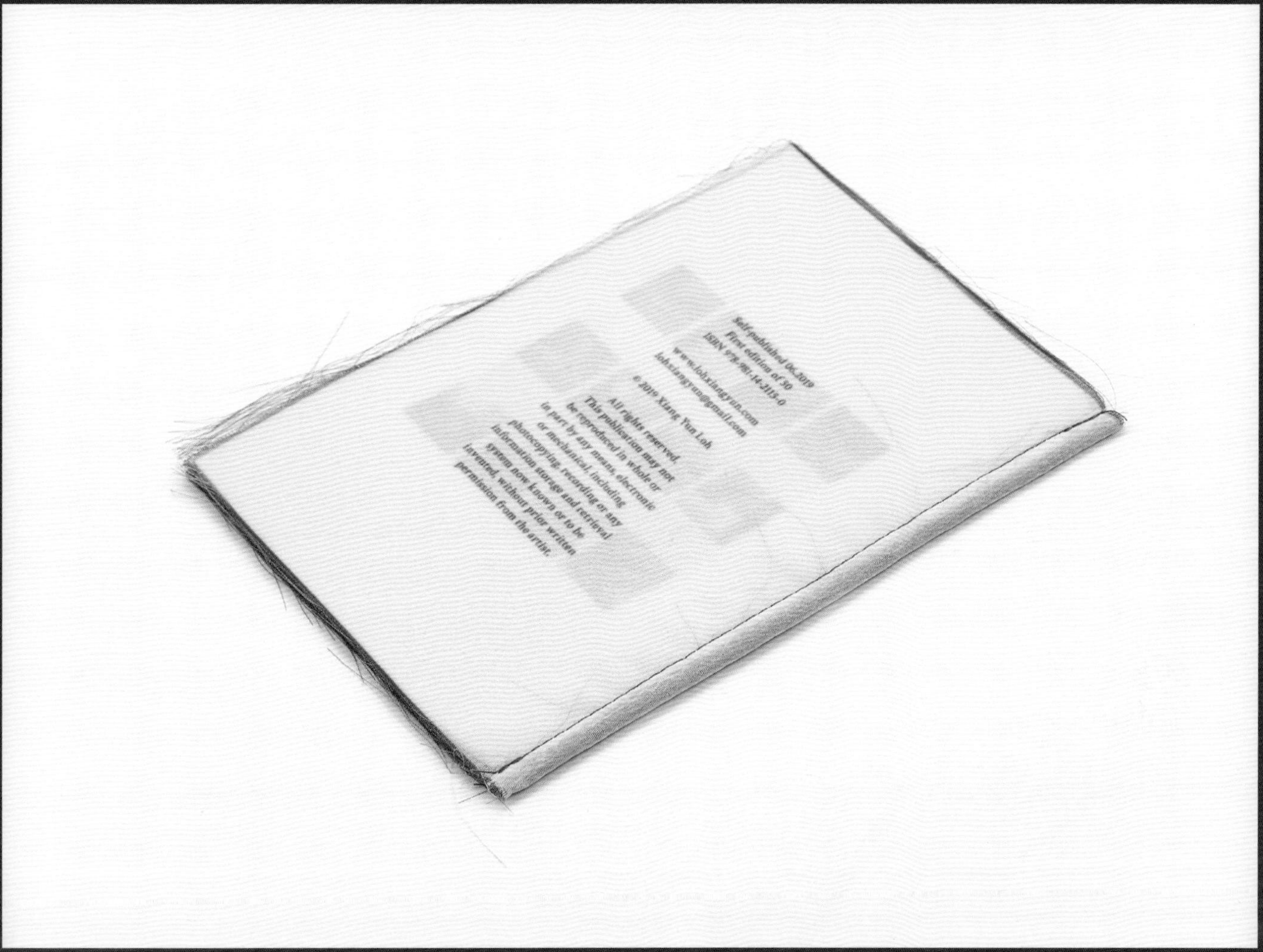

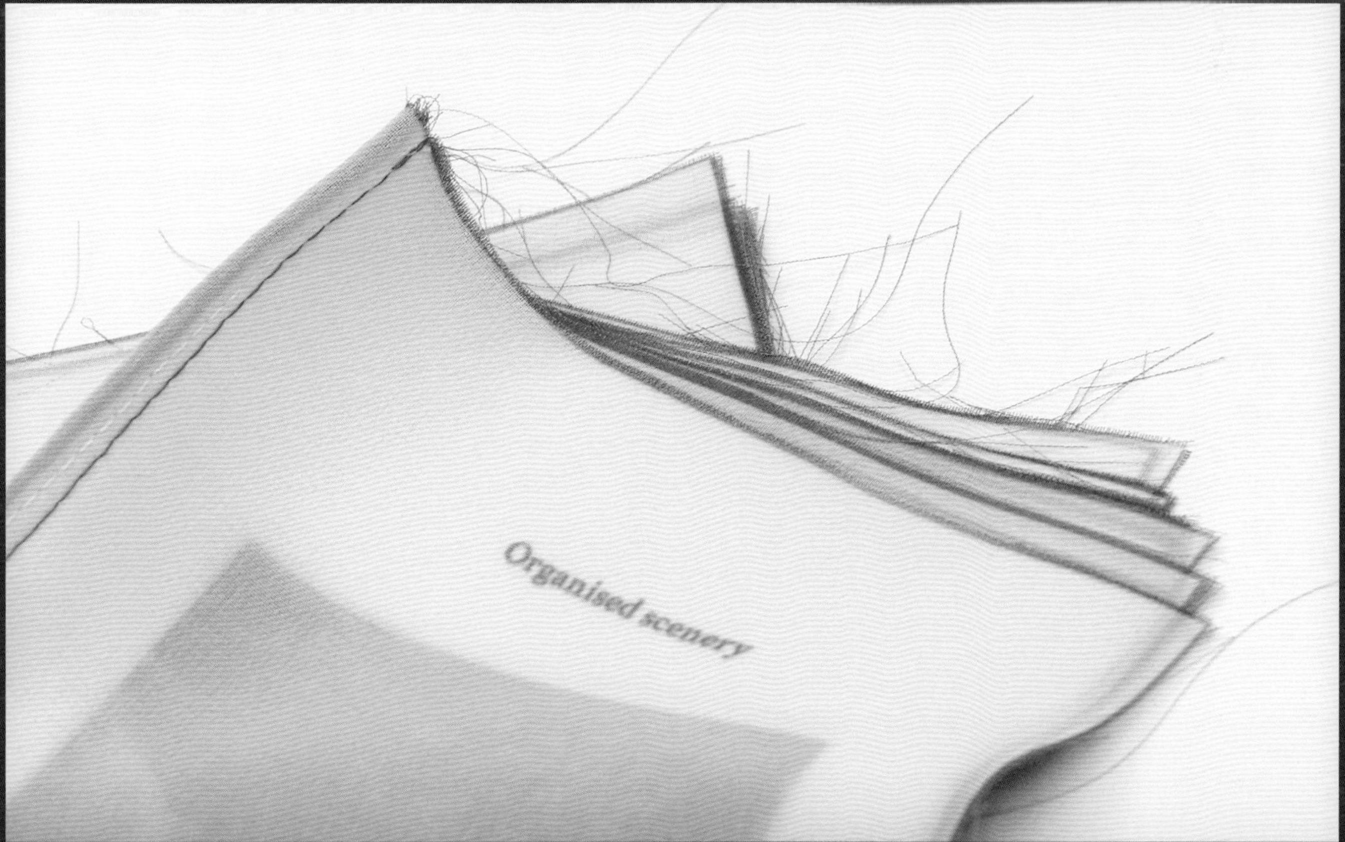

Paper/Material: Chiffon (Fabric) **Binding:** Singer Sewn Binding

Page: 16 **Dimension:** 115×165×3mm **Weight:** 35g

POSTAGE STAMP— CHILDREN & CHRISTMAS

D
0.1 & The object
P
Avec Studio
DS
ADD TO CART

2019

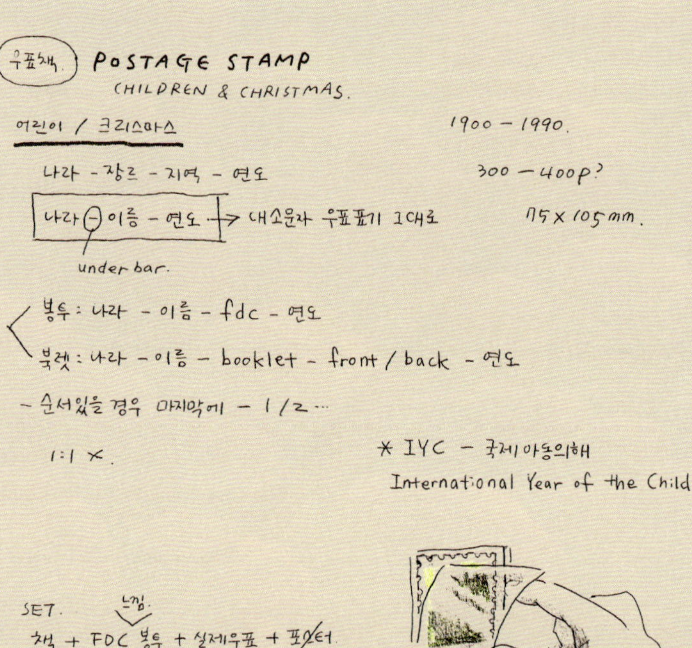

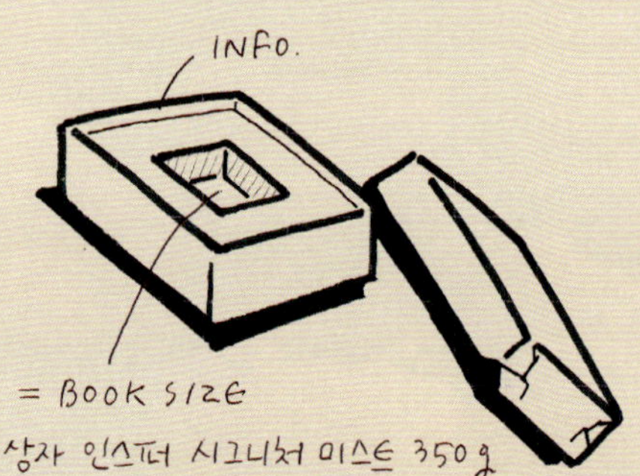

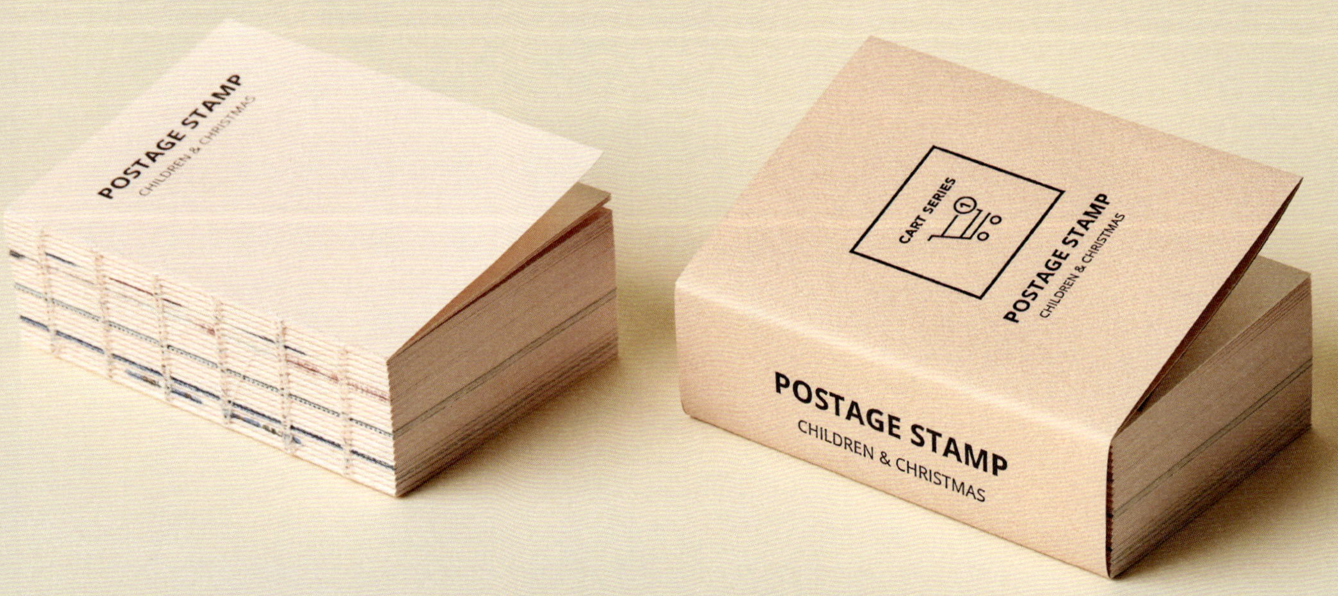

Postage Stamp explores Christmas and child-related themes among a collection of postage stamps from various countries gathered by a studio named 0.1 over a decade. The stamp collection book contains stamps globally from 1900 to 1990. The container recalls old vintage toy boxes and reveals its contents like a gift box. The stamp sheet, envelope, and the book are taken out of the box in sequence, giving the joyful feeling of unwrapping a present.

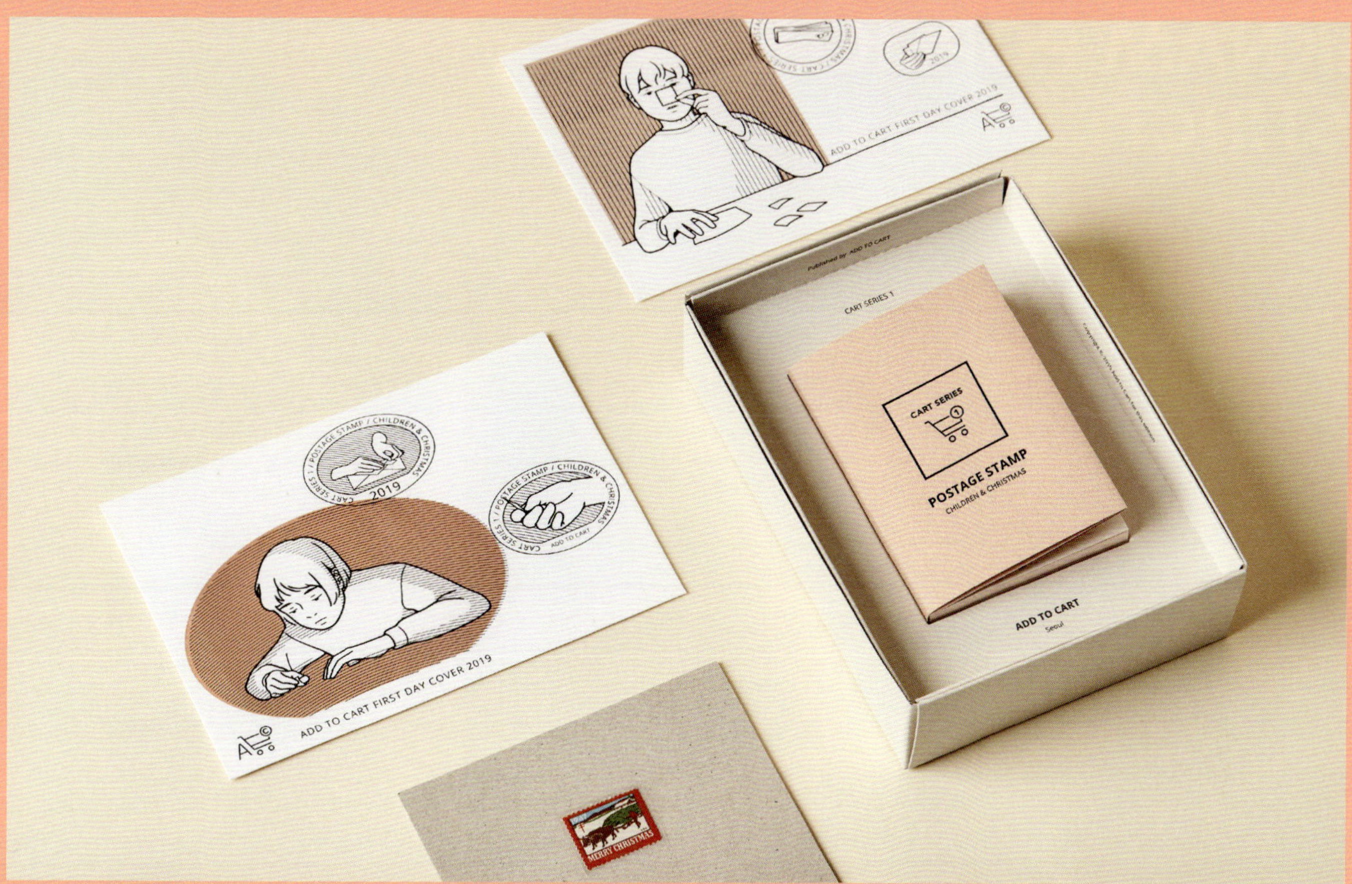

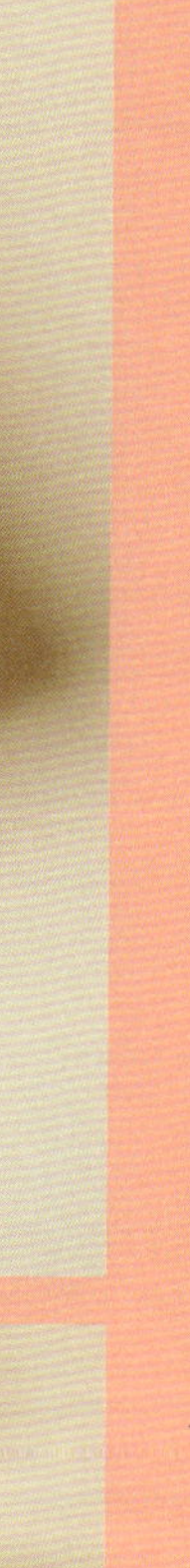

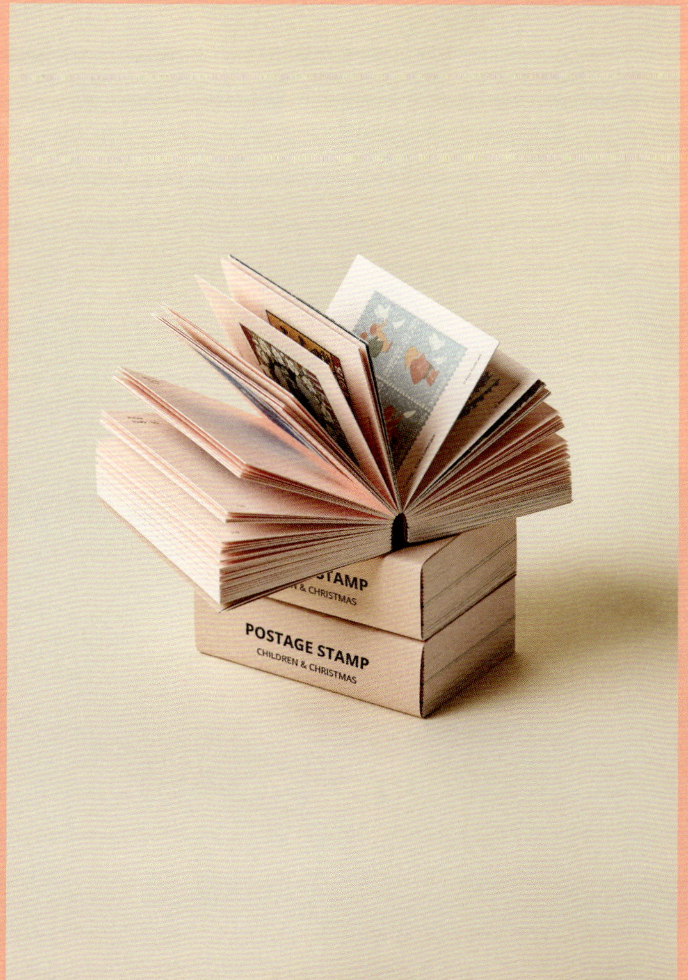

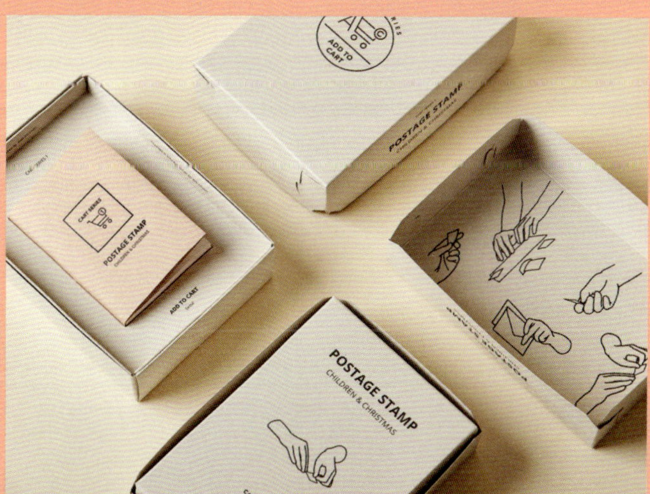

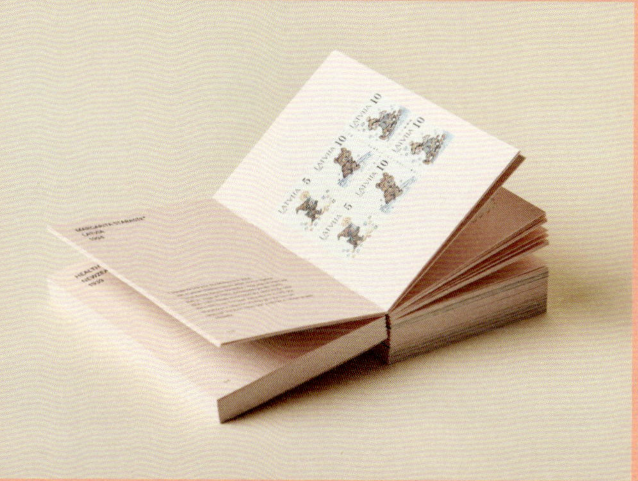

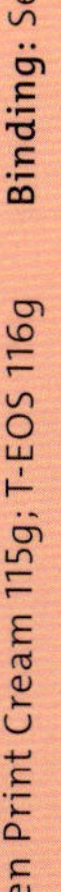

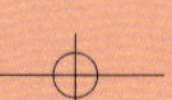

Page: 320 **Dimension:** 75×105mm **Weight:** 250g **Paper/Material:** Insper Signature 350g; Munken Print Cream 115g; T-EOS 116g **Binding:** Sewn Binding

PAKNAM POPSICLE DISTRICT

D
Wuthipol Ujathammarat

2021

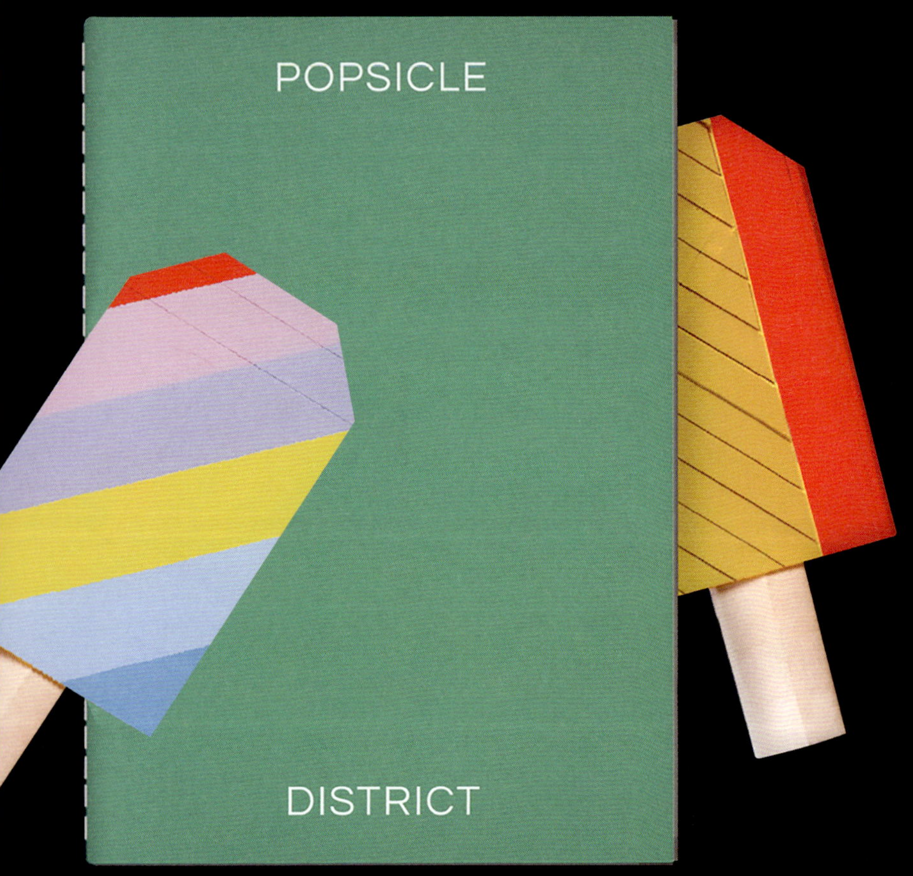

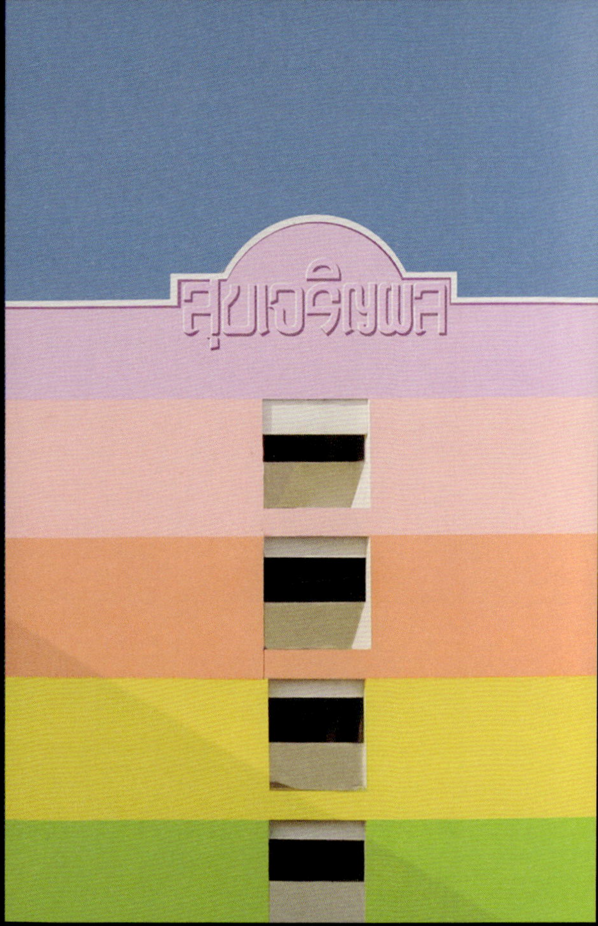

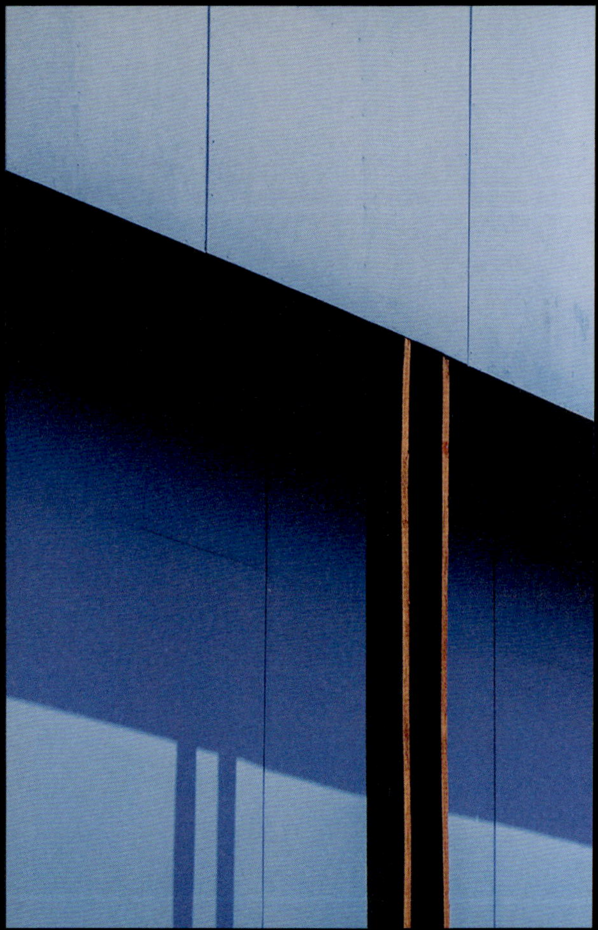

Paknam Popsicle District attempts to fabricate a peculiar visual series based on the designer's hometown—Samutprakarn in Thailand, which has the local nickname "Paknam". He chooses to detail the unexplored aspects of the place, and places emphasis on rhymes involving colors

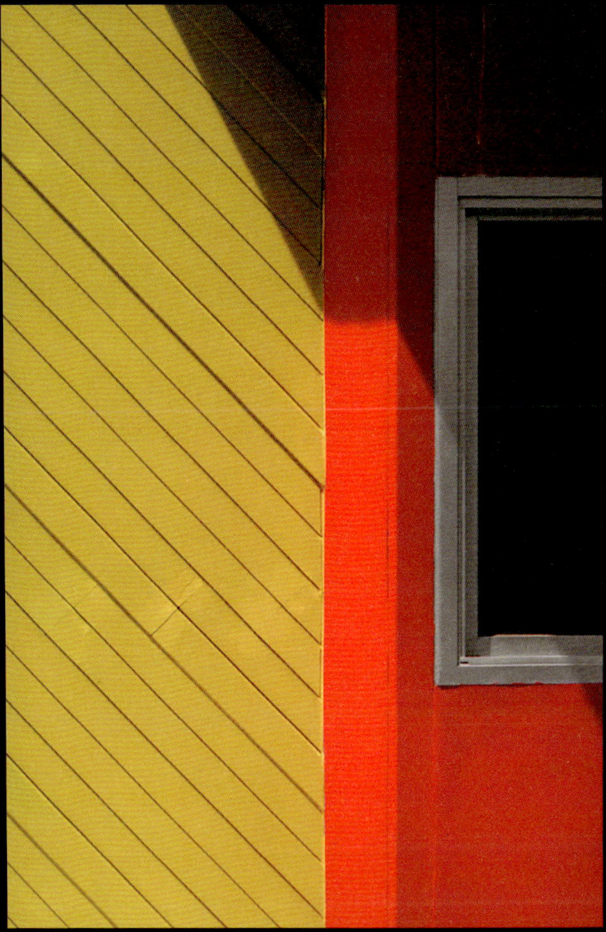

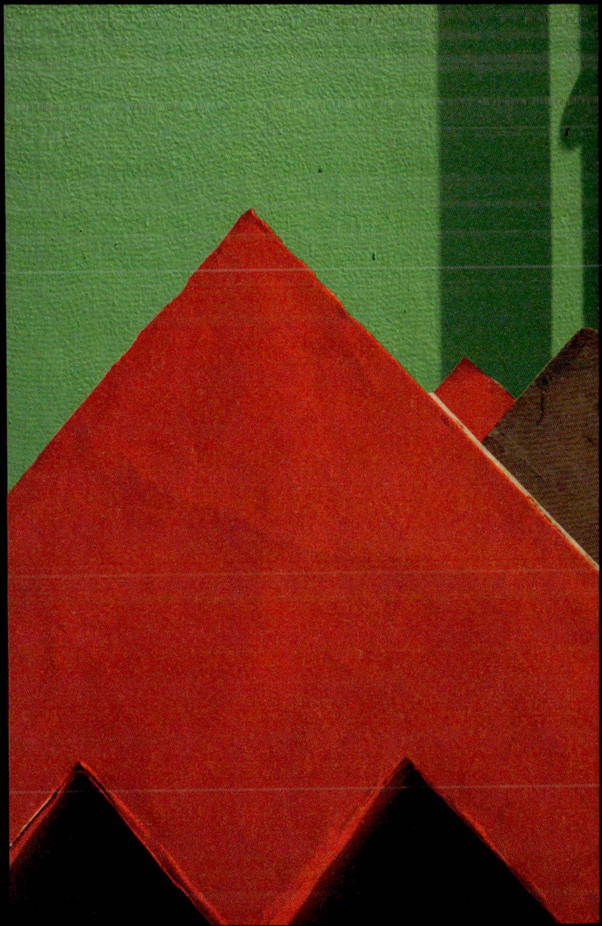

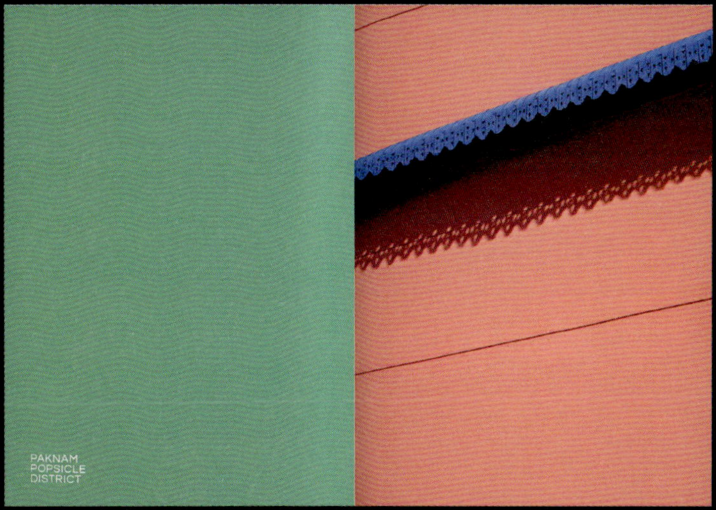

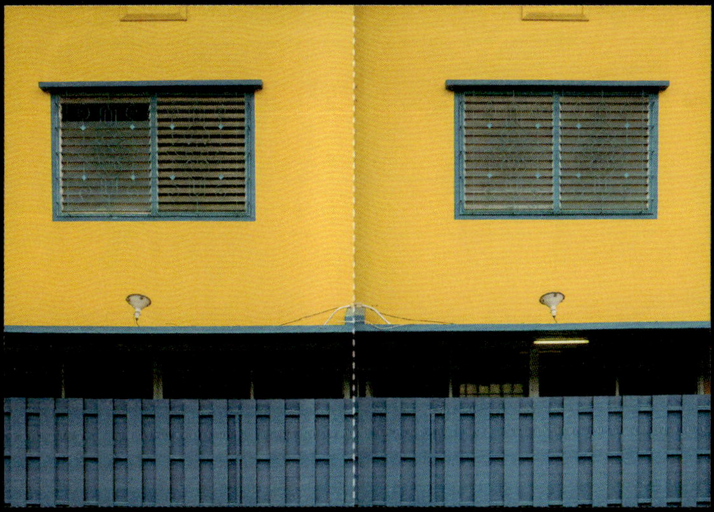

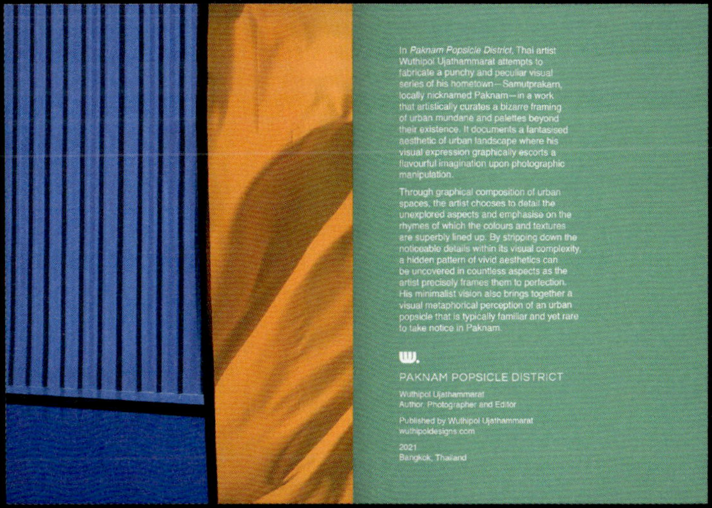

PAKNAM
POPSICLE
DISTRICT

In *Paknam Popsicle District*, Thai artist Wuthipol Ujathammarat attempts to fabricate a punchy and peculiar visual series of his hometown—Samutprakarn, locally nicknamed Paknam—in a work that artistically curates a bizarre framing of urban mundane and palettes beyond their existence. It documents a fantasised aesthetic of urban landscape where his visual expression graphically escorts a flavourful imagination upon photographic manipulation.

Through graphical composition of urban spaces, the artist chooses to detail the unexplored aspects and emphasise on the rhymes of which the colours and textures are superbly lined up. By stripping down the noticeable details within its visual complexity, a hidden pattern of vivid aesthetics can be uncovered in countless aspects as the artist precisely frames them to perfection. His minimalist vision also brings together a visual metaphorical perception of an urban popsicle that is typically familiar and yet rare to take notice in Paknam.

W.

PAKNAM POPSICLE DISTRICT

Wuthipol Ujathammarat
Author, Photographer and Editor

Published by Wuthipol Ujathammarat
wuthipoldesigns.com

2021
Bangkok, Thailand

atiness 150g; Matte White 100g **Binding:** Singer Sewn Binding

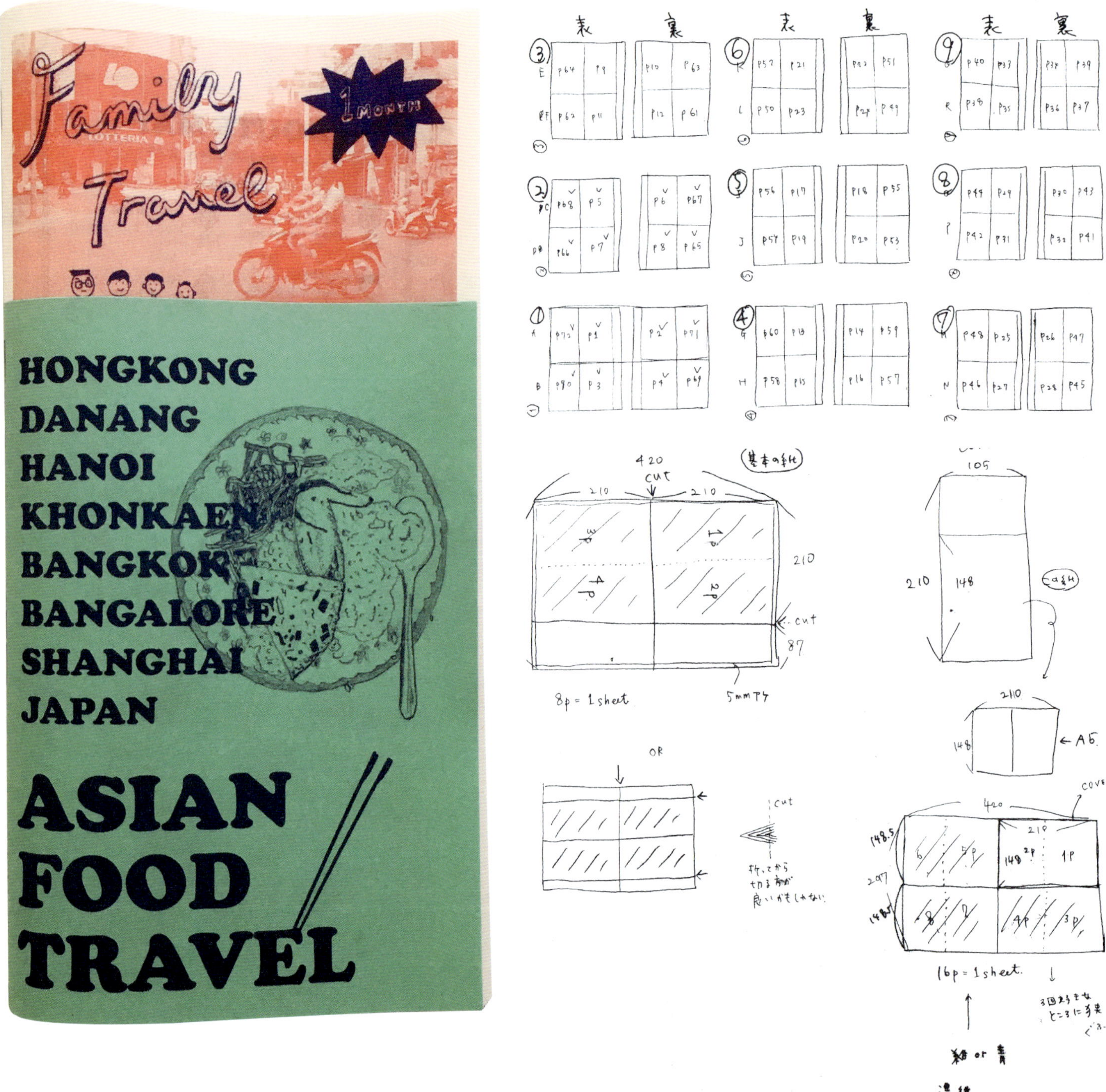

ASIAN FOOD TRAVEL

D
Takako Masuki
DS
Asian Food Design

2020

This zine features the designer's travel in 2019 with her family members. They visited Hong Kong, Danang, Hanoi, Bangkok, Khon Kaen, Bangalore, and Shanghai. She made a zine so as to keep a record of this family trip.

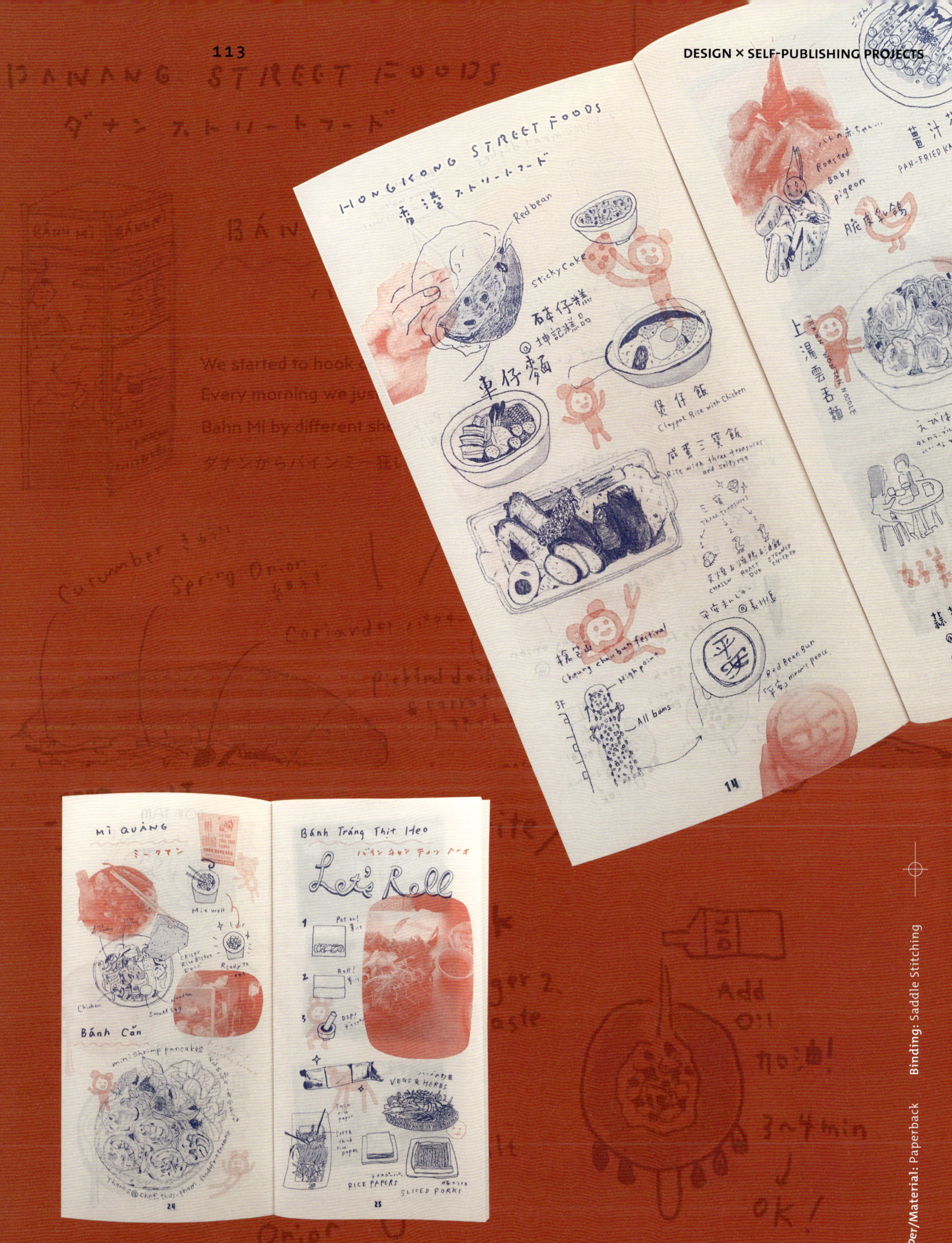

Paper/Material: Paperback Binding: Saddle Stitching

Page: 72 Dimension: 105×210mm Weight: 50g

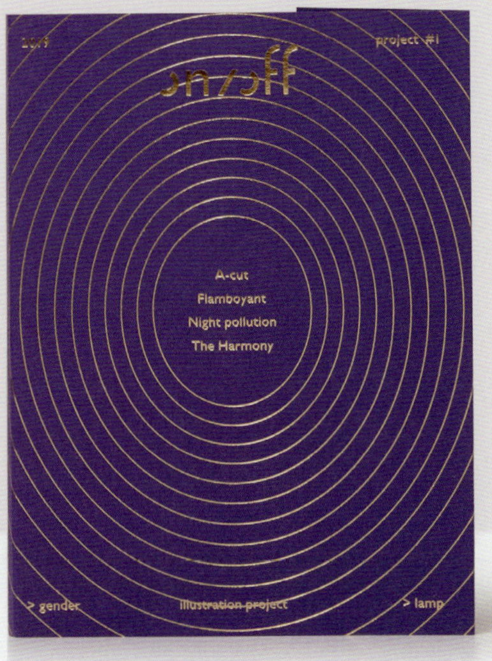

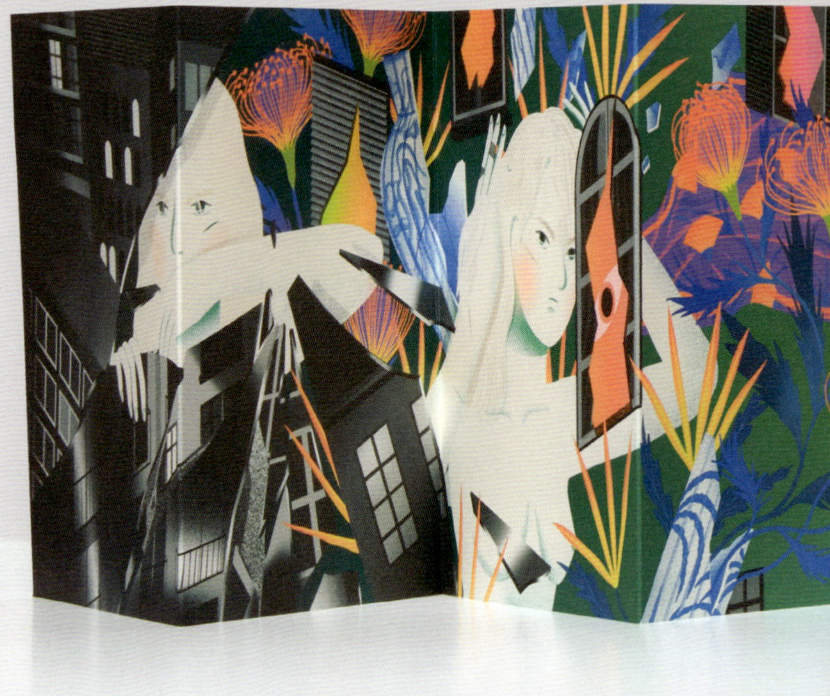

ON/OFF

D
Heehee, Sujan, Eomju & Dalo
P
Ingun Cho

2019

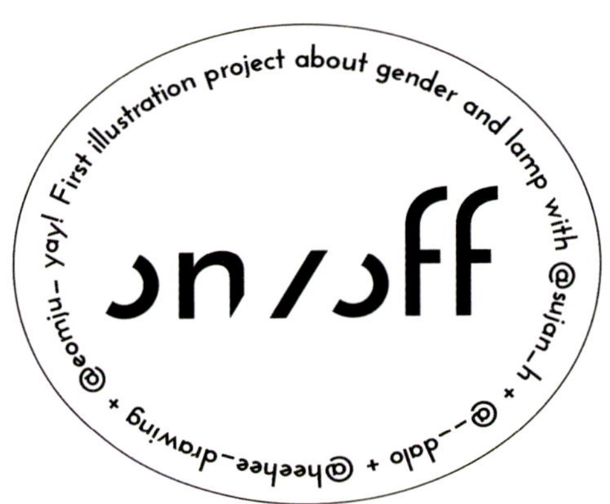

The purpose of the book is to show illustrations with one theme in four different ways. The designers wanted to communicate the theme "The Need for a Spotlight", so they designed a symbolic image of light spreading through each cover. To emphasize the meaning of this design, gold foil was applied on the cover.

There are two ways to read each book. One can read through the story page by page in a traditional way, or unfold the entire accordion book to read the story in its entirety.

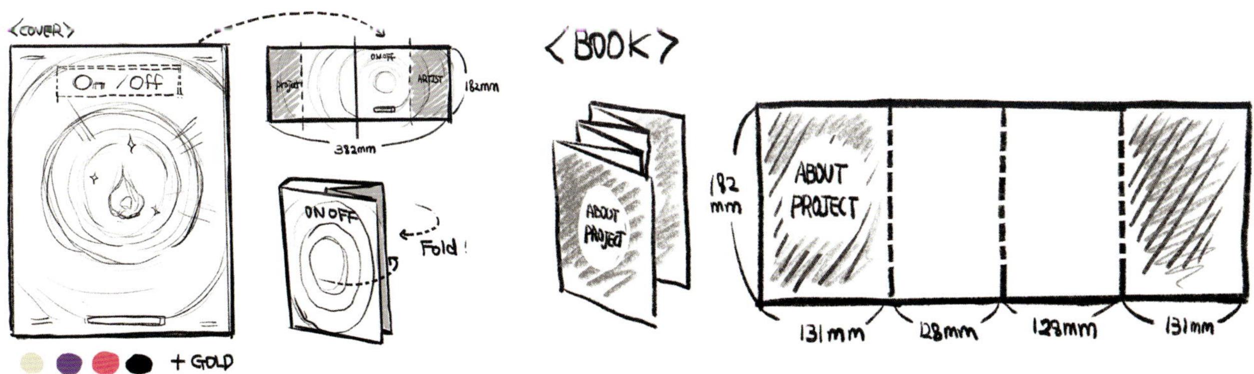

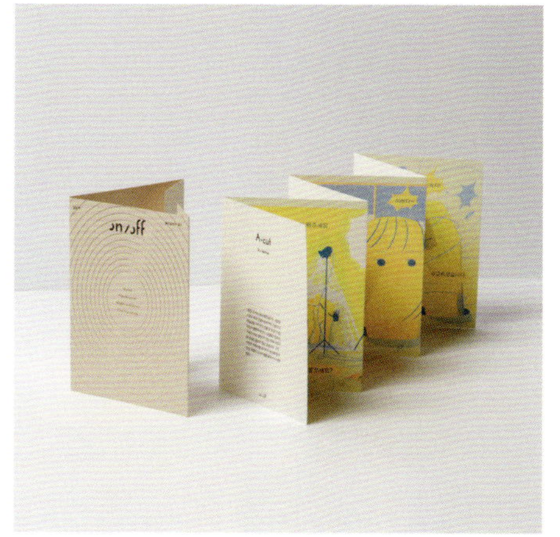

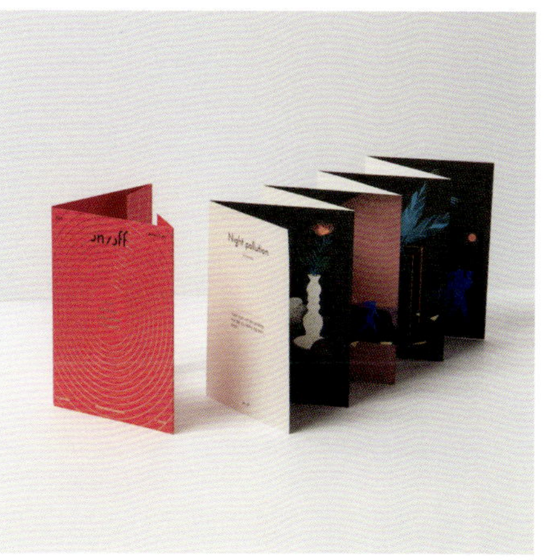

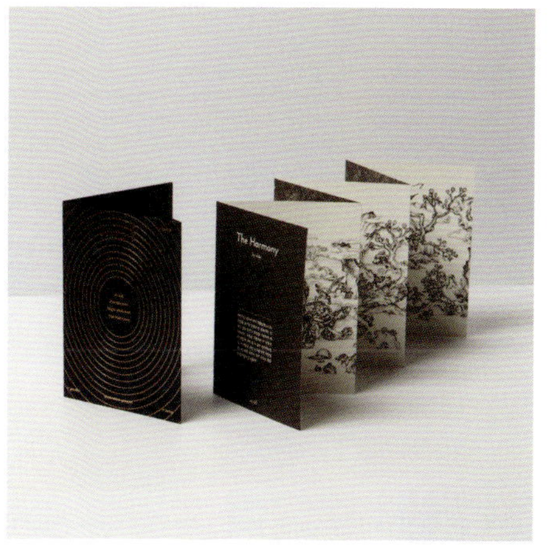

Paper/Material: Munken Pure 200g **Binding:** Accordion Fold

Page: 32 **Dimension:** 134×182×20mm **Weight:** 160g

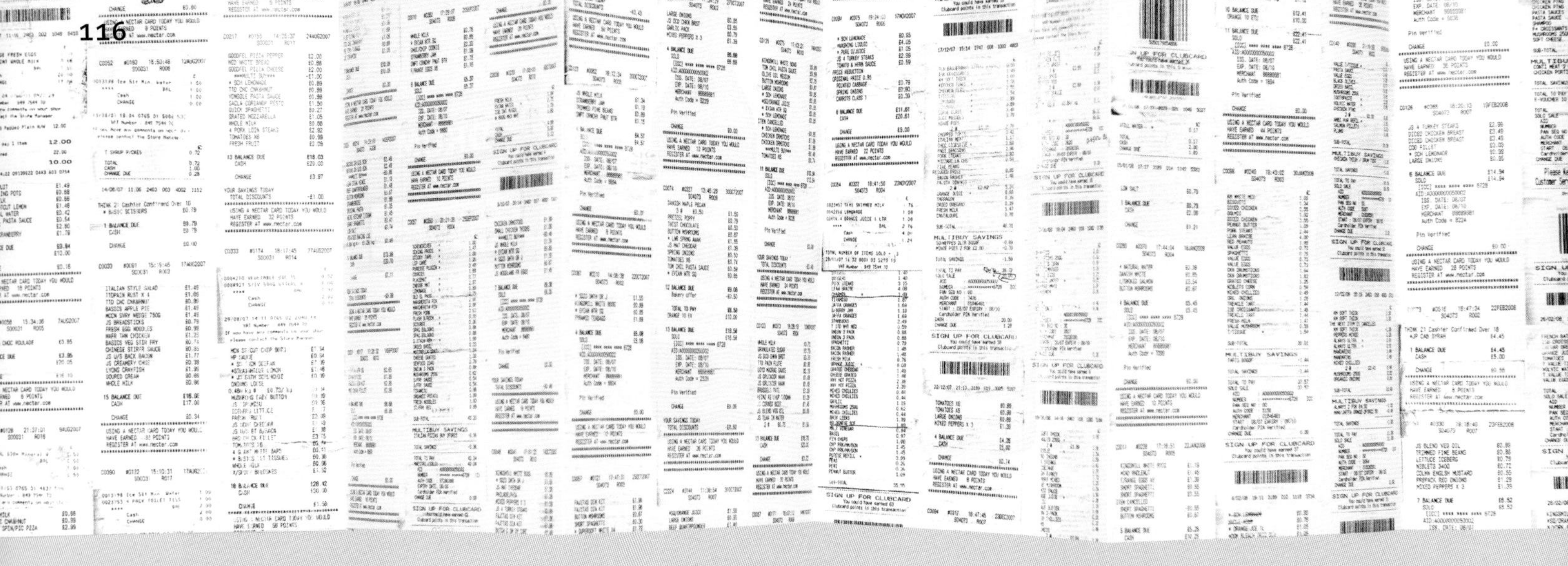

GROCERY

D
Sujin Lee
DS
Piece

2020

Grocery

Lee Sujin

Edition 0 0 0 of 100

Published and designed by piece

ISBN 979-11-91072-00-6

© 2020 Lee Sujin
© 2020 piece

piecephoto.com

「GROCERY」는 4년간 타지에서 생활하며 소비한 개인적인 기호(taste)를 개념적으로 시각화한 작업이다.

슈퍼마켓에서 받은 영수증 속에는 언제, 어디서, 무엇을, 얼마에 구매했는지가 인쇄되어 있다. 수집된 대량의 영수증을 카메라가 아닌 스캐너로 촬영함으로써 종이에 인쇄된 구매 내역을 데이터 이미지로 전환하였고, 이를 마치 구글링 하듯 아이템 별로 찾아 범주화하였다. 범주화된 데이터 이미지 속에는 특정 기간 동안 변화된 개인의 소비 패턴과 기호를 볼 수 있으며, 이를 통해 다양한 해석과 상상을 하게 된다.

책에 실린 슈퍼마켓의 다양한 물품들은 인터넷에서 검색되어진 공산품 이미지를 수집하여 나열하였다.

런던에서 예술사진을 전공한 이수진은 사진 전문 출판사이자 국내외 사진집과 오리지널 프린트를 판매하는 서점인 piece를 운영하고 있다.
piece에서 출판된 협업 출판물인 「Fugue」에서 ≪#≫와 ≪A to Z Categorize by iPhone≫을 작업하였다.

"GROCERY" is a conceptual visualization of the personal tastes that have been consumed over the space of four years in a foreign country.

In the receipt from the supermarket, we can see when, where, what, and how much we spend. By photographing a large amount of collected receipts with a scanner rather than a camera, the purchased history printed on a paper was converted into a data image and then it was searched and categorized by item, like we do when googling. In the categorized data image, we can see personal consumption patterns and preferences that have changed during a specific period, through which various interpretations and imaginations are possible.

Images of supermarket items in this book were listed by collecting images of industrial products searched on the Internet.

Sujin Lee, who majored in art photography in London, runs piece, a publisher specializing in photography and a bookstore selling domestic and foreign photo books and original prints. Her work, "#" and "A to Z Categorize by iPhone" were published in a collaborative publication, Fugue.

FRESH MILK 140
BREAD 418
TOBACCO 65
BRUSSELS PATE 1

624 BALNCE DUE
CASH

CHANGE

Grocery is a conceptual visualization of the personal tastes and consumption patterns over the space of 4 years in a foreign country. The designer uses the form of accordion-fold book to show data in the 4 years. Readers can see how personal consumption patterns and preferences have changed through this book.

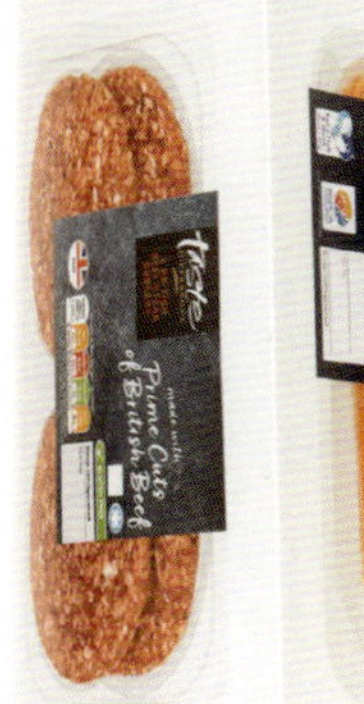

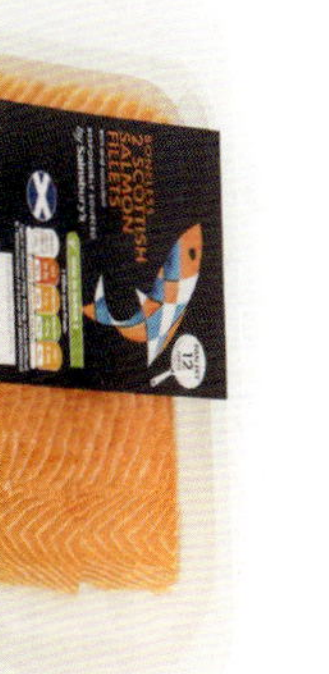

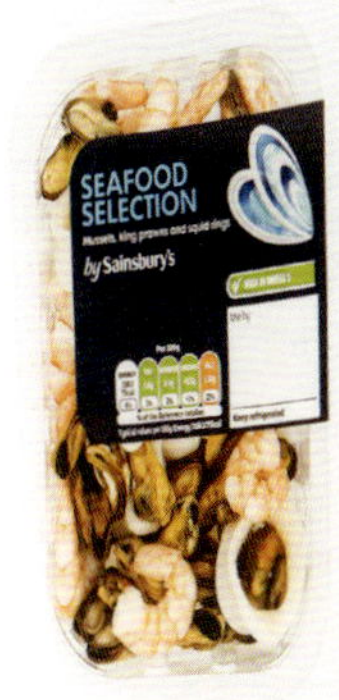

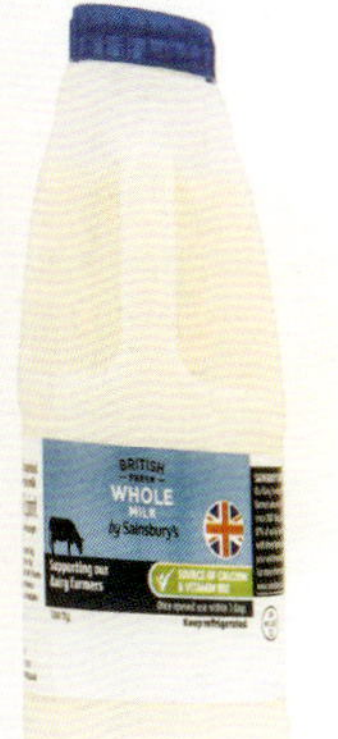

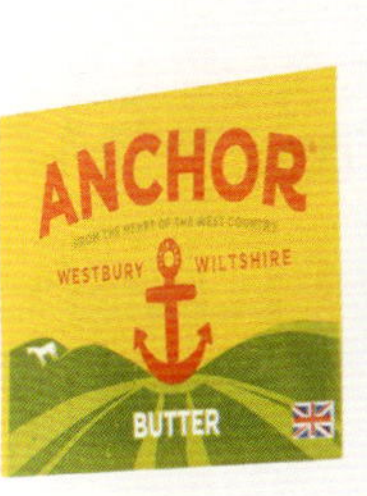

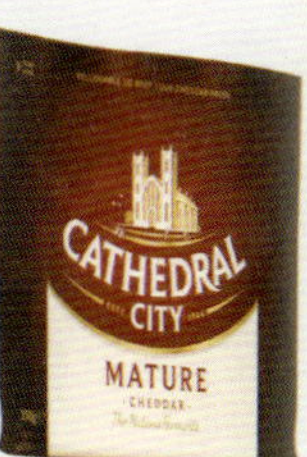

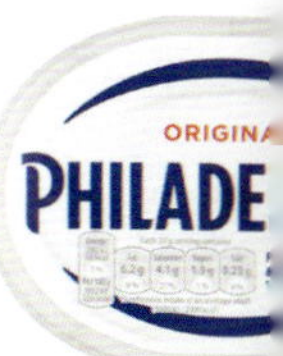

GROCERY

11JUL2007 - 18/10/11

		£
FRESH MILK	140	102.22
BREAD	418	420.75
TOBACCO	65	410.17
BRUSSELS PATE	1	1.09
624 BALNCE DUE		**934.23**
CASH		950.00
CHANGE		15.77

www.piecephoto.com

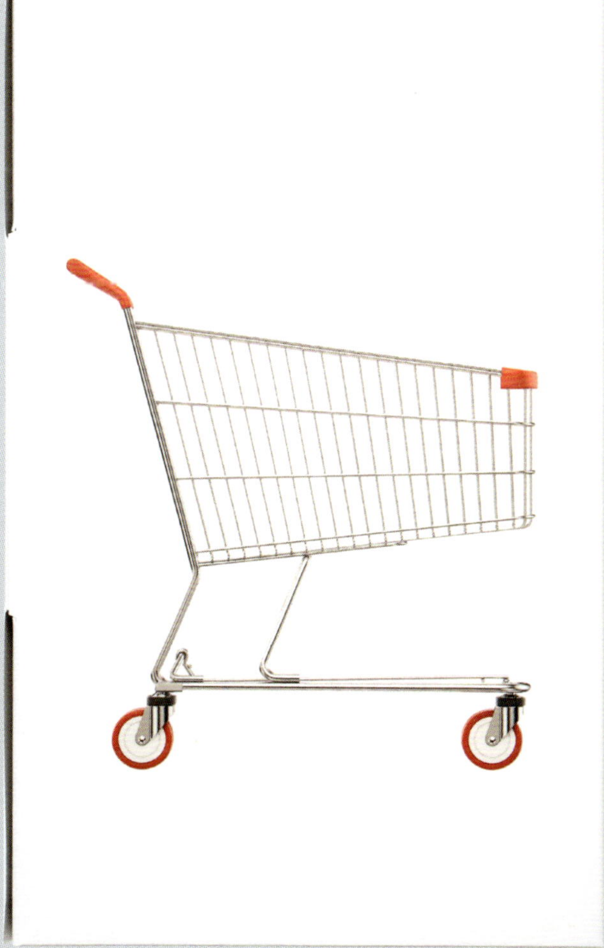

Page: 110 **Dimension:** 117×211mm **Weight:** 650g **Paper/Material:** Grey Eska Board 1.75mm (Cover); Top Kote Matt 82g (Inside Page) **Binding:** Accordion Fold

I AM WATCHING, I AM HIDING

AD, CD, D & P
Ke Xu

2018

Based on a full-size photograph taken in Venice, this publication presents an open narrative driven by zoom-in-and-out perspectives. It is also a discussion about the ways to view a photograph.

The accordion fold limits the speed and creates pauses when turning page, leaving room for the readers' imagination as well as leaving space for narrative diversity. At the same time, the accordion fold achieves a loop within the story. The story restarts when the last page of the book becomes the first page.

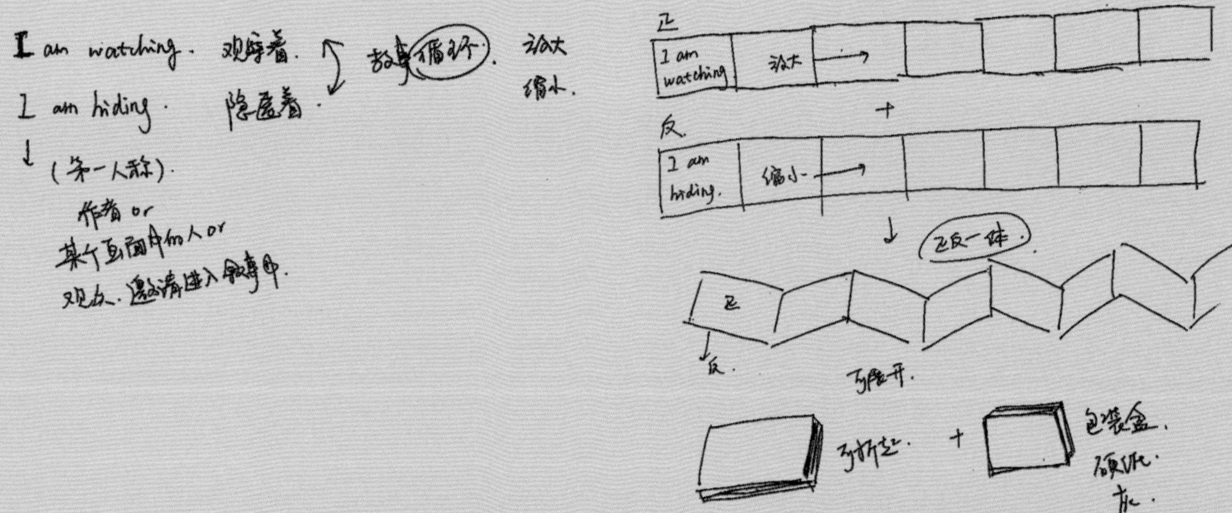

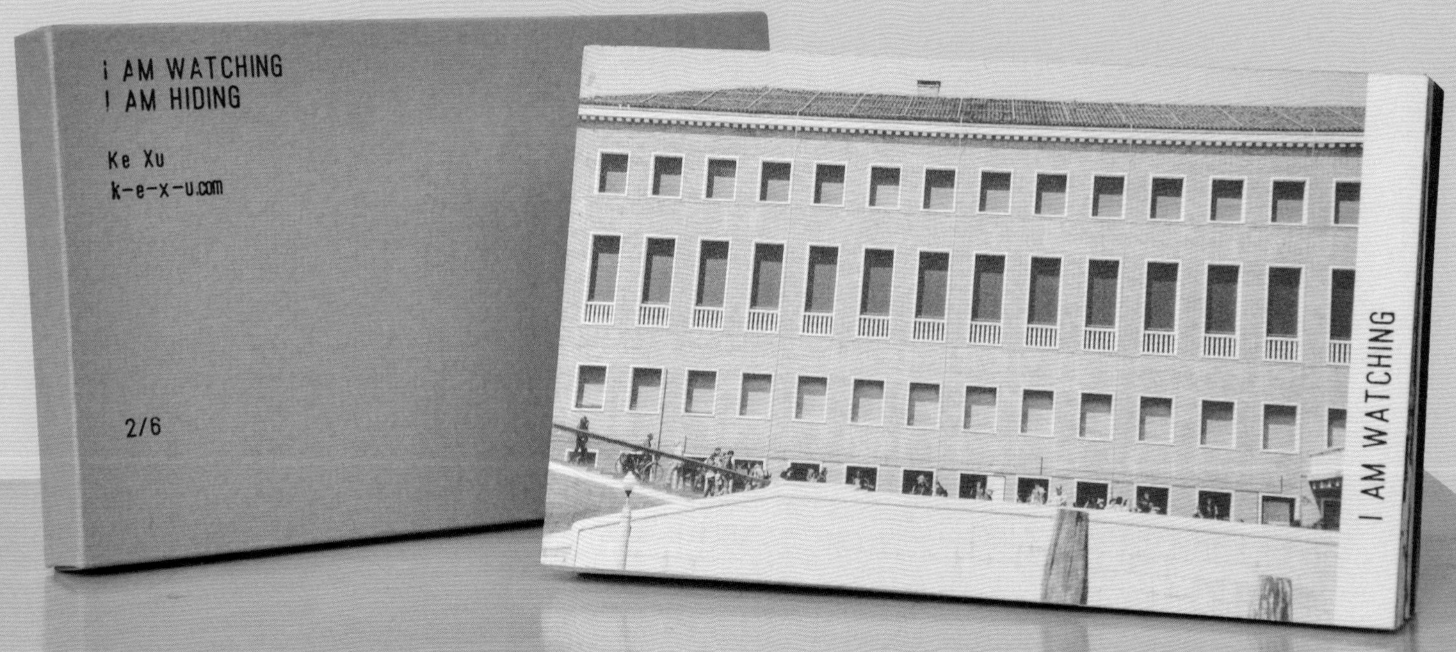

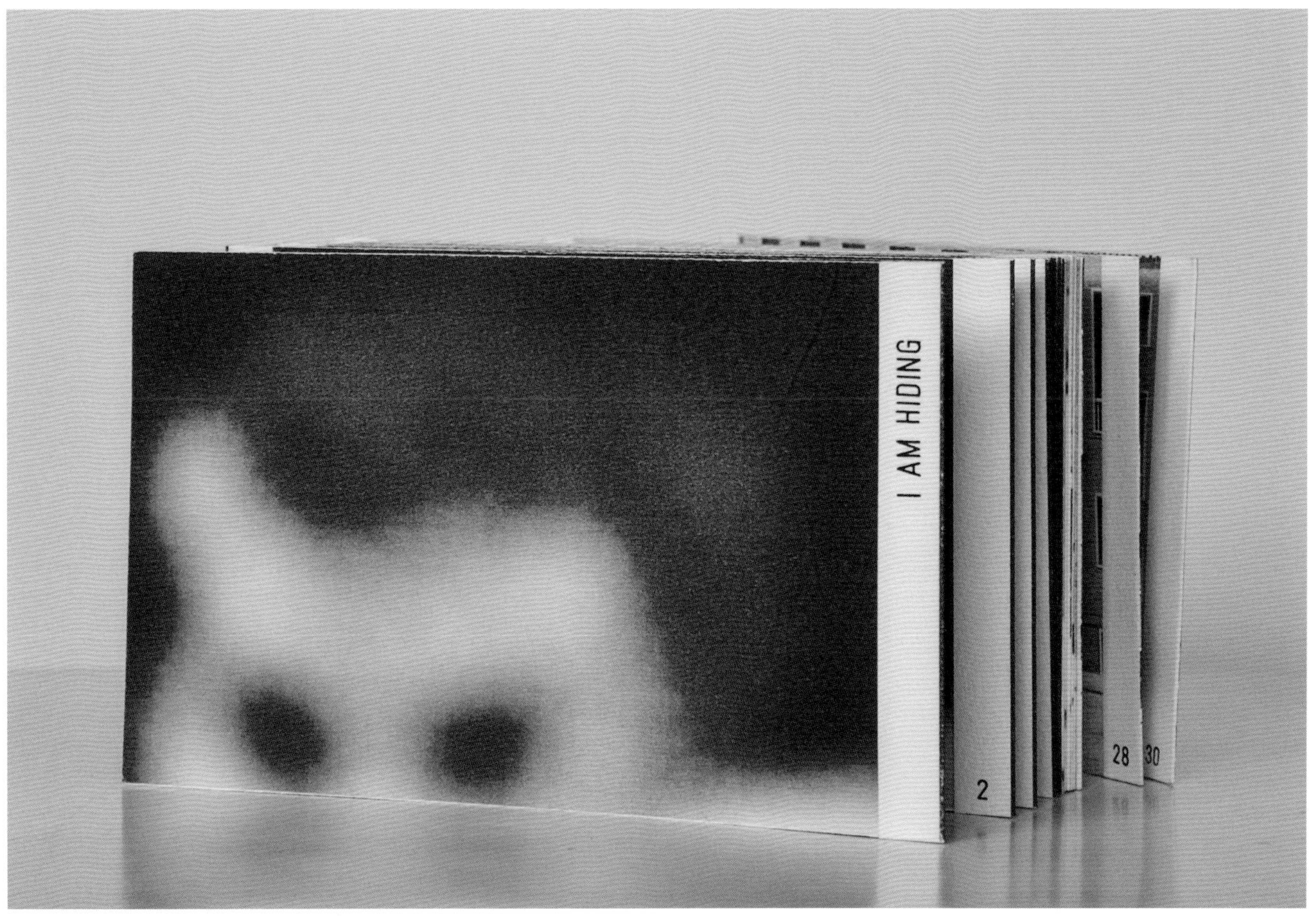

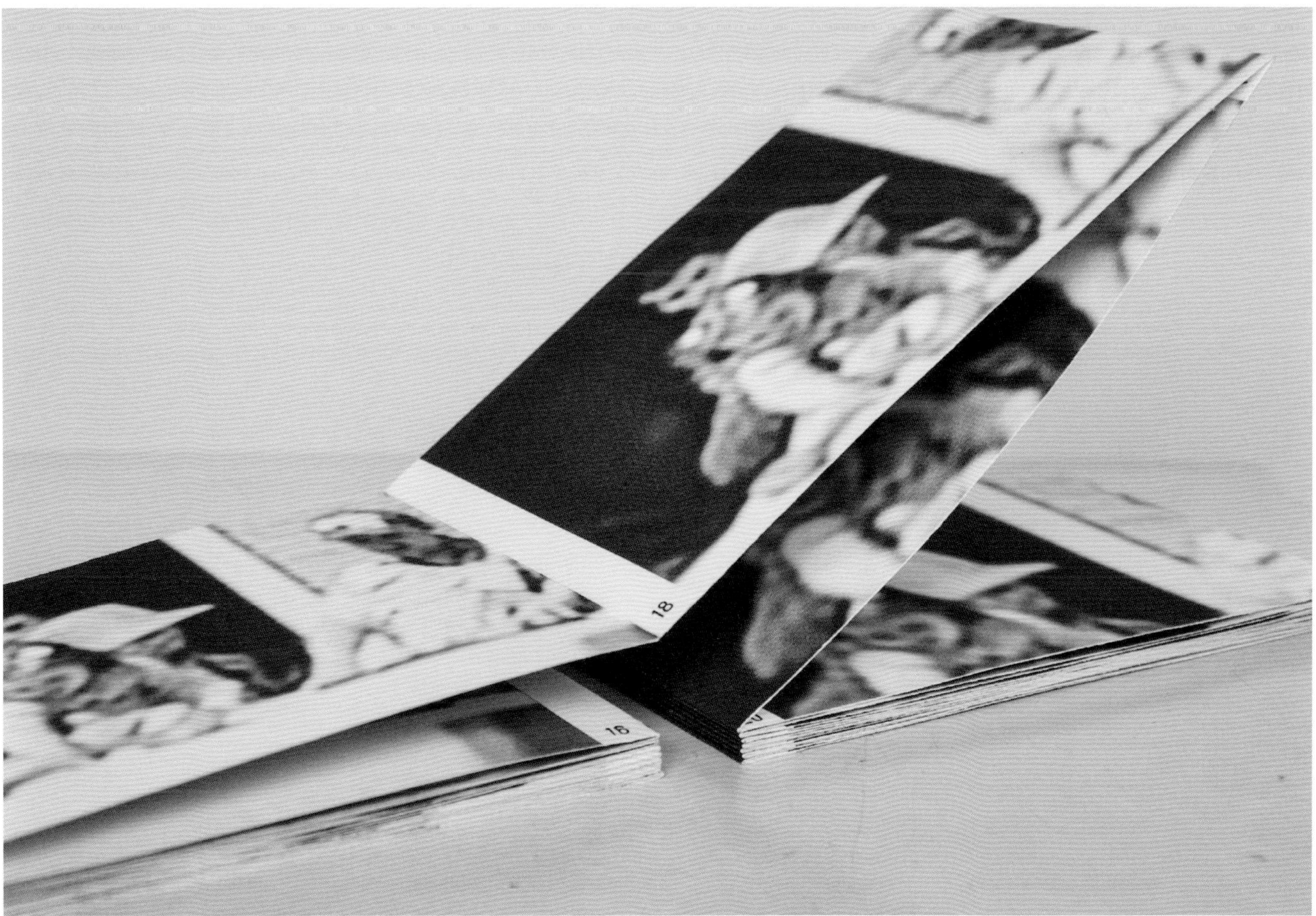

Paper/Material: Cotton Paper **Binding:** Accordion Fold

Page: 64 **Dimension:** 198×126×22mm **Weight:** 208g

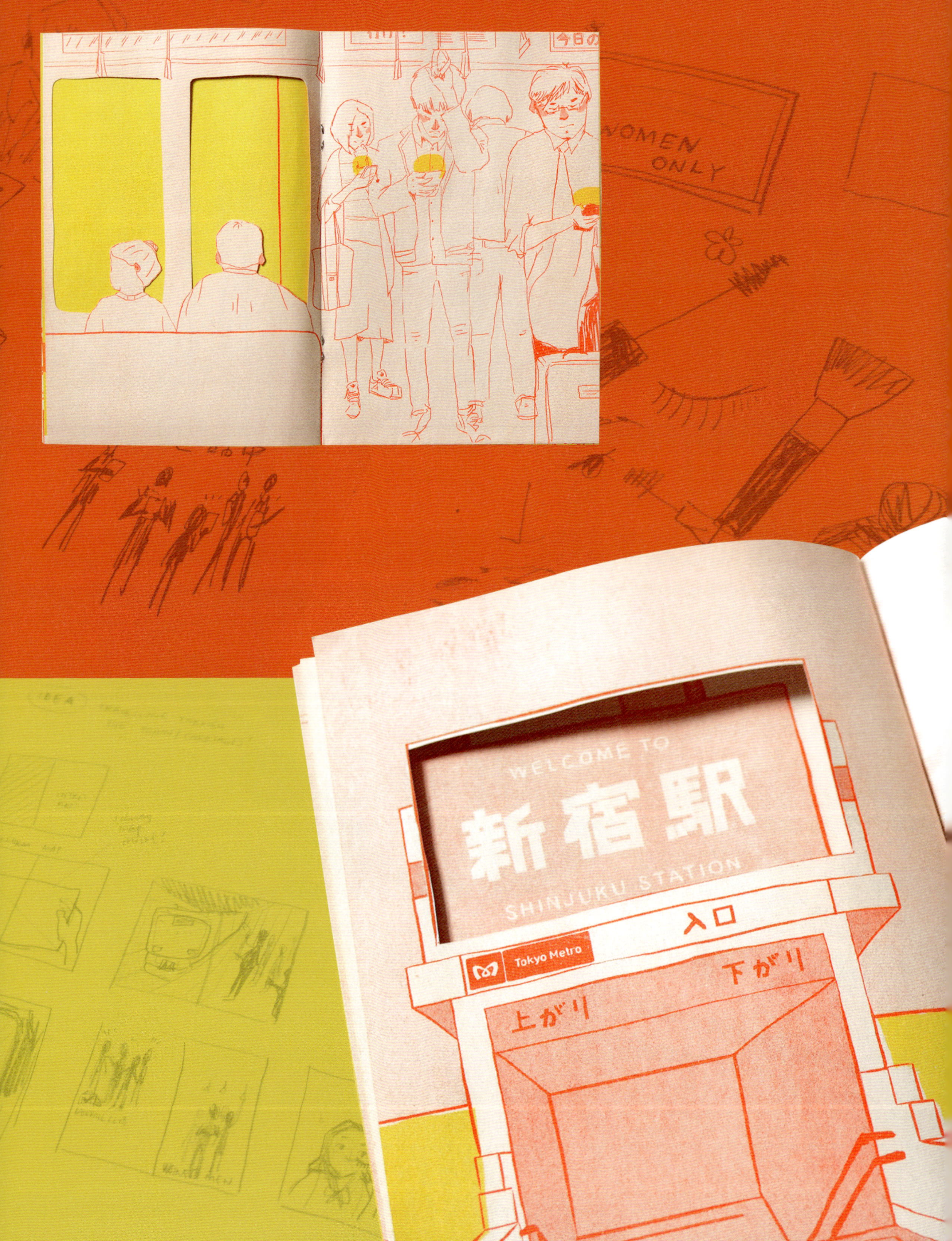
今日の
WOMEN
ONLY
WELCOME TO
新宿駅
SHINJUKU STATION
入口
Tokyo Metro
下がり
上がり

TOKYO UNDERGROUND

D
Emilie Terashi Boyer

2018

Tokyo Underground is an illustrated zine which follows a short journey through the Tokyo subway system, depicting the various carriages and the daily commuters who use the system. It is Riso-printed on newsprint and features sheer tracing paper inserts and cut-outs to create a dynamic experience with each page-turn.

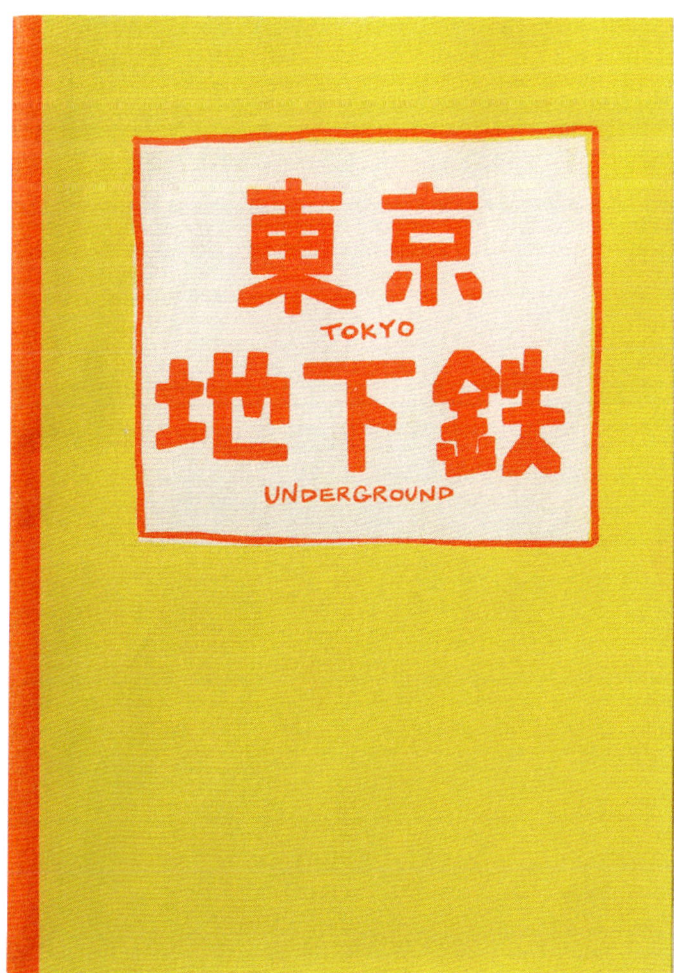

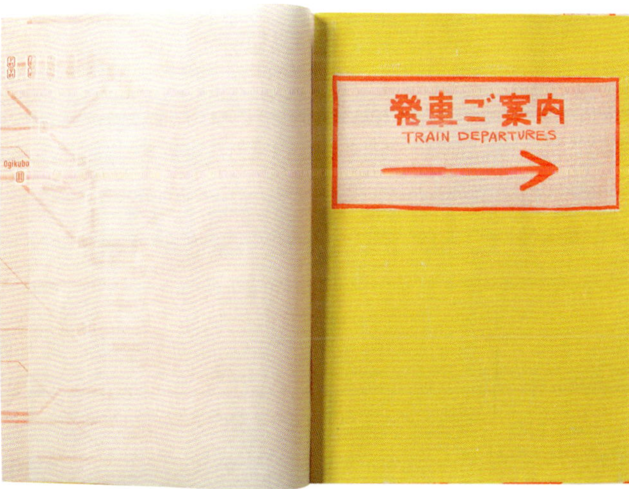

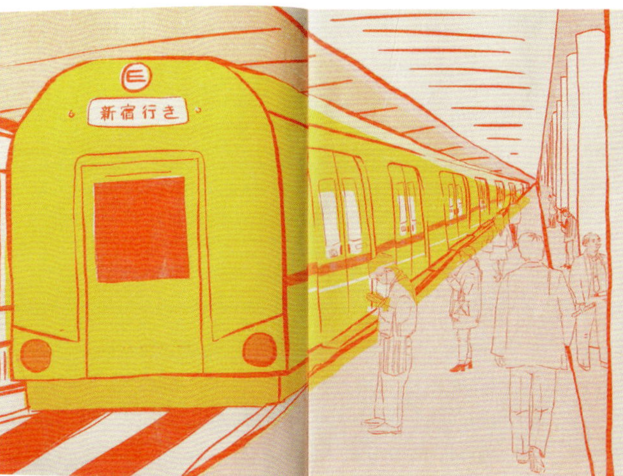

Page: 8 **Dimension:** 135×195mm **Paper/Material:** Newsprint **Binding:** Saddle Stitching

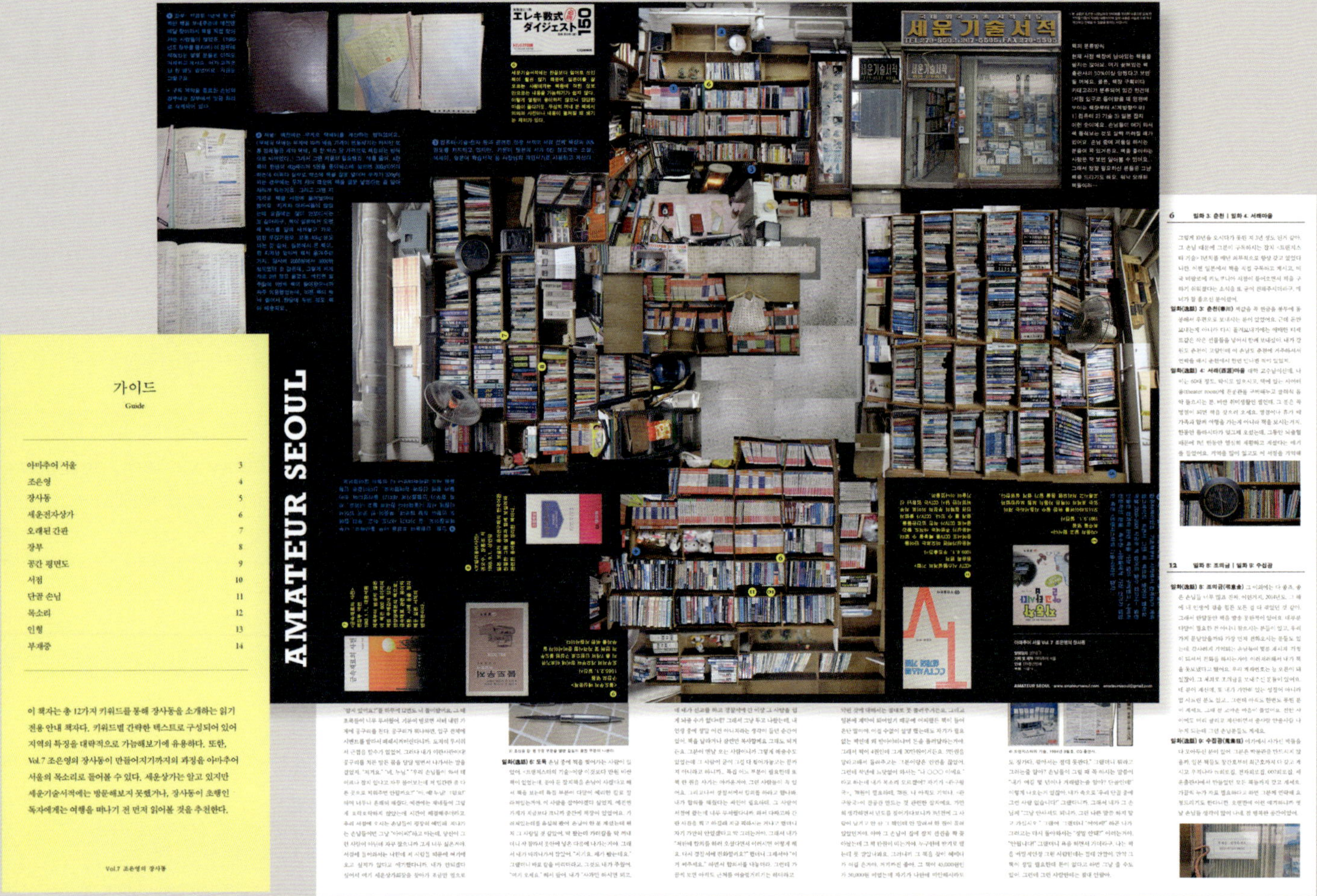

AMATEUR SEOUL

D
Yejin Cho & Hyein You
DS
Amateur Seoul

2009-2021

Amateurs aren't professionals, as they don't earn a living from a certain skill set. Yet, the Latin root "amator" refers to someone who loves something. It is the creators' love for design as well as for Seoul that they find the meaning of the name.

When the designers began to see the rapid development going on and realized that many neighborhoods would not be around for long, they took it upon themselves to build a record of Seoul as it is now. The city, people, and buildings became their focal points and soon they began to look for other outlets like workshops or exhibitions to continue this archive as well as to explore the city they love so much.

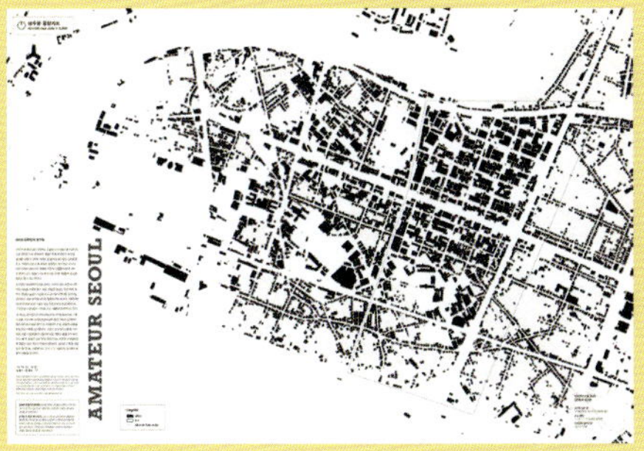

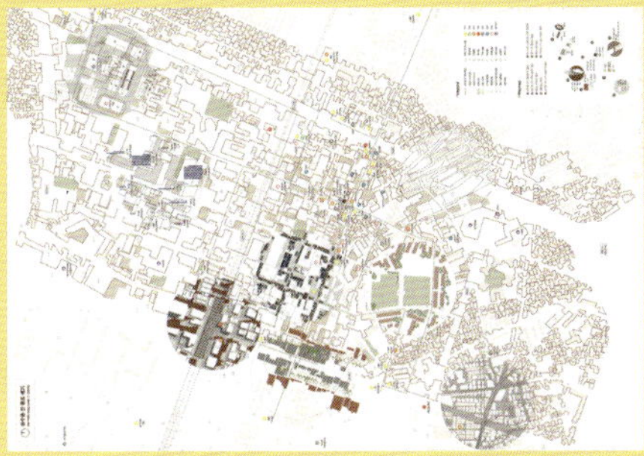

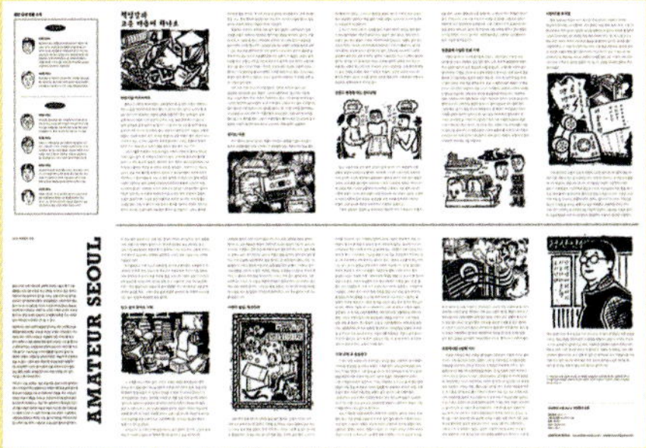

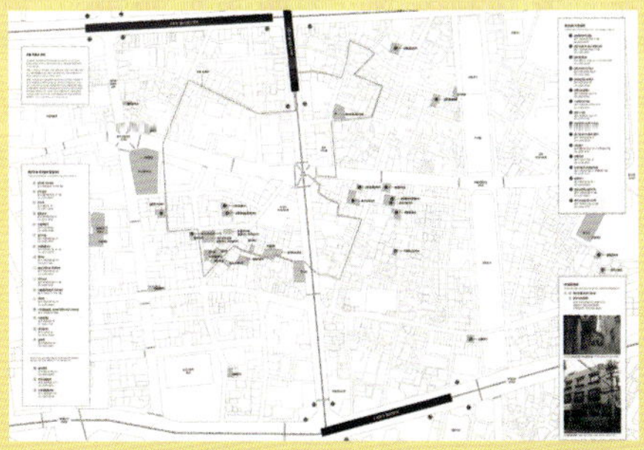

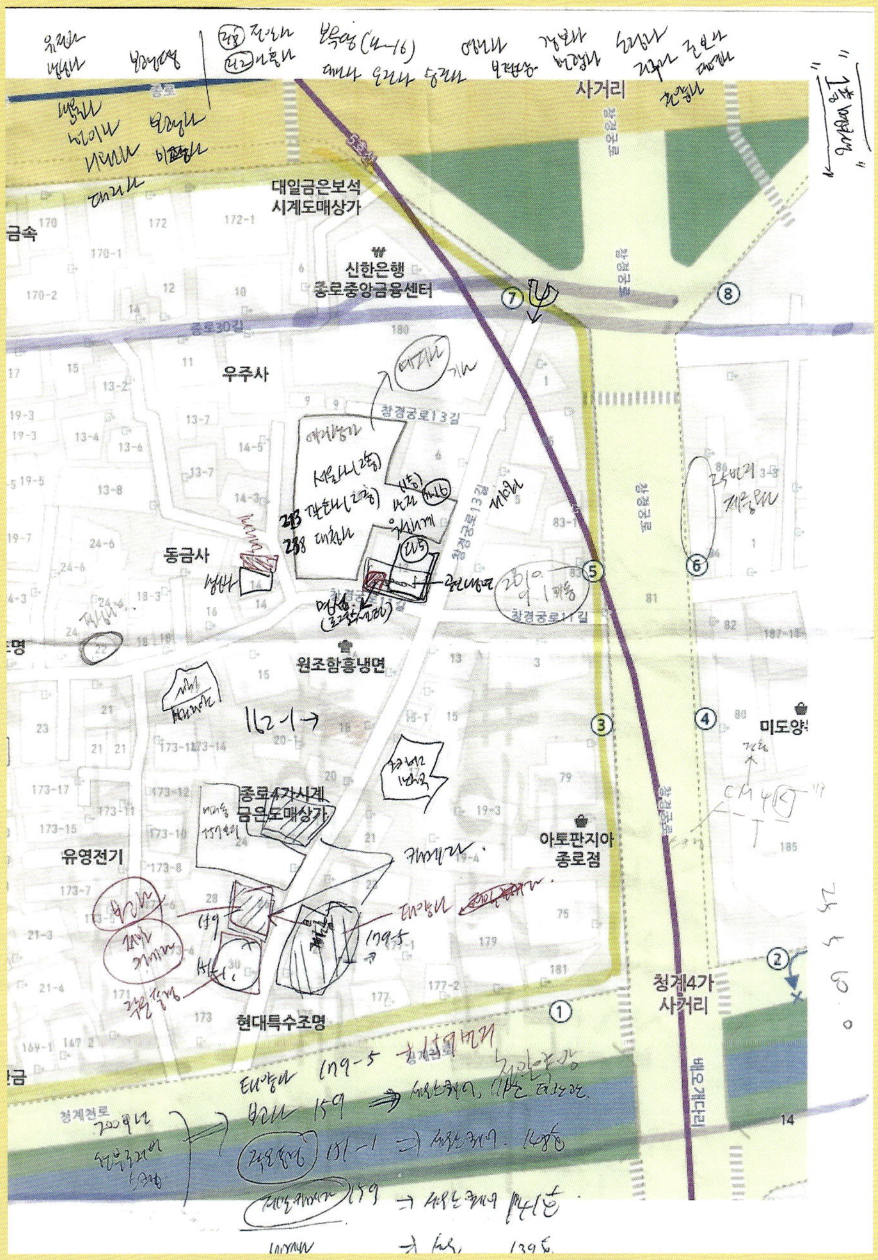

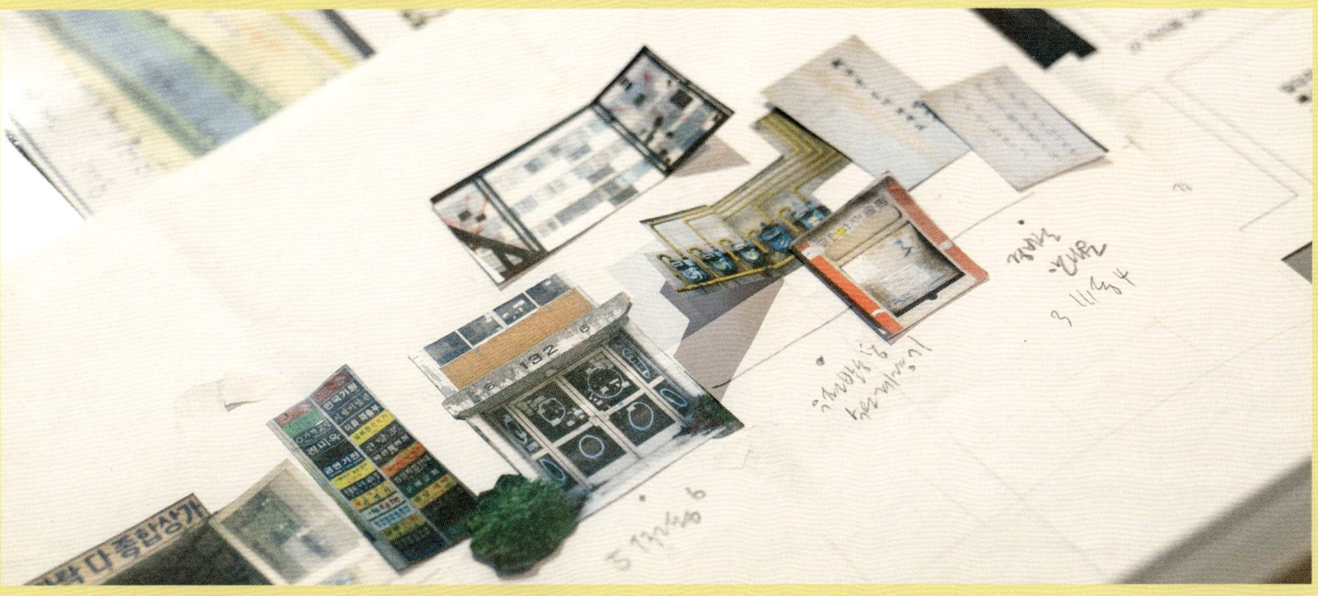

GUIDE BOOK **Page:** 16 **Dimension:** 115×238.5mm **Weight:** 120g **Paper/Material:** Issue Specific **Binding:** Saddle Stitching

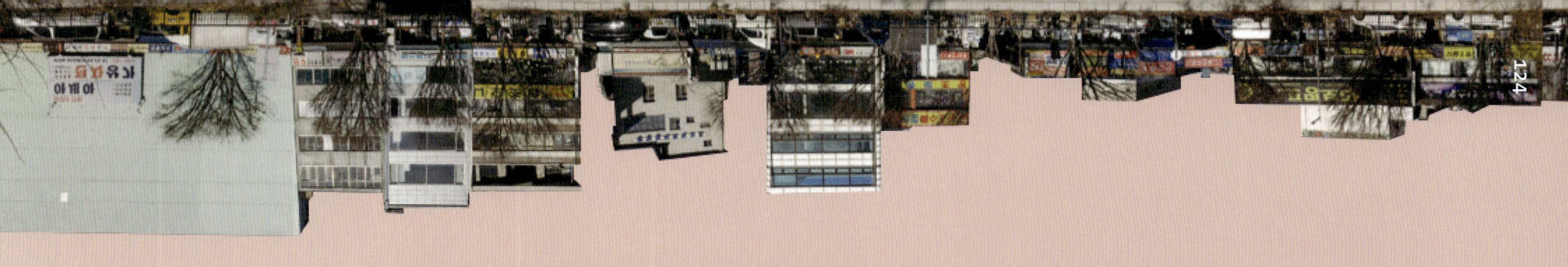

AMATEUR SEOUL

Vol. 8 우리의 예지동 Our Yeji-dong

세운 상가와 광장시장 사이 시계와 귀금속 도매상 거리로 잘 알려진 동네 예지동. 그중에서도 '시계 골목'은 한때 오가는 사람들로 발 디딜 틈 없었던 전성기를 누렸다. 그러나 재개발 바람이 불고 1990년대 삐삐와 휴대폰의 등장으로 점차 잊혀지면서 현재는 영업 중인 곳보다 이전하거나 폐업한 곳들이 훨씬 많다. '오늘'의 예지동은 그렇게 떠나간 빈자리들로 쓸쓸함이 묻어나지만, 1960년 시계 장인에게 듣는 동네 이야기는 활기차고 따뜻했다. 우리는 신문기사나 블로그, 그리고 예지동 사람들에게 전해 들은 생생한 이야기를 통해 '옛' 예지동의 풍경을 퍼즐 맞추듯 어렴풋하게나마 가늠해보려 했다. 2023년 예지동 세운 4구역에 완공 예정인 18층 복합단지로 예지동을 처음 맞이할 '미래'의 누군가에게 이 지도가 흥미로운 단서가 되길 바란다.

Located between Sewoon Mall and Gwangjang Market, Yeji-dong is a well-known district for watch and jewelry wholesalers. Among them, the "clock alley" enjoyed a prime time when it was very crowded with people. However, due to the effects of redevelopment and the emergence of pagers and mobile phones in the 1990s, a lot of stores have moved or closed since the present day.

These days Yeji-dong is desolate due to the empty stores and places left by so many people, but the story of the neighborhood that we heard from the watchmaker with a career of 60 years was lively and warm. We tried to draw what the scenery of Yeji-dong in the old days looked like through the vivid stories from neighbors, newspapers, and blogs. We hope that this map will be an interesting clue to anyone whom Yeji-dong will welcome for the first time in the future when the new 18-story complex is built in the 4th district of Yeji-dong.

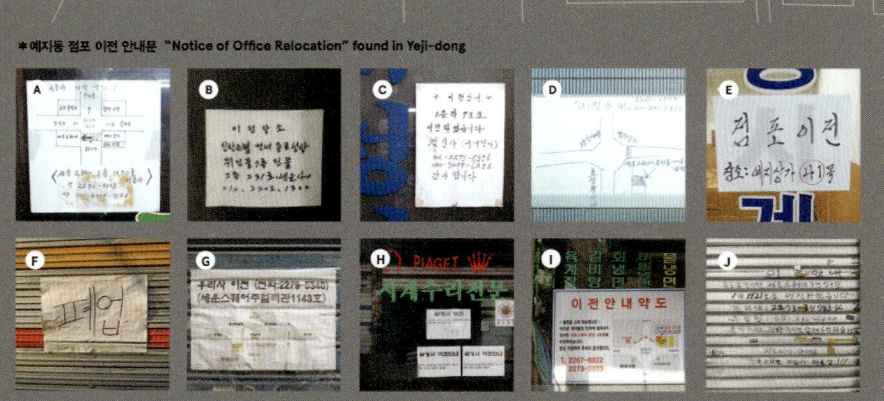

＊예지동 점포 이전 안내문 "Notice of Office Relocation" found in Yeji-dong

③ 종로 Jong-ro

세종로139번지 세종로 사거리에서 종로구 종로6가 79번지 동대문에 이르는 가로로 길이 2.8km, 너비 40m, 왕복 8차선이며 세종로 사거리에서부터 1~6가(街)로 구분되며, 도로를 중심으로 상가가 밀집한 서울의 대표적인 상업지구이다. 네이버 지식백과 – 두산백과

It is an 8-lane two-way street with a length of 2.8km and a width of 40m. It is divided into 1 to 6 streets starting from Sejong-ro intersection, and it is a representative commercial district of Seoul where shopping streets are concentrated around the street. NAVER Encyclopedia-Doosan Encyclopedia

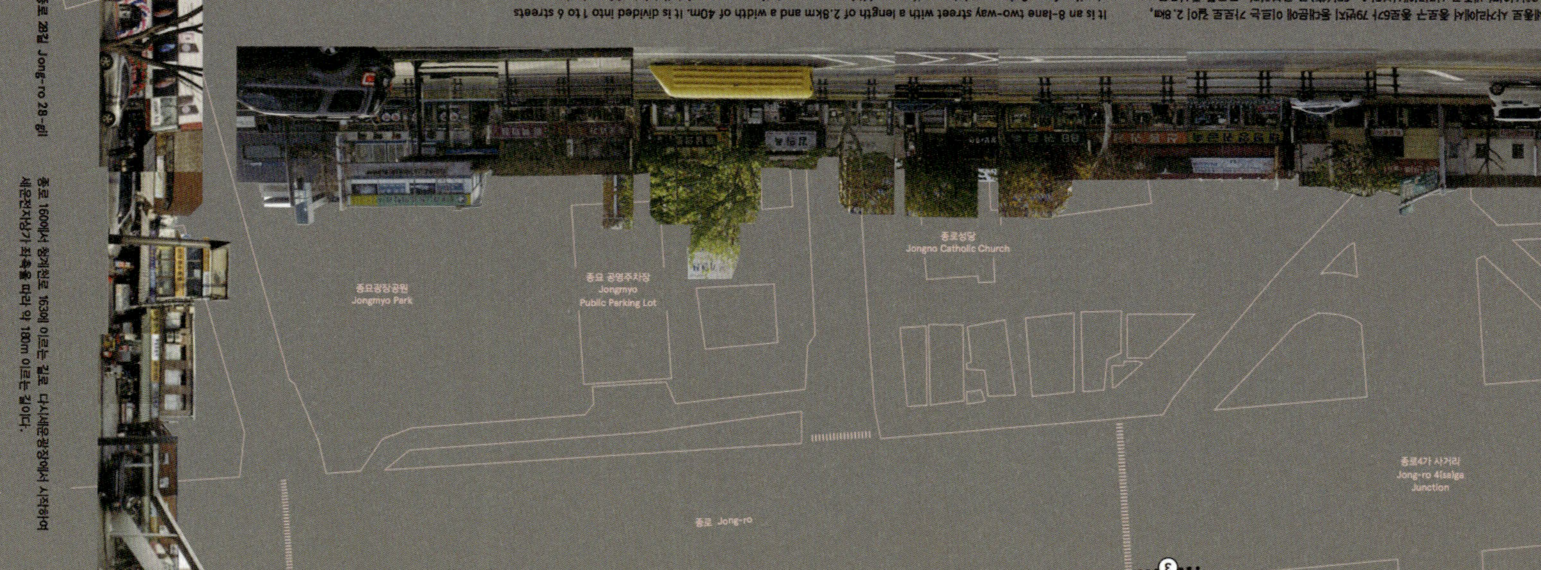

...palaces of the Joseon Dynasty.
...gyo) in Seongbuk-gu.
...ean Encyclopedia

④ 종로 28길 Jong-ro 28-gil

종로 160에서 청계천로 163에 이르는 길로 다시세운광장에서 시작하여 세운전자상가 좌측을 따라 약 180m 이르는 길이다.

It ...
fro...

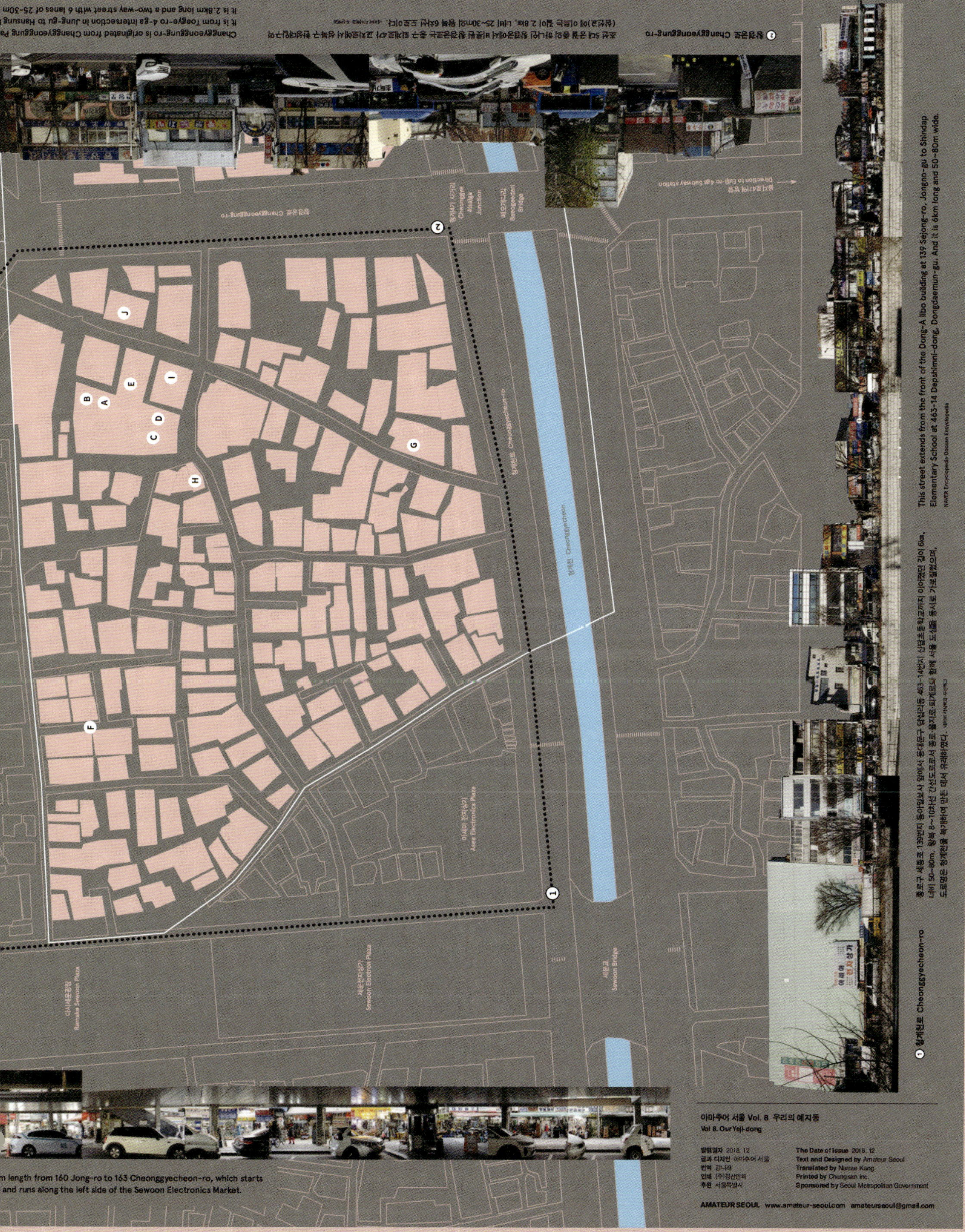

Binding: Accordion Fold

Paper/Material: Issue Specific

MAP Page: 2 Dimension: 690×480mm

MAY I TOUCH YOUR HAIR?

D
Jie Zang

2020

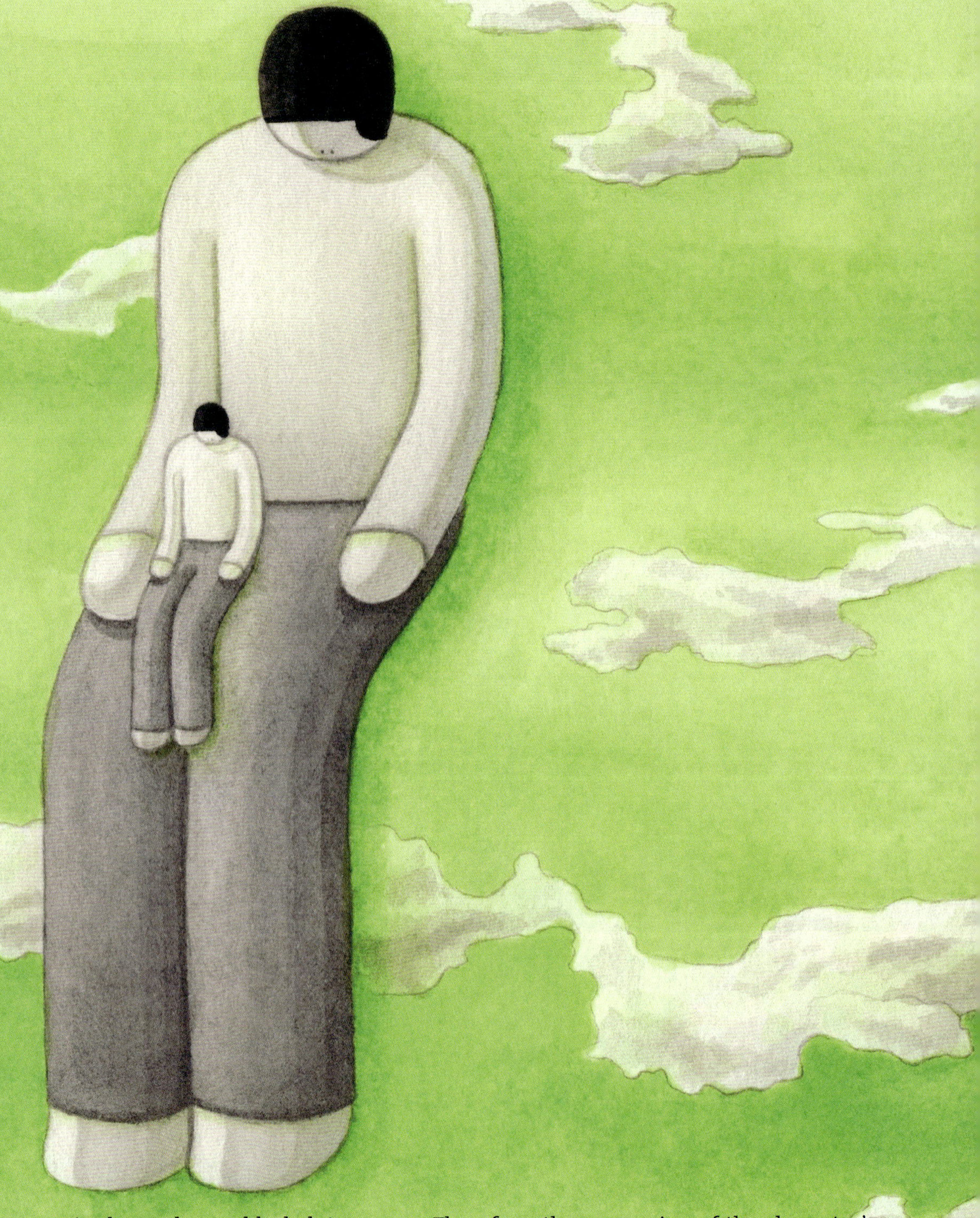

The character in the Butterfly Boy series has only two black dots as eyes. Therefore, the expression of the character's emotion is quite limited, while surprisingly, it can contain more emotions. Most people commonly associate butterfly with innocence, but in this work it represents desire.

The collection includes the designer's individual works in watercolor, acrylic, and clay. The content is a collection of his projects over different periods, so there is no continuous story line in the book. However, readers can view four images at the same time by unfolding the pages to the left and right, which makes reading less of a one-way linear action. The ordering between left and right and the rhythm of reading are determined by the readers, which adds dynamism to the narrative layout.

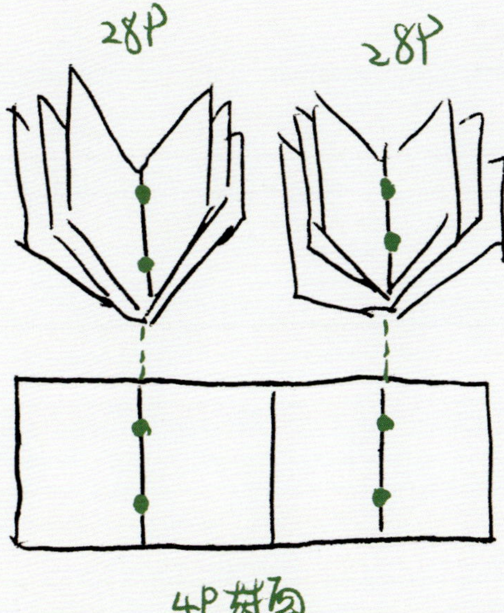

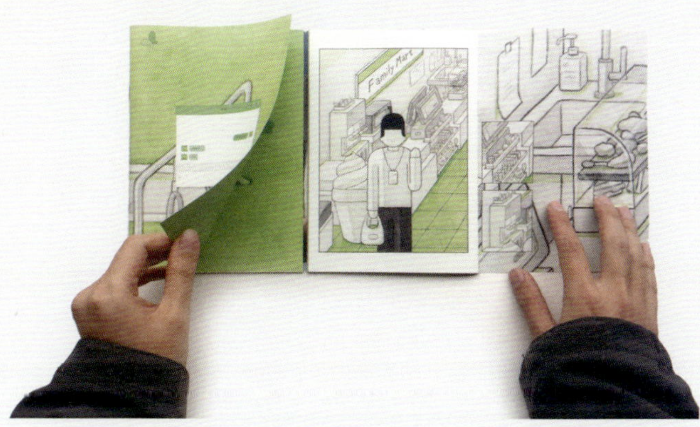

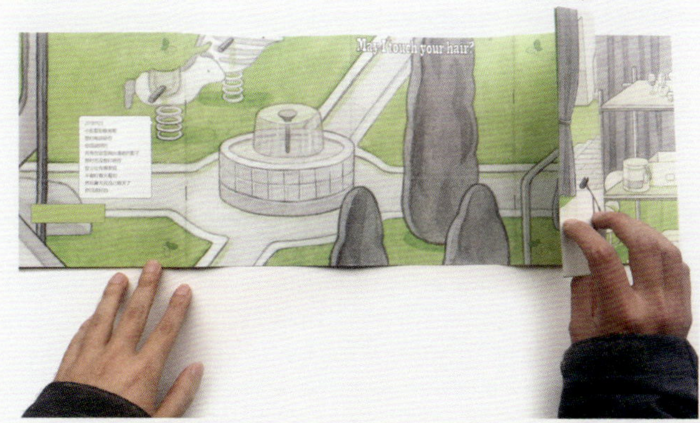

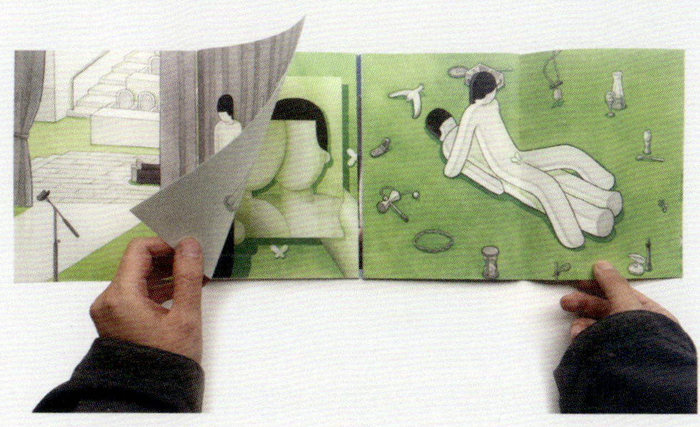

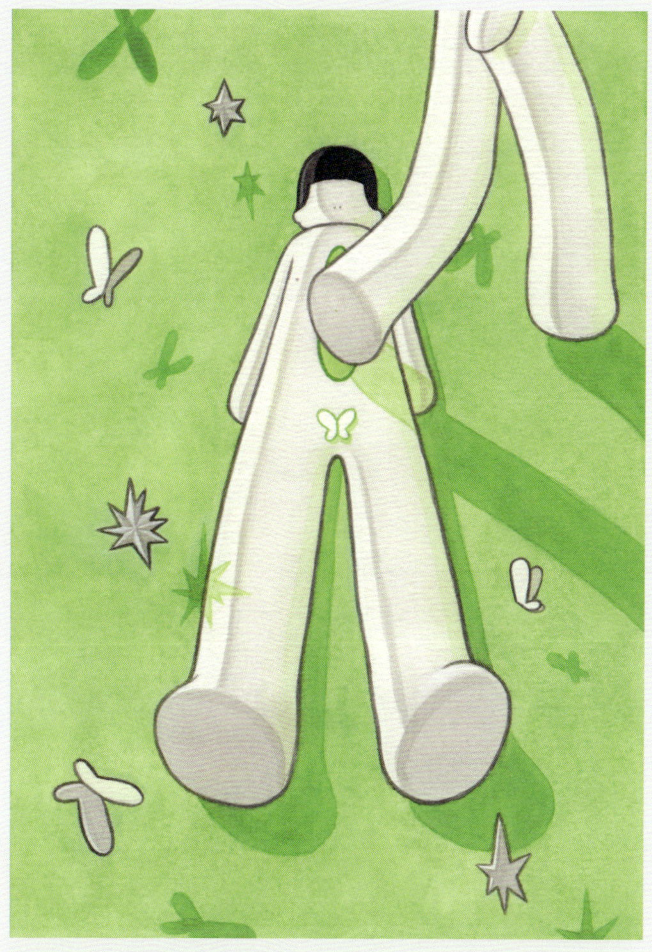

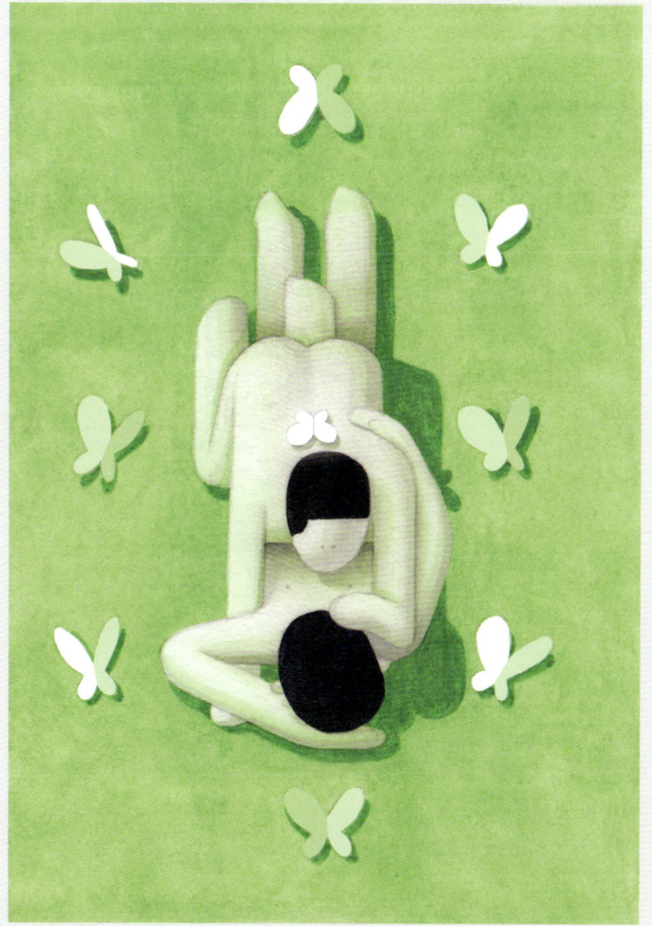

Page: 48 **Dimension:** 140×205×5mm **Weight:** 80g **Paper/Material:** Irish Sensation Paper **Binding:** Saddle Stitching

WANDER OVER HER FACE

AD, CD & D
Rockid Hu
P
Naomi

2020

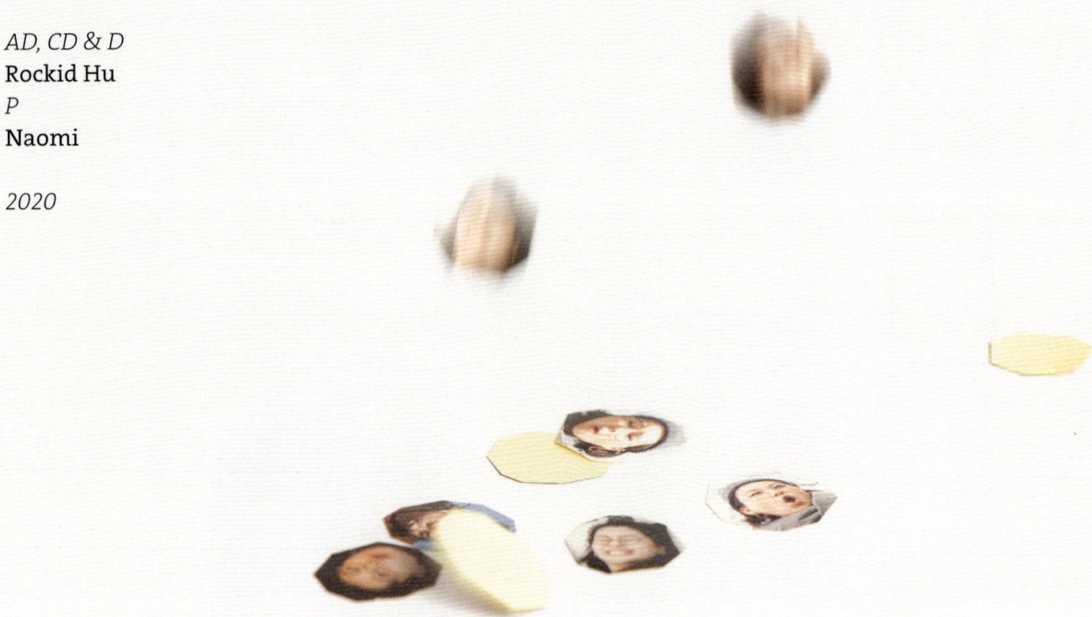

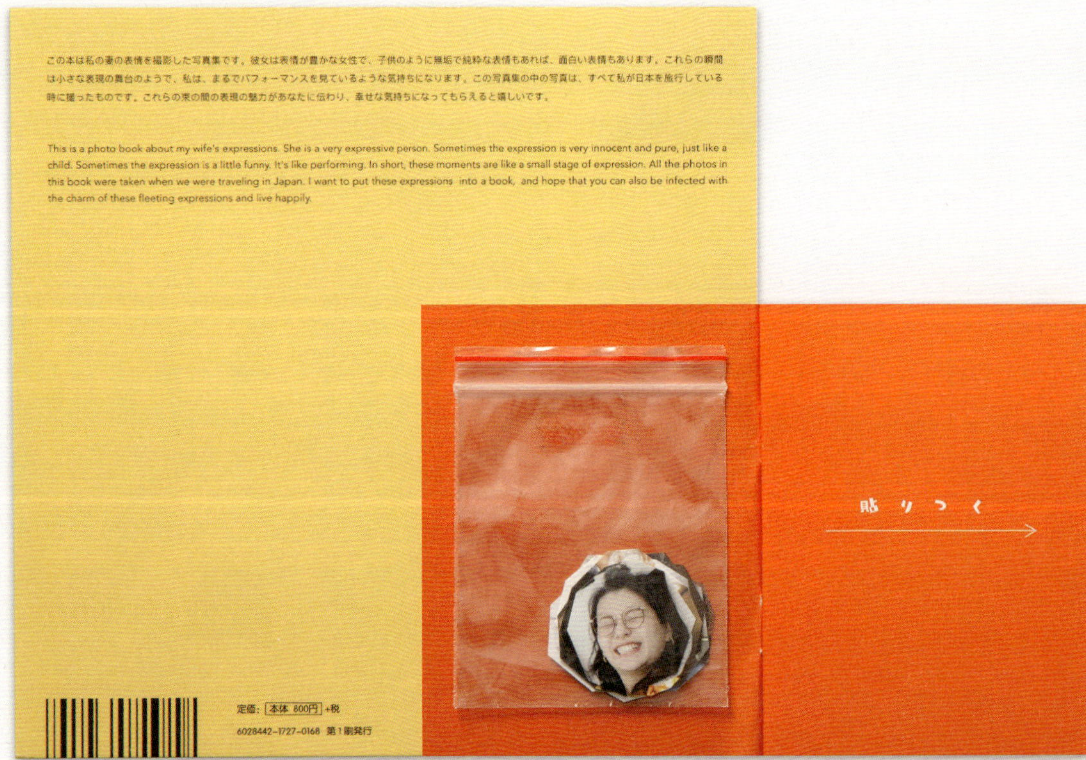

The images in this book were the unposed facial expressions of the designer's wife, which were taken when they studied in Kyoto. The designer created this book as an interactive game book where, as the title suggests, readers can "wander over her face".

The designer turned all the facial expressions in the book into stickers, and the readers have to match these stickers with their original photos. On one hand, the designer hoped to provide readers with a chance to observe the expressions. On the other hand, readers have to pay enough attention to observe everyday images during the interaction process, and appreciate the charm of the expressions we see every day but are easily ignored.

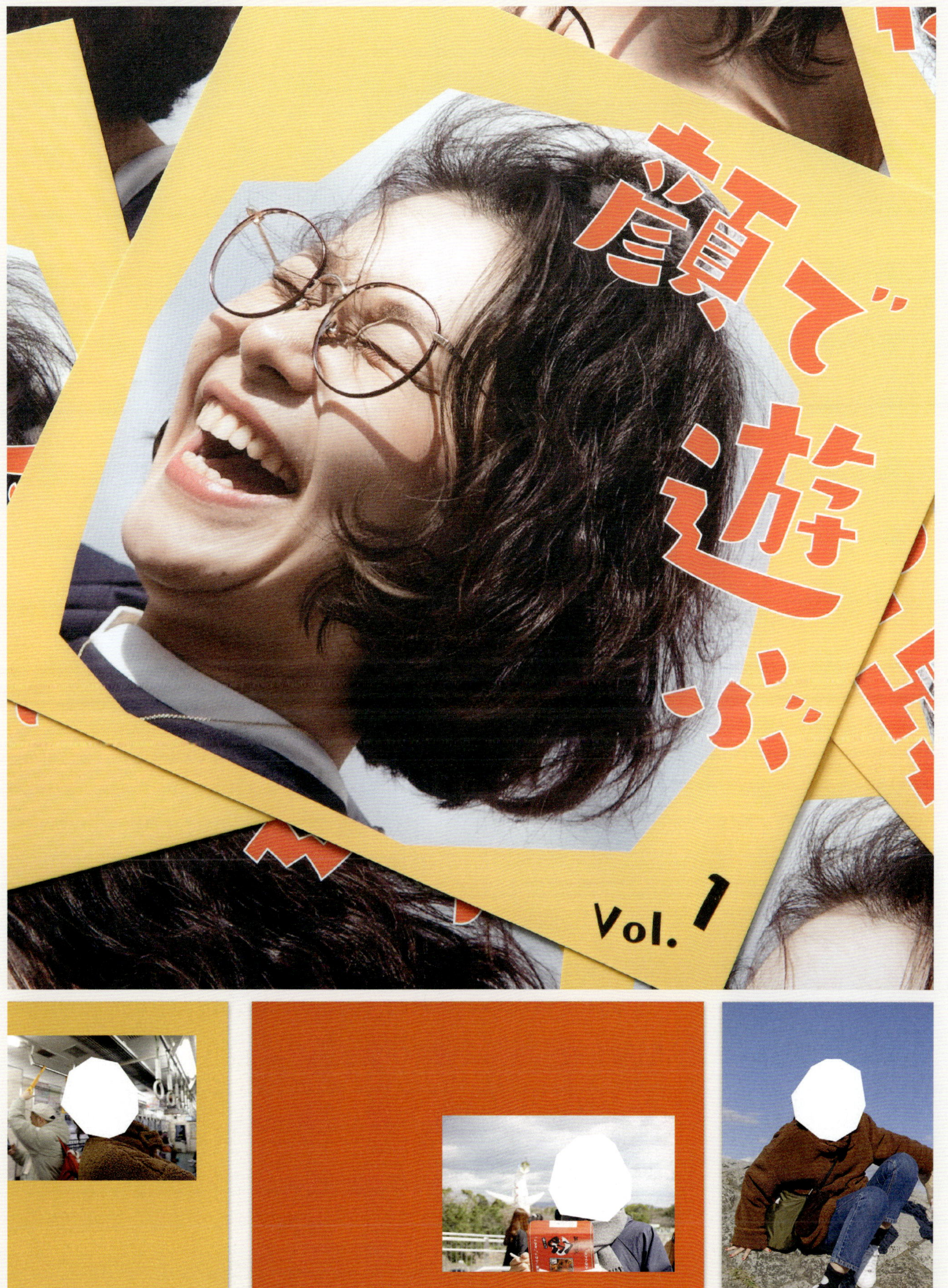

Page: 30 Dimension: 170×170mm Weight: 38g Paper/Material: Sensation Paper 250g (Cover); Matte Art Paper 157g (Inside Page) Binding: Saddle Stitching; Manual Paste

IN•SCAPE

D
Wuthipol Ujathammarat

2019

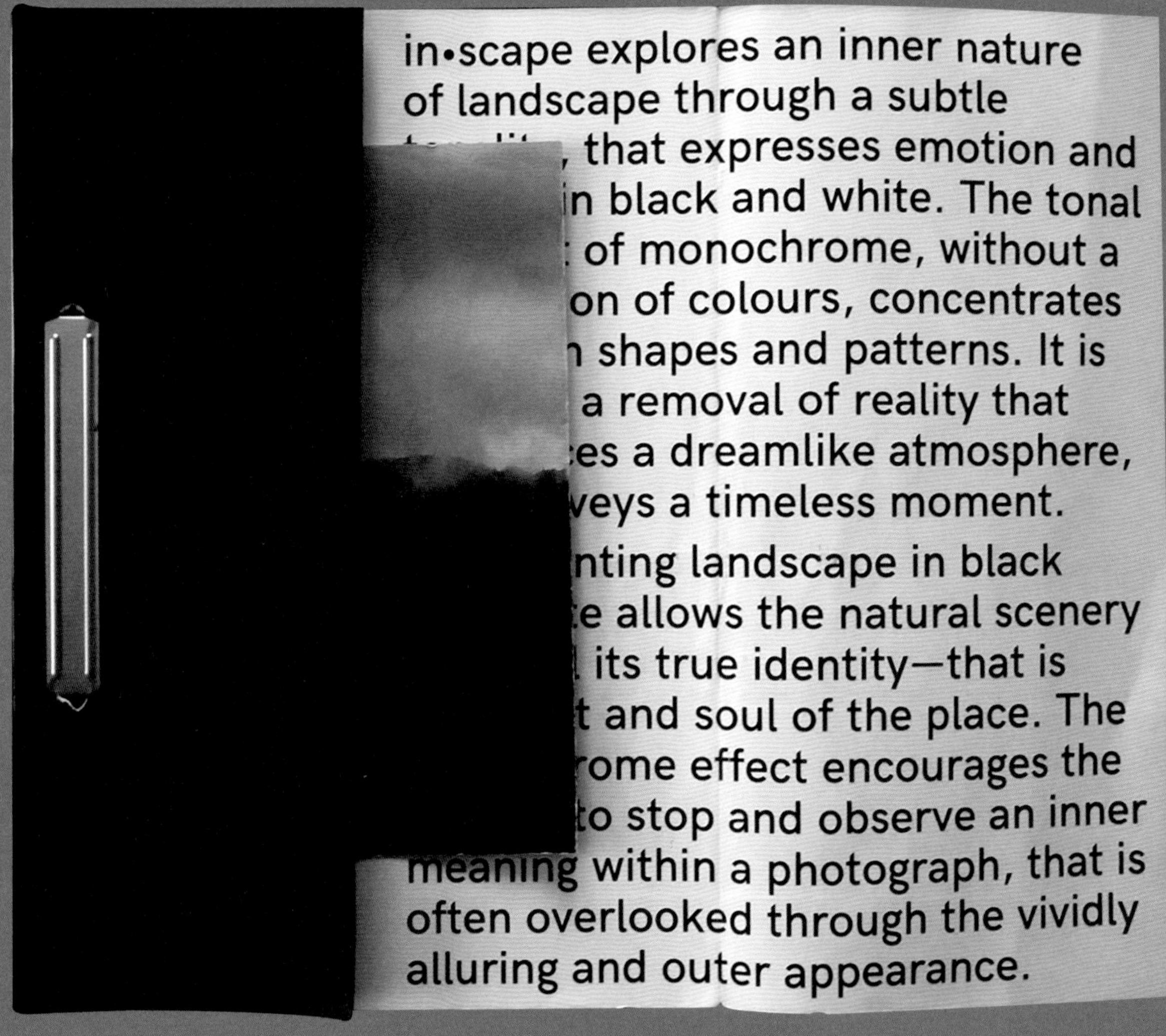

in•scape unveils an interesting way of seeing natural landscape and scenery. It inspires the readers to more closely observe emotions and thoughts that are expressed through sequences of black and white images. Taking away the distraction of color, it explores the inner nature of landscape through a tonal contrast of monochromes, concentrating solely on shape and pattern.

The use of french fold design encourages the readers to seek and peek through the inner pages and between pages, to see what else there is to discover—much like how you would observe natural scenery when you go on a hike. It perfectly blends the reading experience with the content both visually and interactively.

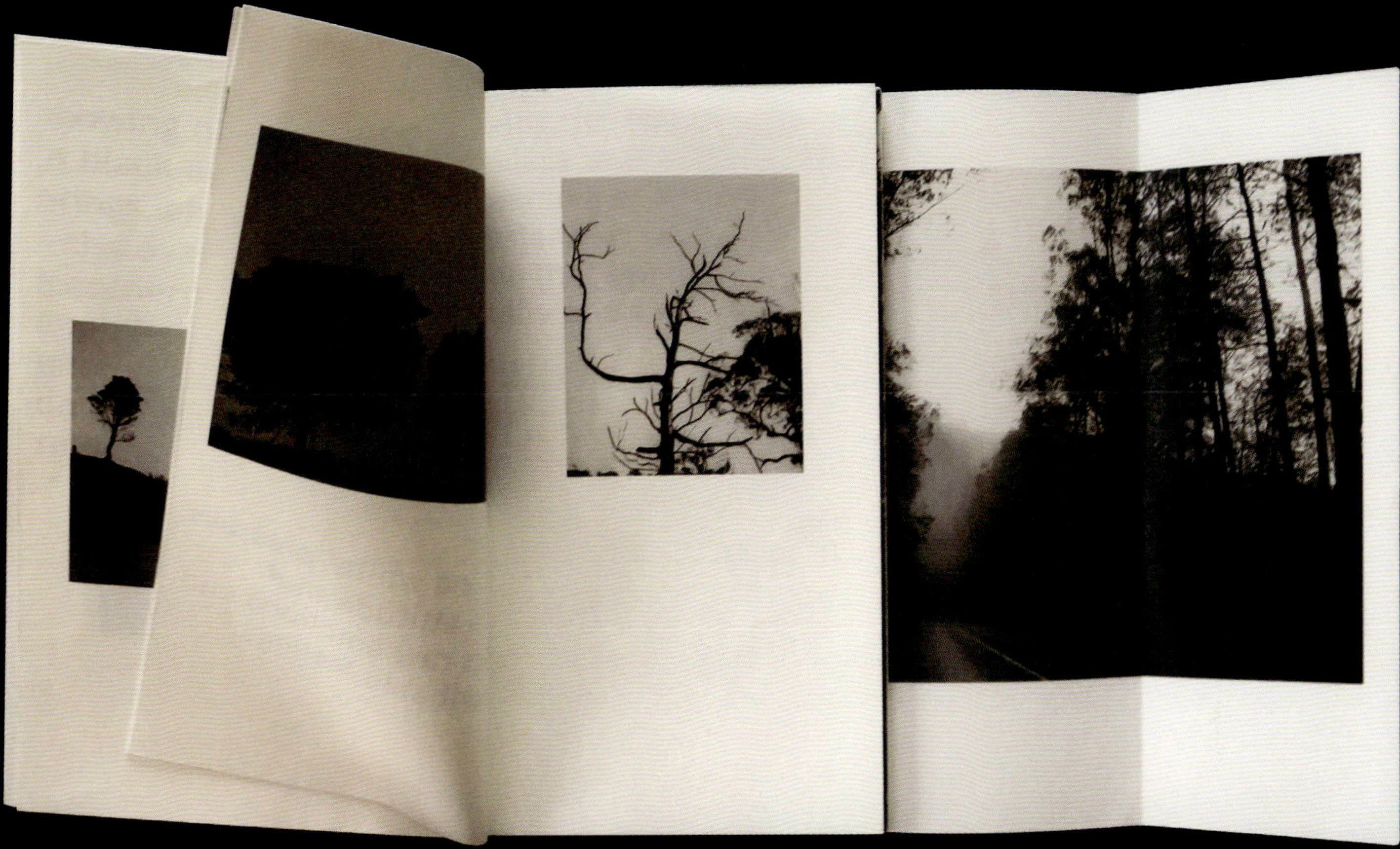

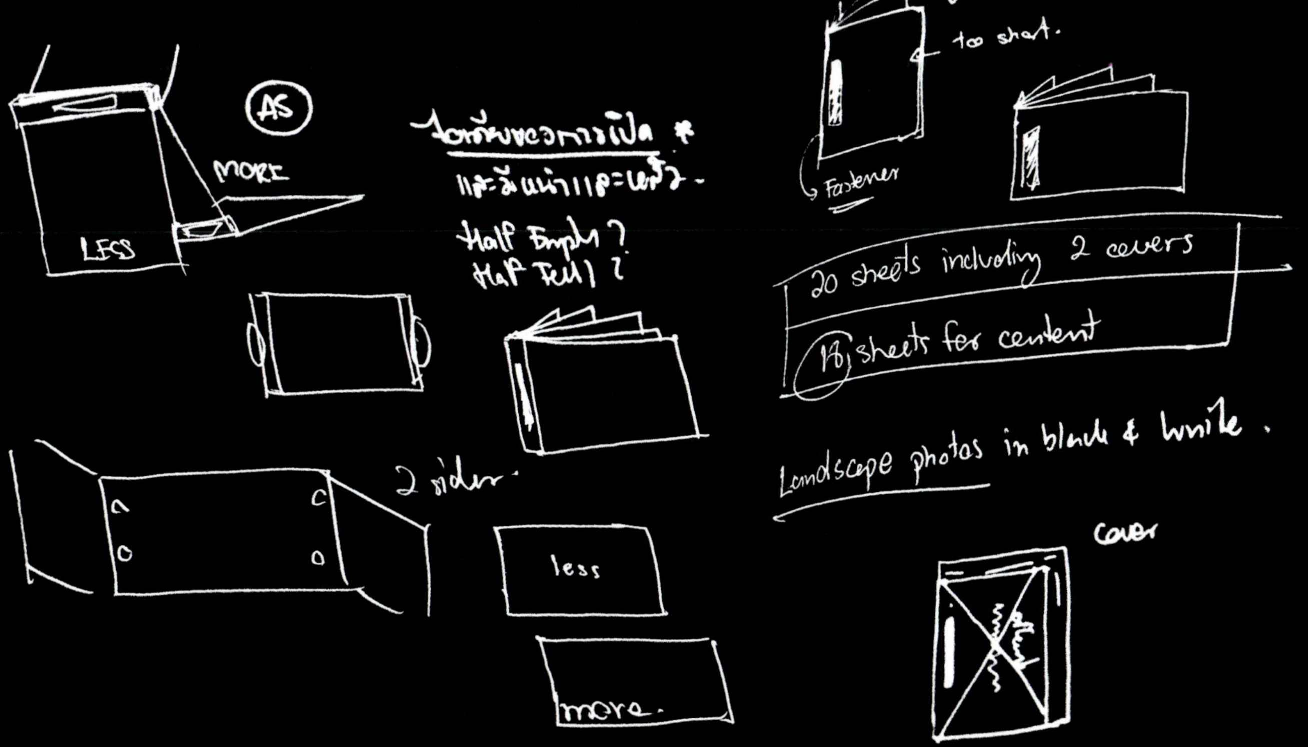

Paper/Material: Green Offset Binding: French Fold

Page: 48 Dimension: 148×210mm Weight: 140g

MY INSIDE GHOST

AD, CD & D
Nozomi Aoyama
P
Ryota Mizusako
DS
non Editions

2019

The designer created illustrations in which a ghost quietly stands in the landscape featuring mountains or houses. The size of the paper is A3, which is folded in four and bound with rubber bands. Each page is a poster when unfolded. This publication is different from typical mass-produced books. The paper, rubber bands, cards, and stamps used in each book are all different from each other, which provides readers with a strong feeling of originality.

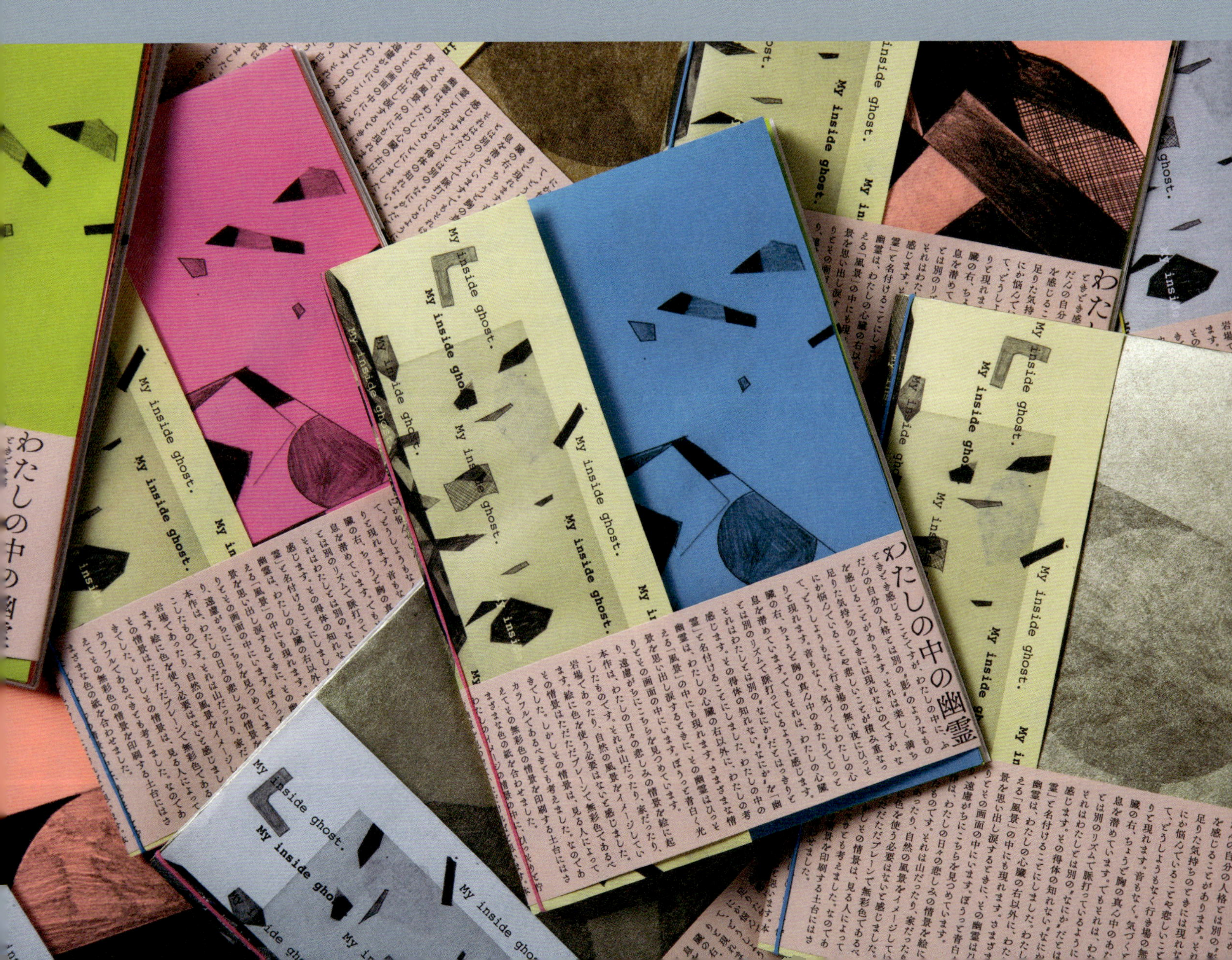

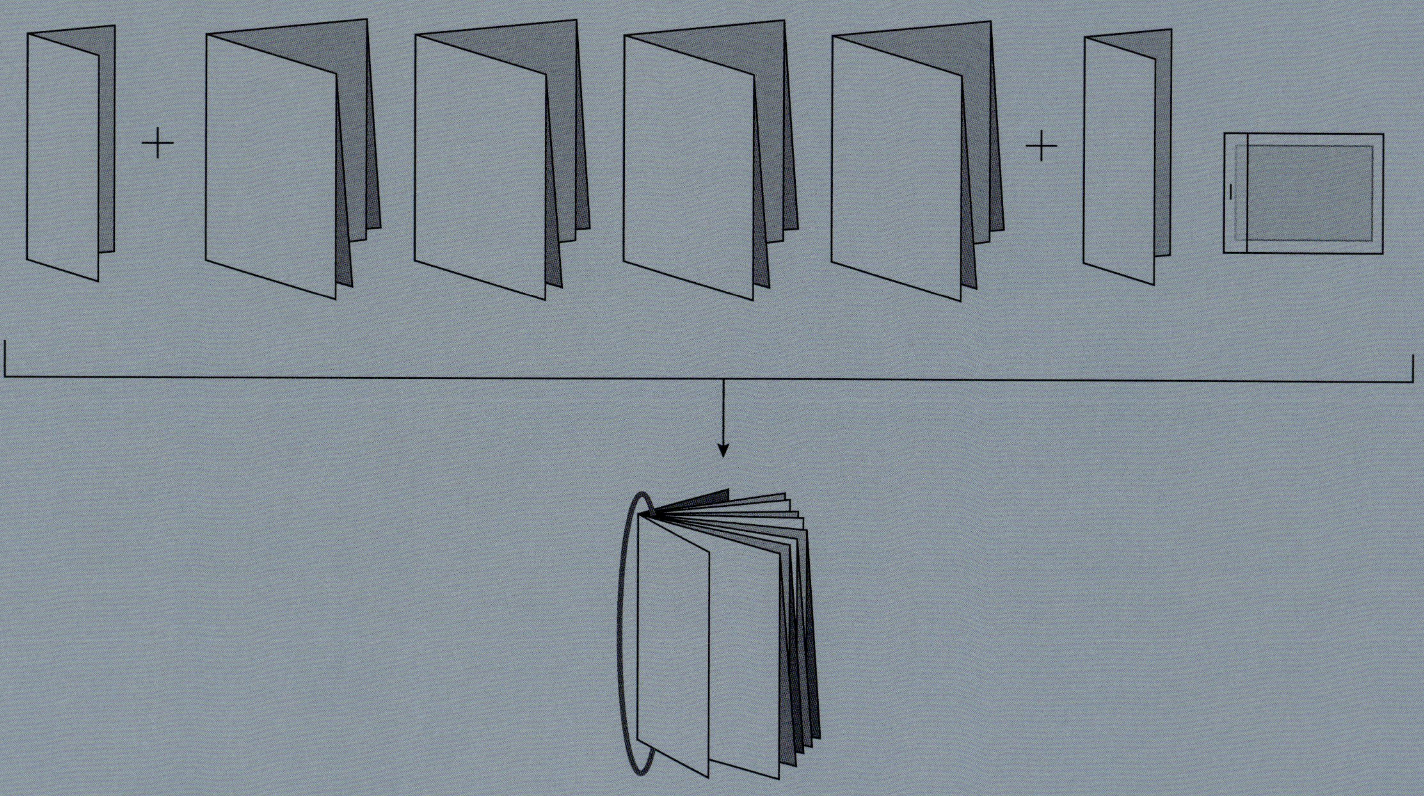

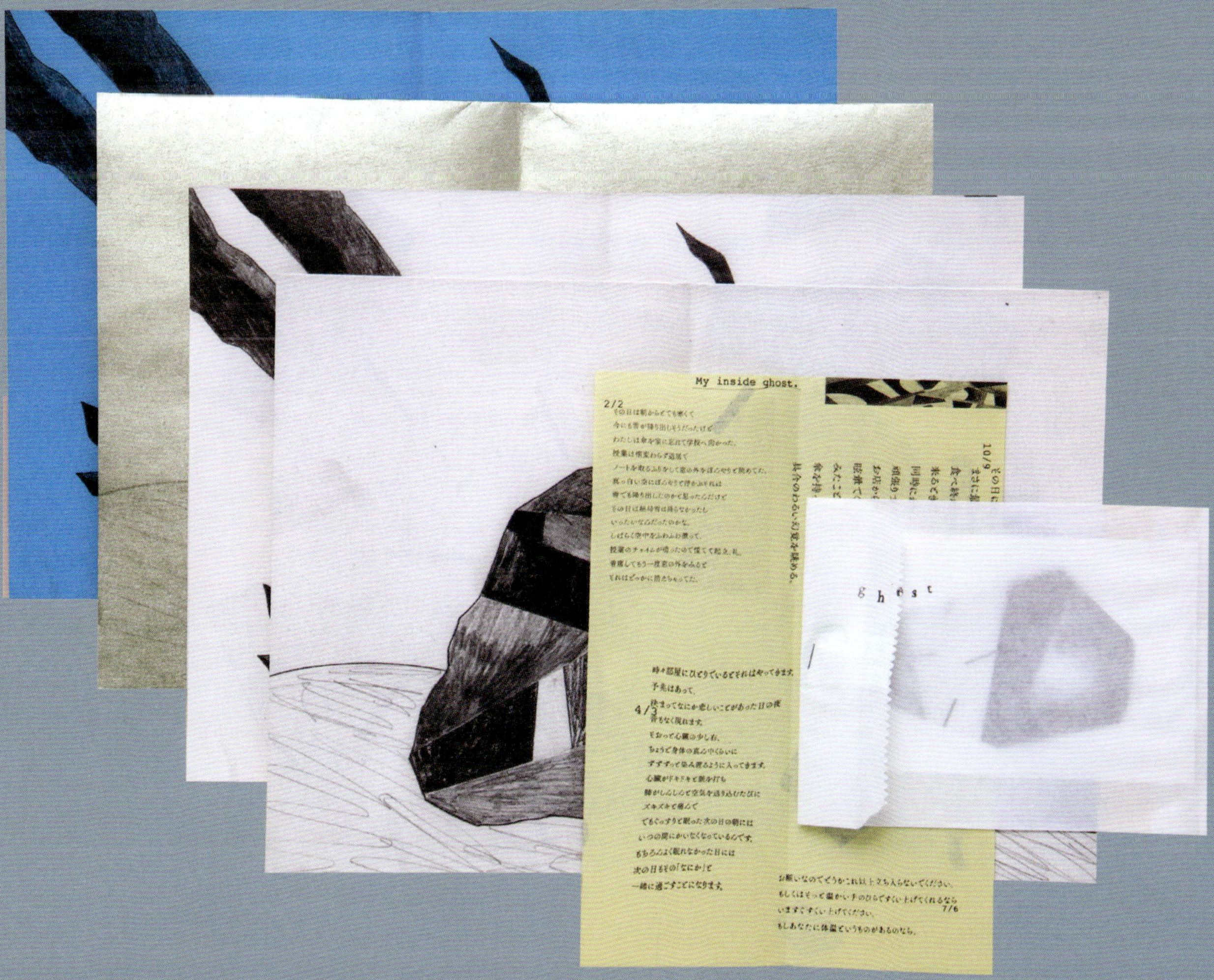

Binding: Rubber Band

Weight: 70g

Page: 20 Dimension: 148×210mm

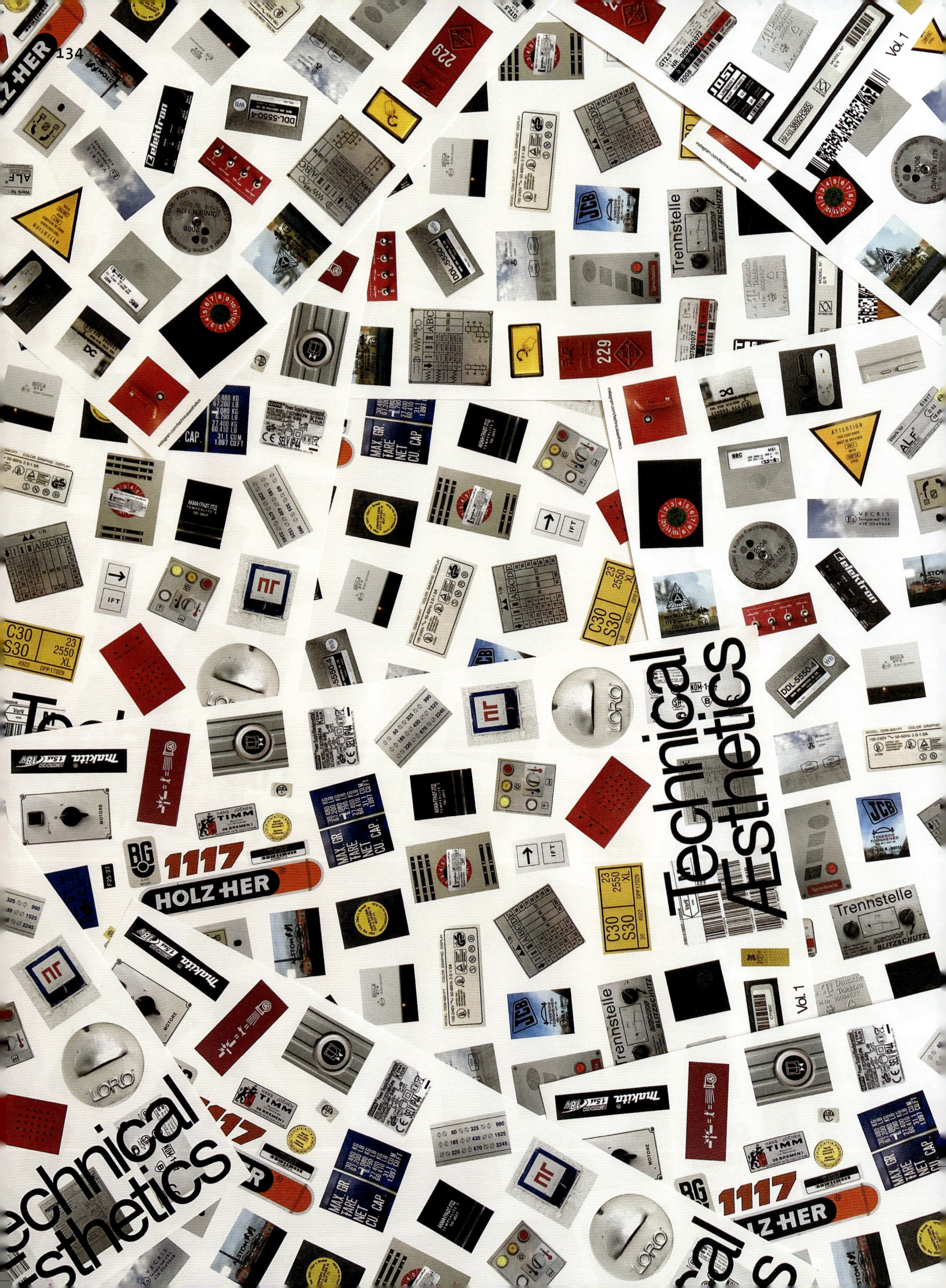
Technical Aesthetics
Vol. 1

AD, CD, D & P
Kseniia Stavrova
DS
Orka Collective

2020

TECHNICAL ÆSTHETICS

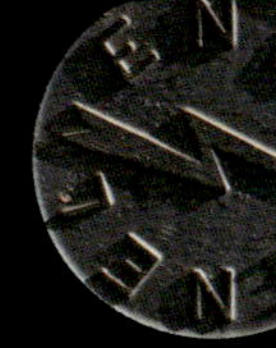

Technical Æsthetics is a personal archive of technical graphics. In 2018 the designer started to collect fragments and samples of technical graphics, a field which the designer has always been obsessed with.

The design of the zine is very minimal and technical itself. It is all about the content and it is in center of everything without any unnecessary decorations. The edition is limited to 20 items. Each one comes with an A3 poster and a sticker set, and each copy is numbered by hand.

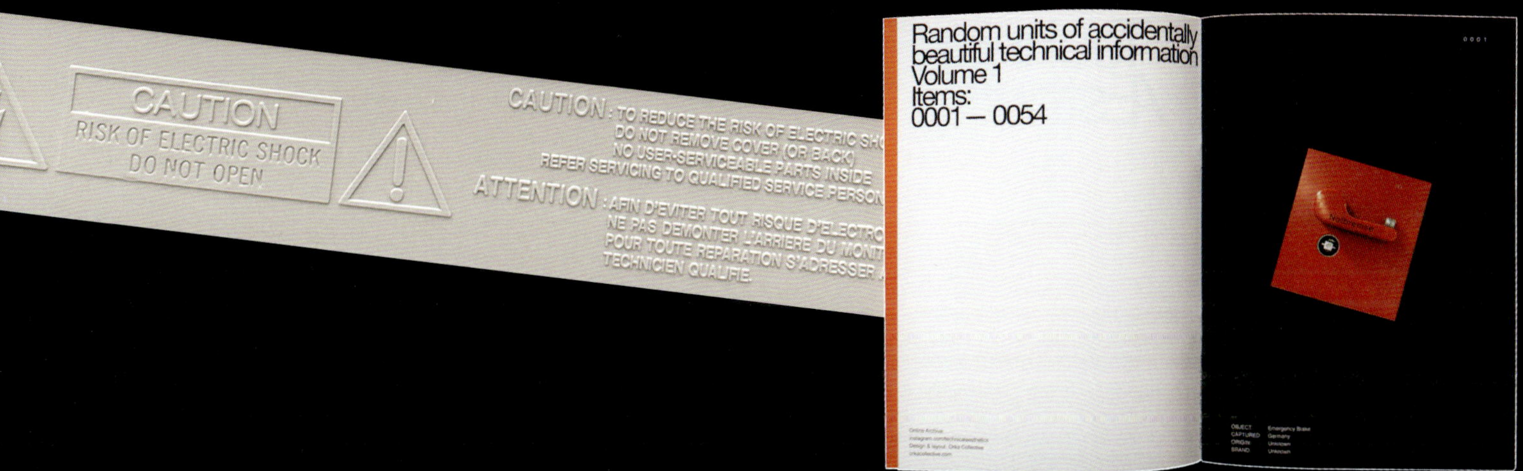

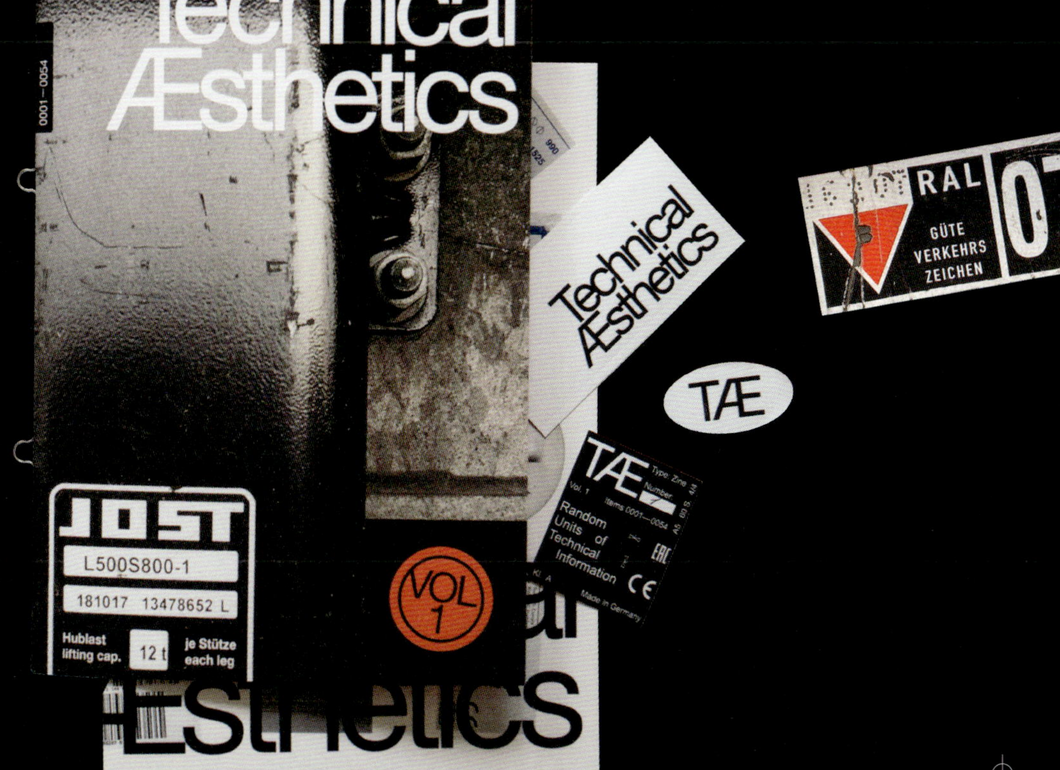

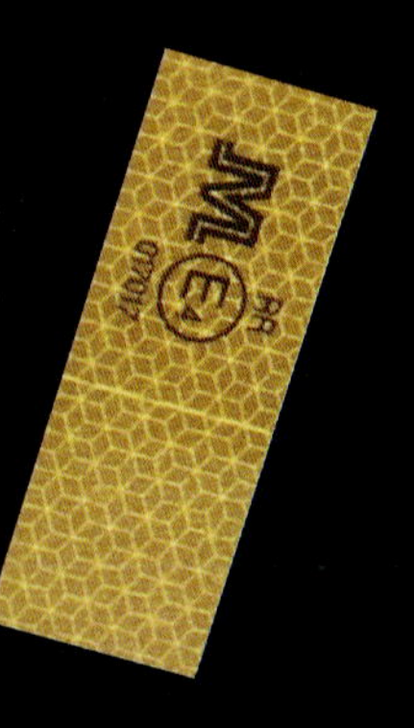

Binding: Loop Stitching

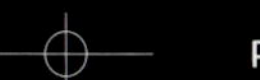

Page: 60 Dimension: 148×210mm

GONGGI

D
0.1 & The object
P
Avec Studio
DS
ADD TO CART

2020

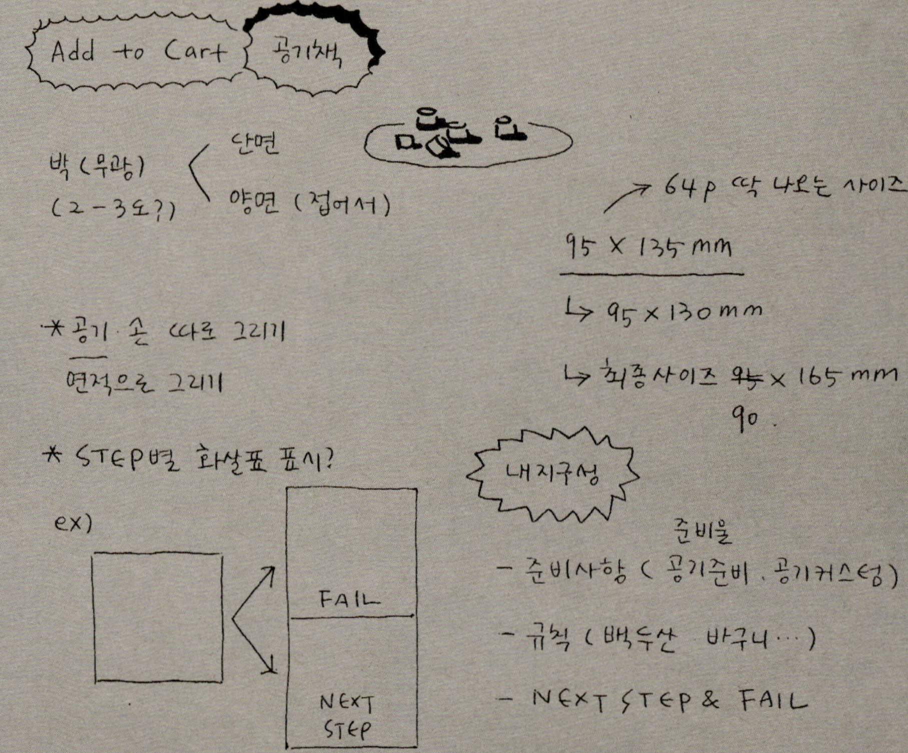

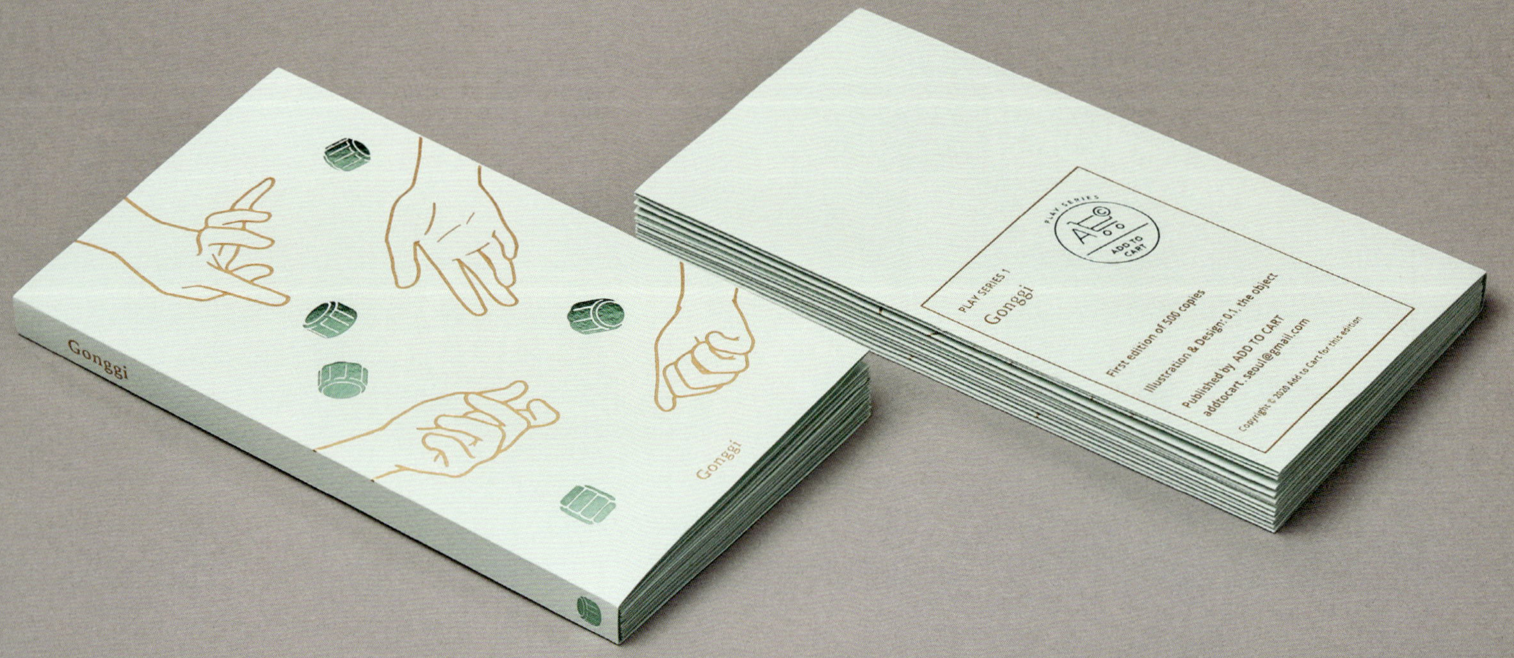

Gonggi is the first play-book series from the studio ADD TO CART. It explores gonggi, a traditional Korean game similar to jackstones. It is printed in two colors using foil stamping so that the angle of the light changes how the book looks. The continuous and repeating images are presented in an accordion book that is hand-bound, so that the beginning and end of the book are all connected as one.

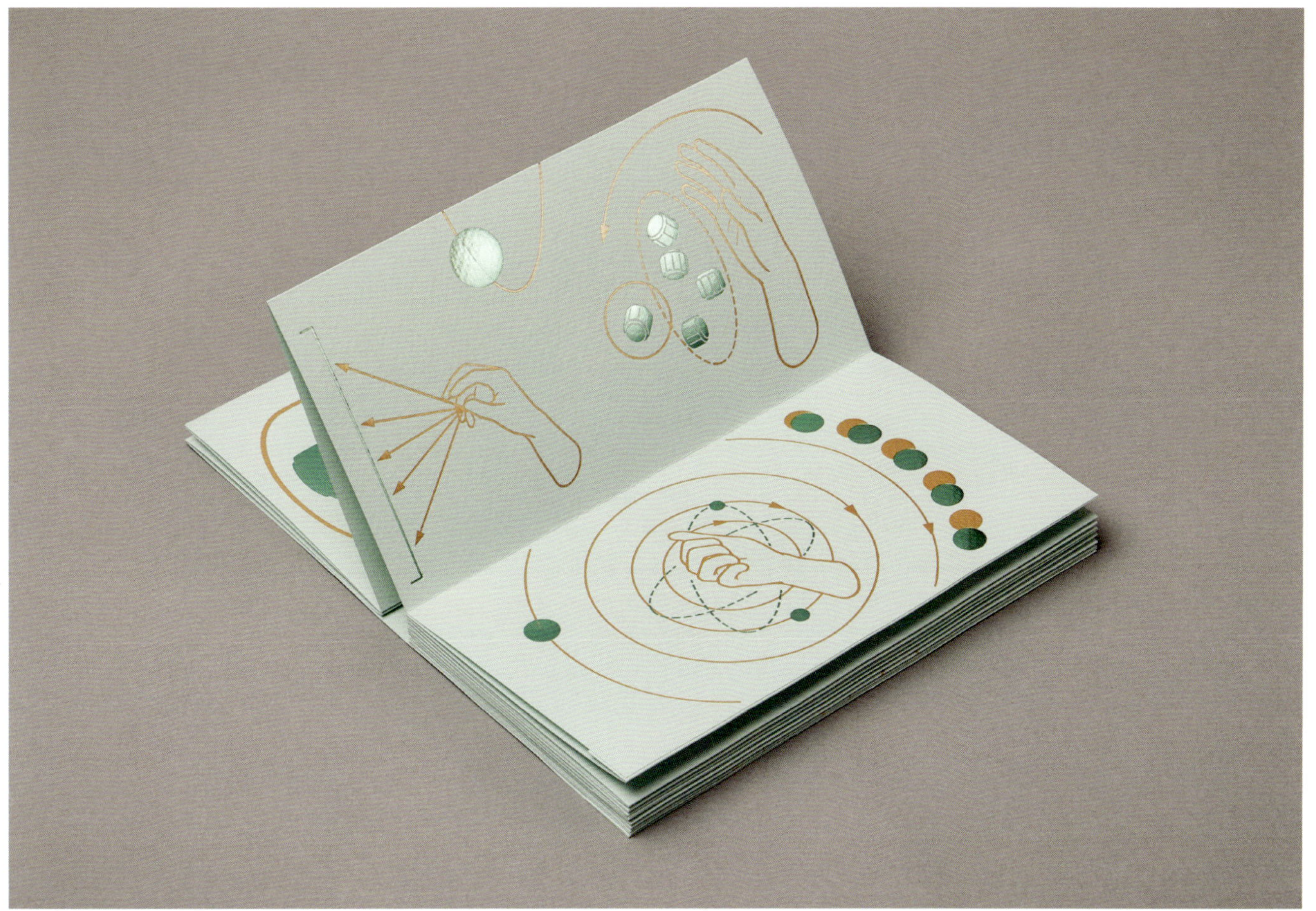

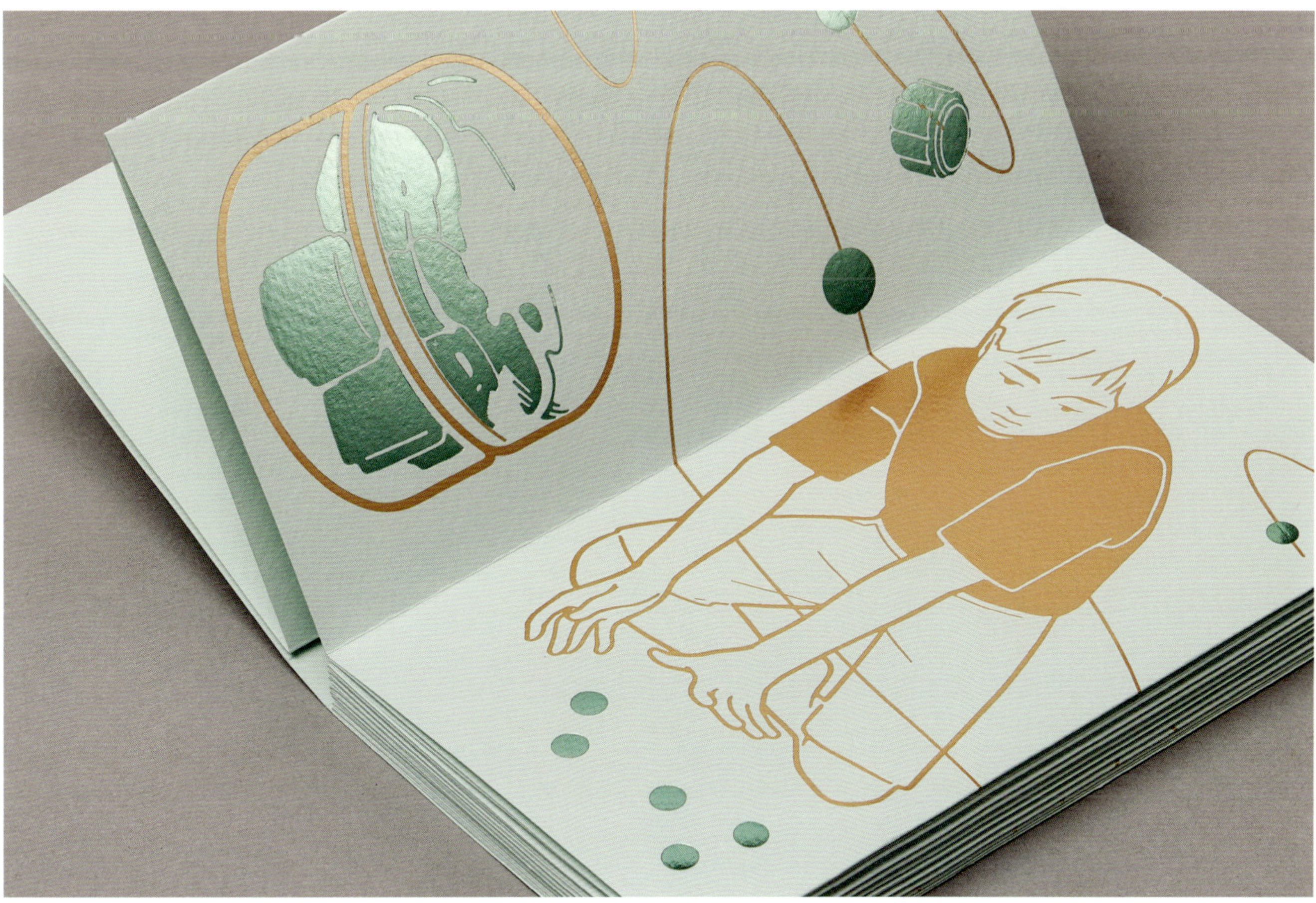

Paper/Material: Magic Touch 180g **Binding:** Accordion Fold

Page: 24 **Dimension:** 150×210mm **Weight:** 70g

THE 70'S — THE ZONE

AD
Francisco Ortega
CD
per(r)ucho
D
Jaime Ortega & Francisco Ortega
DS
per(r)ucho

2021

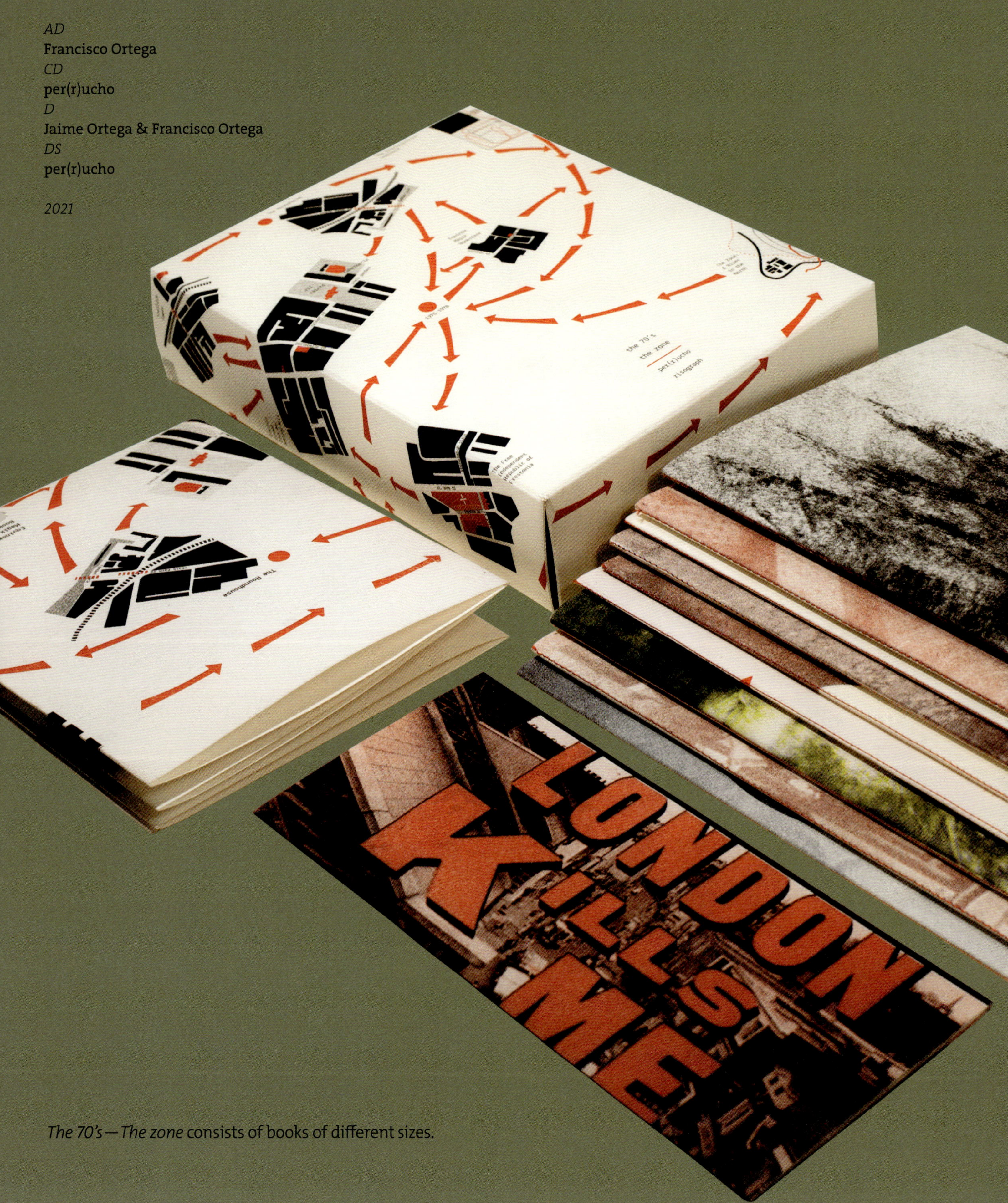

The 70's — The zone consists of books of different sizes.

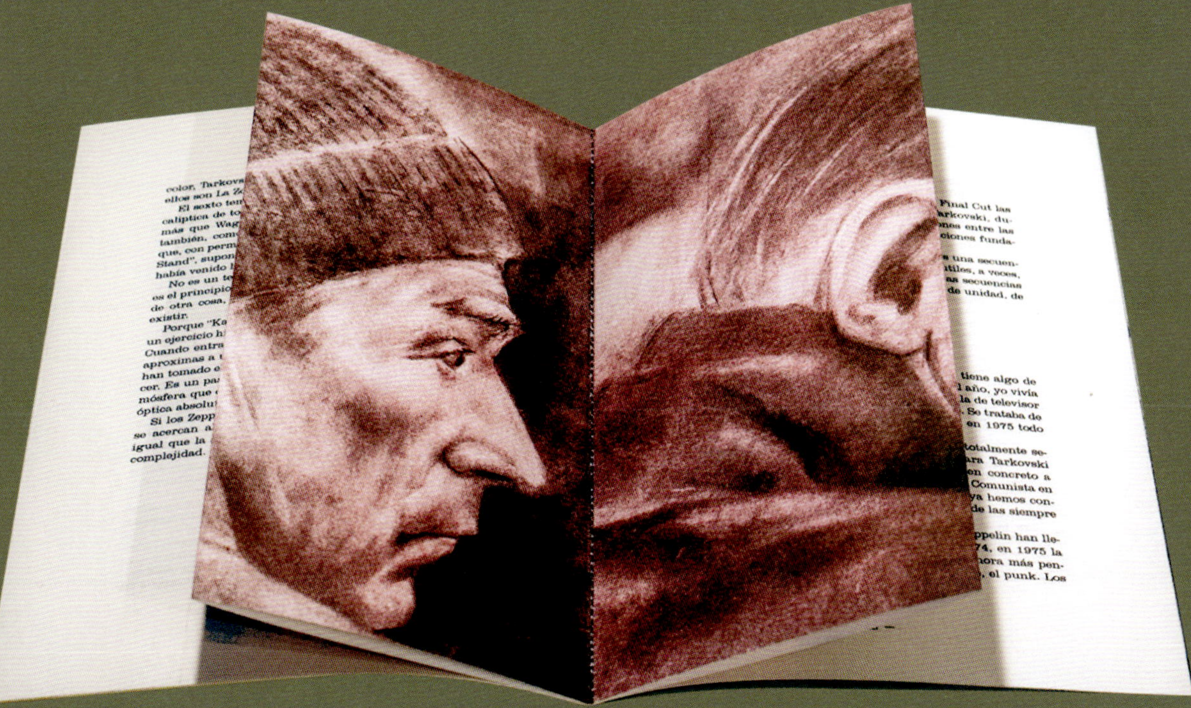

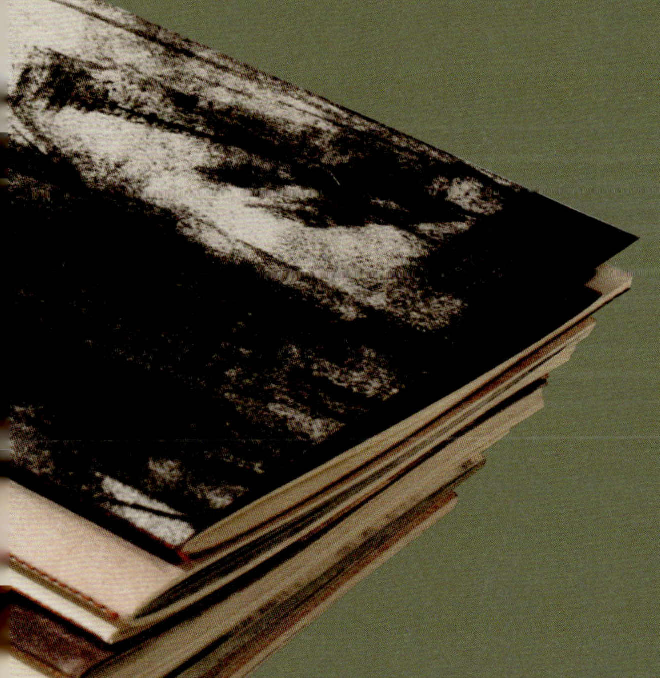

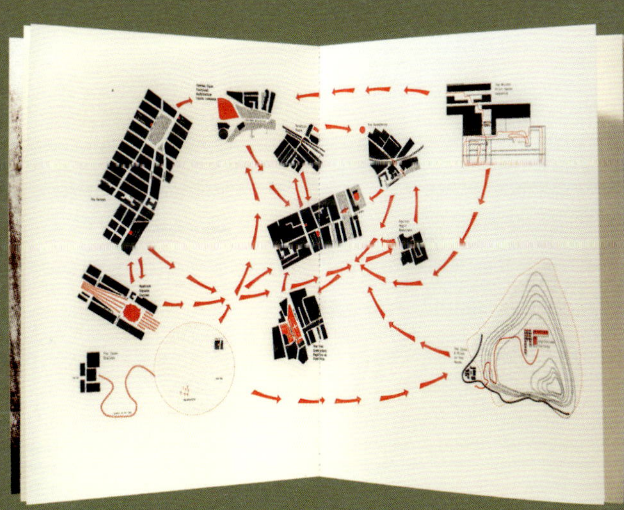

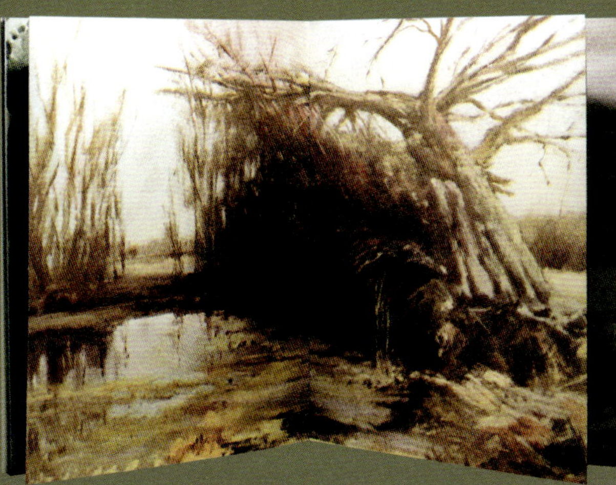

Page: 240 **Dimension:** 160×200×55mm **Weight:** 500g **Paper/Material:** Fedrigoni Arena **Binding:** Singer Sewn Binding

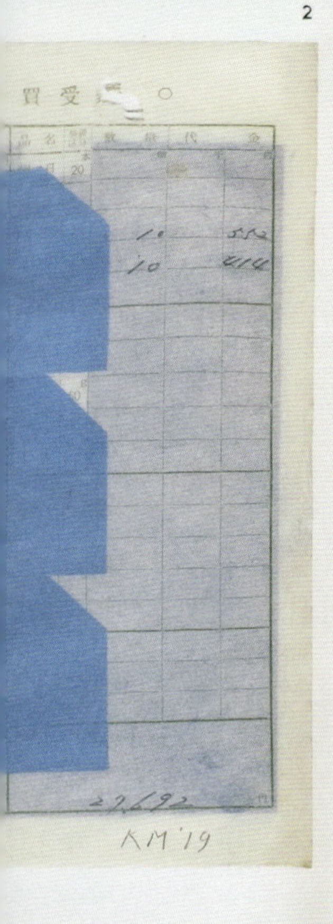

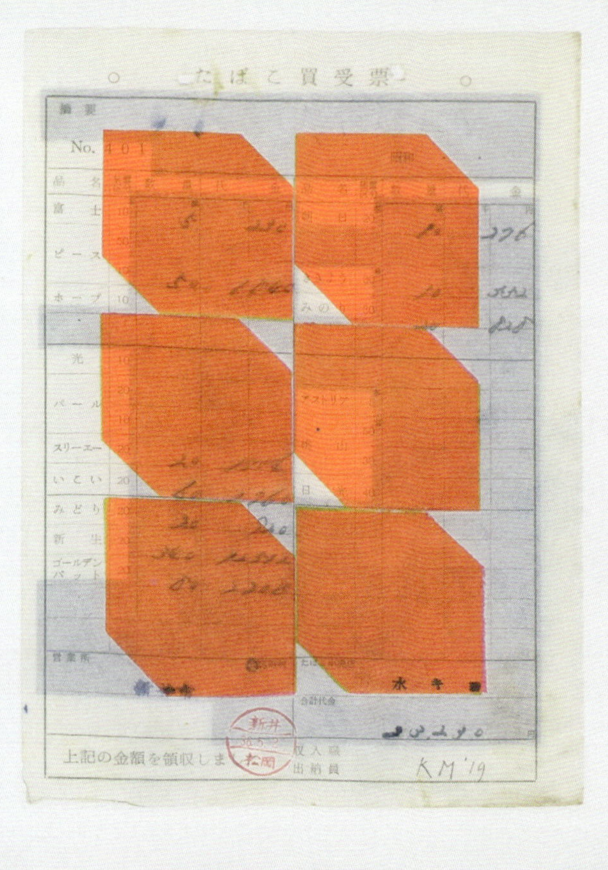

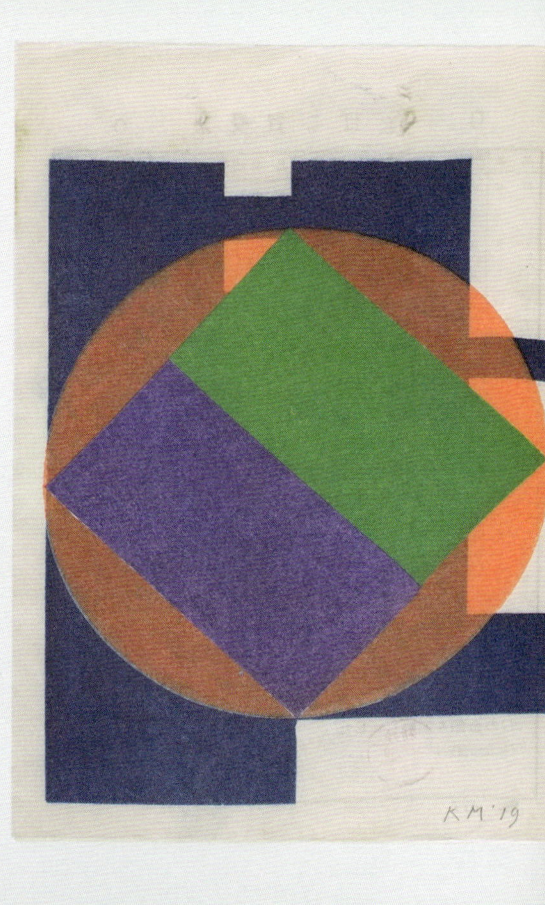

TOKYO PAPERS

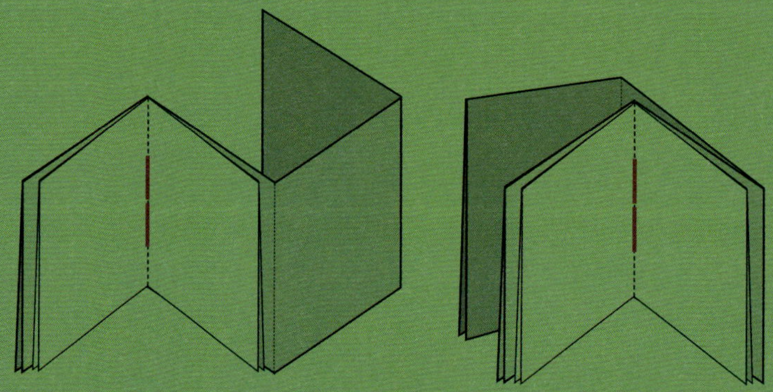

D
Karel Martens
DS
Karel Martens & Roma Publications

2020

Reproduced in its original size, this is a collection of 41 monoprints created by Karel Martens in 2019 and 2020. In 2018, Martens received a package in the mail from Pierre Leguillon with a small pile of used Japanese forms which he had found at a street market in Tokyo. This was an intriguing collection of documents—printed on thin paper with a rectangular blue-black layer of carbon on the back. Initially in 2019, Martens started to print on these back sides, but because the overprinting on the carbon layer caused unwanted damage, Martens eventually started printing on the front sides as well.

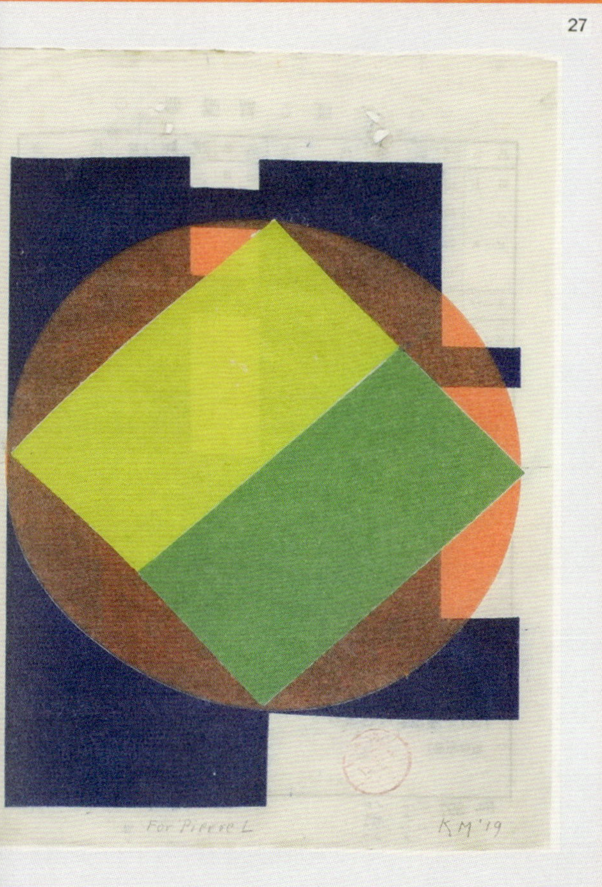

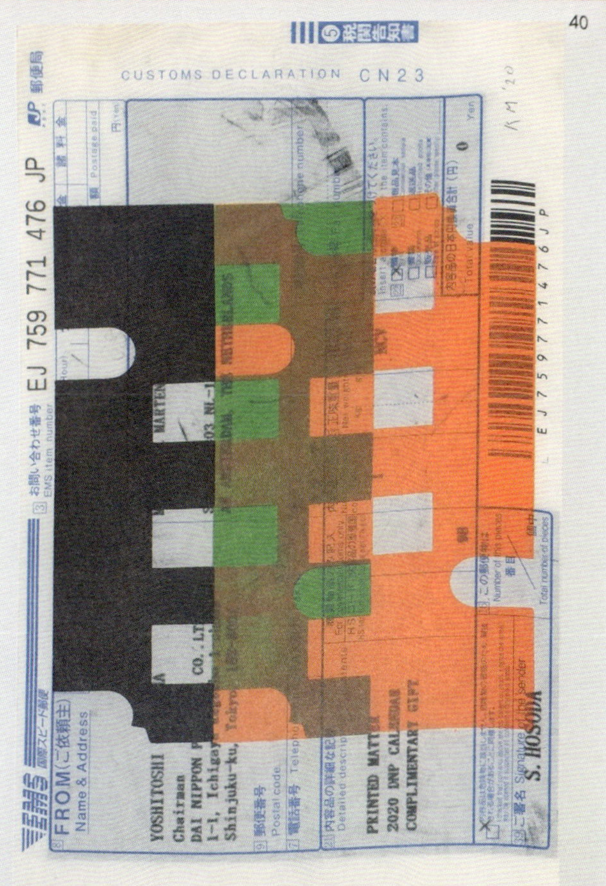

© Karel Martens
Publisher: Roma Publications, Amst
Printing: Lenoirschuring, Wormerve
Binding: Voetelink, Haarlem
Distribution: Idea Books, Amsterdar

ROMA 394, 2020
ISBN 9789492811837

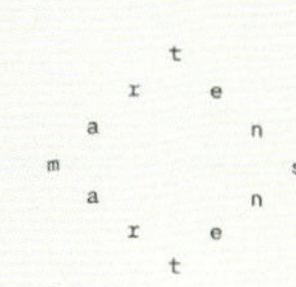

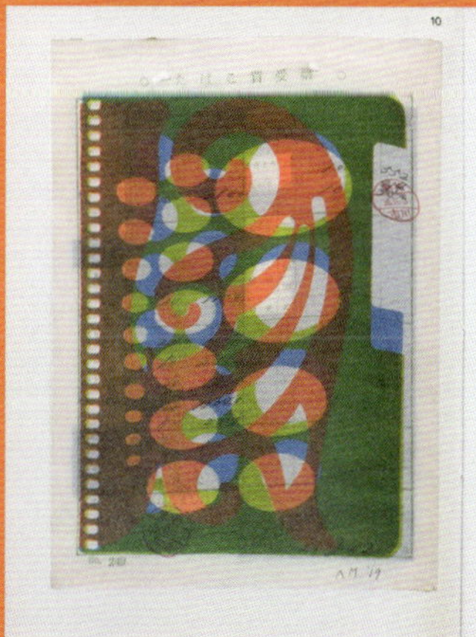

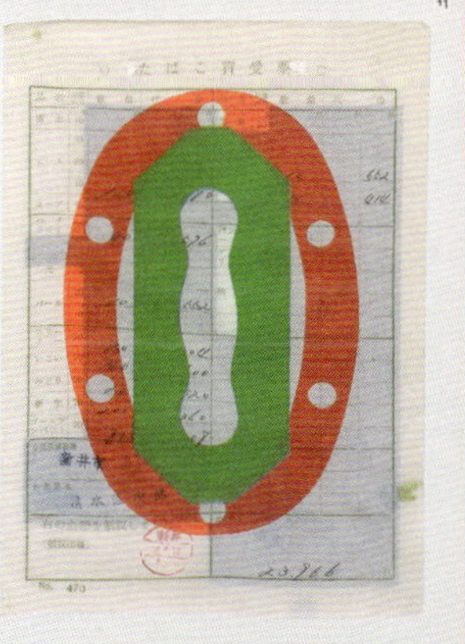

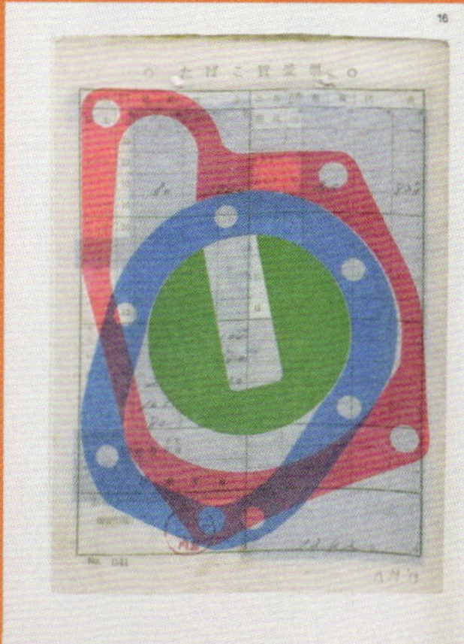

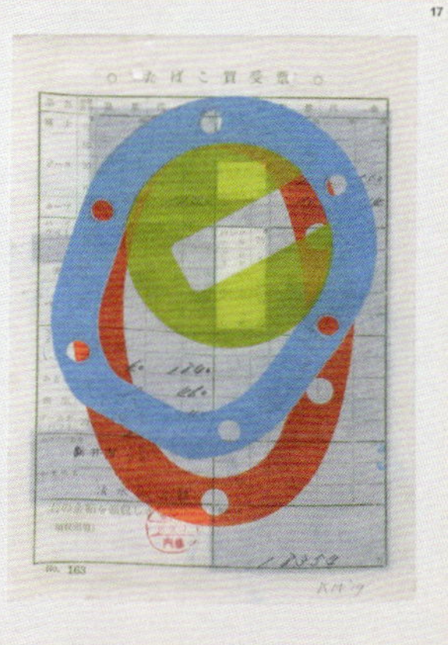

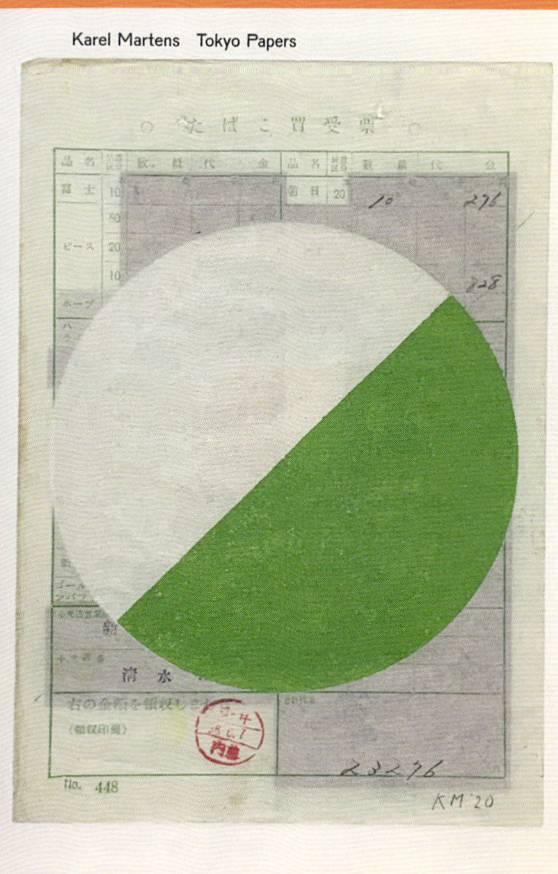

Page: 40 **Dimension:** 155×215mm **Weight:** 150g **Paper/Material:** Thin Opaque 60g **Binding:** Singer Sewn Binding

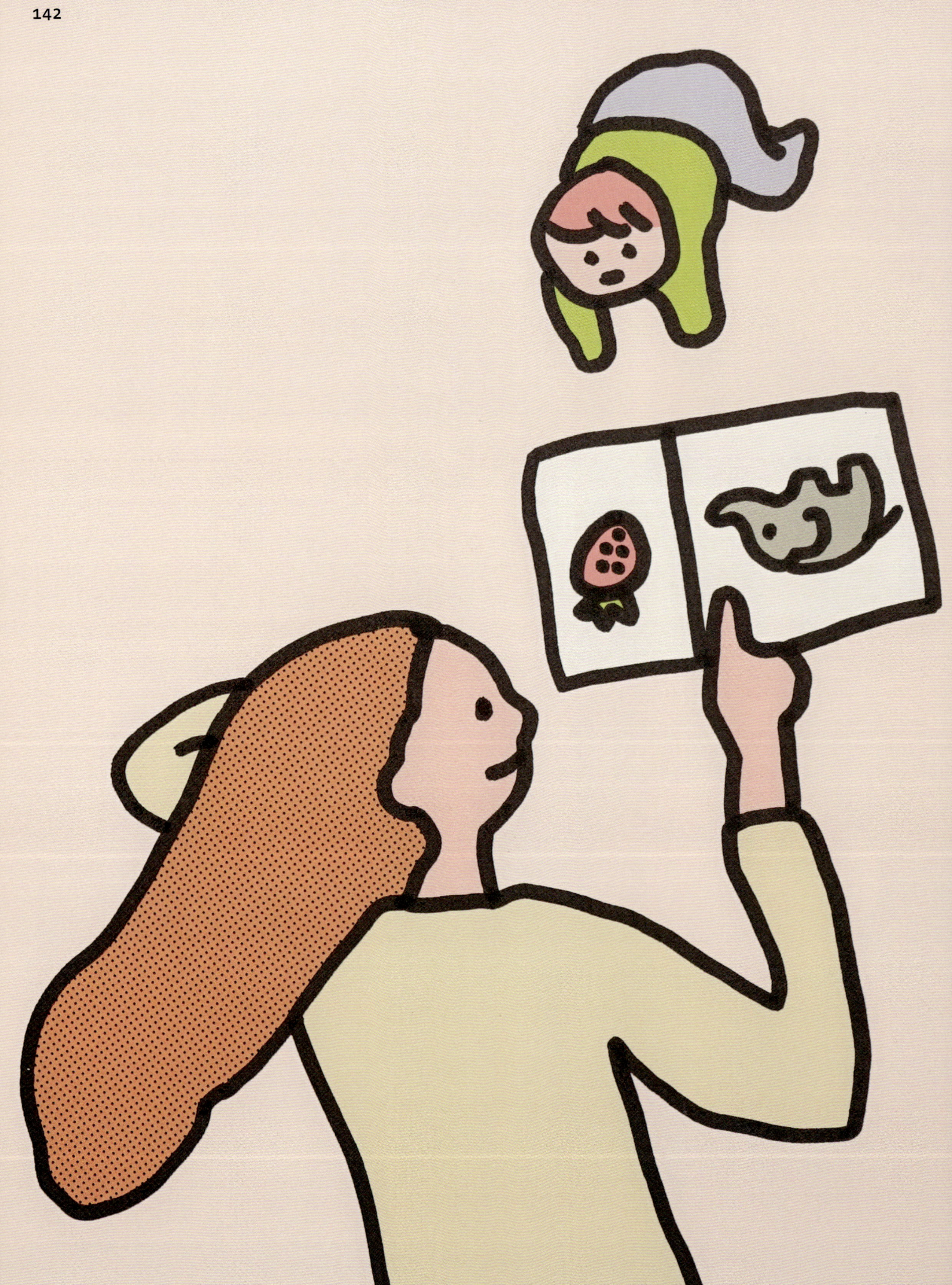

MOTHER AND DAUGHTER

AD & D
Jihwan Kim & Sol Jin
P & DS
Zero Per Zero

2015

The book *Mother and Daughter* describes moments when emotions and feelings are exchanged between a mother and a baby daughter based on the author's experience of feeling connected with her child in 2014. The most significant feature is that all 32 pages of paintings are composed of images with no text, allowing parents to tell their children stories in their creative ways.

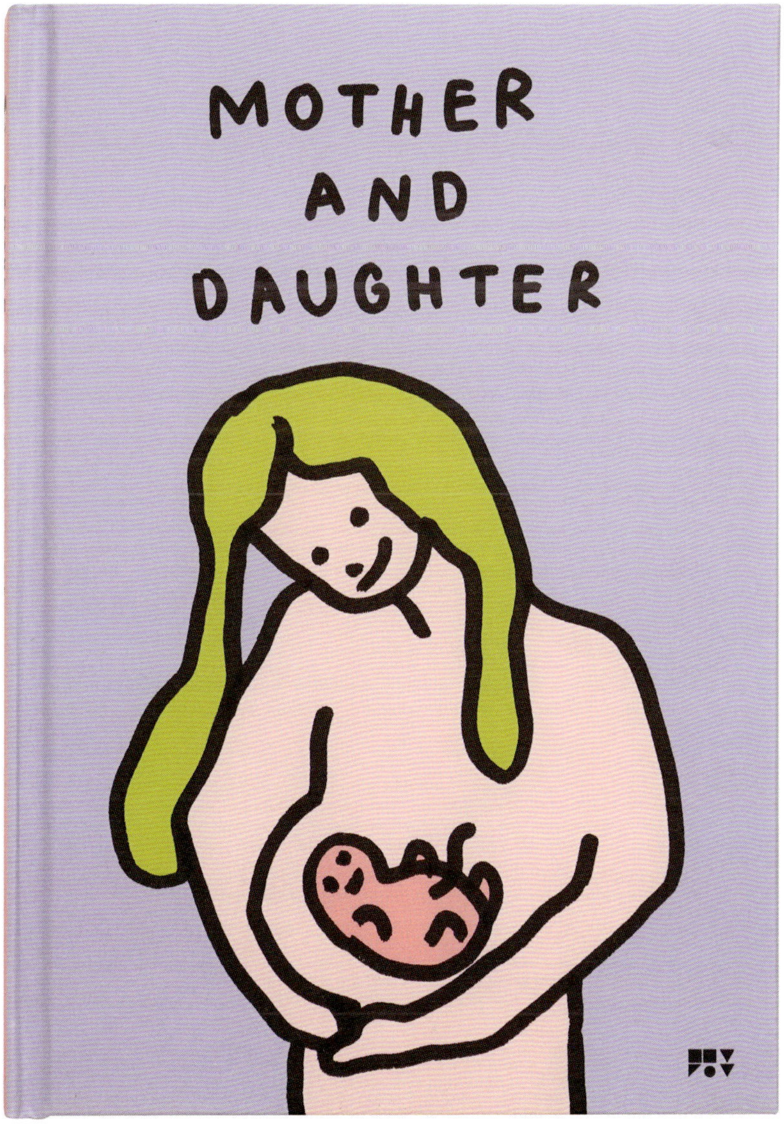

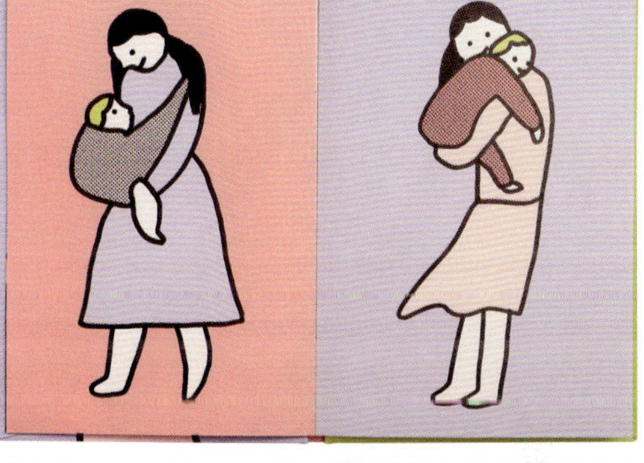

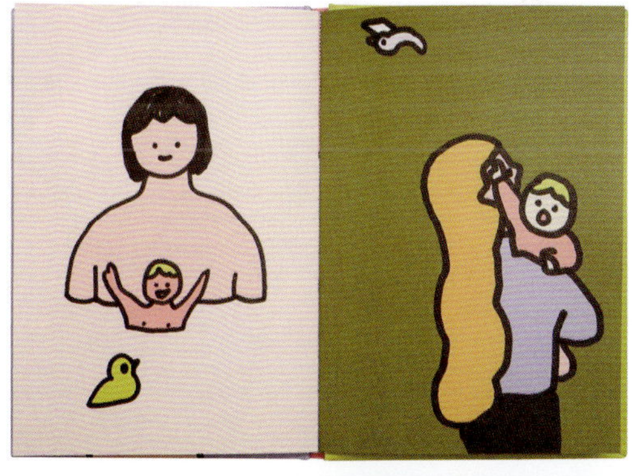

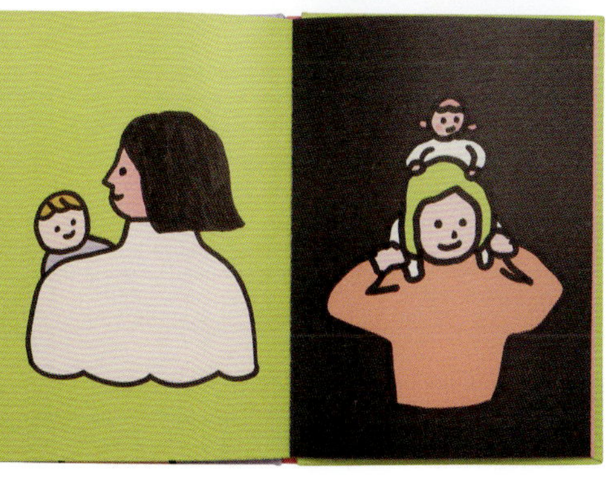

Page: 32 **Dimension:** 153×218mm **Weight:** 220g **Paper/Material:** Uncoated Paper **Binding:** Case Binding

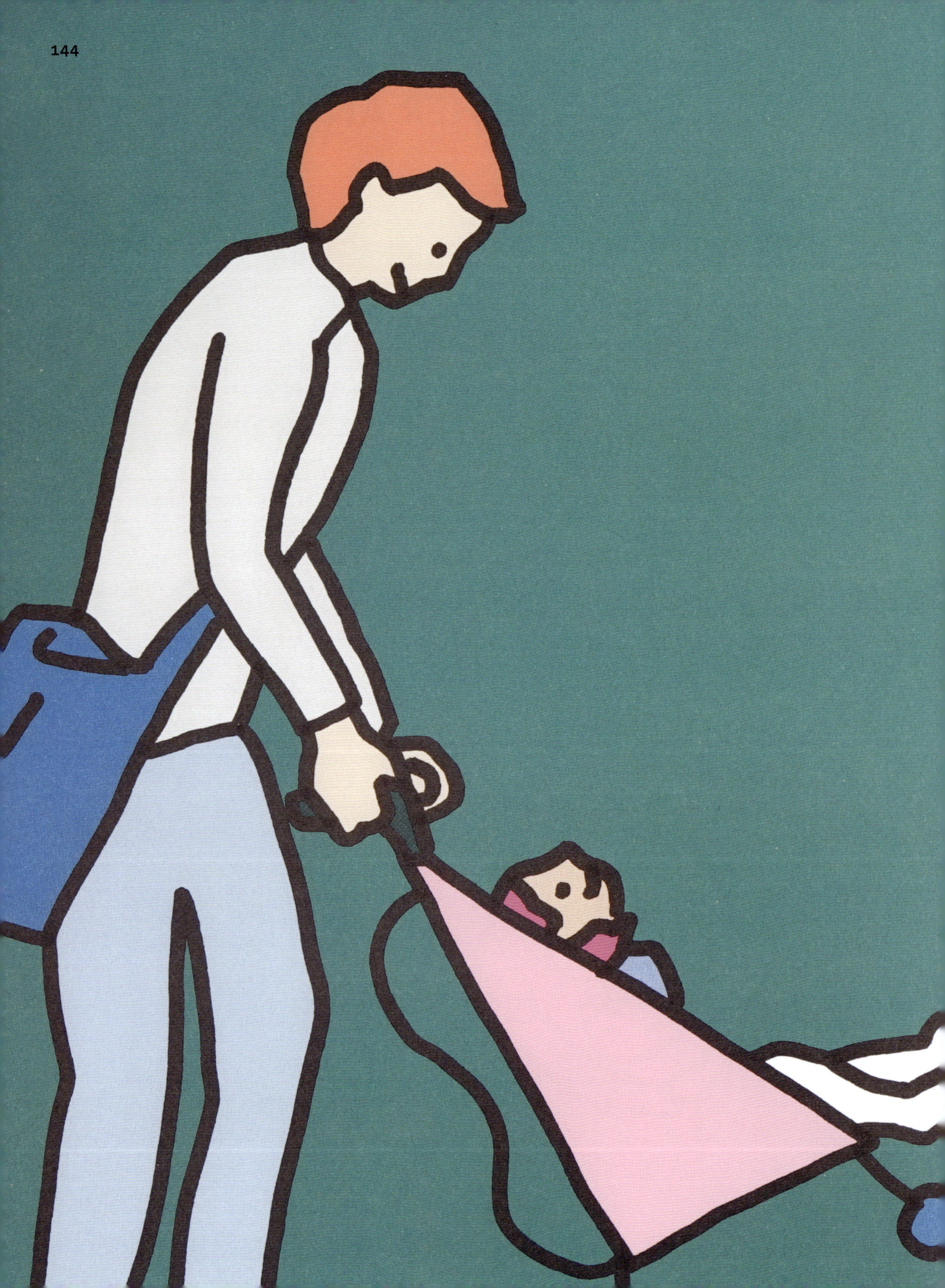

FATHER AND DAUGHTER

AD & D
Jihwan Kim & Sol Jin
P & DS
Zero Per Zero

2015

Doodle-like picture drawn with a thick pen is the essential character of this book. The designers believe simplicity in drawing can convey the feeling of connection with the children to readers more honestly and clearly.

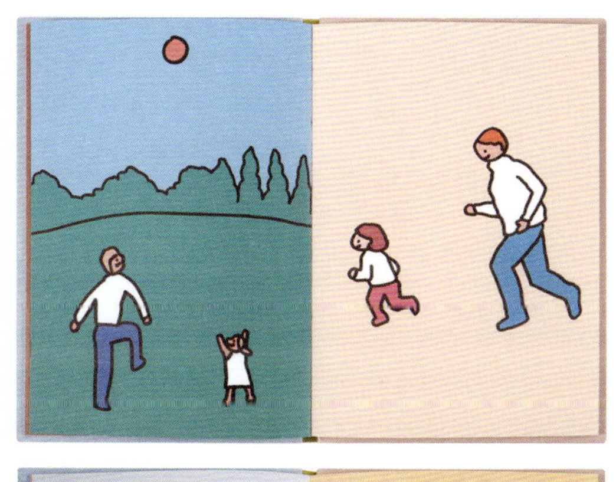

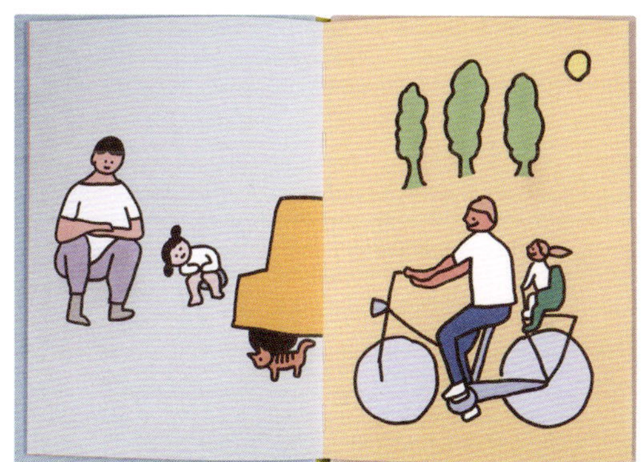

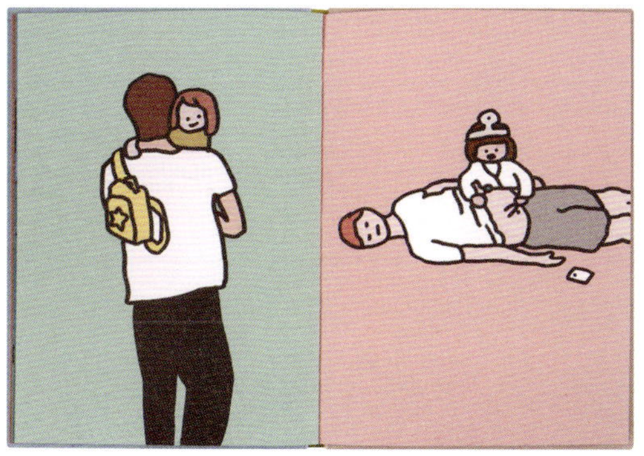

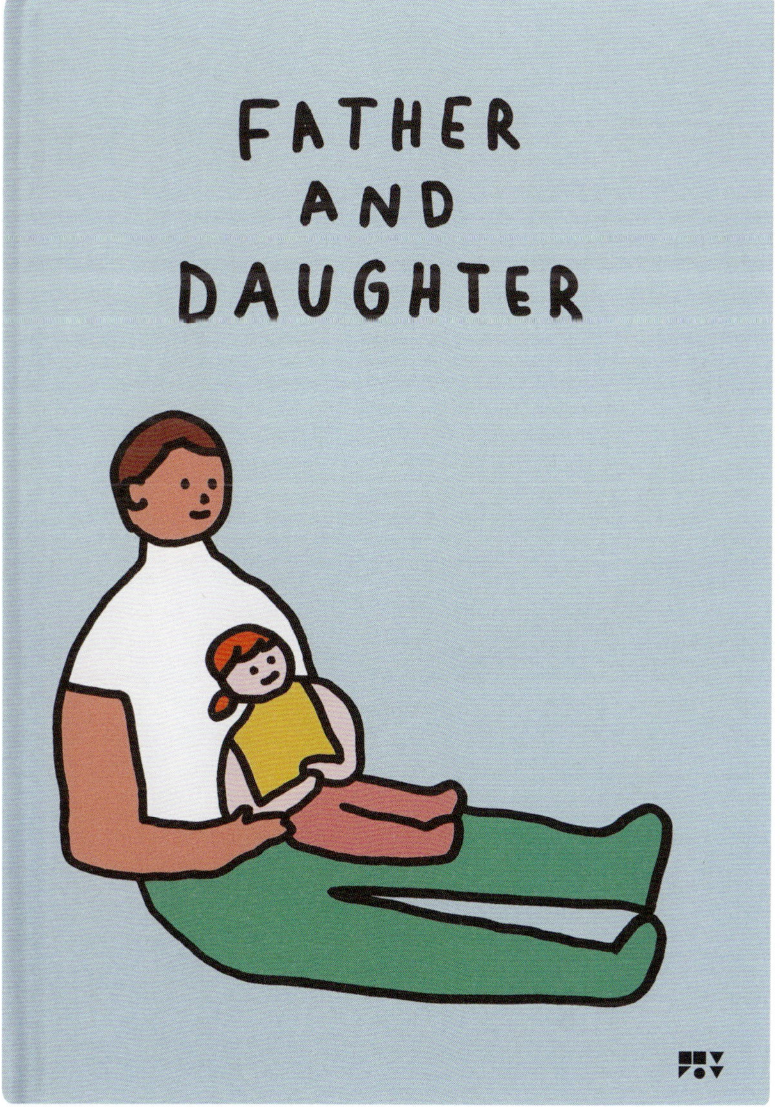

Binding: Case Binding

Paper/Material: Uncoated Paper

Page: 32 **Dimension:** 153×218mm **Weight:** 220g

LALATA NO. 17

AD, CD & D
Manuela Martínez & Carmen G. Palacios
P
Ramón Peco Muñoz

2015-2018

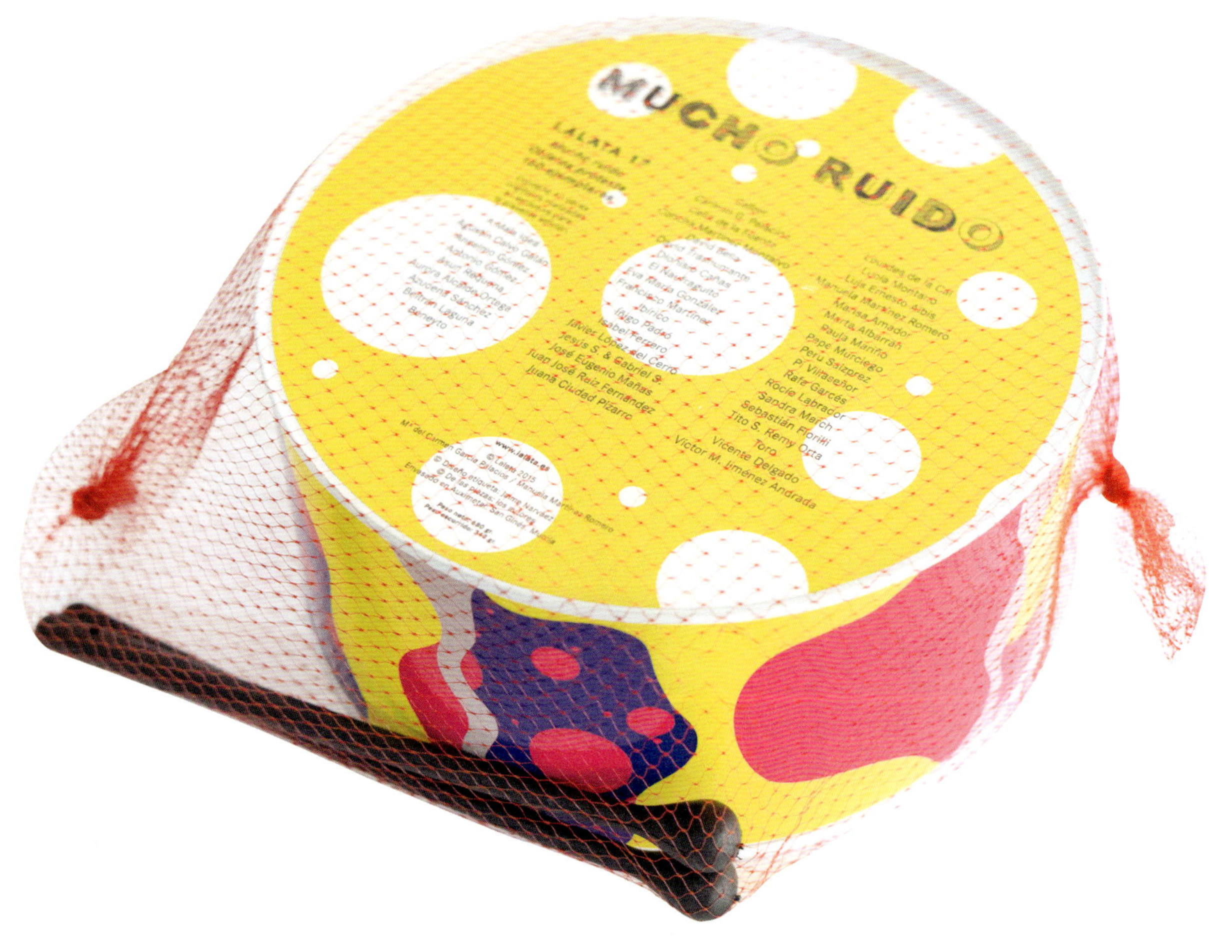

The team of *LALATA* magazine wants to give readers a different experience that goes beyond written text.

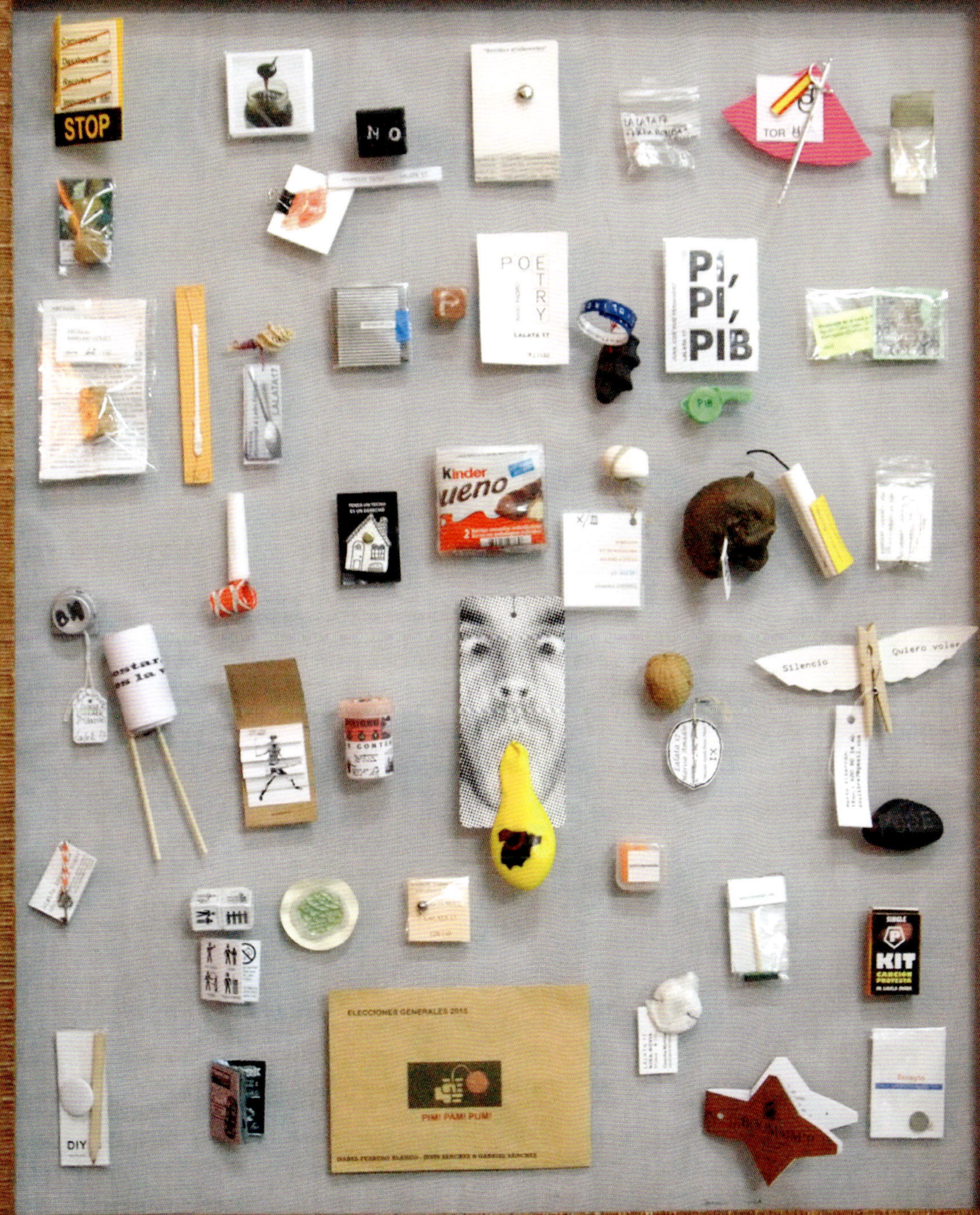
STOP
NO
POETRY
LALATA 17
PI,
PI,
PIB
Kinder
ueno
Silencio
Quiero volar
ELECCIONES GENERALES 2015
PIM! PAM! PUM!
KIT
CANCIÓN PROTESTA
DIY

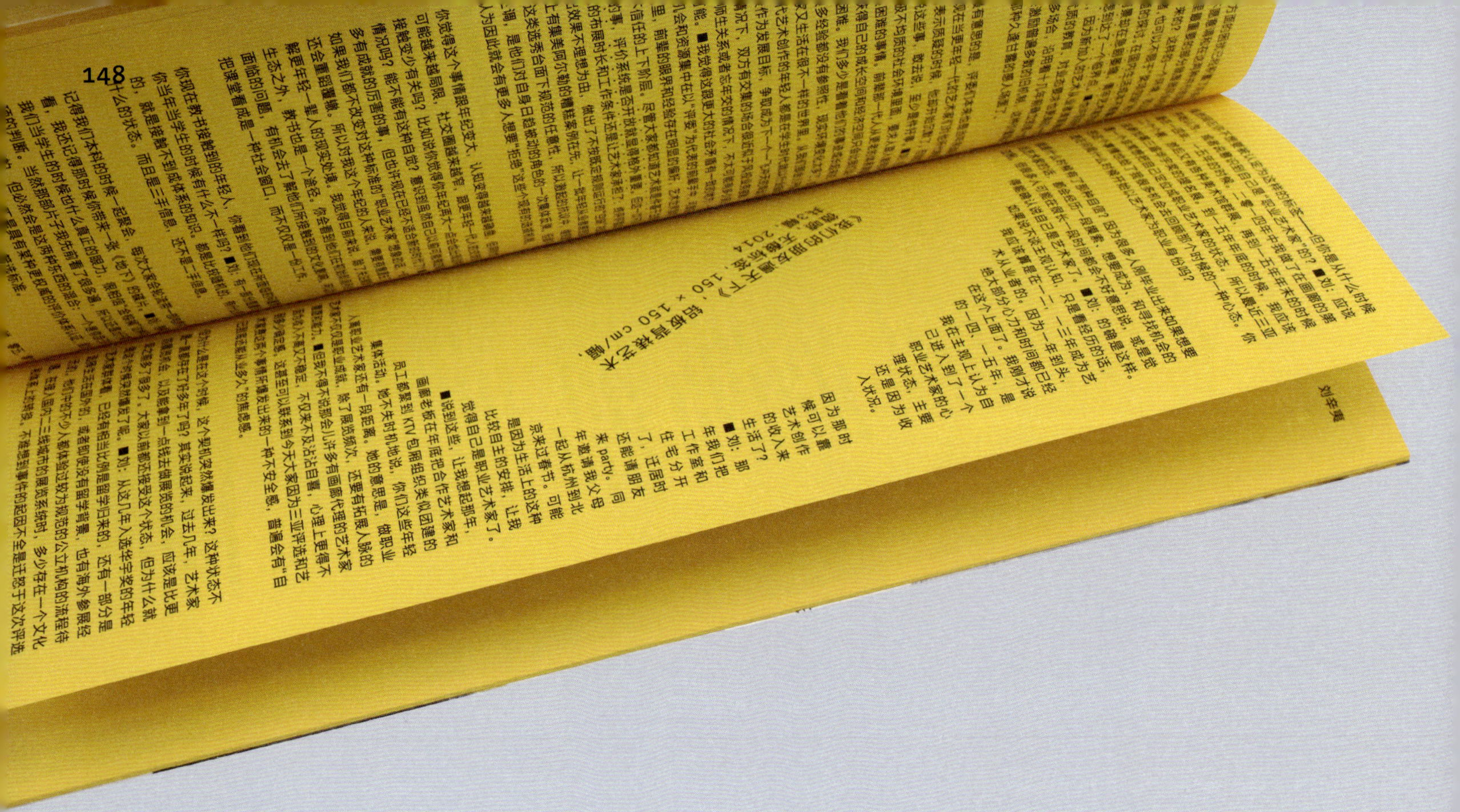

[SOFT] MAGAZINE

D
Pianpian He
DS
Studio Pianpian He & Max Harvey

2020

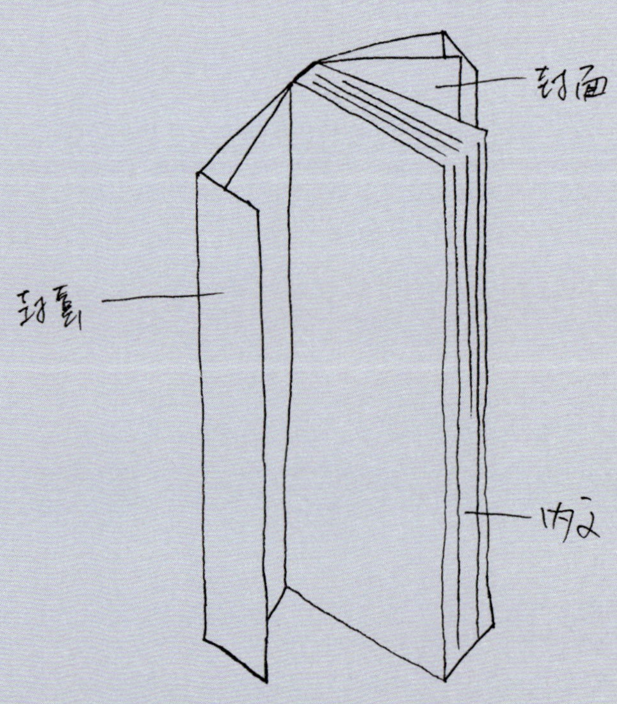

A disintegrating and confrontational world influenced by the global pandemic is presented in this work. The designers divided the magazine into 2 parts. They fragmented the images, and left the space for positive and negative division during the process of typesetting, which was the way they sought to respond to the theme. They deliberately offer a difficult reading experience for readers, hoping to provoke readers' anxiety and contemplation. *[soft]* magazine is published by OpenArt Studio.

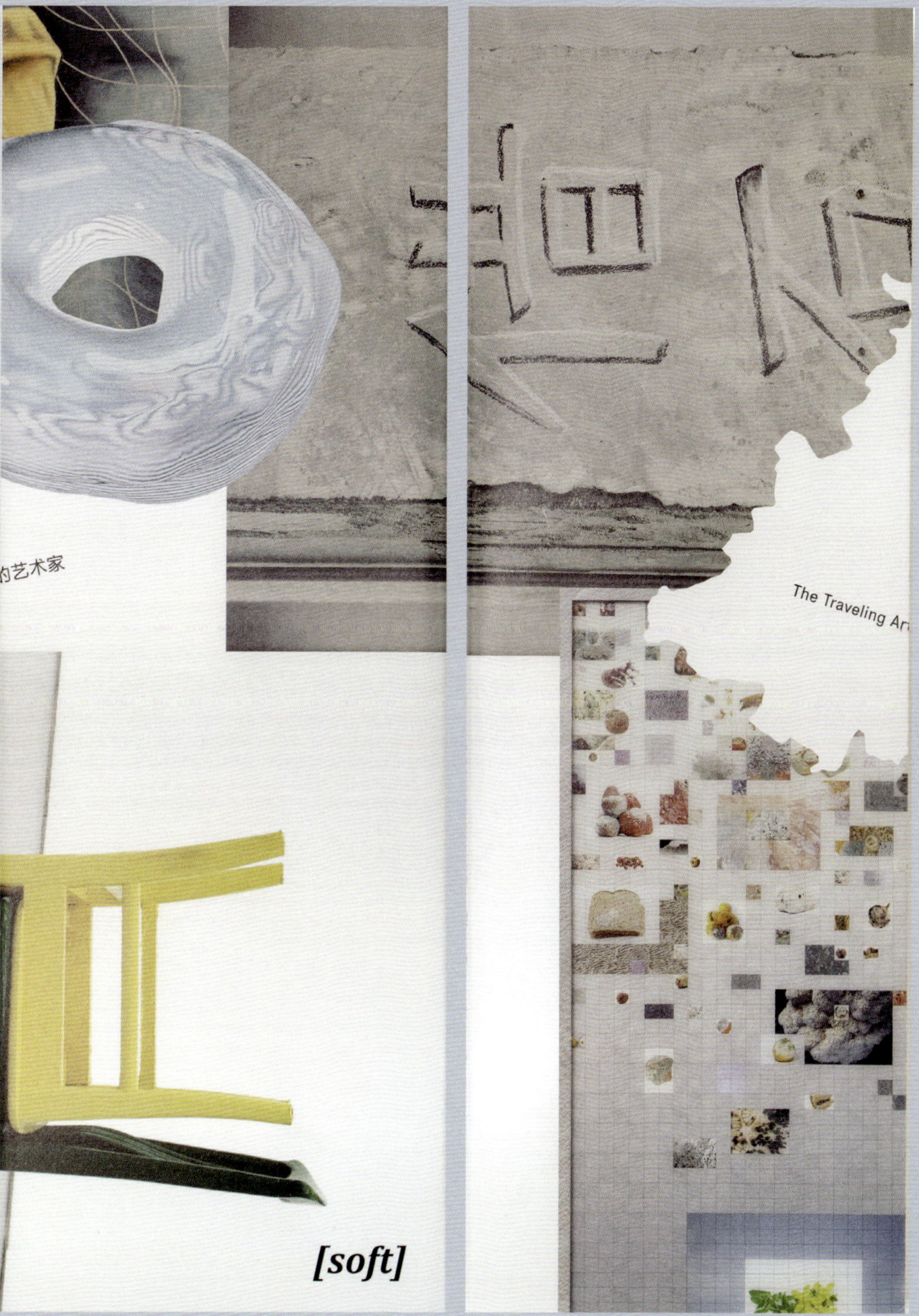

Page: 180 **Dimension:** 112×330mm **Weight:** 285g **Paper/Material:** Art Paper 240g (Cover); Kishu 80g (Inside Page); IP 120g (Book Jacket) **Binding:** Coptic Binding

DEATH IN A GOOD DISTRICT

AD & CD
Will Anderson & Corina Reynolds
D
Will Anderson & Diana Ross
P
Will Anderson
DS
Yewtree Press & Small Editions

2015

The book is inspired by a poem that the designer's grandmother wrote around 1956. The project has seen a few different forms. Firstly, there was a box of photographs in 1996. Then an exhibition was held in New York in 1999. After that the designer began to start thinking of making it into a book which was finally published in 2015. The whole book run of 70 copies was handmade.

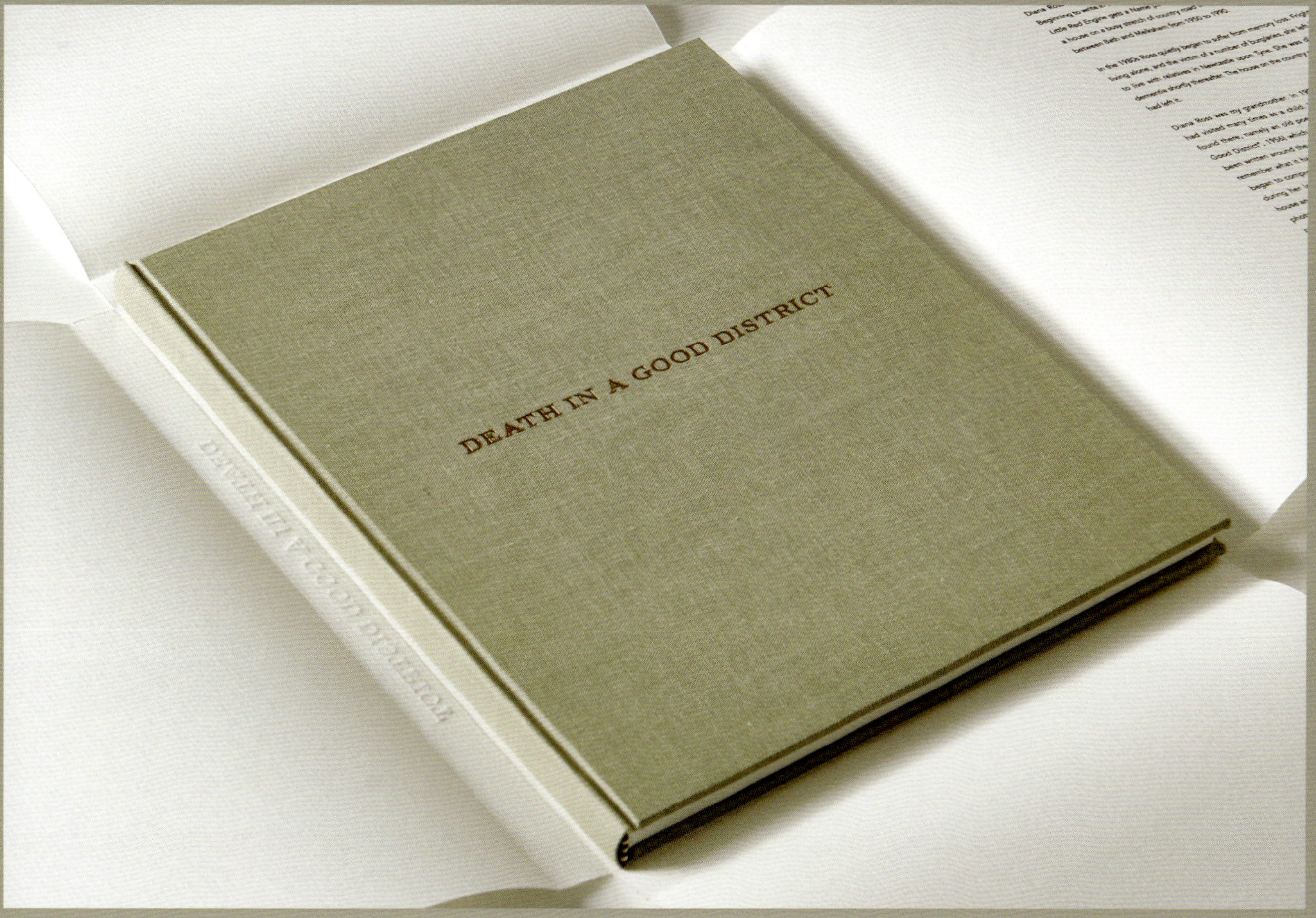

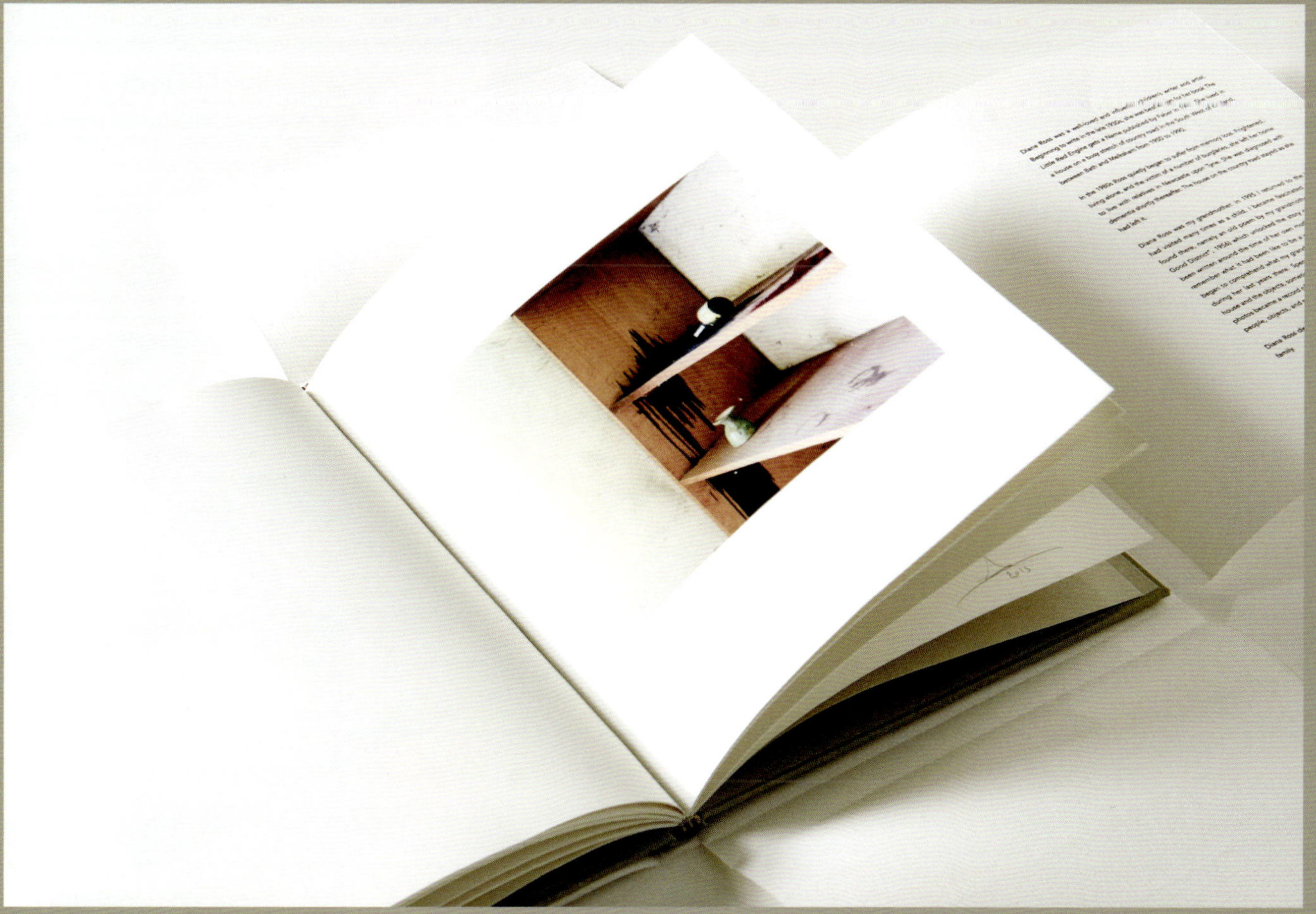

Page: 56 **Dimension:** 178×216mm **Weight:** 226.8g **Paper/Material:** Pheonix Motion 170g **Binding:** Sewn Binding

TITULO NON VERBALE

AD
Simone Virgini
CD
per(r)ucho
D
Simone Virgini
DS
per(r)ucho

2020

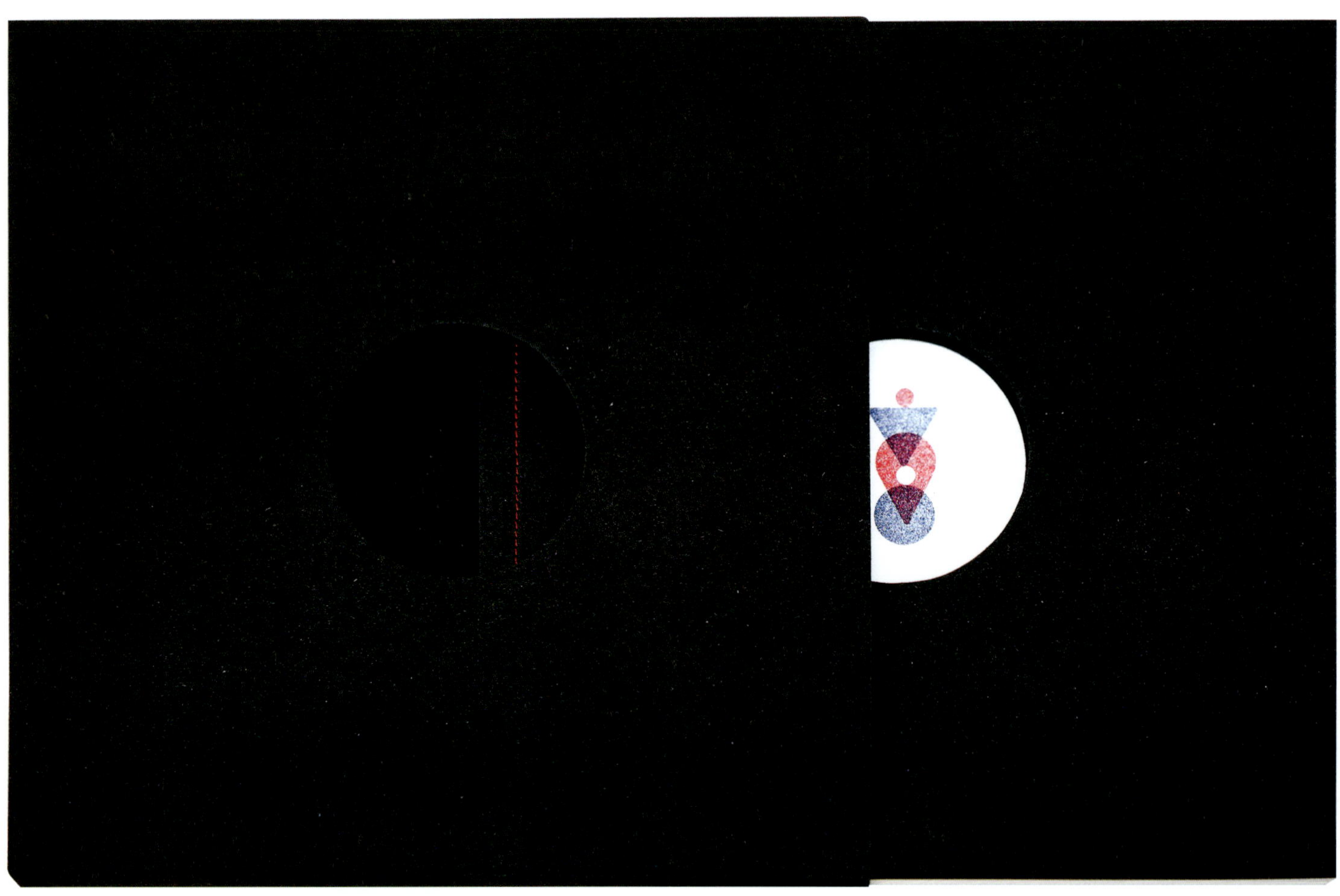

Titulo Non Verbale is a book created by the Italian artist Simone Virgini in which a new graphic language is proposed through the superposition of two Riso inks.

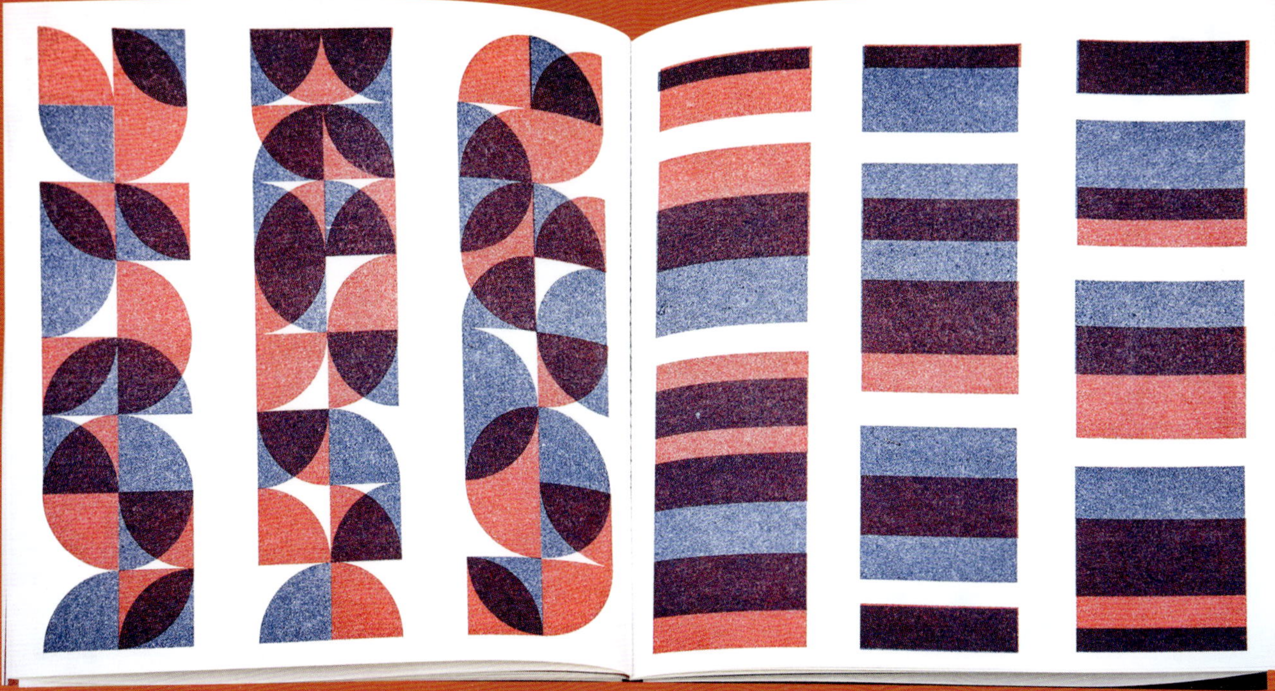

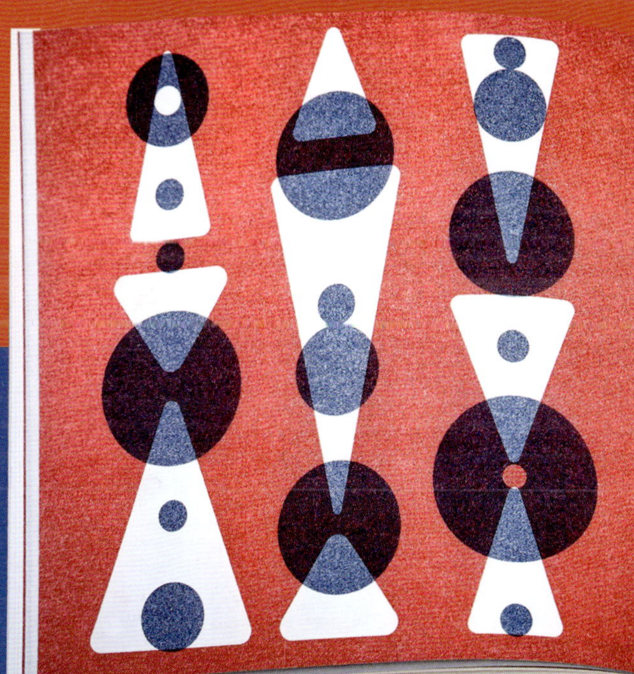

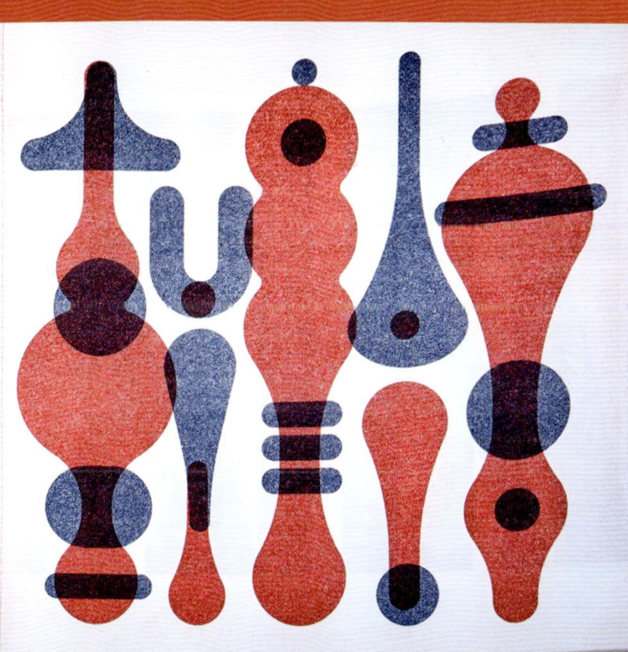

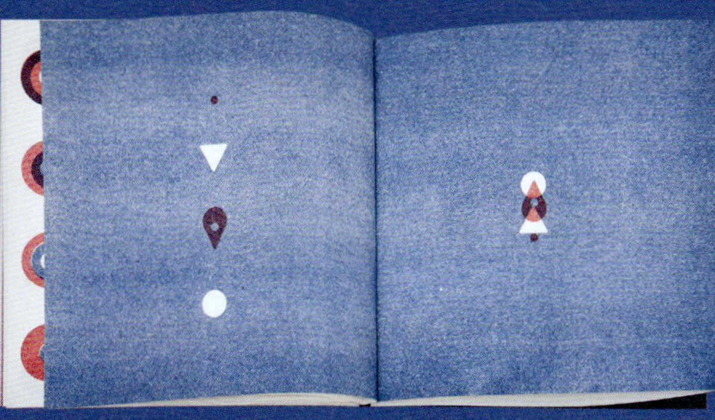

Page: 72 **Dimension:** 200×200mm **Weight:** 300g **Paper/Material:** Fedrigoni Old Mill **Binding:** Singer Sewn Binding

SUBTLE BODY

AD, CD & D
Lauren Clay
P
Small Editions, NYC
DS
Small Editions, NYC &
Corina Reynolds

2016

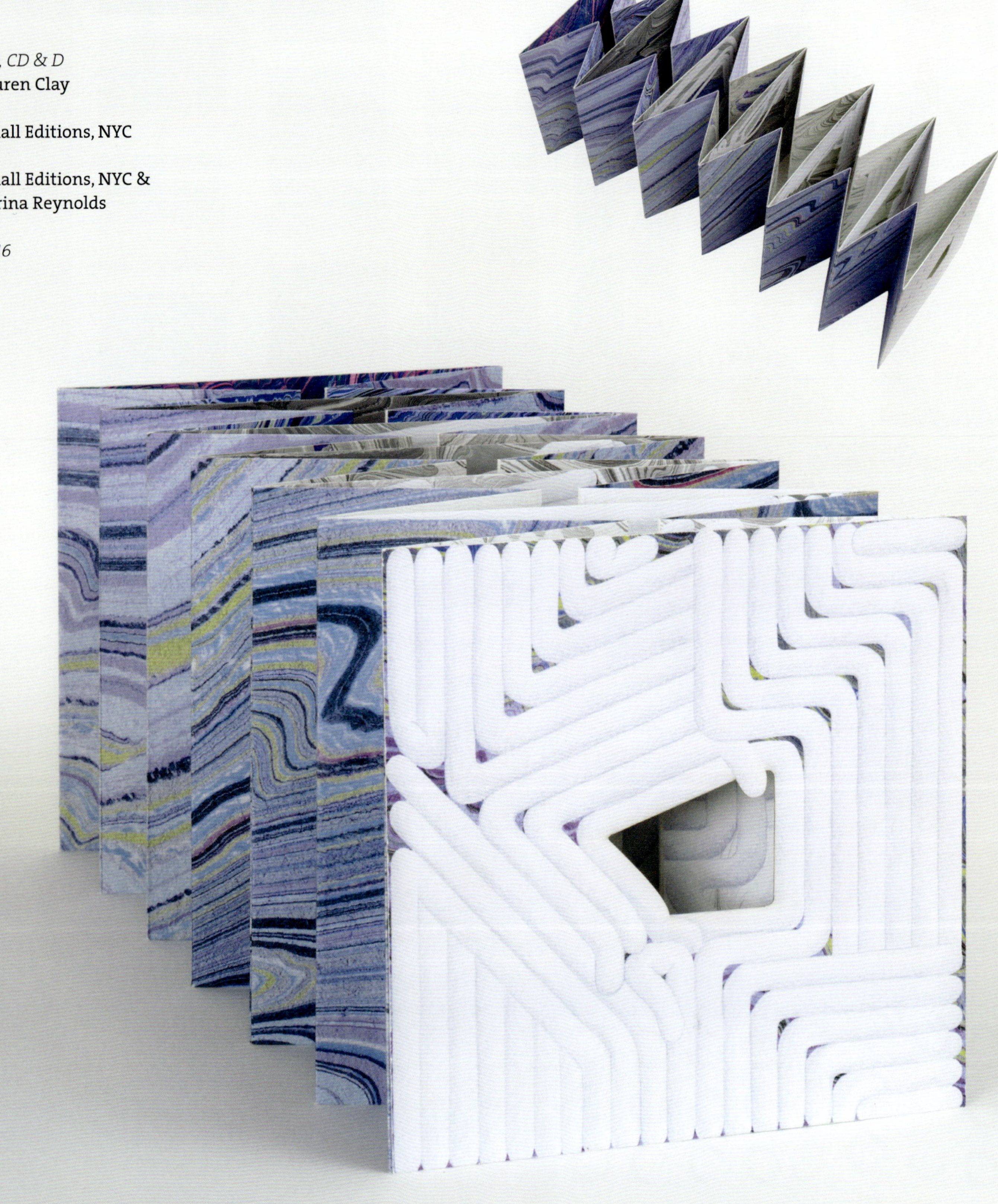

The designer is an artist who creates sculptures and immersive installations. Creating this tunnel book was a way for the designer to expand the creation of experiential space similar to the spaces in exhibitions. The book's layered pages and cut-outs create a cinematic effect for the viewer as the book expands and contracts, giving the illusion of traveling into the work.

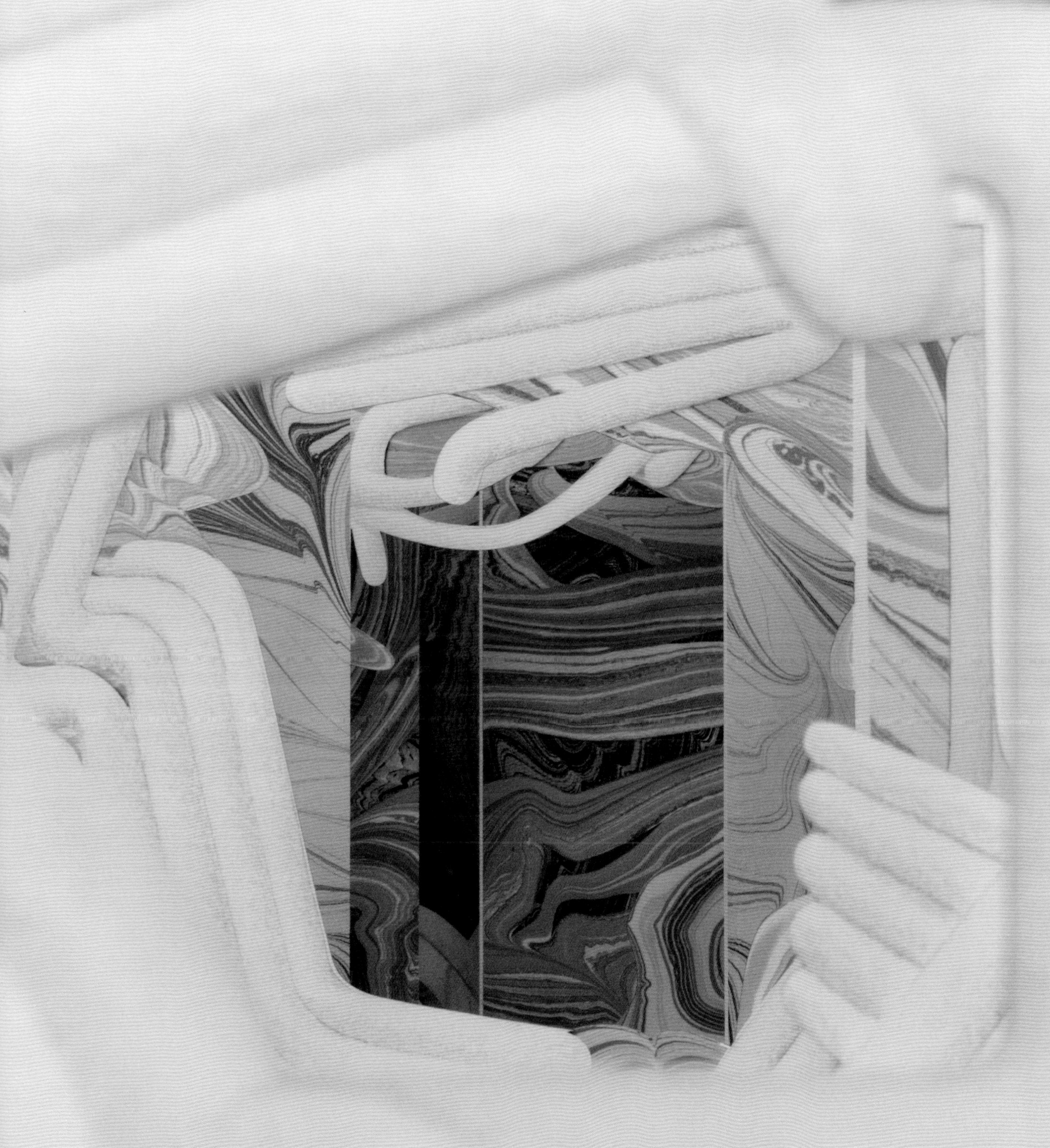

Page: 7 **Dimension:** 203×203×117mm **Weight:** 453.6g **Paper/Material:** Moab Entrada Rag; Kozo Paper **Binding:** Hand Bound

LITTLE YELLOW SPOTS

D
Wuthipol Ujathammarat

2019

Little Yellow Spots consists of four scattered photography zines that are intentionally designed and assembled to irritate the readers, in a way that is reflective of the phenomenon of random dumping of shared bicycles. This bundle of work does not come with any literal descriptions. Instead, the readers need to scan a QR code to access details about the work—this is also a conceptual play on how bike sharing works.

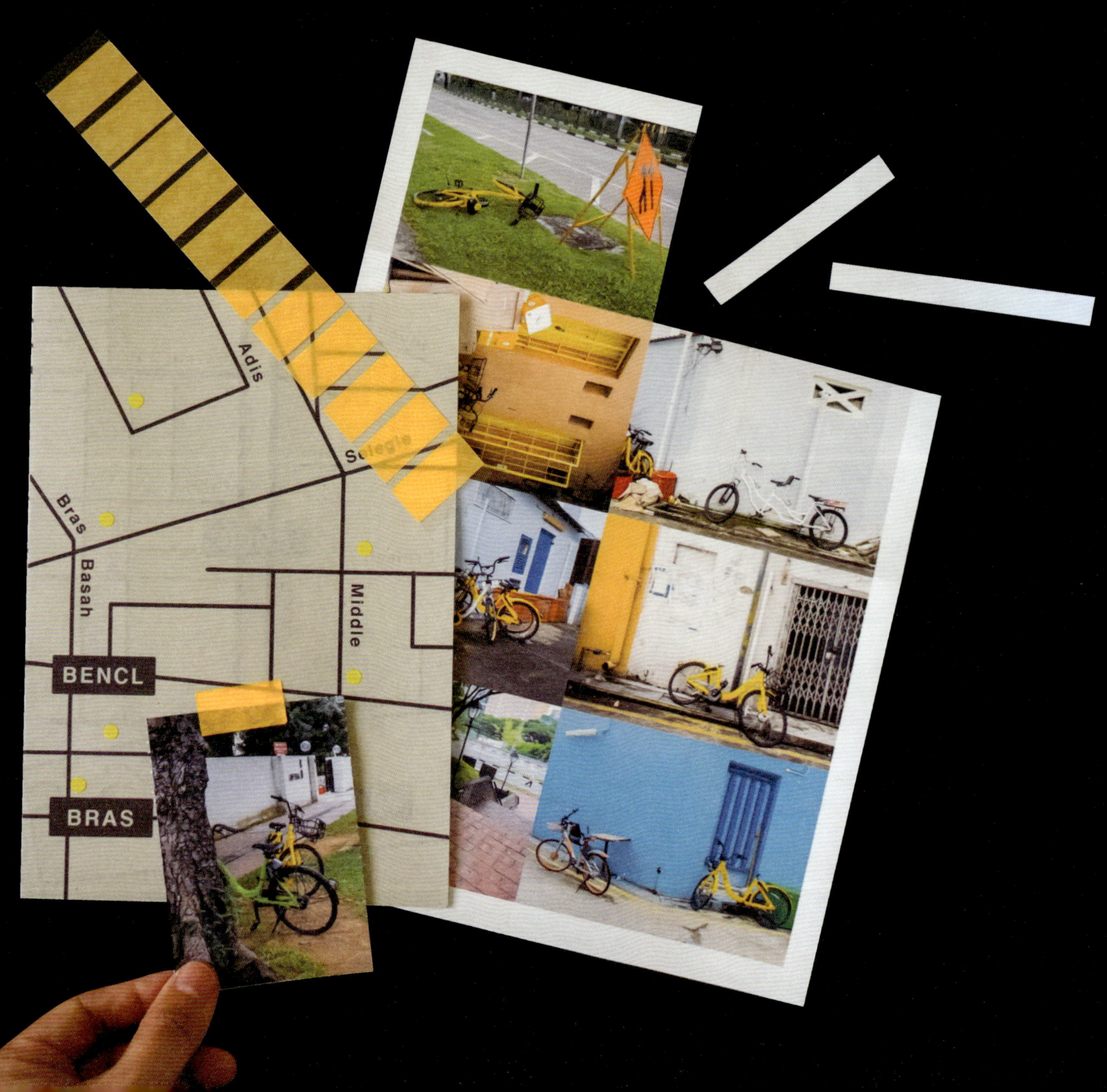

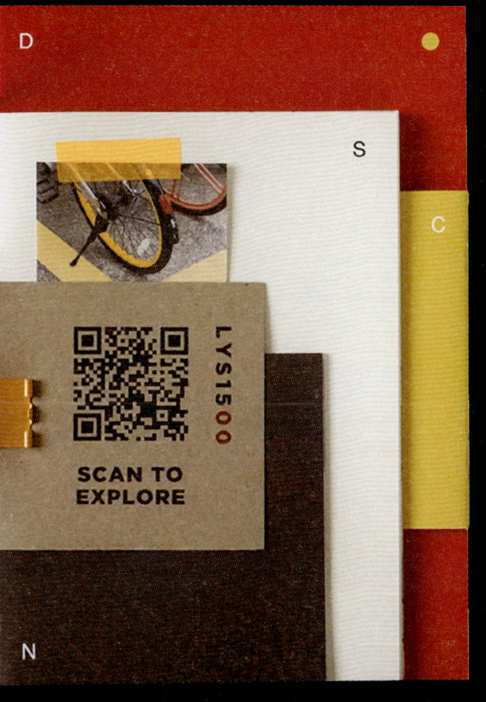

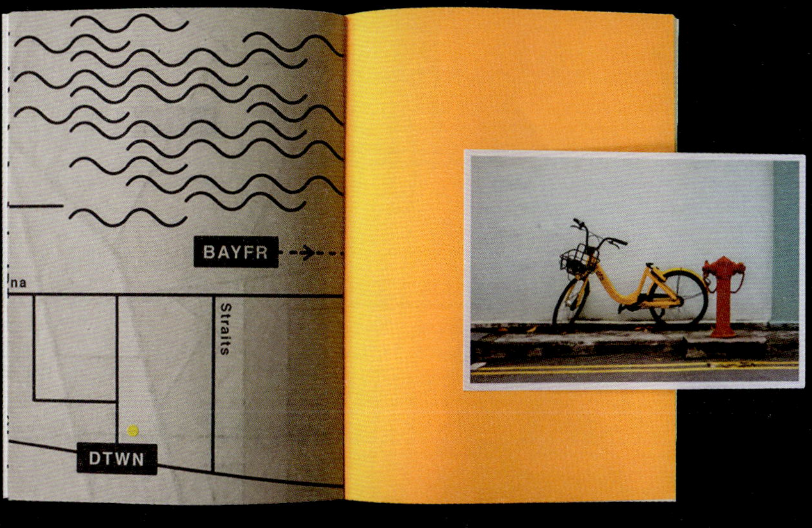

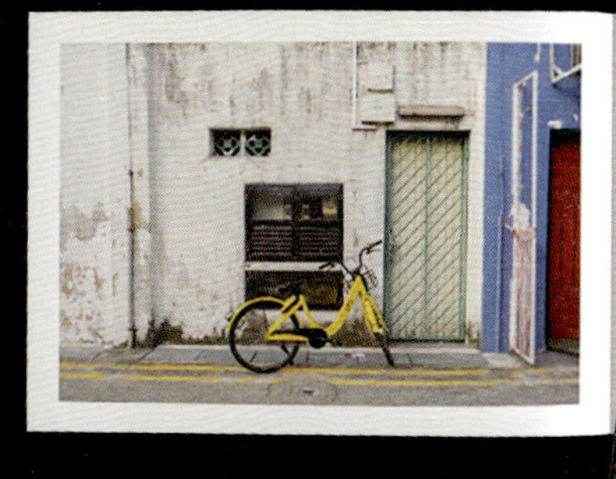

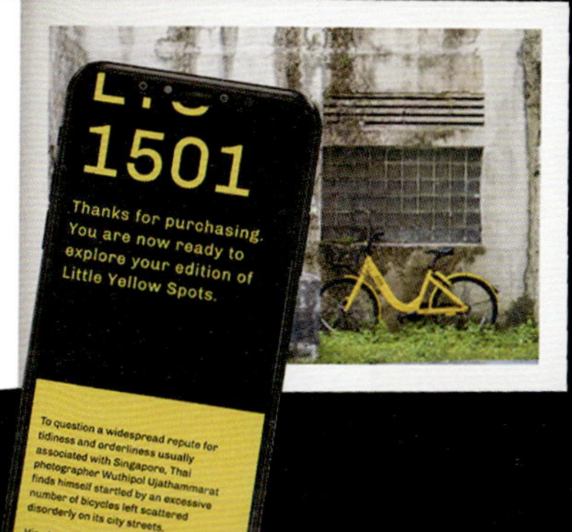

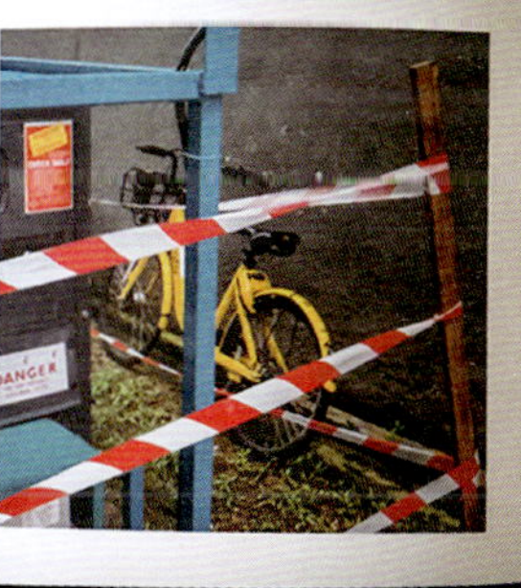

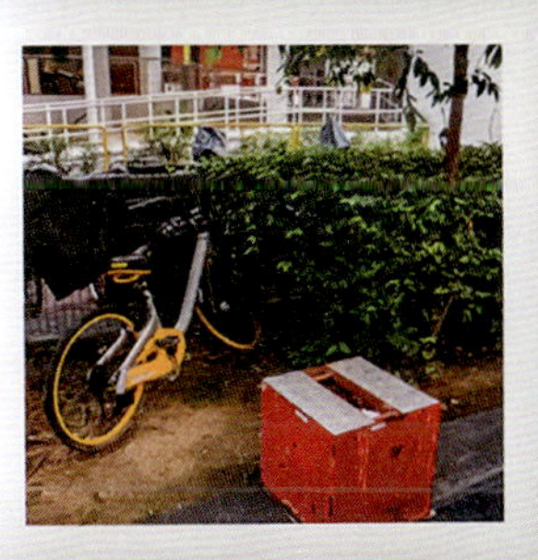

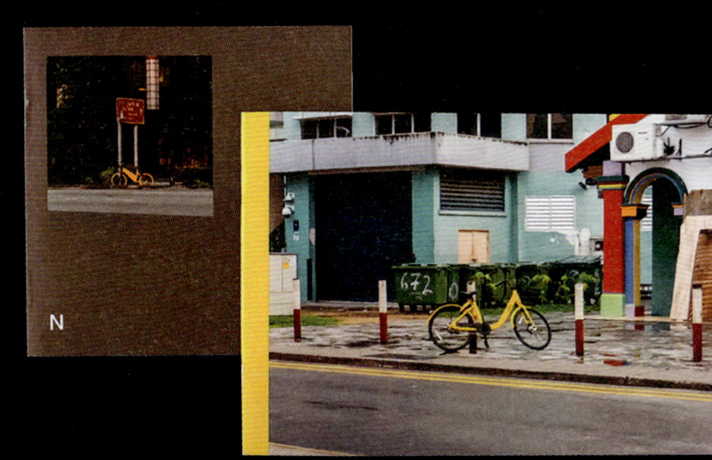

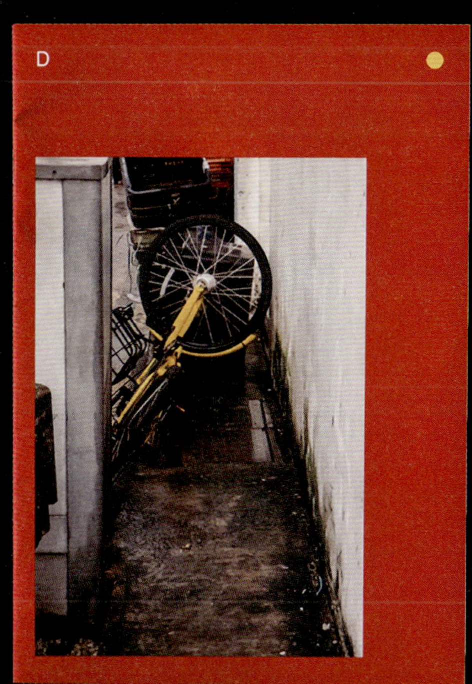

ed Matte; Matte White Binding: Saddle Stitching; Binder Clip

LALATA NO. 18

AD, CD & D
Manuela Martínez & Carmen G. Palacios
P
Ramón Peco Muñoz

2015-2018

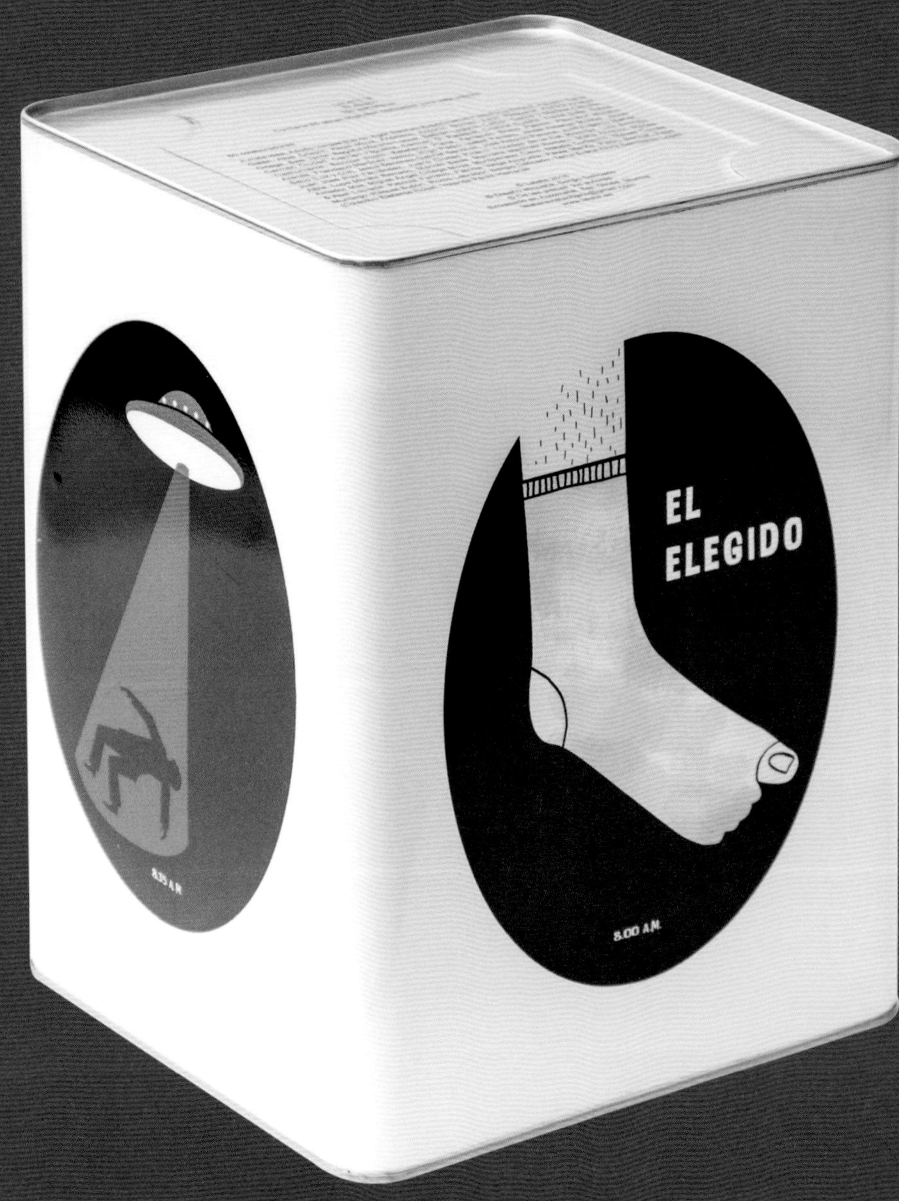

LALATA magazine hopes to provoke an artistic and sensory experience when readers open a can that contains artistic objects inside.

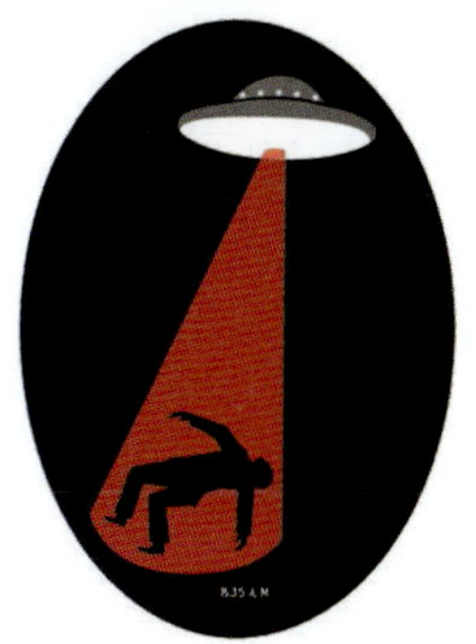

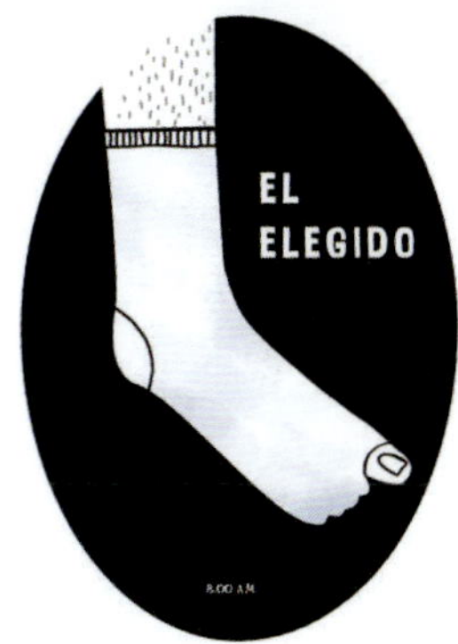

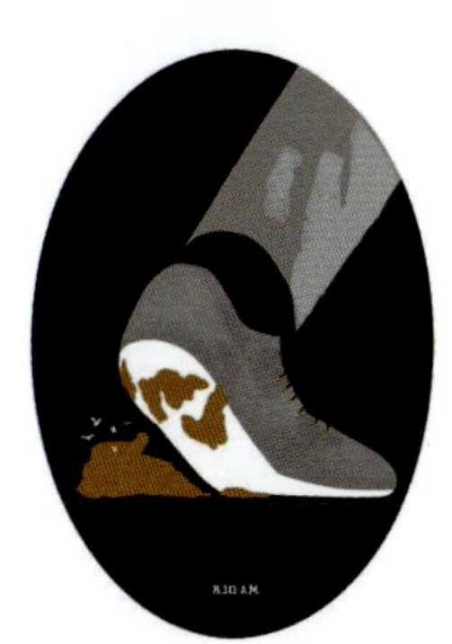

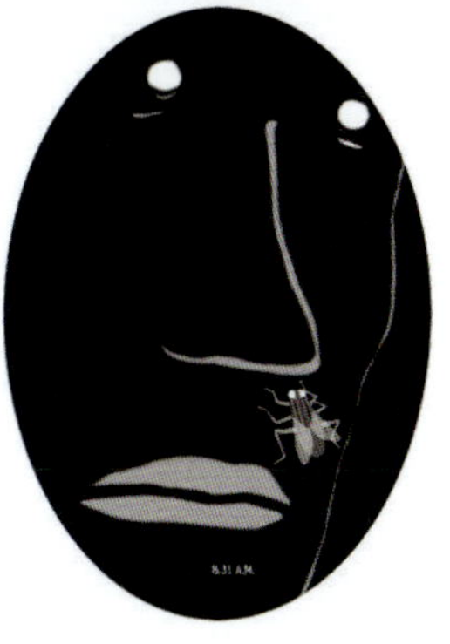

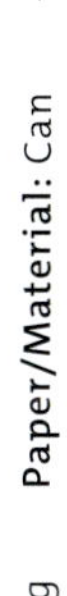

Paper/Material: Can

Weight: 1kg

Dimension: 170×260×190mm

GUILTY PLEASURE

CD & D
Nao Mi & LWT
P
Huanyu Lin & Wei Fang
DS
bonbonedition

2020

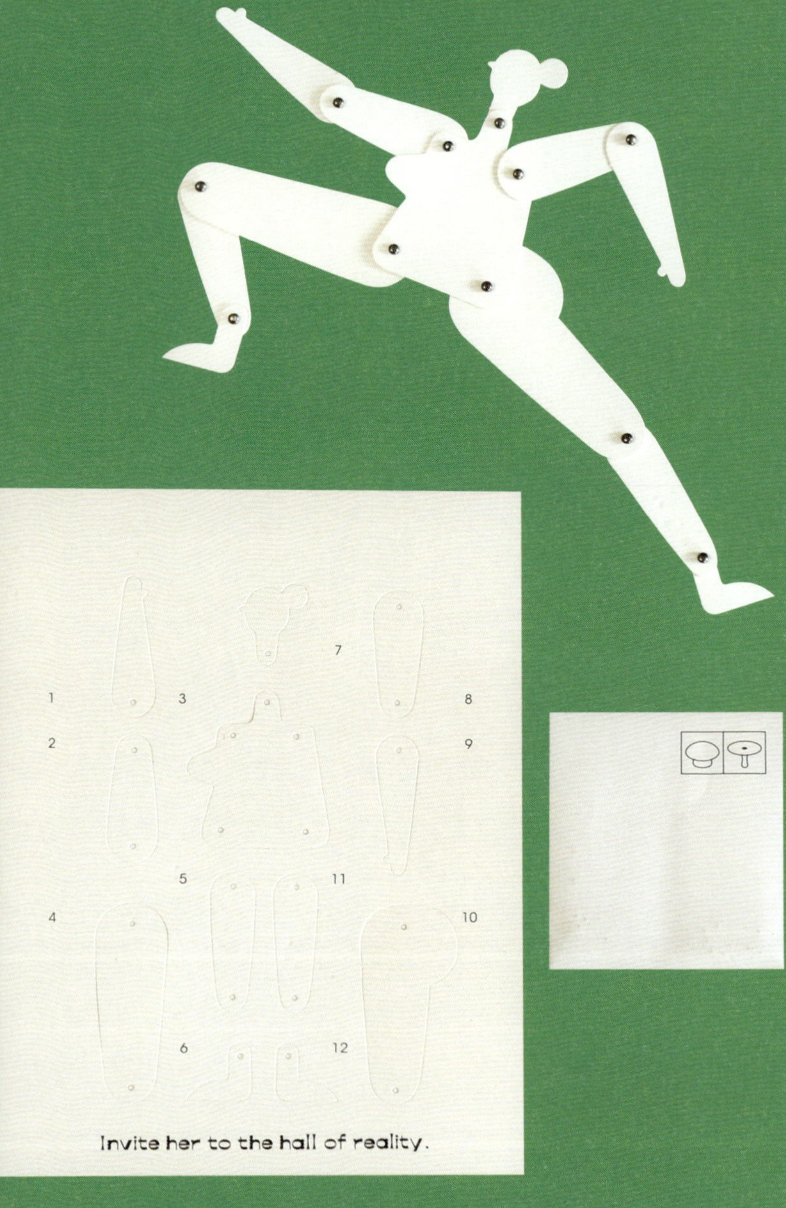

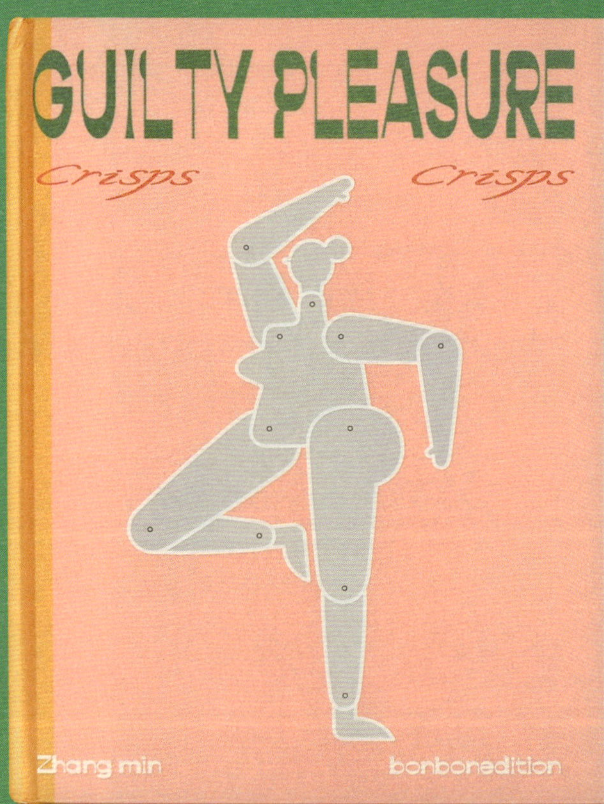

The book is about guilty pleasure, describing trivial and insignificant behaviors that can cause embarrassment or mild guilt, such as biting nails or squeezing acne.

The designer wanted to lead the readers to re-imagine this topic through design, and provide space for a game. At the end of the publication, there is a kit of handmade materials for readers to put together a paper action figure. The main character is outside of the book, with which readers can interact. It tries to explore the possibilities of publication with readers.

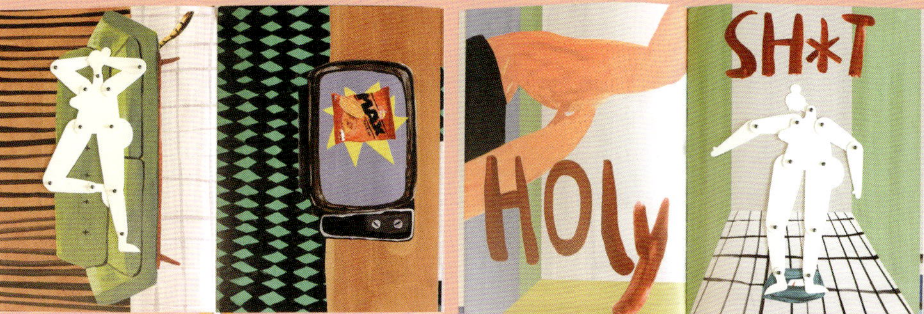

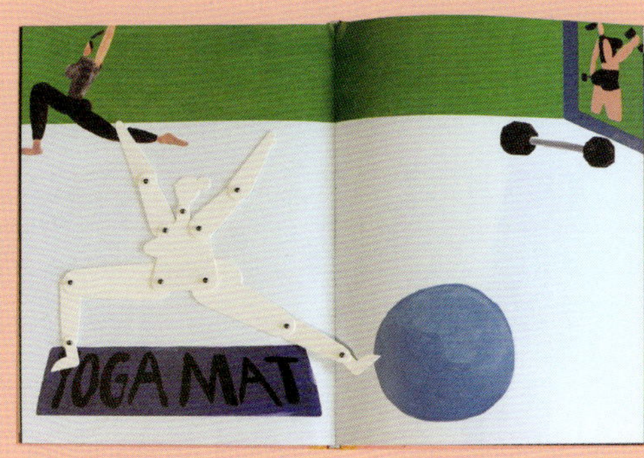

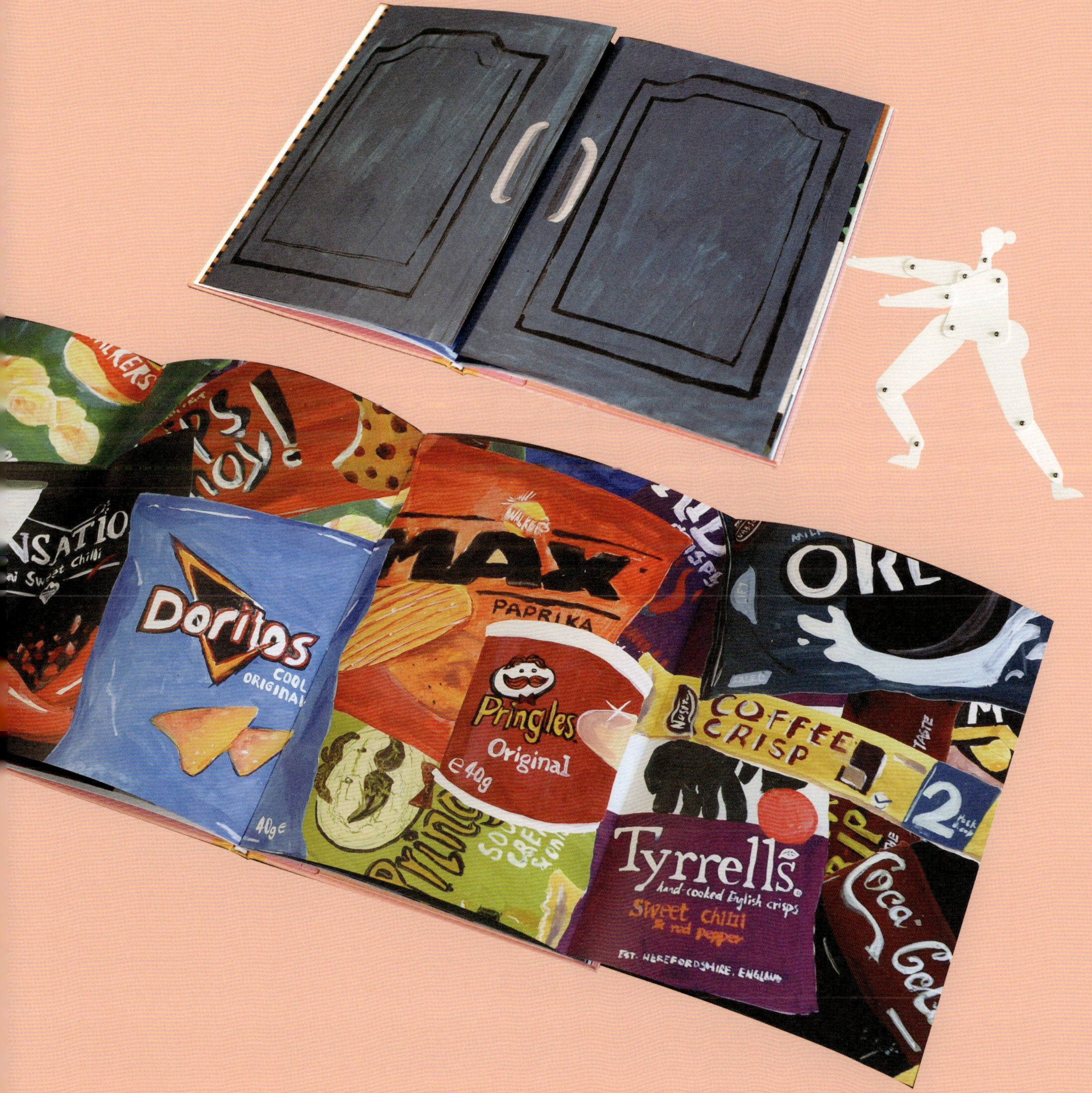

Page: 32 **Dimension:** 180×250×15mm **Weight:** 230g **Paper/Material:** Gao Jie Ying Hua Paper 140g; Coated Paper 157g **Binding:** Case Binding

IN BED

D
Yunqi Peng

2019

This work tries to carry the ideographical expression of book in the form of an installation. The designer amplified the overall visual power by materializing the key graphics, which is an experimental attempt based on her thinking on the concept of "book". She hopes readers can be attracted by the invisible form of this work. As an installation book, it is hard to hold it in the hands and read. To read this "book", readers have to stand in front of it, which is the special concept of this work.

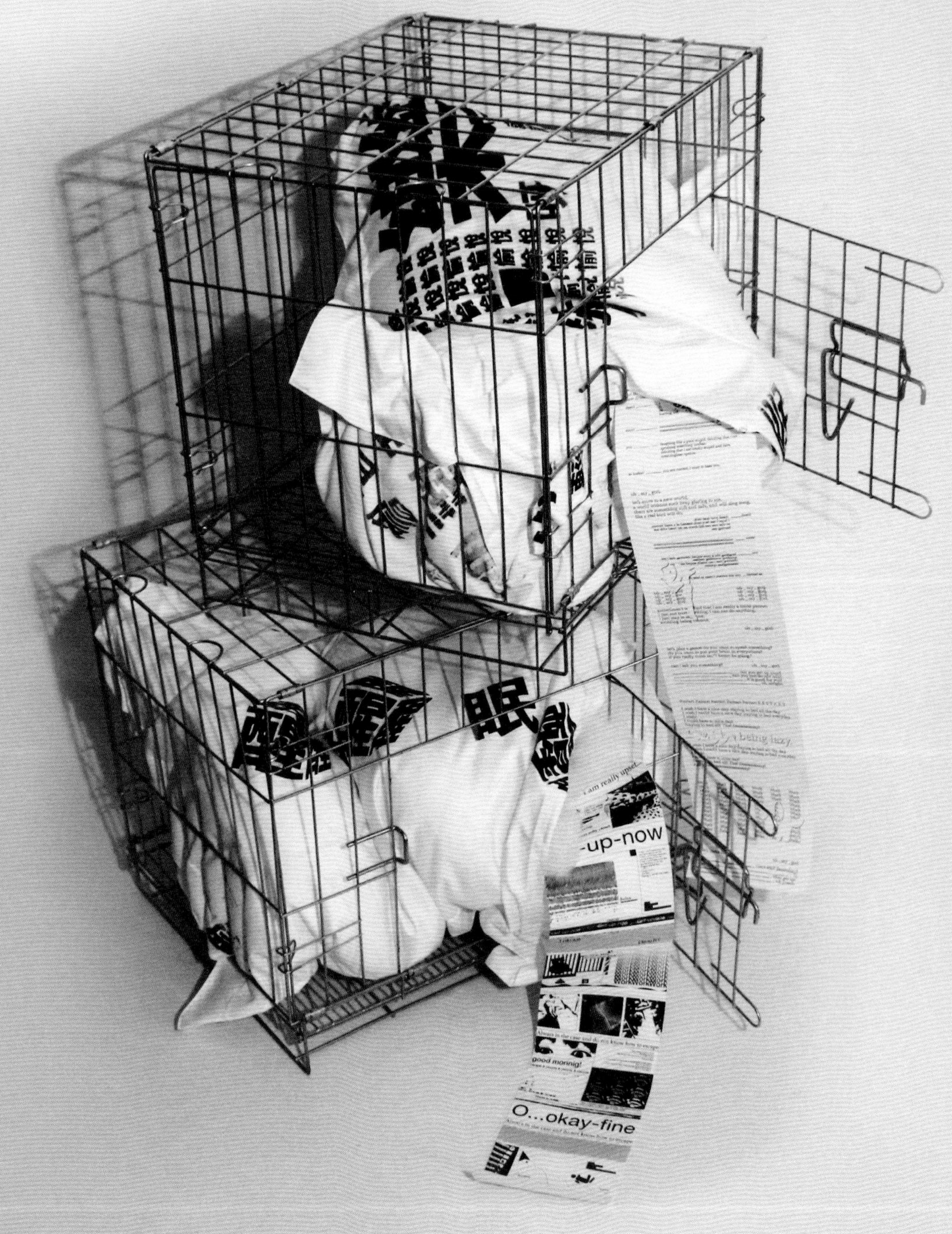

Dimension: 330×460×390mm

Weight: 4kg **Material:** Iron Cage; Pillow; Cotton

RM :1 .9

流水号：0421
打印时间 1 /08/11 18:03

他們不知道如何回復，卻又不肯認輸，我愉快地繼續躺在床上。

流水線上

商品名称
颜色商品

你願意成為流水線上的
一顆永不停息地拐彎兒的螺絲釘嗎？
你如果願意的話，
現在從床上爬起來也不是不可以。

（話說我只是想買瓶水欸）

品名	净重 (Kg)	单价 (元)	金额 (元)
	0.120	79.60	9.56

我想做從前不敢做的

合计：2.00元
优惠：0.76元
实付金额：1.24元

我想做從前不敢做的事，最簡單的就是，
在有事的時候也能賴在床上不動。

如果生活的目的就是為了保持快樂，那就好了。

（登記好了請再排隊，謝謝合作）

总计

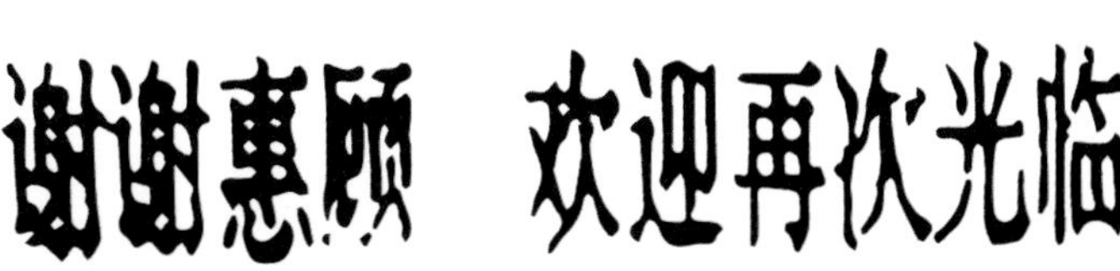

a rock is waiting for my life
i am not sure how many time it has been waiting,
but it is obviously waiting.

i tried to use printer to record my shouting,
but the printer was broken,
how dramatic.

thank ____________ thank you! dear rock.
i hope i can be a rock, instead of a weak human.
so that you can fall down on my head with not
hurting me.

101110 ____________ 10101010000011110101011010
1010101000001111010101110000001

you ____________ laughing like a pure stupid, thinking that i am
speaking somthing useless.
thinking that i am totally stupid and have
meaningless opnion.

as human ____________ you are correct, i want to hate you.

oh _ my _ god.

let's move to a new world,
a world without rock keep glaring to me.
there are something soft and safe, and will sing song,
like a real bird will do.

oh _ my _ god.
oh _ my _ god.
oh _ my _ god.
oh _ my _ god.

sometimes i find that i am really a timid person.
i can not hurt anything, i can not do anything,
i just stay in my zone,
avoiding being control.

oh _ my _ god.

let's play a game! do you want to speak something?
do you want to put your brain in everywhere?
if you really think so, "i better be going."

can i ask you something? oh _ my _ god.

____________ can you get up now?
____________ can you just do not talk?
____________ it is good for you!
____________ ok, alright.

Restart Restart Restart Restart Restart R E S T A R T

I wish I have a nice day: staying in bed all the day.
I wish I could have a nice day: staying in bed everyday.
I wish!
I could have a...nice day!
Staying in bed all! The! Daaaaaaaaay!

being lazy.

I wish I have a nice day: staying in bed all the day.
I wish I could have a nice day: staying in bed everyday.
I wish!
I could have a...nice day!
Staying in bed all! The! Daaaaaaaaay!
All! The! Daaaaaaaaaaaaaay!

Work Work Work Work Work Work
Work Work Work Work Work Work
Work Work Work Work Work Work
Relax Relax Relax Relax Relax Relax

ciao, come stai? oh _ my _ god.

____________ come stai? Benissimo?
____________ Sì.
____________ then get up!
____________ ok, grazie.

ALONE TIME

D
Youngchae Lee

2020

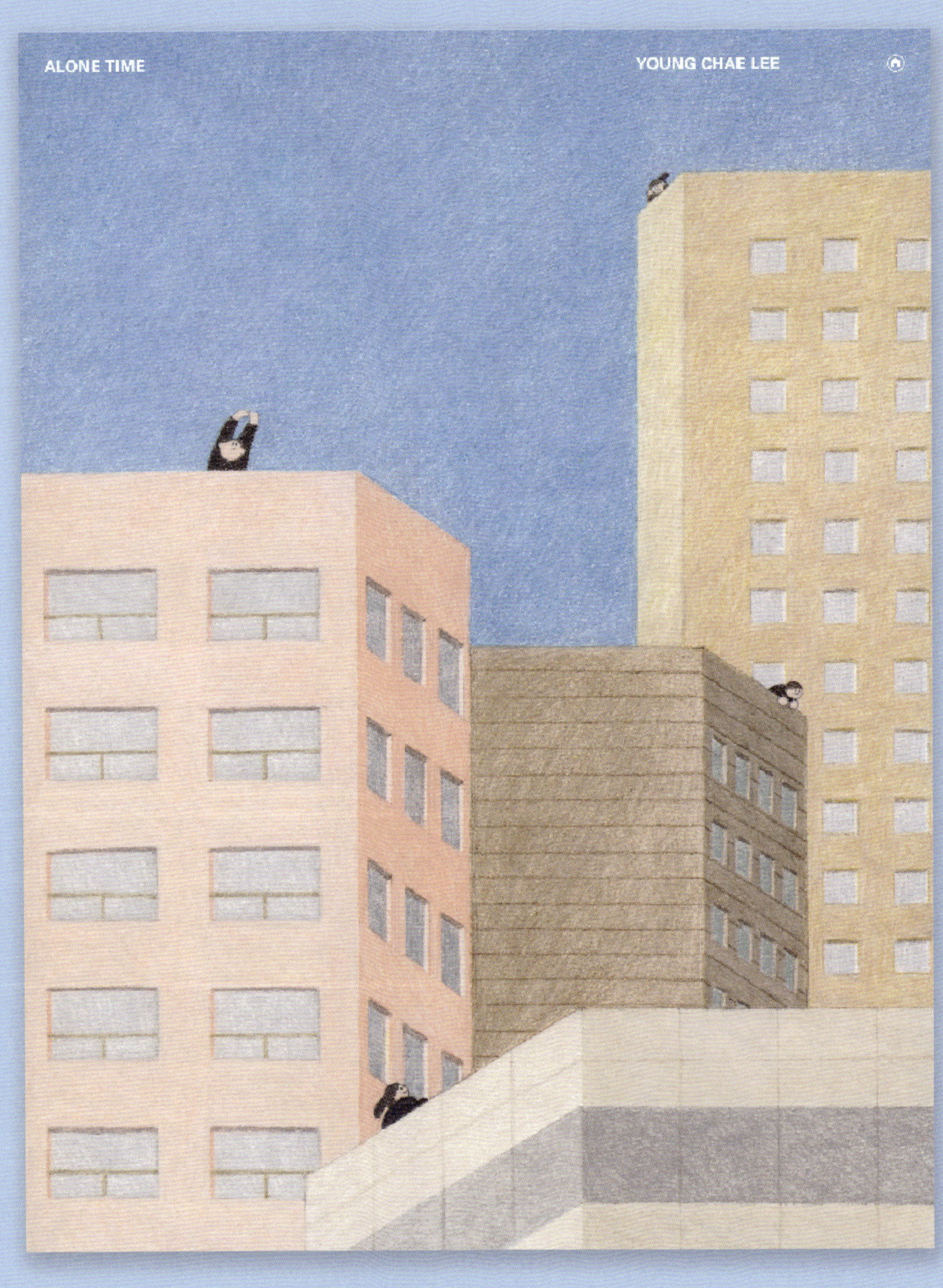

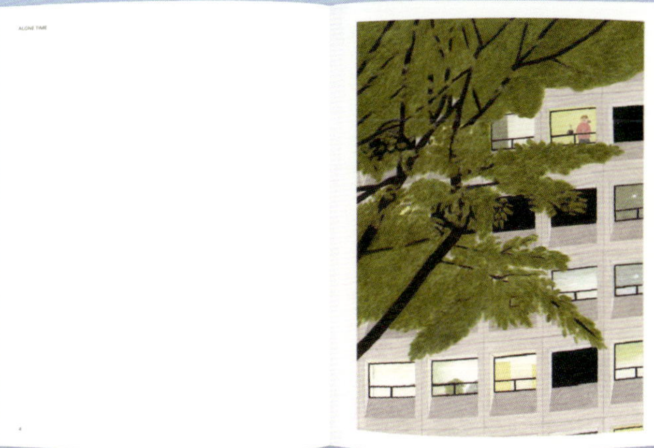

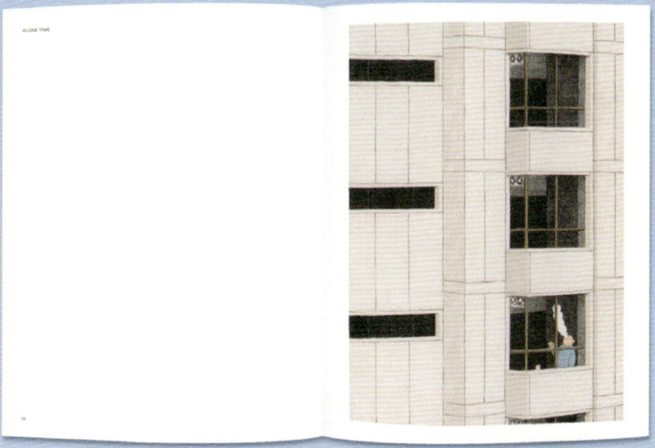

ALONE TIME

6

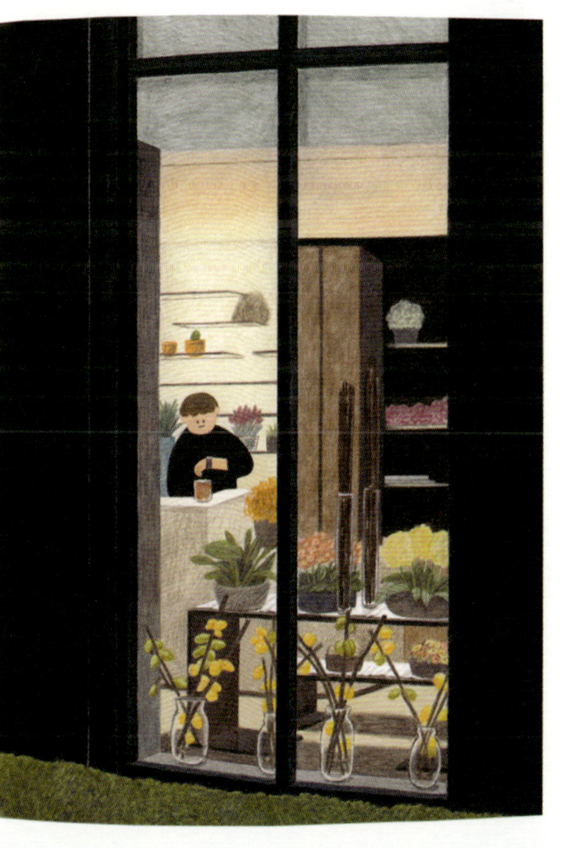

Page: 20 Dimension: 240×320mm Paper/Material: Uncoated Paper Binding: Saddle Stitching

GITAI ARCHIVE—MEAT MAP MARKET

D
Tomoyuki Koseko
DS
koseko design & press

2016

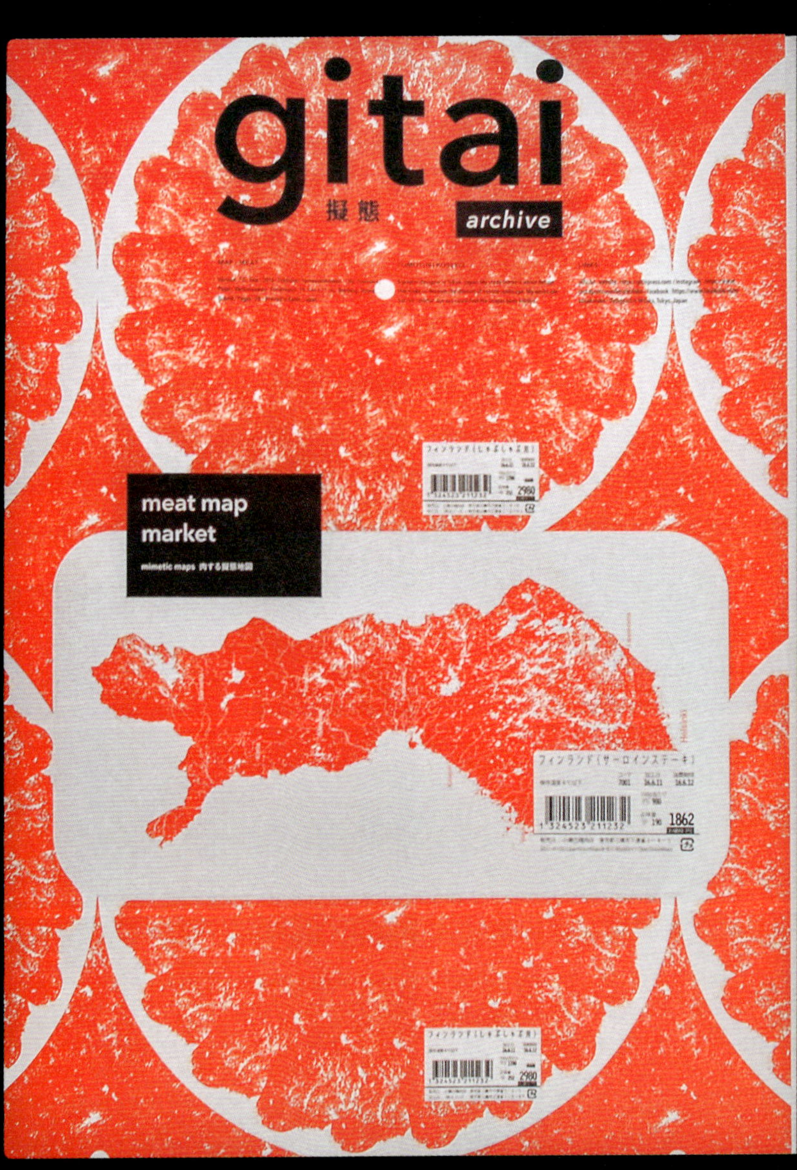

The theme of the *Gitai* project is "visualizing the mimicry hidden in daily objects through the power of design", and has been published since 2016. While mimicry is usually discussed in the context of biology, the aim of this magazine is to design new mimicries from daily objects in order to share new points of view with readers.

Each issue presents a new mimicry, such as "Meat Map Market", in which a map of the country is represented as meat; or "Tree Rings in Maps", in which a map of mountains is represented as tree rings.

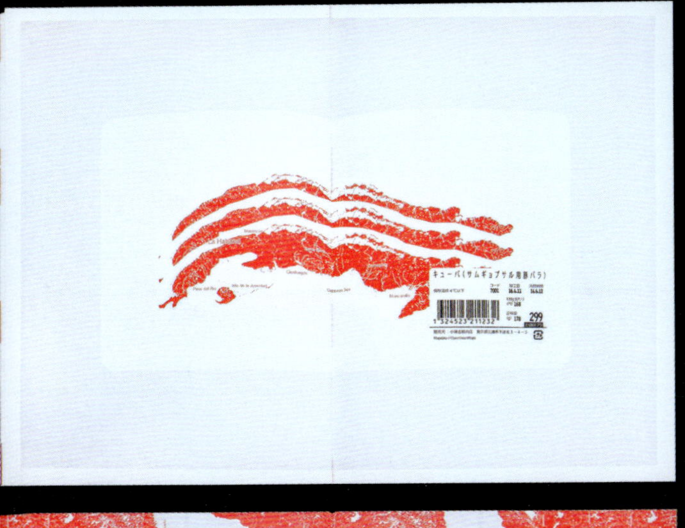

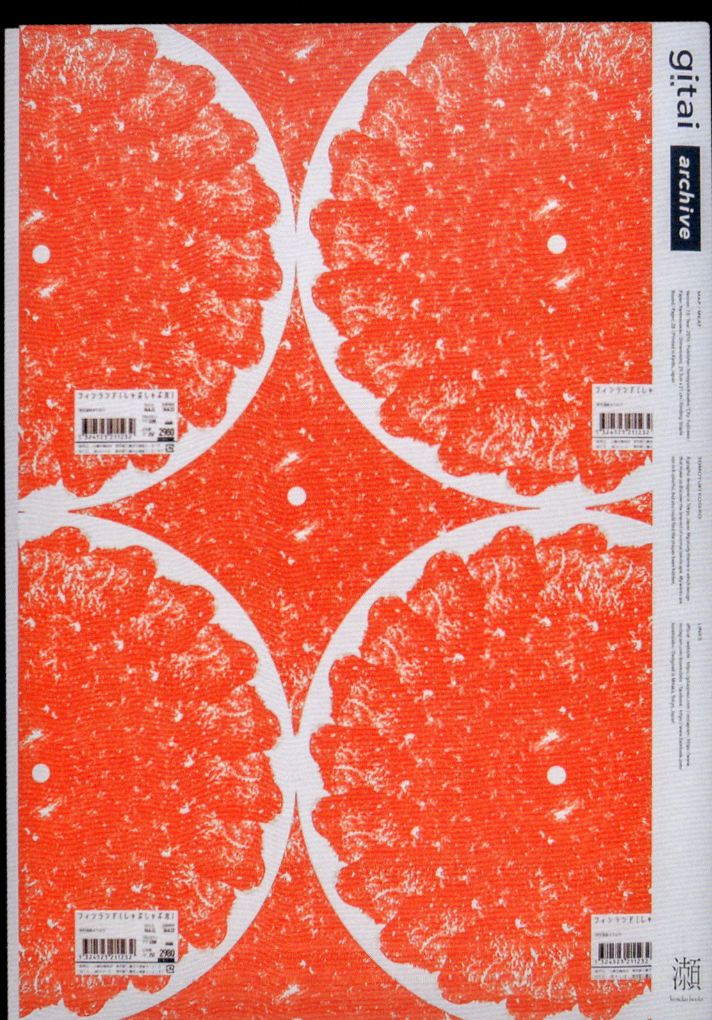

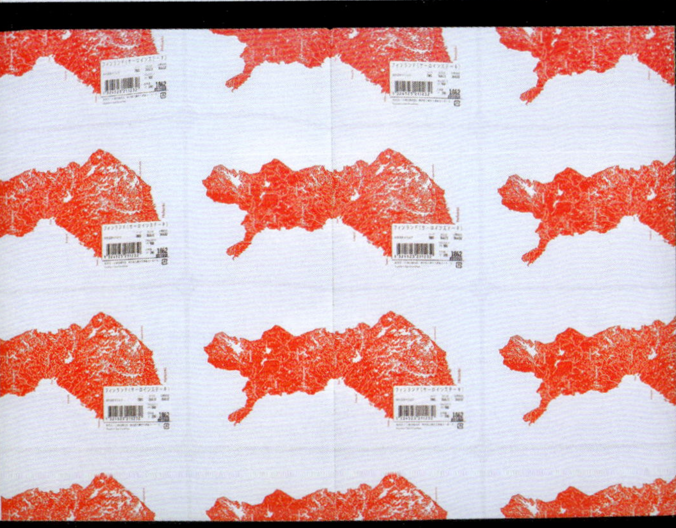

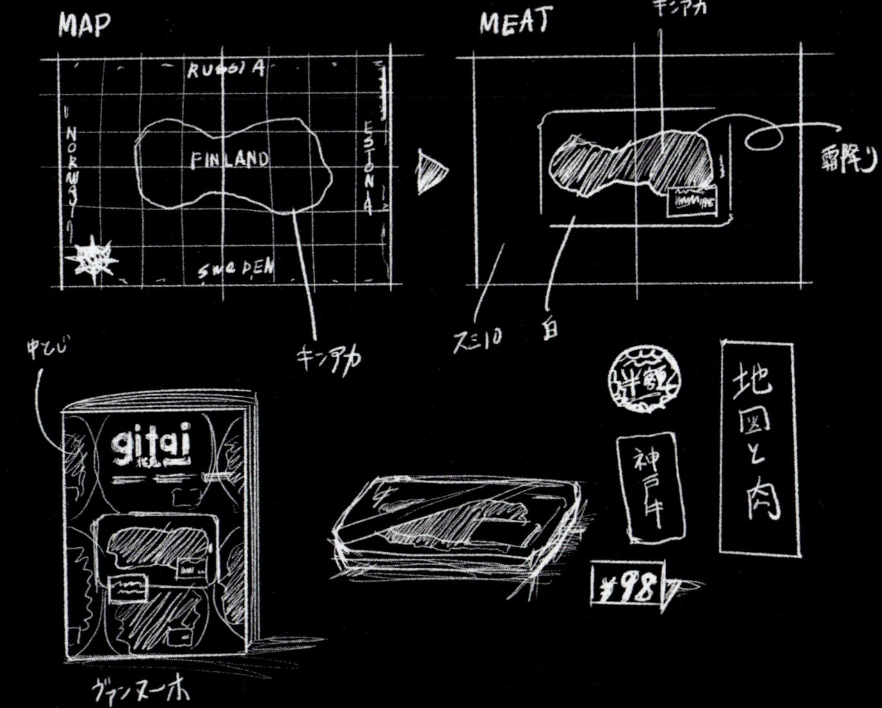

al: Ventnouveau Binding: Saddle Stitching

GITAI ARCHIVE — TREE RINGS IN MAPS

D
Tomoyuki Koseko
DS
koseko design & press

2017

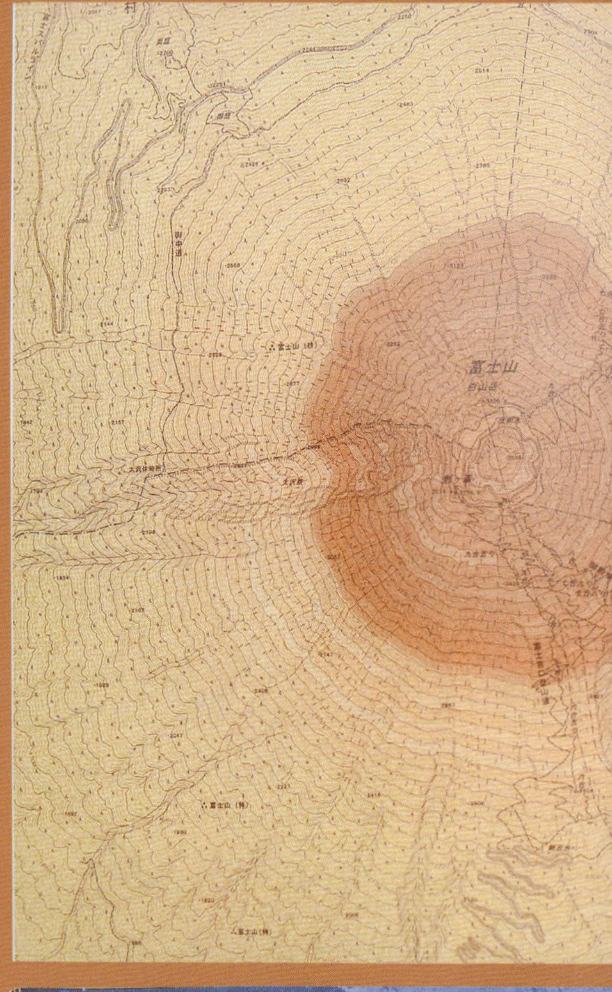

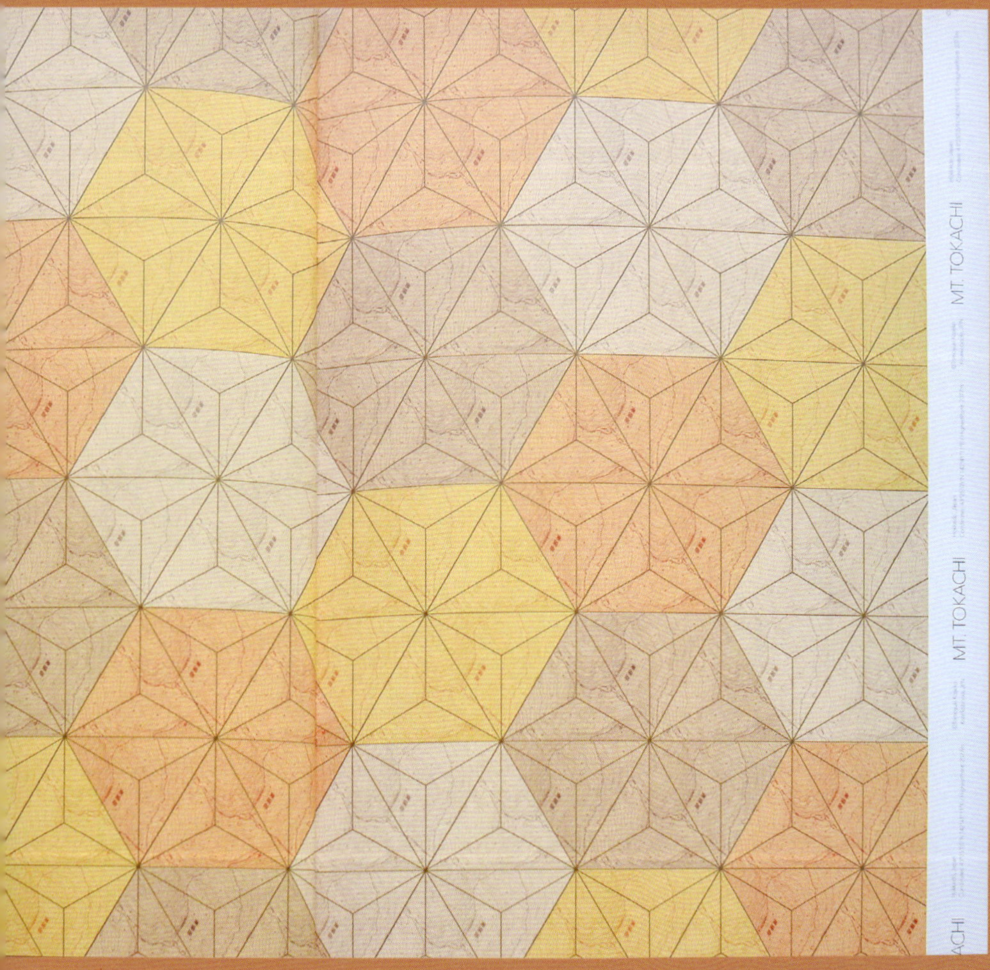

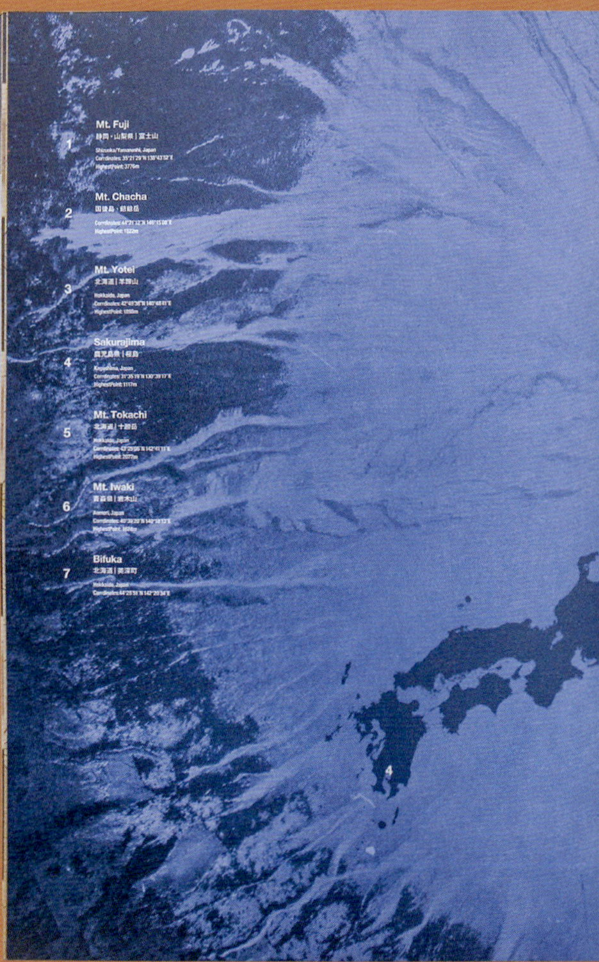

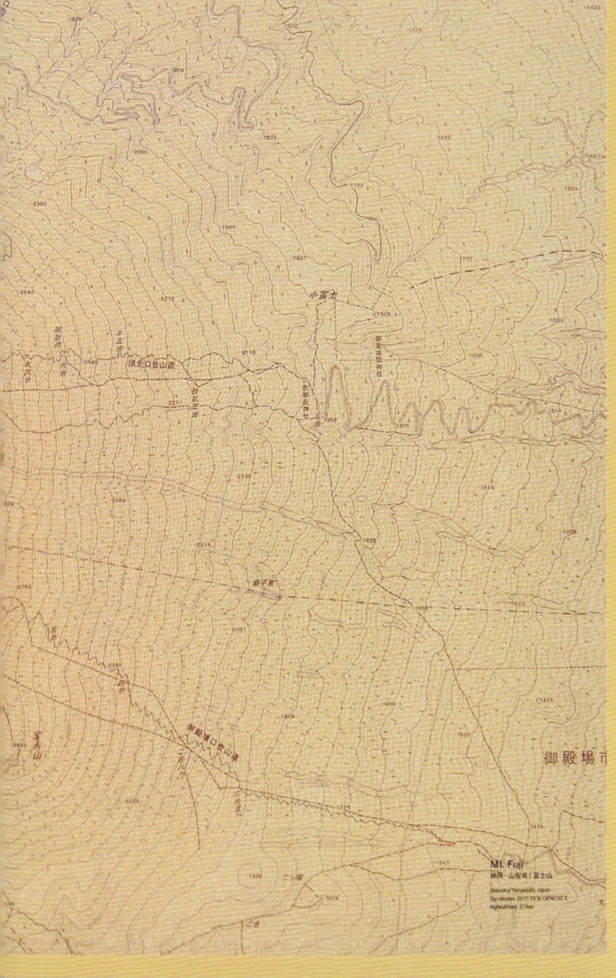

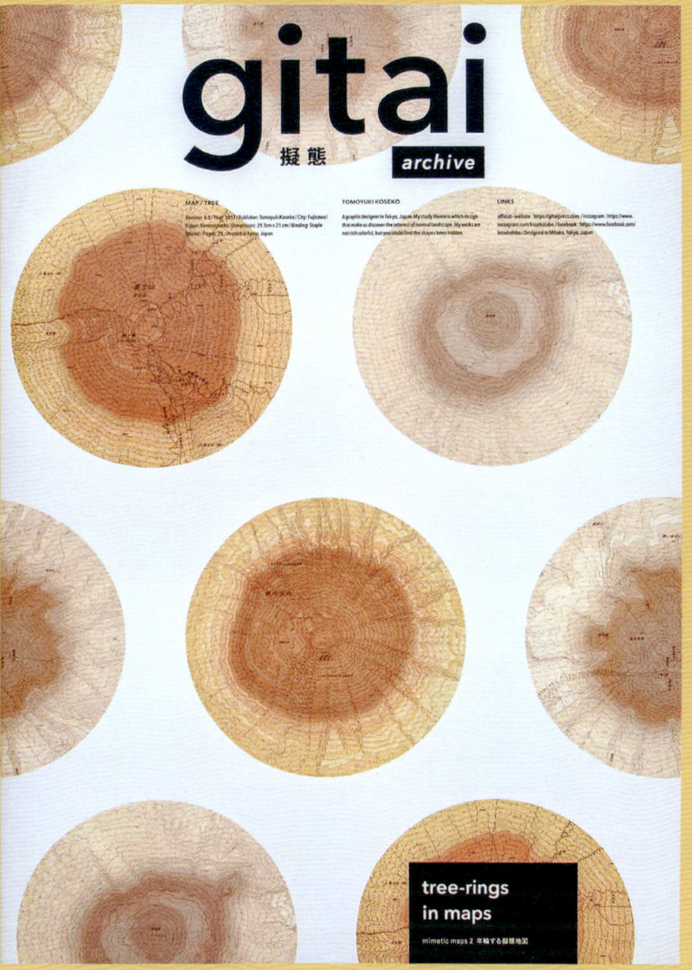

The Mimetic Maps 2 is a new work of the series "Mimetic Maps" which is continuing the experimental mix of art and graphic design.

Recording the process of how to simulate the topographic maps such as the well-known symbol of Japan: Mt.fuji to the colored tree ring patterns that everyone is familiar with. The unexpected similarities between tree rings and maps will be remarkable.

Koseko books
Fujisawa, Kanagawa, Japan
https://kosekobooks.com
Edit/Design: Tomoyuki Koseko 小瀬古智之
Printed in Japan

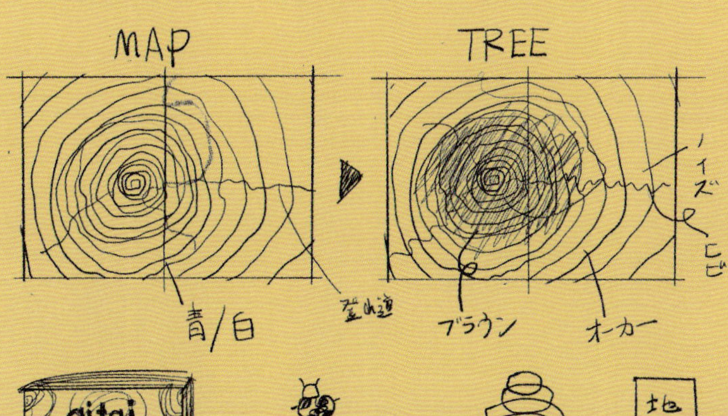

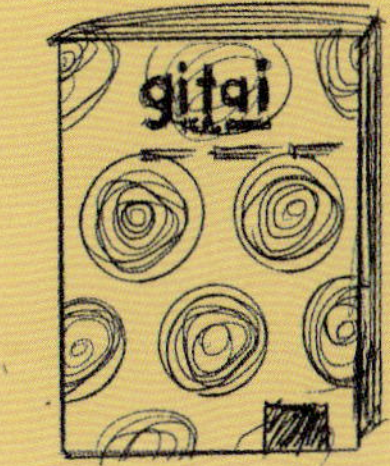

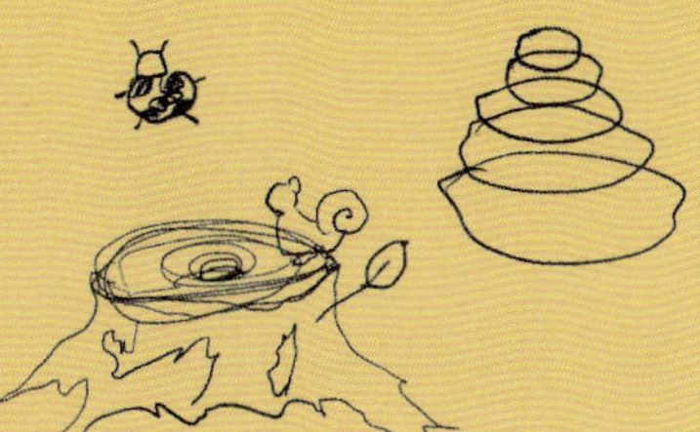

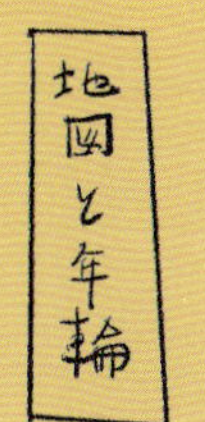

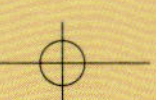

Page: 28 **Dimension:** 210×297mm **Weight:** 150g

Paper/Material: Ventnouveau **Binding:** Saddle Stitching

GITAI ARCHIVE— SNOW CRYSTALS OF MAPS

D
Tomoyuki Koseko
DS
koseko design & press

2019

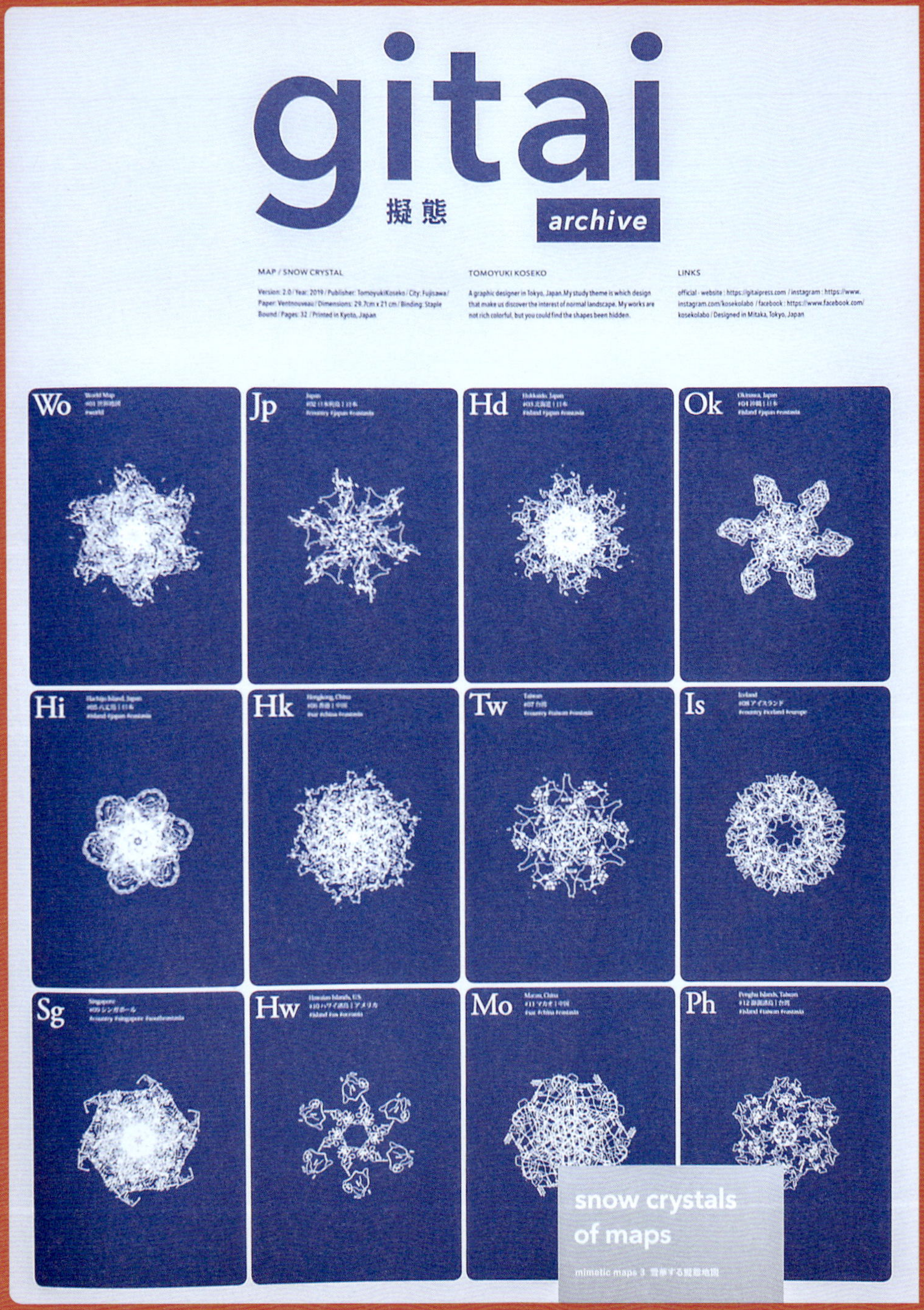

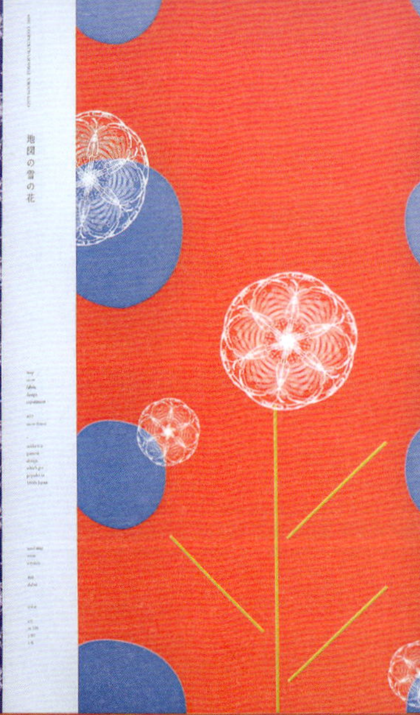

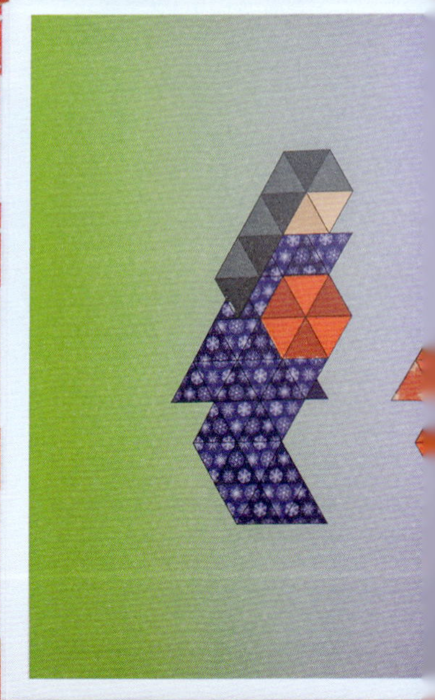

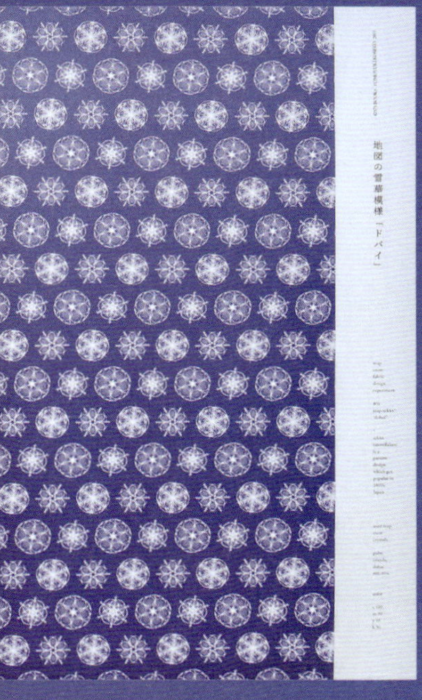

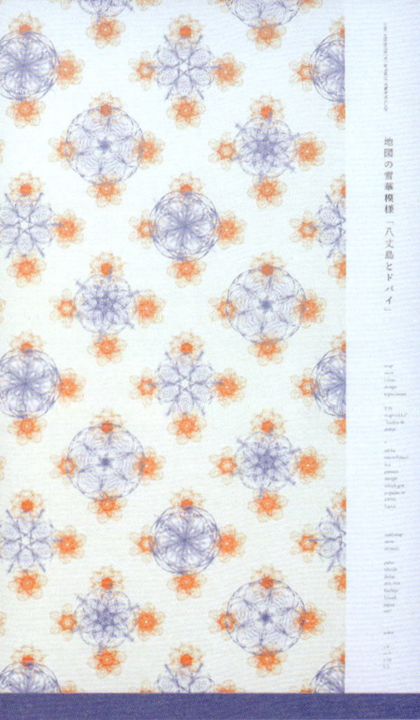

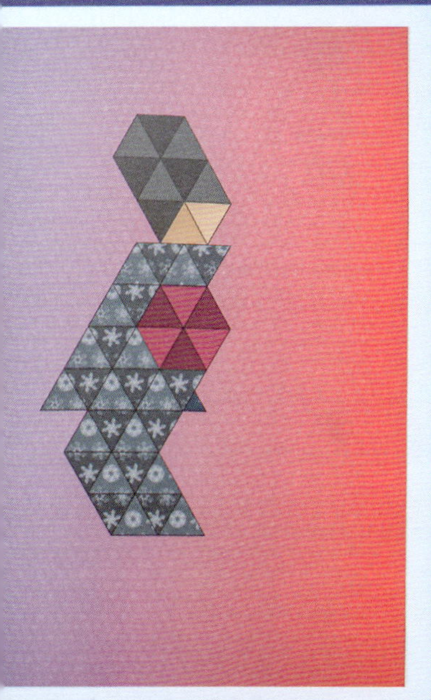

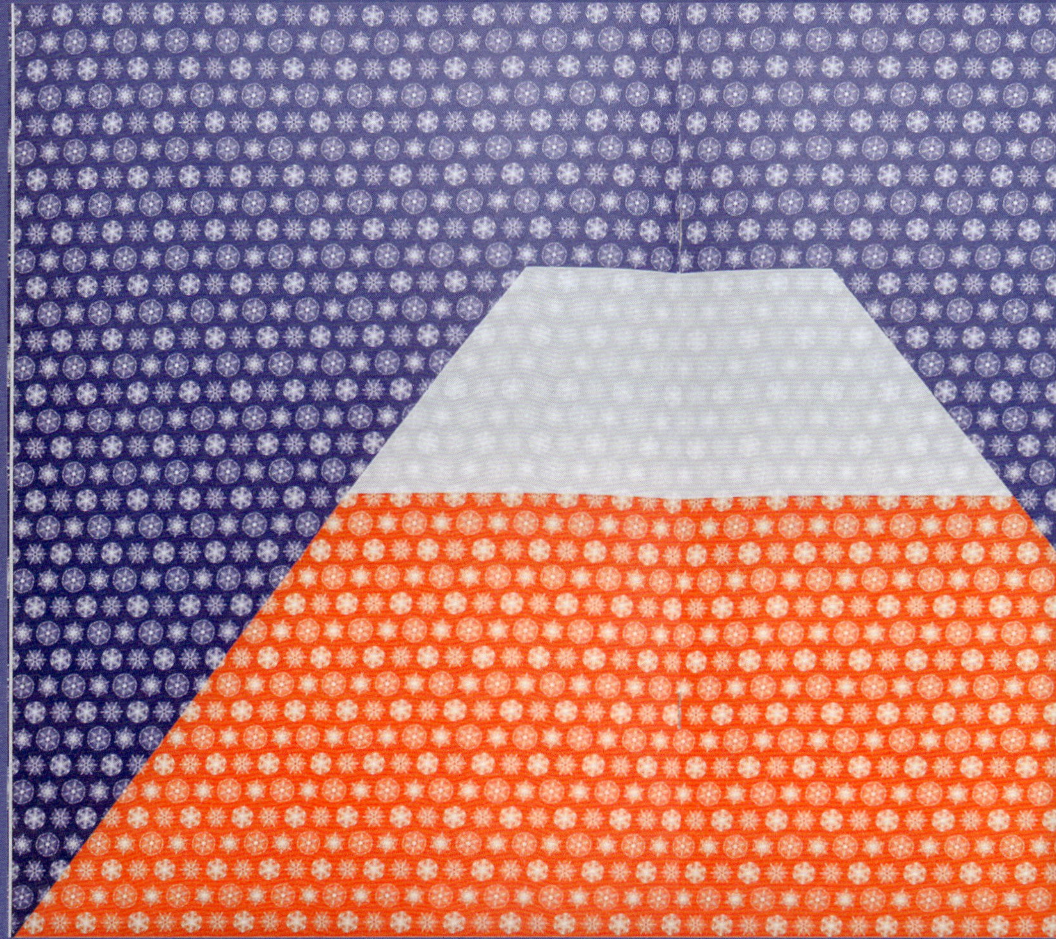

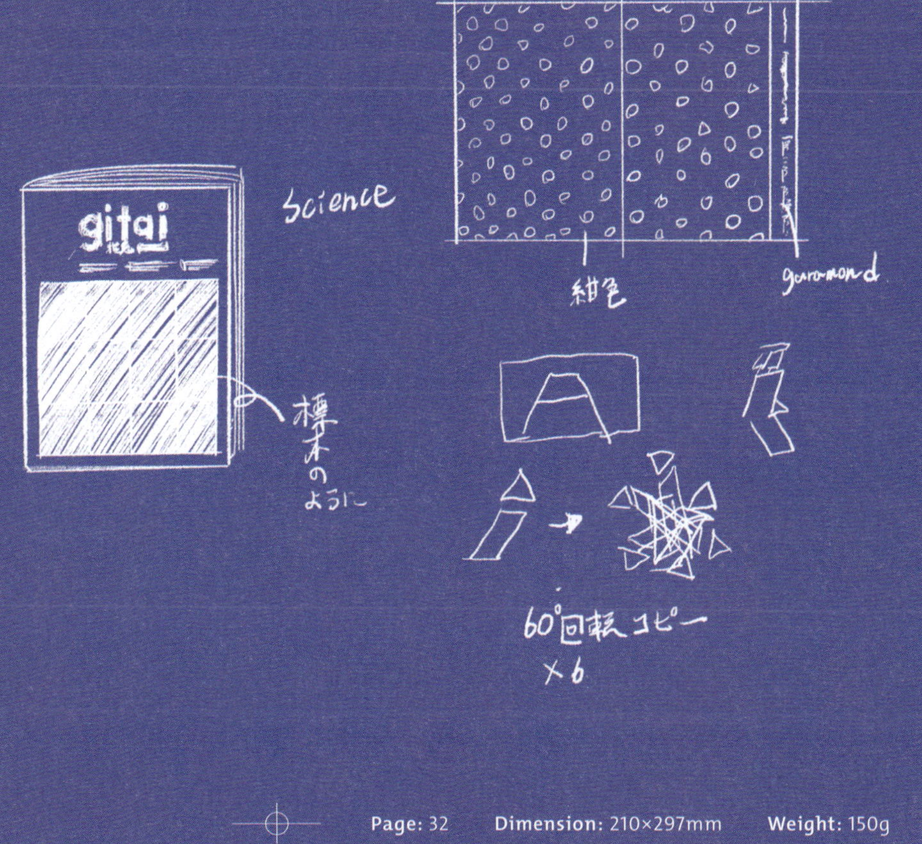

Page: 32 Dimension: 210×297mm Weight: 150g

Paper/Material: Ventnouveau

Binding: Saddle Stitching

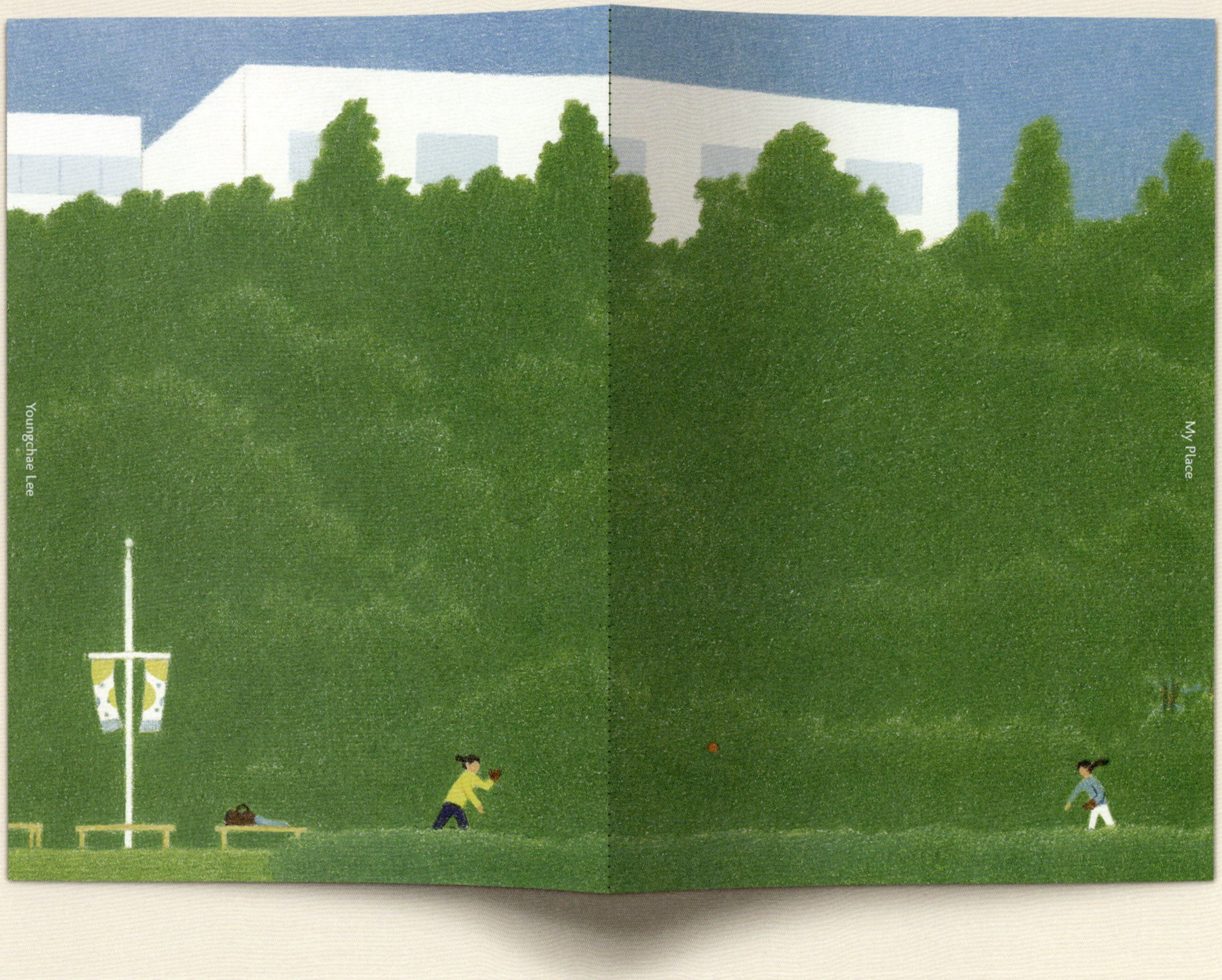

MY PLACE

D
Youngchae Lee

2020

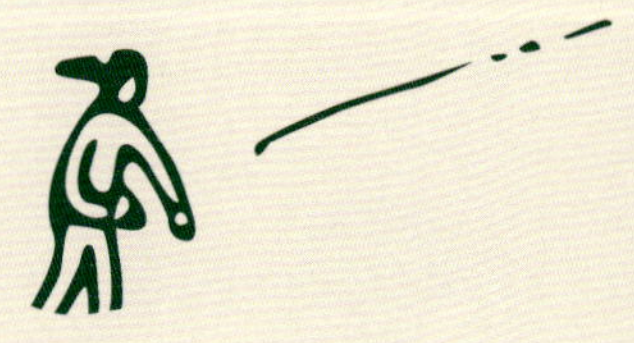

The book shares various observations of unseen beautiful scenes from the neighborhood. It is important that every illustration can be seen without interruption, so the designer leaves a space between pictures and uses a minimum font size in the pages.

The type on the cover is designed so that the picture could stand out firstly. The color of the thread used for binding is chosen for the same reason, and the binding makes the whole picture easy to look at.

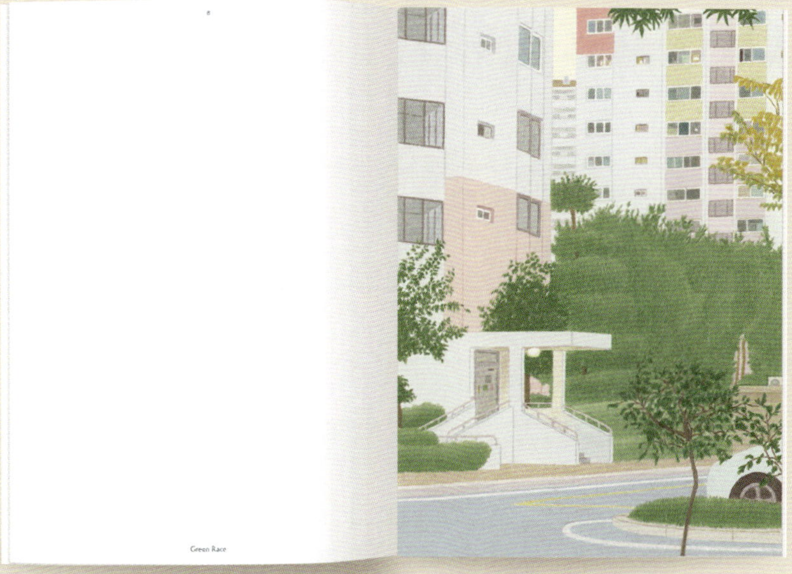

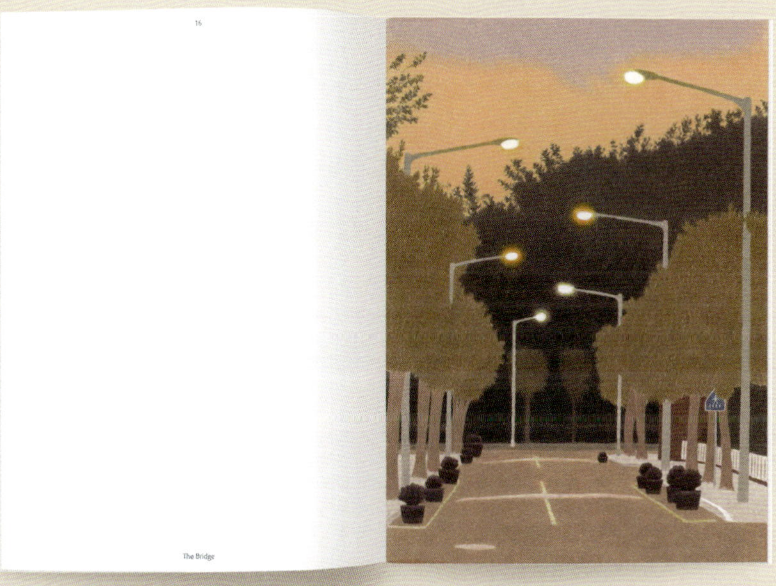

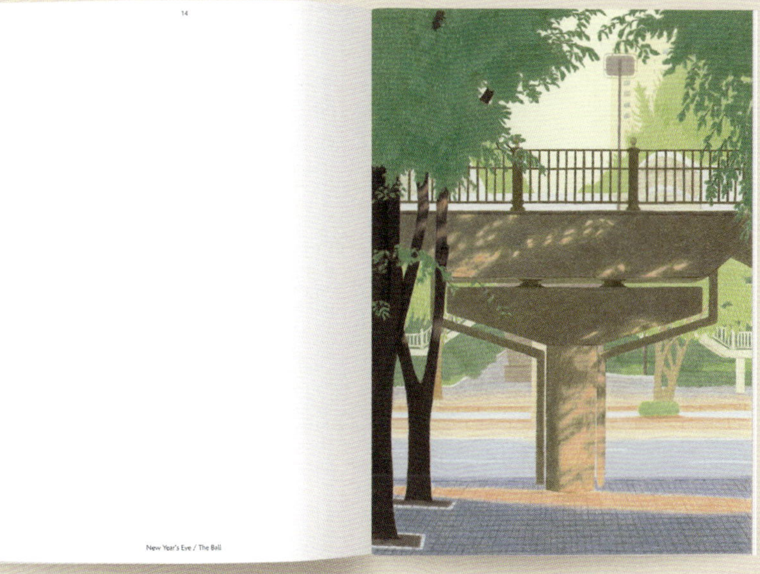

Page: 24 **Dimension:** 210×297mm **Paper/Material:** Rough Gloss Paper **Binding:** Singer Sewn Binding

ORDINARY #7

D
Yuki Kappes & Max Siedentopf

2016-2021

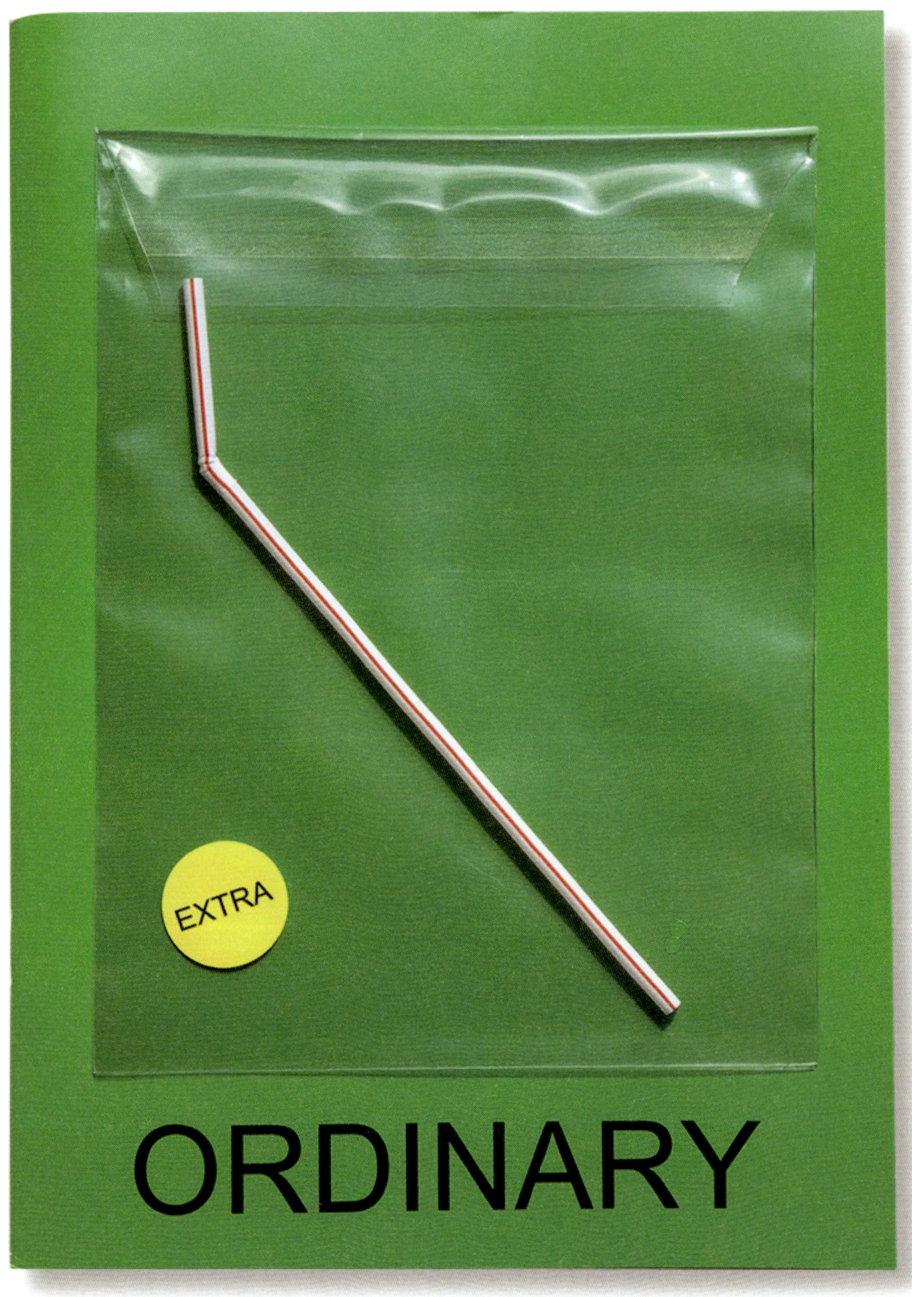

Ordinary is a quarterly fine art photography magazine featuring over 20 artists around the world who are sent one ordinary object, which comes as an extra, and tasked with making this object extra-ordinary.

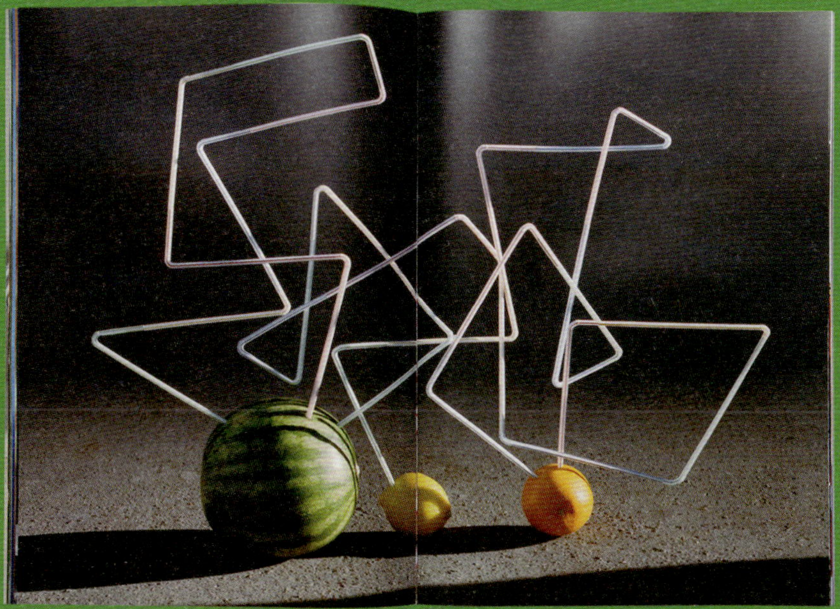

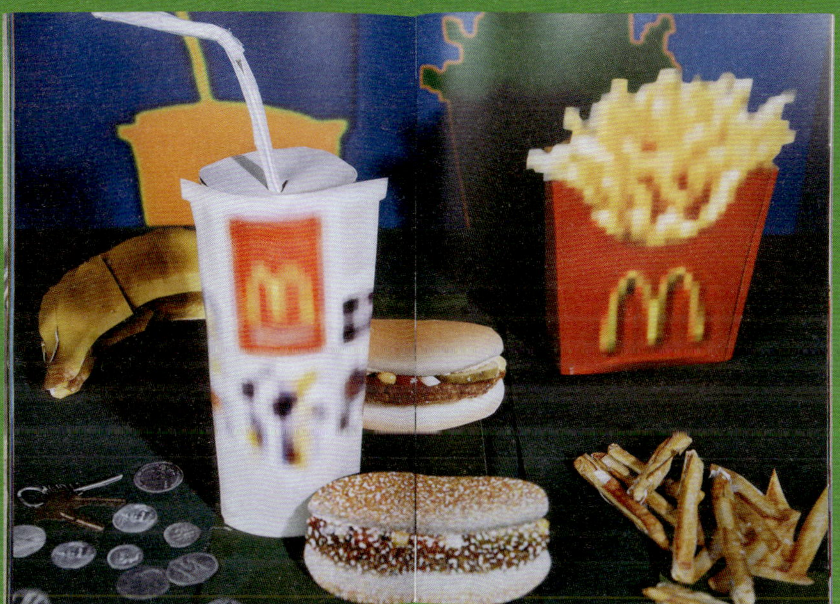

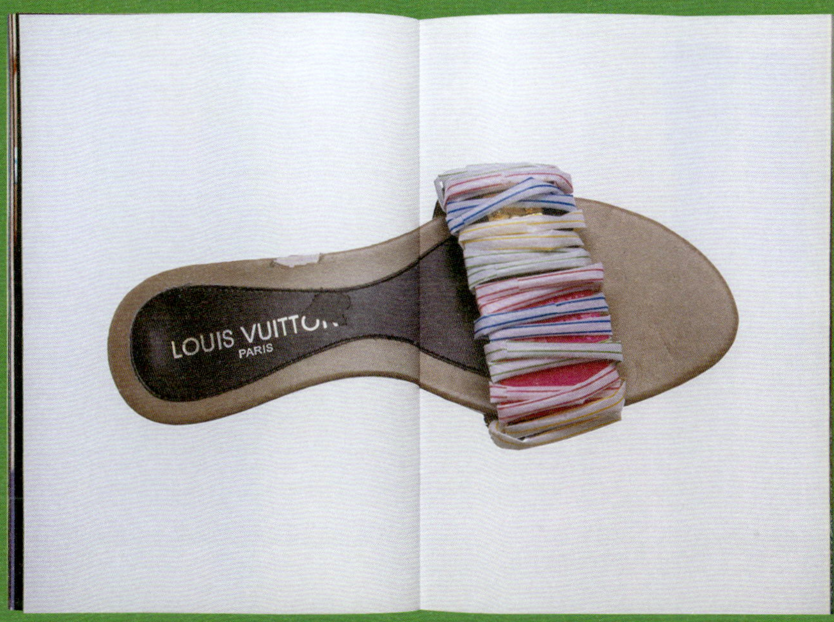

Page: Issue Specific **Dimension:** 210×297mm **Weight:** Issue Specific **Binding:** Saddle Stitching

ORDINARY #8

D
Yuki Kappes & Max Siedentopf

2016-2021

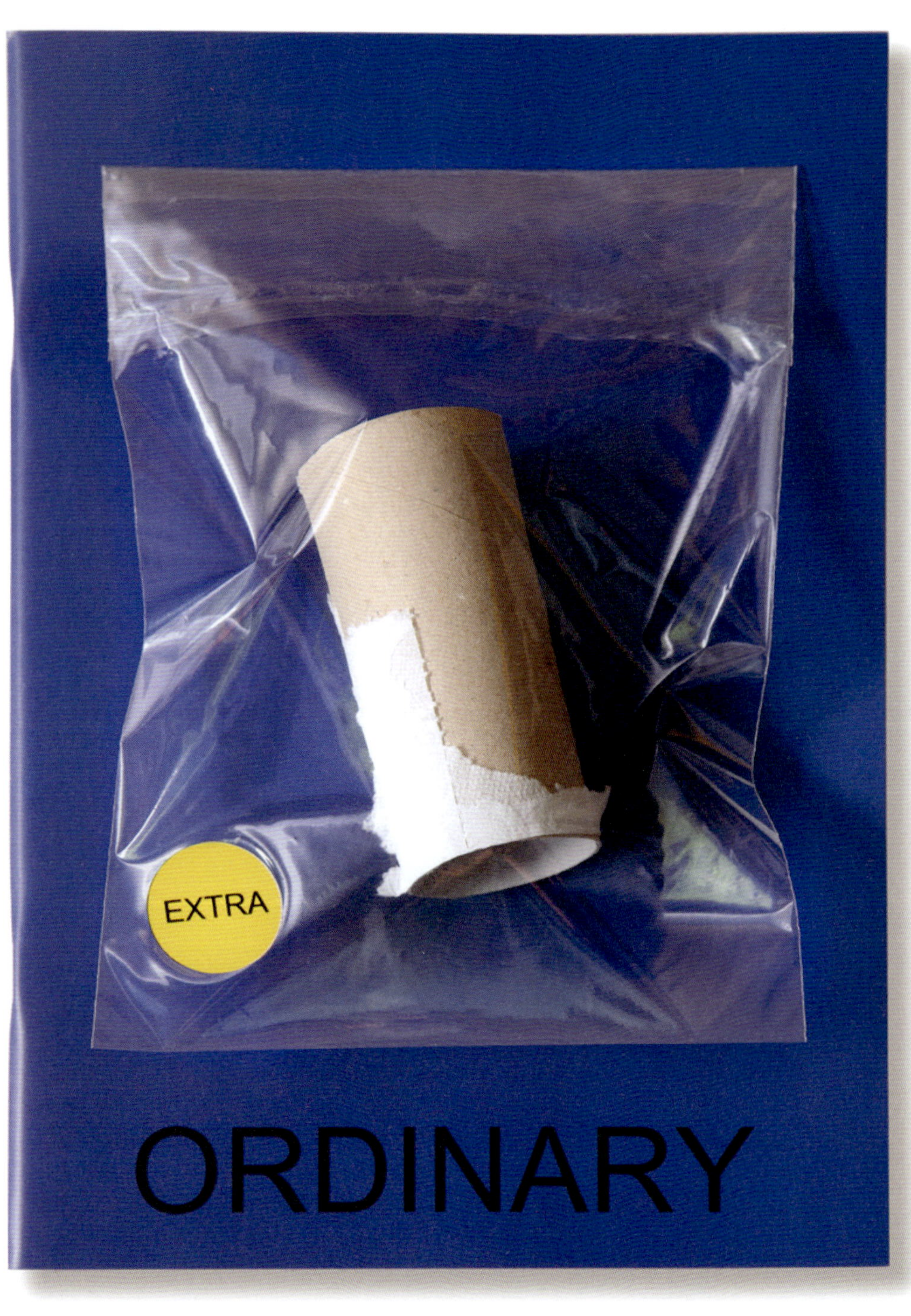

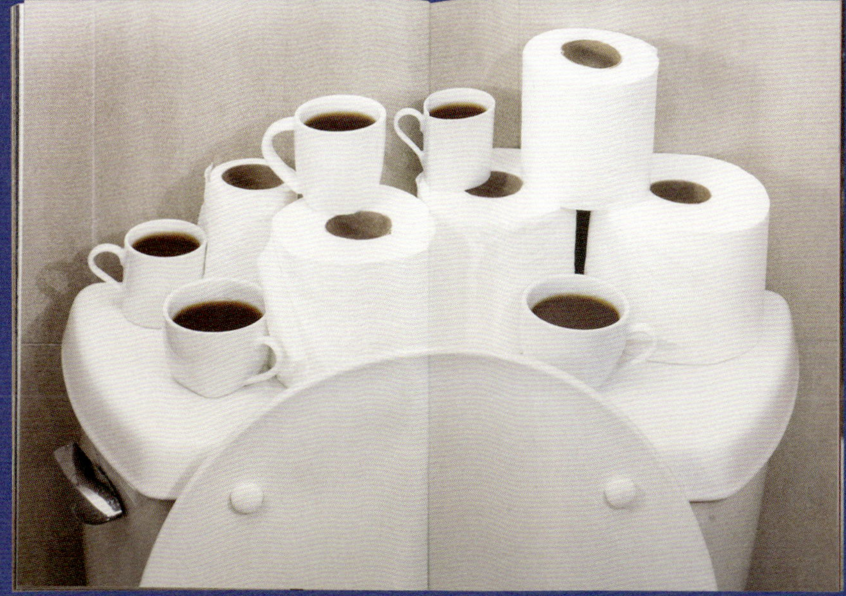

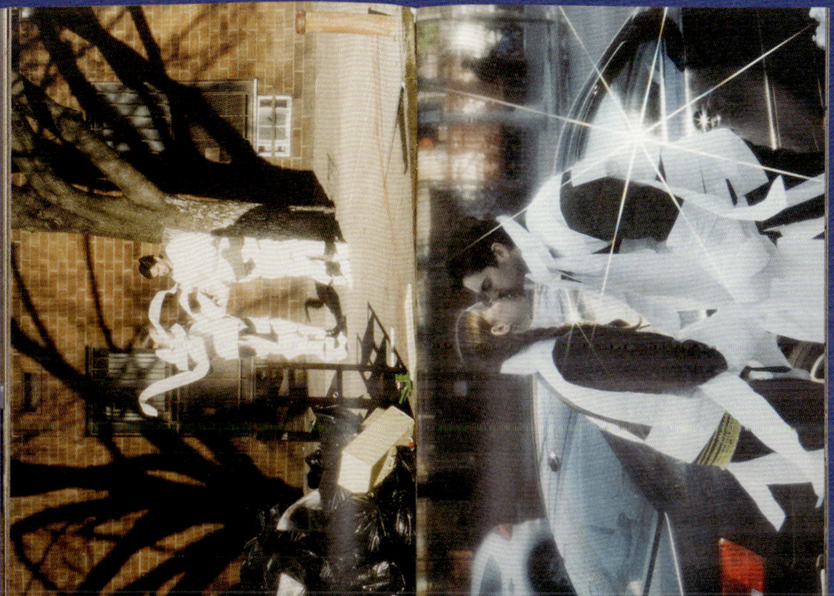

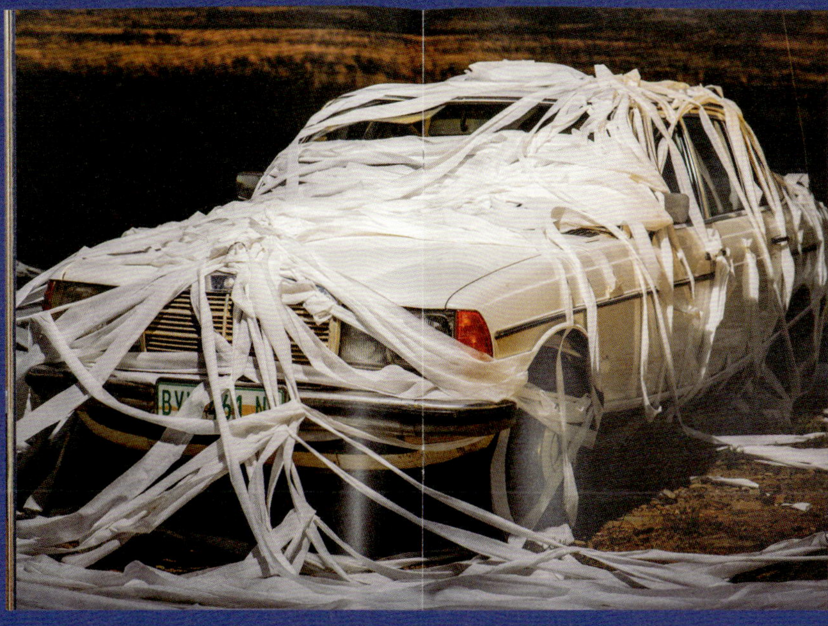

Page: Issue Specific **Dimension:** 210×297mm **Weight:** Issue Specific **Binding:** Saddle Stitching

ORDINARY #9

D
Yuki Kappes & Max Siedentopf

2016-2021

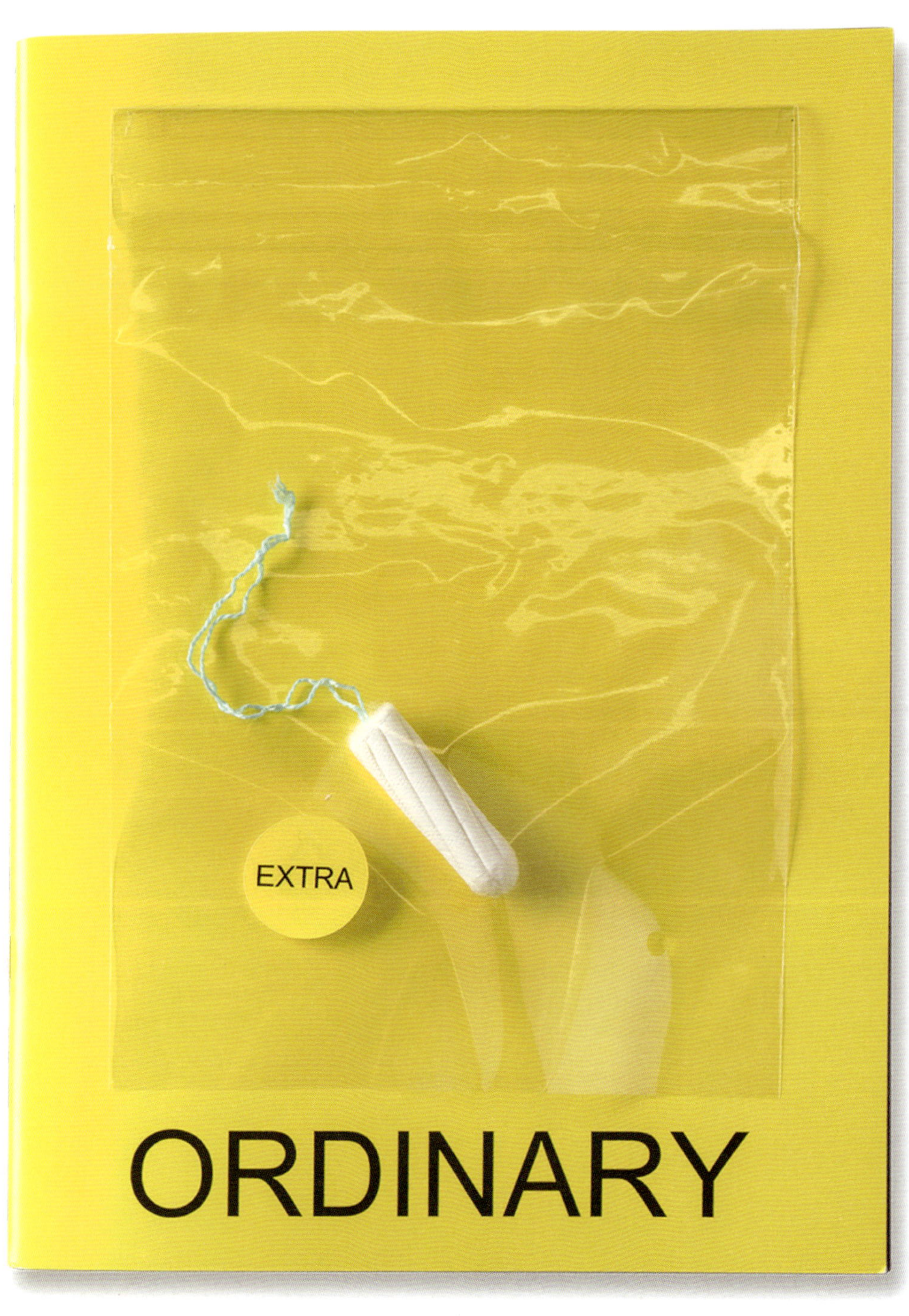

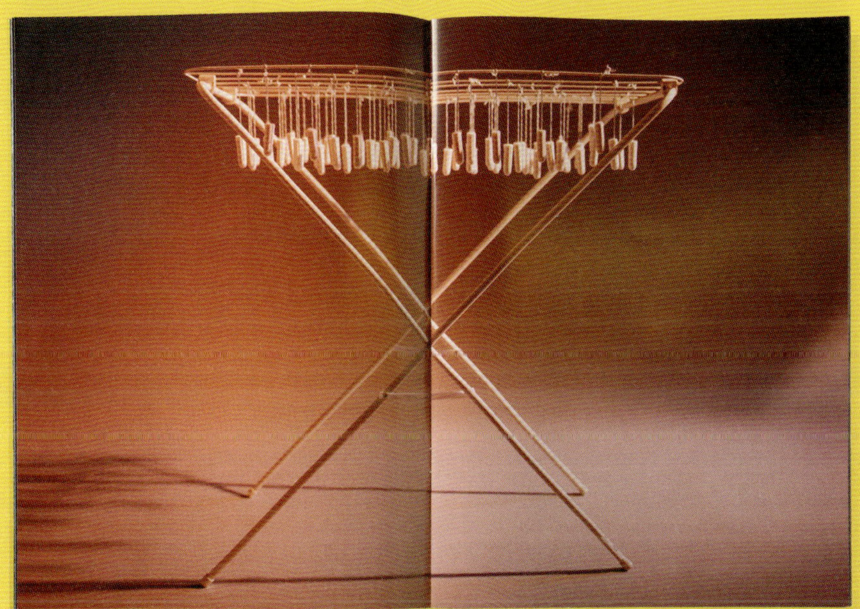

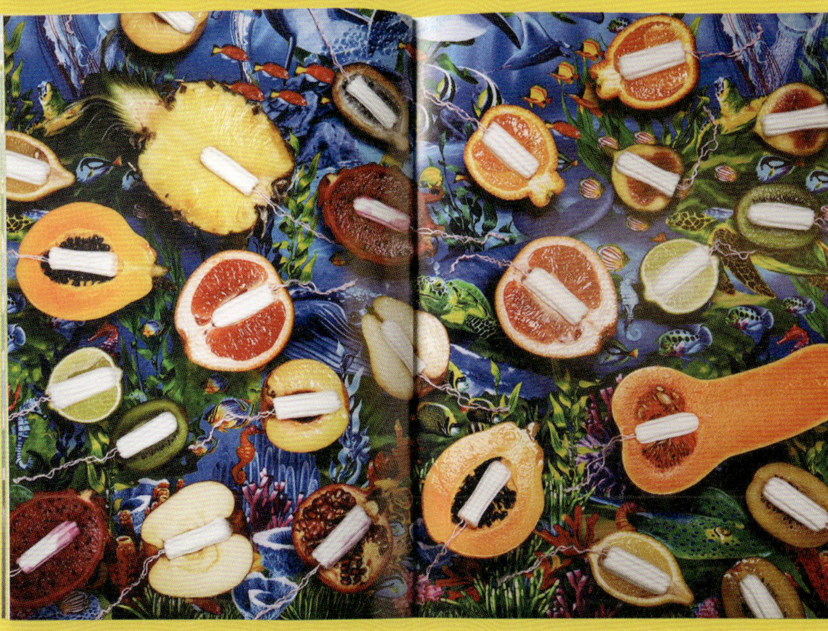

Page: Issue Specific **Dimension:** 210×297mm **Weight:** Issue Specific **Binding:** Saddle Stitching

ART HOLE

D
Bird Pit

2019

Art Hole is a doodle book that humorously satirizes modern art and summarizes the reality of visiting museums and galleries today. In museums and galleries, people decorate themselves with cell phones, selfie sticks and art-related goods (hats, T-shirts and phone stickers). Art works become secondary to the potential of online appreciation. The designer chose cartoon paper as the text page, hoping the overall impression of the book to be read in a comic and humorous way.

ART HOLE

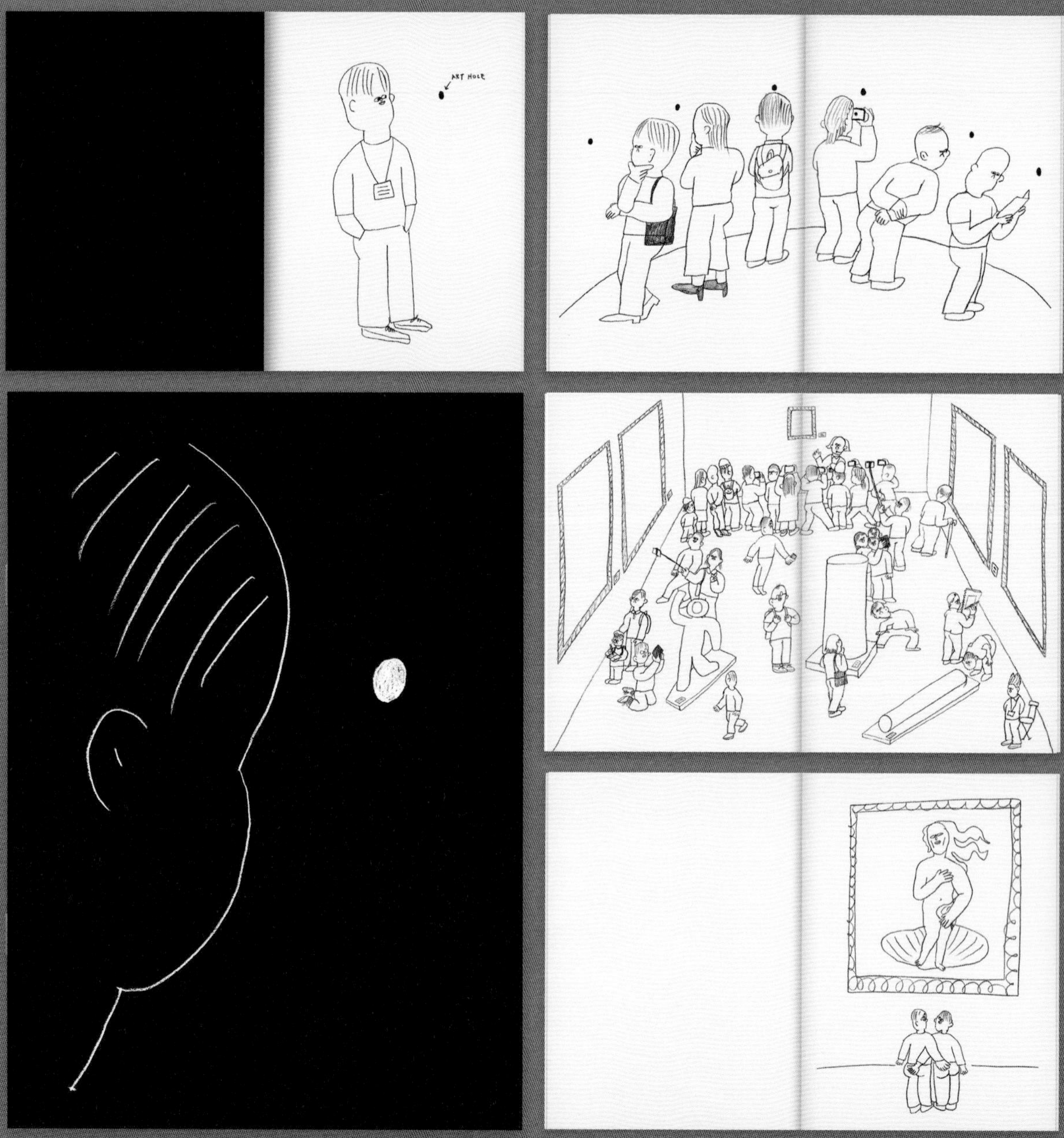

Page: 68 Dimension: 210×297mm Weight: 50g

Paper/Material: Cartoon Paper **Binding:** Saddle Stitching

D
Bird Pit

2017

BIRD PIT

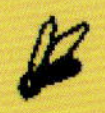

Bird Pit is a book made up of a series of drawings entitled "Portraits of the Ugly". It portrays people who are dissatisfied with everything and express their complaints in their own way. The cover of the book shows the tense situation just before the human catches the bird.

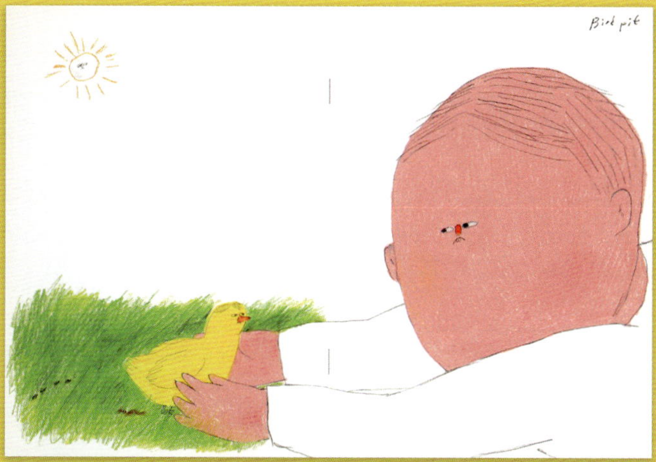

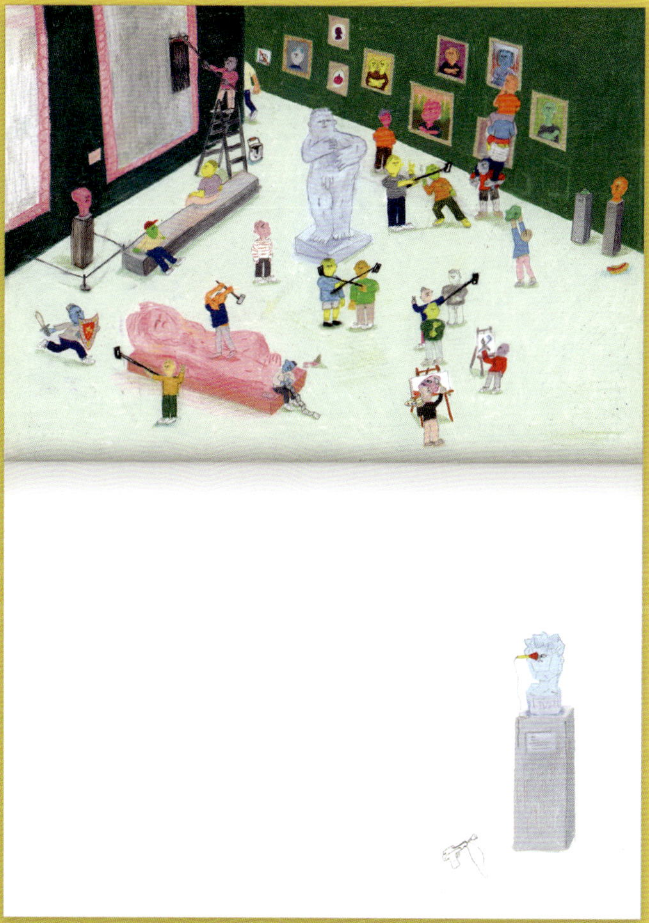

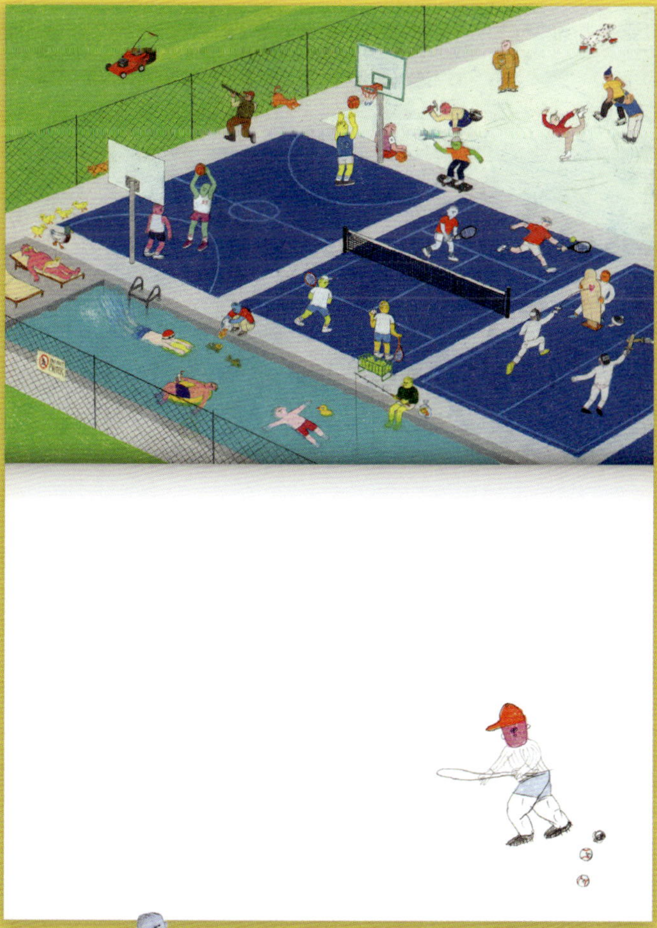

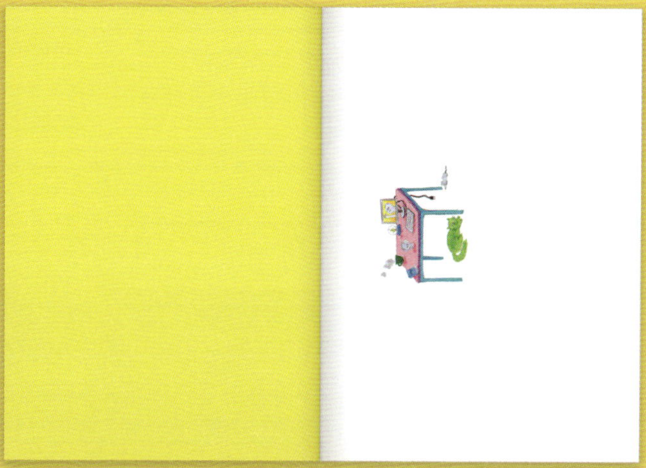

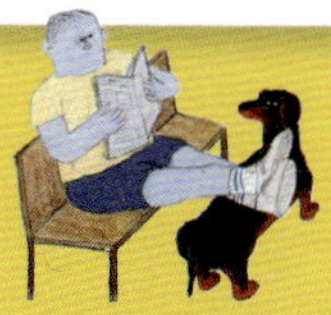

Page: 60 **Dimension:** 210×297mm **Weight:** 50g **Paper/Material:** Munken Polar Rough **Binding:** Saddle Stitching

ABYSS STARING

D
Yunqi Peng

2020

This publication is a visual expression based on the issue of "female gaze on social media". The content of the big volume is an abstract graphic visual experiment based on the key phrase—abyss staring. There are some messy patterns, which explore an environmental metaphor. The small volume is a collection of images with a sense of "being peeped", which were collected from many females. The pink PVC makes these images feel somewhat covert. The seal provides two choices for readers when they read. They can tear it, so that the publications cannot keep its shape. They can also pull the volumes out of the seal and pretend nothing has happened after reading and putting them back as the original statement.

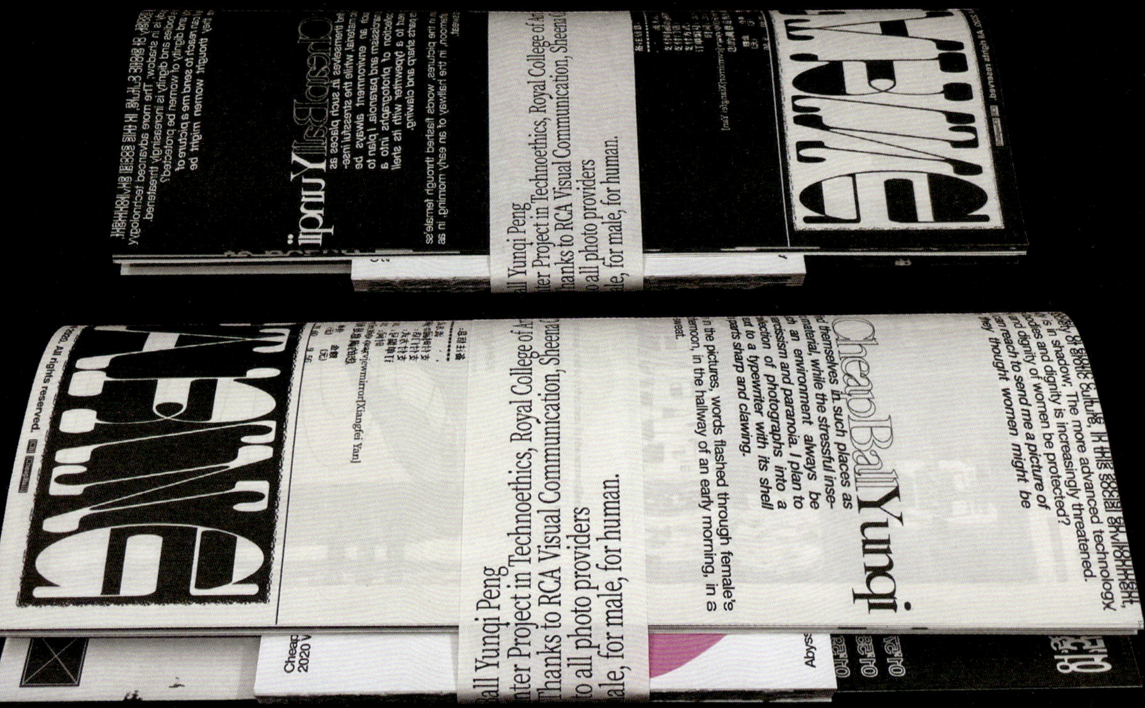

NEWSPAPER **Page:** 12 **Dimension:** 210×297mm

Paper/Material: Sensation Coated Paper 120g **Binding:** Saddle Stitching